College Education
as
Personal Development

Margaret B. Fisher

Jeanne L. Noble

Prentice-Hall, Inc.

Englewood Cliffs, N.J.

1960

PRENTICE-HALL PSYCHOLOGY SERIES
Arthur T. Jersild, *Editor*

PRINTED IN THE UNITED STATES OF AMERICA
14500-C

Contents

part two: The student's role

part three: Choices and values

Introduction:
forewarned is forearmed

The great choices
of the college years

During the college years most students face the three most important decisions of life: the choice of a vocation, the choice of a mate, the choice of a way of life. Their experience in the college years may help them move toward the crucial decisions, or it may bog them down in indecision. But colleges afford resources to help students make decisions that can open up a happy and effective life.

For instance, the college curriculum offers courses that develop interest and skill in various fields of knowledge related to many occupations. College courses are organized in sequences that lead to the choice of a major field in which to specialize, and to an occupation in which the knowledge and skill can be applied. The student has a course mapped out for him to follow, leading to an occupational choice and a career.

The college years also provide close and frequent association with students of both sexes. On a coeducational campus, or during weekends at a men's or women's college, association with students of the opposite sex offers unsurpassed opportunity for acquaintance to ripen into friendship, friendship into courtship and marriage. Perhaps never again will a student find so many people of his age and of like abilities and interests so conveniently grouped together. Even the inevitable rules and regulations, the organizations and committees, that seem so confining or boring, help students develop enduring patterns of living and working with others. The values found in college life also endure as a foundation of the way of life followed in later years.

Of course, a freshman does not arrive at the dormitory, unpack, and begin at once to think about these important matters. The history of these decisions begins with birth. Ever since that first day, the attitudes about himself and others that will shape his decisions have been forming and growing. From childhood, he has had dreams of himself as policeman, nurse, fireman, teacher, lawyer. He has had fantasies about himself being in love, getting married, being a parent. By the time he enters college, sober reality has begun to take over some of the material of his dreams. He usually has done some realistic thinking about a vocation, a mate, a way of life.

Many students come to college with these decisions substantially settled, ready to follow a plan to carry them out; others have not made final decisions, but are pretty clear about the direction they want to move; and some are confused and unready to commit themselves yet. But all feel that college in some way is important in their plans and decisions. The course of college life is expected to move them toward choices and decisions about themselves and their life's plans.

Whether or not a clear decision is made before college, questions and shifts of direction occur during college years. "Am I bright enough to be a chemist?" "Do I really want to spend forty-five years of my life running the family business?" "Do I really have what it takes to have a happy marriage?" "Can I give up some things that make me uncomfortable in my religion and still have some standards that will help me be a decent person?" "Am I really in love?" Each student arrives at college with some clear ideas about the kind of person he is or could be, some feeling about what he can do and cannot do, some idea of what is pleasing and displeasing to himself and others. But he also confronts new experiences that will pose new questions, color his view of himself, and affect his decisions.

College offers a student fresh opportunities to learn, to explore new ideas about himself, to modify those he already has. He is away from home, wholly on his own if he is in residence at college. If he is commuting, he spends most of his days in surroundings quite different from home, and he is on his own in his role as a student. What he makes of his college years, the interests he develops, the choices he makes, are his own responsibility.

SELF-UNDERSTANDING AS PART OF COLLEGE EDUCATION

Most students enjoy the experience they have in college and use it to improve their knowledge of themselves. They do not have parents around to warn, comfort, correct, protect them. They are responsible for their own self-understanding. They enjoy the freedom and responsibility to estimate their own abilities, emotional reactions, intellectual, social, and vocational interests. The college provides rigorous tests of competence in scholarship against which a student can measure himself. He also measures his self-understanding and self-development in other ways: every activity from campus politics to dating, parties to advanced experimental psychology can serve as a test of his understanding of the kind of student, friend, or citizen he really is or wants to become.

Opportunities for self-understanding, however, both beckon and threaten. Students are both eager and frightened at having to make these important and irreversible decisions. They are eager to get a degree and find an interesting and lucrative job; but they are also frightened and anxious over the pressures that force an occupational choice. They look forward to the last fling of youth, the last surge of fun, pranks, rebelliousness, frivolity; yet they feel harried by social and administrative pressures on them to emerge from the college years *self-directed* and *mature*. They like the idea of extracurricular activities that make them well-rounded persons, but they face the inexorable requirement of the college to maintain a solid grade-point average; they sometimes feel they are expected to be well-rounded with a large academic bulge on top.

These pressures of threat and opportunity, freedom and responsibility, independence and conformity become intolerable for some students. They cannot follow the opportunities that beckon because the threats loom too large. Evasive action seems more attractive than painful decision. Sometimes, therefore, they make hasty choices without consideration of their own interests or the realities of life. Other students try to avoid decisions by declaring a moratorium, putting off the choice to some unspecified tomorrow. One student, for example, avoided choice of an occupation by going into the army "to think things through." Another pursued one graduate degree after another, not for love of learning, but as a way to avoid a marriage he felt unready for and yet somehow committed to.[1] College itself may be used as a moratorium by some students, who put off decisions "until I finish college." But the moratorium must one day come to an end. The choices have to be made if a student is to be fully himself.

SELF-UNDERSTANDING AS A FACTOR IN DECISION

The decisions of the college years often appear more threatening because they seem to be binding. For instance, college students eventually have to choose a major. The later the decision is made, the harder it is to complete the required sequence of courses. The longer it is postponed, the less chance there is of correcting an unsatisfactory choice. Rising enrollments and increasing costs make "hedge-hopping" from one major to another, or from college to college, more difficult, more expensive, and less rewarding. Academic decisions are binding. Marriage, in our social system, represents a contract that binds both parties to their choice, and imposes continuing obligations, even though it may be dissolved by divorce. Although many students are marrying younger, even during the undergraduate years, they seem to regard marriage as a lasting attachment, seriously undertaken. And studies of moral and spiritual values show that college graduates carry into life the personal values they demonstrated to be important to them while in college.

Precisely because they are serious and enduring, the great choices are best made on the basis of clear self-understanding. Whether or not anyone else likes them, the student has to be satisfied with his choices. He has to live with them for the rest of his life. So he had best know something about himself and about the effect of these decisions on his life and happiness. Self-understanding, however, is both a pleasure and a pain, a threat and a necessity. So some students avoid decisions because they fear the pain of self-understanding, which looms larger than its pleasures. Rushing into decisions may be a choice of the lesser of two evils; a bad decision may be preferred to the threat of self-understanding.

To understand and use the opportunities for self-development available in college, the student has to have some awareness of three factors that affect his development and the choices he makes. Such awareness may increase his wisdom and his pleasure in making decisions of enduring significance for his future life and present happiness.

First, he can use some understanding of the nature of the self and the way it develops toward maturity. Second, he can understand the nature of the college and the resources it offers for his own self-development. Third, he can try to anticipate the choices he must make and use the resources of the college to help make wise ones.

WHAT THIS BOOK IS ABOUT

This book is divided into three parts, each intended to describe in detail these three aspects of college life. It is not just a handbook or "do-it-yourself" guide to success in college. It introduces some concepts about the student as a self, college and its resources, and choices in the student's life plan. These concepts provide a picture of the course of personal development in the college years. From this picture, a student may be able to anticipate some of the experiences he will encounter and the choices he must make in his own college career.

Naturally, this picture has had to be drawn in the most general terms. Students differ, colleges differ, so that only the most general ideas can be developed about things that are common to most students or to most colleges. To be a student requires developing some general patterns of behavior and habits; these are described so far as they apply to what makes a student recognizably a student. There is still a great deal of room for individual differences in behavior, habits, and decisions. To be a college means having some general institutional resources, purposes, and patterns of organization; these are described so far as they distinguish colleges from other kinds of institutions. There is still a great deal of variation among colleges in purposes, patterns, and resources.

Each student, therefore, must seek to understand himself and his college by direct experience and observation. Being a student means having a general style of life, out of which an individual style develops. It is this general style that is described in this book. But what makes a student an individual, he himself must supply. The distinctive character of his college will have some effect on a student's individual character. Some general characteristics of colleges are described in this book. But each student must discover for himself the distinctive character of his own college.

The student as self

To be a student implies, first of all, being a self, an individual, a person different from others. The self is a concept that can be described as something everyone has, but something which makes everyone different because he has it. Consequently, it can be described in general terms that apply to most people; but knowing oneself is the individual's own task, which cannot be delegated to others.

The first part of this book takes up the subject of the self as a general concept. It explores the nature of the self, the way to discover and understand the self. It describes the "developmental tasks" of the college age, the steps that complete the process of becoming an adult, as they have been defined in developmental psychology. It applies some concepts of mental hygiene to the understanding of the tasks of self-discovery and self-direction. It takes up some methods of self-appraisal through tests and measurements, counseling and guidance, that aid in self-direction.

The student as a member of the college

To be a student also means being a member of a college, enrolled for a regular course of study. It implies accepting the disciplines and habits of college study. It means working with faculty members. It means gaining skill in various intellectual disciplines and fields of subject matter, and understanding what is being learned. The second part of this book takes up this role of the student as student. Habits of study and personal disciplines of academic work are described as a means of dealing with stress and standing up to pressure so that the student may seize the opportunities of college work while reducing its threats. The reciprocal role that student and teacher must play are discussed, showing how each helps the other play his part in the college. Different intellectual skills and methods are discussed in terms of the different roles the student must play in using them. The relation of college resources to self-development is suggested.

The student as adult: the choices and resources of college life

The third section takes up the three great decisions: choice of work, choice of a mate, choice of a way of life. These decisions are so closely related to each other that it is almost impossible to discuss them separately. So the stages of vocational development are described in relation to the process of college education, the development of a life plan, and the considerations of marriage and family life. The patterns of personal relationships in college are discussed in terms of their effect on the student's concept of himself; the way in which the college serves as a resource for self-realization is related not only to academic interests and activities, but also to the growth of friendship and the development of intimate personal relationships leading to a choice of mate. The way the student body is organized, the patterns of government and leadership, and the standards of community life in college are related to the development of common interests and standards of value among students that affect vocational choices, friendships, and marriage. Finally, the development of values and the service of great causes, as they emerge out of the choices and personal relationships of the college years, are related to the use of intellectual methods in understanding one's own values and choosing a way of life.

SOME DEFINITIONS AND LIMITATIONS

The idea that prompted this book is that college education offers more than intellectual table fare. Intellectual methods and academic disciplines have historically developed as a way of mastering the tasks that face students. To understand oneself as student is easier if one has some fairly clear idea of what these tasks are and of what a college education can contribute to mastering them.

It is not easy to find terms for some of the tasks, the resources, the patterns of college life. Some old-fashioned terms have been adopted since they seem to convey the principles involved. They have a traditional meaning, which may be useful in thinking about the self, the roles played in college, the college as an institution.

So in this book, the role of student is sometimes spoken of as that of "scholar." This term is intended to convey the concept of the commitment a student has to his college and the loyalty he bears toward its purposes. The college is referred to as a "community of scholars." This is a short way of saying that the college, like a village, town, or neighborhood, has an inner life of its own. Reference is made to "the vocation of scholarship," or just to "scholarship." This term is intended to convey the commitment of the student and of the college to more than just the immediate courses offered or research done—it suggests the whole task of preserving and extending learning in society. This commitment to the very hard and serious work of extending learning is sometimes referred to as "the scholarly enterprise," or "academic work." So, when these terms are used, the student should think of himself as a scholar, a person who has taken on a real job in the scholarly enterprise, and become a member of "the community of scholars," to which contemporary faculty members and students belong with scholars and thinkers of ages past and ages yet to come. The college years are a brief part of the life of a student. But they are an important part of the scholarly enterprise, the never-ending job of learning and teaching the facts and principles that make civilized life possible.

The way in which colleges share the scholarly enterprise among themselves has led to the appearance of a bewildering variety of institutions of higher education. American colleges, perhaps more than those of some other nations, show an unusual range of difference. So what is said in this book about "the college," in general, may or may not apply to a particular college.

Each student will, therefore, have to get acquainted with his own college, its traditions and organization, and understand it in its own terms. It may be a junior college, giving two years of education beyond the high school, from which some students go into occupations and others into the final years of a four-year degree-granting college. It may be a four-year college, granting a bachelor's degree in one or several fields. It may be an undergraduate college or school in a large university, one of several such "colleges" or "divisions" offering various kinds of degree programs, both graduate and undergraduate. It may provide dormitories and dining halls for all students who must live on campus. It may house some resident students and accept others as non-residents or day students. It may provide no housing at all, but only academic facilities—classes, laboratories, libraries. It may be a center of research, or a college in which faculty devote themselves principally to teaching. It may offer only courses leading to degrees, or it may also offer instruction to people who are not interested in a degree, but in extension or adult education study. It may be privately controlled and financed; it may be controlled and supported by another institution such as a church or fraternal order; it may be an agency of local, state, or national government. It may be located in a city, in a small town, or in the country. It may enrol students from all over the country, from many foreign countries as well, or only students who are resident in a particular area. It may restrict enrolment to men or to women; it may admit both. It may restrict its courses to the liberal arts or to scientific and technical subjects; or it may offer both.

All of these different types of colleges—and many more—have developed because of the variety of interests that colleges serve in American life. They have answered some special needs for teaching, research, professional education, leadership, cultural enrichment, or social service. The history of American colleges and their purposes are as varied as the history of the American people. Each student should enjoy finding out about the history and purposes of his college, and the place it plays in the life of the state and nation it serves. Unless he understands its history and recognizes its purposes, he cannot relate his personal interests and purposes as a student to the life of the college very effectively. And he will miss much of what his college has to offer.

When "the college" is spoken of in this book it means any type of institution of higher learning, enrolling students upon graduation from high school. Anyone enrolled for full-time study in such an institution, who has not yet received a bachelor's degree, is referred to as a student. These terms are to be understood in the most general way; they do not refer to any particular college or any particular student. The examples given hold good only for the particular type of student or college mentioned.

This book is for college students, or for high school graduates about to become students, or for people who are interested in students. It is written in the hope that it will help students understand themselves and their college better. It is written in the hope that it will help them find more meaning and more pleasure in their college years.

The college years are rightfully expected to be among the busiest, happiest, and most productive of a person's life. Those who have been students look back on college as a time when they found the work, the friends, the causes that have continued to enlist their interest and service ever since. It is this sense of being part of an important enterprise, of being engaged in significant work, of enjoying the new experience and interests that unfold in the college years, that we hope you may come to understand and share in your years as a college student.

ACKNOWLEDGMENTS

The authors express their grateful appreciation to their student and faculty colleagues at the University of Buffalo, Mills College, City College of New York, and Hampton Institute, from whom they have learned so much that is in this book. Special thanks are due to Dr. Arthur T. Jersild, for his encouragement and advice; to Mrs. Katherine Caldwell, Dr. Evelyn Urrère, Miss Elizabeth Pope, Robert M. Roth, Gordon Klopf, and Alonzo G. Morón, for useful criticism in their fields; to the eagle-eyed typists, Misses Sheila Weibert, Dorothy Wright, Mary Virginia Massey, and Mrs. Christine Bouldin and Mrs. Louise Coulbrit; and to the many students who helped the authors compare their concepts with the hard reality of contemporary college life.

JEANNE NOBLE
MARGARET FISHER

part one

Understanding oneself

1

Me, myself, and I

*Self-discovery and
self-development*

A Princeton senior expresses an idea as old as time, and as new as tomorrow:

Each of us who wishes to assert himself significantly has first to discover what constitutes his "self." He must root out and reevaluate his most basic desires and beliefs so that he can plan a future which will most adequately give expression to his nature.[1]

Socrates put it more succinctly, saying, "Know thyself." Shakespeare put it more elegantly: "This above all, to thine own self be true . . ." Dr. William Menninger says from the psychiatric point of view:

You may feel that understanding about yourself is not important. You may say that after all, you can drive a car without knowing how a gasoline engine works. Which is quite true, except that the more you know about a car, the longer you can keep it working at its top efficiency. If you are taking Latin, the more vocabulary and grammar you know, the faster you can translate . . . And the more you understand about yourself, the better you can manage yourself and your life.[2]

Philosophers, poets, psychiatrists—and Princeton—attest to the ancient, common human need for self-understanding.

Self-understanding requires understanding of the emotions—how they develop and how they affect our actions. Most people go through life without paying much attention to this emotional aspect of the self. And, for all practical purposes, many of them appear to lead relatively productive and happy lives, despite occasional disquieting psychosomatic disorders, anxiety, and ulcers. If it becomes absolutely necessary to call their attention to their emotional reactions, they are likely to respond offhandedly: "So I got emotions! So what?" Or else, "Why pick on me? I'm not bothering anybody and I'm making a living." Some natural-born pessimists may be acutely aware of unpleasant emotions, and enjoy pointing out that life is not meant to be happy, 'tis folly to demand it.

There is much talk these days about developing the intellectual potential of people, especially of gifted students. The shocking gap between intellectual powers and performance must be closed; all students should work up to capacity, however limited that may be. This is the college's business. When it comes to "working up to emotional capacity," however, we get a different picture:

. . . . we seem to feel that the individual should be able without much help to acquire knowledge of his own inner life and impulses, to understand them, and to learn to use them automatically. In fact we act as if we preferred that the individual think and learn about the former group of skills [intellectual] to the exclusion of the latter [emotional].[3]

Only recently, science has uncovered how closely the development of intelligence is related to emotions. There is a parallel relationship between learning and emotional development. One does not wait for the development of the other. By November, the college freshman may have mastered the slide rule, but not his temper. By December, he may have brilliantly passed a test on the evolution of man from an arboreal to a terrestrial creature; but he may be so caught up in hours of daydreaming that he cannot get his own feet on the ground long enough to make a choice of a major. Unless emotional development goes along with intellectual development, the most brilliant academic performance will get the student exactly nowhere.

THE EXTENT OF EMOTIONAL PROBLEMS AMONG COLLEGE STUDENTS

There are rather disheartening statistics about the extent to which emotional problems beset people. Conservative estimates suggest that one out of every ten youngsters alive today will have need of treatment for a serious emotional problem or personality disorder sometime during his life. Probably many of this unfortunate group will not get to college, but there is no indication that students are exempt from the probabilities.

. . . . that an appreciable percentage of college students in American institutions of high learning are disturbed by problems of an emotional nature is evident. These problems can be described as occupying a continuum extending from mild anxieties or feelings of inferiority through psychosomatic disorders or manifestations of hostility, to symptoms of psychoneurosis or even psychosis. That colleges and universities are aware of this situation and that they have taken steps both to cope with and alleviate such a stumbling block to the mental health of their student populations also is a matter of record. At the rate counseling centers, mental hygiene clinics, psychiatric services, and other accoutrements of a comprehensive mental hygiene program in college have been developing, it is safe to say that the future augurs increasingly well for the personal and social adjustment of the nation's potential college graduates and more highly educated scholars.[4]

One mental hygienist asked a group of normal students in a psychology class to list some of the conflicts and problems that troubled them. These are a few of the most frequently chosen responses.

1. Wish to marry one of an equally strong but different faith.
2. Desire to follow a profession other than the one the family intends.
3. Making a dinner date, but finding that a parent is planning to visit and also wants a dinner date.
4. Desire for financial and economic independence opposed to the love of home and parents.
5. Desire for wise social activities—extracurricular—versus recognition of need for studying.
6. Desire for scholastic attainment opposed to strong feelings of inability to understand or accomplish the work.
7. Fear of performing in public opposed to genuine and strong interest in the stage, radio, and so forth.
8. Desire for marriage opposed to circumstances which make it impossible or difficult.
9. Desire for athletic attainment opposed to a physical limitation.
10. Desire to express oneself through the medium of the arts opposed to the necessity of working hard for a living.
11. Giving in to a dominant person versus trying to outdo him.
12. Where to call a halt in affection with the opposite sex.
13. How to adjust when fellow companions smoke, swear, and so forth.
14. Problem of being disgusted with people's actions, but trying not to show it.
15. What to choose as a life's work.
16. Meeting a situation by pleasing one's family, or by pleasing oneself.
17. Conflict of whether to break a date at the last minute because someone else much nicer has just asked for the same night.
18. Conflict of changing religion (from Catholic to Protestant, or from Protestant to Catholic) to marry someone of the other religion.[5]

TABLE 1-1
Situations Feared by a Group of College Students

Situation feared	Number of students mentioning situation (174 in the study)
Insecurity	64
Illness	47
Failure	46
Disapproval by others	42
Loss of friends or relatives by death	32
Unhappy marriage	31
Frustration (being unable to do as desired)	30
Unhappiness	20
Poverty	18
Death	15

From Lynde C. Steckle, *Problems of Human Adjustment* (New York: Harper & Brothers, 1949), p. 16.

Another psychologist, Lynde Steckle, asked a group of 174 bright students to list (anonymously) the things they feared (see Table 1-1). Steckle classified these responses as unnecessary concerns. All these fears might be removed or reduced by facing the need to understand the emotional and psychological aspects of personality development.

But the observant student does not need statistics to make him aware of emotional problems around him. On every college campus there are students who are obviously intellectually gifted and yet dissipate energy in social activities. There are those who have "off days" and become unapproachable. A glance around the reading room of the library shows those who "daydream" for hours while the book before them goes unread. There are the angry ones; the ones who embark upon a crusade against the administration because to them the real meaning of life seems to assert itself only when there is something to fight. There are the shy and withdrawn, the belligerent and overbearing ones. The student has to get along with all of them. And he can avoid or solve problems like theirs, for himself, only if he understands what makes *him* tick.

Therefore, one major goal for the enterprising college student is to discover his own unique personality. "Discover," admonishes the Princeton senior, "what constitutes . . . self!"

THE SELF: WHO AM I? ME!

According to psychologists, the *self* is a useful concept for explaining behavior. We have certain beliefs about ourselves, and try to act in ways that are consistent with them. We try to act ourselves. This organization of ideas about who and what a person believes and feels himself to be as an individual is called the self-concept. It answers the question, "Who am I?" as well as the inquiry, "Who does he think he is —anyway?"[6]

The self is the referent of the pronoun "I." It includes all that *a person believes about himself*—his attitudes toward his body ("Oh," said an attractive coed, "I am so plain"); his intellect ("I'm averagely bright, I guess," replied a student who tested in the top ten percent of all students in the country); his emotions ("I get along well with everybody," said a student who argued constantly); and general limitations and strengths ("I think I will become a social worker because I have no scientific talent, but I love working with people," concluded John after a session with his counselor). Though it may be obvious to others that the student's belief is inconsistent with the way in which others view him, his actions are motivated by his own beliefs.

Included in a person's self-concept or knowledge of "I" are his *beliefs concerning what others think of him*. Does he see the people in his environment as kindly disposed toward him most of the time or as continuously hostile? Or, does he see them responding negatively or positively depending on how he himself behaves? ("I can't seem to make friends at this college. Everybody just sort of goes his own way, not caring about anybody else." The counselor asked: "Have you tried to approach any of the students in your class and strike up a conversation?" "No indeed, I heard before I came here that the best way to get along at this college is to mind your own business!") Again, beliefs concerning others may be valid or invalid; nevertheless, they motivate actions.

The expectations others hold for him are another part of an individual's self-concept. The others must be "significant others"—family, friends, and associates whose opinions and ideas matter. Does the student believe that they expect him to be a good student? ("I know my mother will die if I don't get into medical school!") Or, what do they expect of him altogether? He will be motivated, not by their actual expectations, but by his understanding of what they expect of him. This understanding of what others expect may or may not be accurate.

An understanding of a person's self-concept also includes his *beliefs concerning social demands on him*. Social demands, opinions, and expectations differ from the expectations of the "significant others" in that they are not related to specific persons who are close within his family or acquaintance group. Social demands are the ways of thinking, behaving, or achieving expected because of membership in a sex group, religious group, or socio-economic group. "Nobody expects me to do very much, since I'm a Negro," said Joe. "I have to really get on the ball; after all my family stands for something in the community," said Jim.

"I would like to be a physicist, but I also want to get married and have children. Do you think I could really do all that, as a woman?" asked Carol.

Often such remarks reflect an acceptance of stereotypes. For example, there are women who combine a marriage and career. But Carol believes that such a life is unusual for women, and feels the need to seek further understanding of herself before making a decision concerning her place in society. The "significant others" may include in their expectations of Carol the societal demands upon women, but they tailor them to Carol as an individual. In other words, Carol incorporates within "herself" values she selects from society and also others she selects from her family and friends.

What a person believes about himself is colored by feelings. The self is not a public matter, subject to purely rational understanding. The self constitutes the private, intimate "inner" life of a person which only he can know directly. It is a composite of both *thoughts* and *feelings*. And often the feelings can be observed by others without knowing what causes the person to react that way.

The self includes among other things, a perceptual component: The way a person perceives himself—the image he has of his appearance of his body; the picture he has of his impressions he makes on others. It also includes a conceptual component: The person's conception of his distinctive characteristics, his abilities, resources, assets, lacks and limitations; and his conception of his background and origins, of his future and what he might become. There is also an attitudinal component of the self, including the feelings a person has about himself and his origins and background; his attitudes toward his present status and future prospects; his tendency to view himself with pride and shame; his convictions concerning his worthiness; and his attitudes (which may be mixed) of self-acceptance or self-rejection. As a person reaches maturity, these attitudes relating to self include also the beliefs, convictions, ideals, values, hopes, and commitments that comprise what we speak of as a person's philosophy of life.[7]

The image a person has of himself includes a picture of the way he looks, of his body as part of himself. This is called "the body image." It includes feelings as well as bodily sensations. He does not look at his body as if it were in a test tube; *he has it*. He also has feelings, good or bad, hostile or indifferent, about that body. These feelings affect what he believes about himself, and are part of the body image. An understanding of these feelings matters to him, for they affect what he will do with the body in which he dwells, and to a large extent, determine his behavior. If he likes his body image, he is likely to move out toward people in a genuine, spontaneous way, feeling that they will accept and like him as an attractive person. If he dislikes his body image, he may dislike himself; he may withdraw from other people in order to avoid the rejection he expects because they may not find him attractive. Feeling miserable, he acts miserable. He may want to make others miserable. Being sure that others dislike his looks, he interprets their behavior toward him as meaning that his looks are disagreeable. He feels like a disagreeable person. He behaves disagreeably. Others respond disagreeably to him, and thus confirm his impression. Misery breeds misery!

All too often what a person believes about himself and what others believe about him (as near as we can tell through the use of objective measurements such as tests, associations, and observation) may be widely different. The discrepancy between (1) self as known by the

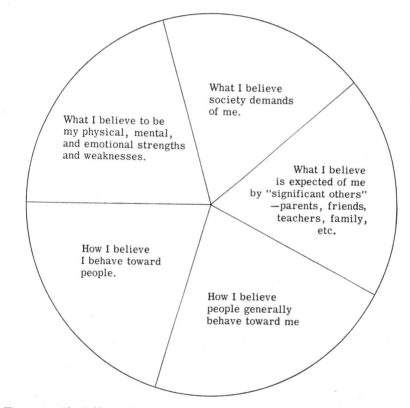

Fig. 1–1. The Self or I. If you imagine this wheel in progress and circular motion, it will illustrate the interaction of aspects of the self. Both inner feelings (urges, drives, physiological processes) and outward events or persons motivate behavior. That is, they account for the action of the person in a situation. The person may or may not be aware of all the aspects, of the reactions that account for his behavior, or of the self. He may not understand the self in these terms, but may have a picture of an idealized self that takes the place of a real self image. But in self-understanding, some insight into all of these factors is needed.

student and (2) self as seen by others can often provoke confusion. When decisions have to be made out of such confusion, the outcome may not be very satisfying.

The real and idealized self

When a person says, "I want to know myself," he should mean that he wants to see himself *as he really is*. This means that he must be willing to look at each component of the self as objectively as possible. For instance, this would mean that he could see each section of the wheel (see Fig. 1-1) as if it were part of himself. He should be in search of a *real self* as contrasted to an *idealized self*. The idealized self is the image of oneself in the "irrational imagination."[8] A person may get this irrational image because he believes he should be something that others in his life expect him to become. Without bothering to make a decision in his own interest, or a choice that is his own, he makes plans and moves into situations in an effort to satisfy the wishes and desires that other people have of him. He tries to be the person they want him to be. But he does not develop his own identity that way. He does not understand his real self.

Of course, many of the purposes and expectations that give a person his identity originate with "significant others"—with parents and family, teachers and friends. These expectations are internalized, as the psychologists say; that is, as a person tries to live up to them, they soak in and become absorbed in the self. He is largely unconscious of them, because he has made them his own, and does not have to think twice about acting in such a way as to achieve them. They are, in practice, indistinguishable from the purposes and expectations that he originates independent of outside influence.

However, some of these internalized elements fit him better than others. Those wishes, desires, and patterns of behavior best fitted to him are most readily internalized. But a person may also be forced to live up to other expectations that are incongruous, that do not fit his real self, and that he cannot make his own. These may form an idealized self. They are most likely to do so when a person finds some satisfaction in meeting these expectations, over and above the pressure that is brought to bear on him to live up to them. For example, a student who is gifted in art and interested in painting may study law instead, in order to enter his father's firm after graduation. His parents make it clear that they expect him to follow in his father's footsteps. Financial support and the prospect of a successful career, as well as subtle parental pressure, move the student to make such a choice. Furthermore, he finds satisfaction for himself in living up to his parents' expectations and satisfying their desires, as he sees them. So he tries to see himself as a lawyer, and tries not to see himself as an artist. He is, then, living up to an idealized rather than a real self.

Because the struggle for identity is largely unconscious, it is often difficult to distinguish between the real and the idealized self. But the person seeking the idealized self may be aware that there are things in his life that somehow don't fit. He may have a sense of inadequacy, a feeling of being unable to achieve anything in life. He may feel excessive anxiety or dissatisfaction. "Nothing ever comes out right for me," he moans. Or he may be unable to enjoy himself, to accept pleasure; he has to do something, preferably something strenuous, difficult, even painful. "I've got to get busy," he says, "I can't just sit around and enjoy myself, I've got things to do." He may actually feel the lack of self-direction. "I am driven instead of being the driver."[9] The idealized self drives the person to become something different from what he is or could be. He can be neither himself nor the idealized self, because his interests or abilities or temperament incline him in another direction. The idealized self is a driving force, not a driver. Unless the person *himself* takes control, the drive is likely to be wild and erratic, getting nowhere, and risking a crackup.

According to Horney, "the real self is the 'original' force toward individual growth and fulfillment, with which we may achieve full identification."[10] This original force is the spontaneous energy which flows from the true abilities and interests which every person has. The real self represents a person's actual or potential abilities and resources for growth and self-fulfillment.

The real self is, of course, something that can only be known to the individual. There are some common characteristics that can be used as a check. Certainly, a real person assumes responsibility for his acts. Others influence his life, and he is aware of their influence. He is aware of his behavior and feelings in different situations. He will take the consequences of his actions and decisions. He knows it is up to him to do something about his difficulties without relying on fate, time, or other people.

In contrast, a "pseudo-real" person shifts responsibility, blames everything and everybody for his plight, and feels others are responsible for helping him achieve his purposes. He spends his energy in fruitless activity or idle excuses. The real person comes closer to an objective analysis of his abilities to achieve his goals, either academically or vocationally. Consequently, his energies are neither dissipated nor over-extended.

An idealized person is keeping up a pretense of some sort. He usually works either below or above his natural potential; his idealized self is not related to his true capacities. His energies are harnessed, not to real, achievable goals, but to impossible bolstering of a false and unnatural self. He is driven, not the driver. He lacks the inner direction that takes a real person through channels of opportunity without stepping on his own feet, without serious or continuous inner conflicts.

The idealized person operates from a blueprint, usually copied from somebody else; efforts toward putting the blueprint into operation usually engender strain and stress. The real person is alive, motivated by special, individual interests and energies.

But there are also forces in him which we cannot acquire or even develop by learning. You need not, and in fact cannot, teach an acorn to grow into an oak tree, but when given a chance, its intrinsic potentialities will develop. Similarly, the human individual, given a chance, tends to develop his particular human po-tentialities. He will develop then the unique alive forces of his real self: The clarity and depth of his own feelings, thoughts, wishes, interests; the ability to tap his own resources; the strength of his will power; the special capacities or gifts he may have; the faculty to express himself, and to relate himself to others with his spontaneous feelings. All this will in time enable him to find his set of values and his aims in life. In short, he will grow, substantially undirected, toward self-realization . . . the real self as that central inner force, common to all hu-man beings and yet unique in each, . . . is the deep source of growth.[11]

Accordingly, Horney takes the position that . . . . "the actual self cannot de-velop according to its potentials unless its holder is truthful to himself about who and what he is; unless he is active and productive, unless he relates himself to others in the spirit of mutuality and only if he assumes responsibility for him-self."[12]

The way toward this goal is through an ever-increasing awareness and understanding of ourselves. And the first step toward this aware-ness is to understand the factors responsible for the development of self.

The ideal self and the idealized self

We have spoken of the real and idealized self. Some psychologists indicate that having an ideal self is healthy—as long as it is consistent with one's abilities, interests and capacities. There is an important dif-ference between an ideal self and an idealized self. The former is healthy, the latter unhealthy.

The ideal self, according to Havighurst and MacDonald[13] is devel-oped in several ways. First, there is a period of identification with a parent or parent substitute. The boy wants to be like the father and often imitates him. This is why the father should spend time with the son and enable him to observe and practice manhood. The same is true for the daughter-mother relationship.

Later there is the unrealistic, moonstruck stage in which the person wants to become a movie star or singer or something glamorous. This is understandable because the adolescent sees the culture rewarding and advancing these persons. Then, there is a stage of identification with an attractive young adult or an imaginary character who has a combination of many admirable qualities. The imaginary character may come from biographies or books. But there is greater realism in an ideal self modeled after a warm-blooded human who is present in the immediate environment or was there long enough to leave a personal impact.

Adults provide models for young people, who tend to identify with admired adults whom they come to know in their acquaintance, their reading, the movies, magazines, and TV. They imitate these models and try to develop a style of life or behavior like what they imagine the models have.[14]

One bright college woman discovered a model—a bit late, but soon enough to support a wise vocational choice.

"Well, I would get a Ph.D., but those female professors at ———— are such a dreary monotonous lot. They wear flat shoes—spend all their time on cattle boats or bicycling through Europe. Me—I like luxuries. Say, when you went to Europe did you go like that?"

"No," replied the new found Ph.D. friend. "I went cabin class. To me a vacation means a few luxuries also."

"No kidding? Well, I . . . . . . well . . . . . . I wouldn't mind going to all that trouble to get a Ph.D. I guess it really would be the logical thing to do since I am tremendously interested in this field. And, I would enjoy going further. But honestly, you are the only female Ph.D. I know who wears high heels and seems interested in other sorta normal things. . . ."

It is healthy to have an ideal self against which one measures his growth and progress. The idealized self, however, cannot serve as such a model because it is impossible to attain. But the ideal self, which is helped along by identification with adults, can be realistic. In the first place, the person chooses his own models, and he analyzes their behavior, actions, and achievement rather critically. He is not necessarily trying to become *exactly* like his model. Rather, he enjoys matching qualities, finding similarities and differences between himself and his model, and discovering that certain qualities tend to bring certain rewards. The ideal self then can present a realistic goal, because others have achieved the qualities and rewards it represents.

THE DEVELOPMENT OF SELFHOOD

How does one get to be a self, a person who differs markedly from others and yet shares many human traits with others?

The natural inheritance

First of all, nature makes its contribution by laying down the ground rules of self-development. Geneticists are discovering more and more about the influences of genes, the tools of heredity, upon human development.[15] Genes are responsible for more of our physical, mental, and emotional makeup than most of us realize. For example, the union of genes at the moment of conception determines the color of our eyes and skin, the size and shape of our facial features, the length of our limbs and fingers, the general level of our mental capacity.

Despite this, however, no one can accurately predict what kind of personality will result when genes of the father unite with those of the mother. Leonardo da Vinci, often called the world's most outstanding genius, was born of a peasant girl and an obscure notary in a little Italian village. On the other hand, highly gifted persons may have children of low mentality. Heredity is a gamble; the distribution of genetic factors is governed by laws of probability. One classic example is George Bernard Shaw's reminder to Isadora Duncan when she proposed that they have a child: "Wouldn't it be wonderful if our child had your brains and my beauty," said the beautiful dancer. "Yes," Shaw replied, "but what a tragedy if the child had *my* beauty and *your* brains."

Though there is a breath-taking element of chance—producing anything from genius to moron—a study of the heredity of parents gives a fair prediction of the general intelligence of their children. Children of brainy parents are more likely to have higher IQ's than children of fathers and mothers who are not normally intelligent.

One biochemist indicates that:

On the basis of (1) common observation, (2) what appears to me to be irrefutable biological evidence, and (3) specific objective psychological findings . . . Every newborn baby has a distinctive and complex pattern of inborn mental capacities. Each item in this pattern is derived from his human forebears, but the pattern with its interactions is unique.[16]

Not all traits are hereditary. And not all hereditary traits appear in every generation. The outcome of particular combinations of genes depends upon their dominant or recessive character, and upon chance distribution of paired genetic factors. Table 1-2 shows some examples of hereditary characteristics and the outcome of the distribution of genetic factors.

TABLE 1-2
Some Examples of Human Hereditary Characteristics

Dominant characteristics	Recessive characteristics
(Trait variants which are always visible when the proper gene is present. These are not necessarily transmitted to the next generation.)	(Trait variants which are visibly manifested only when both parents contribute the same kind of gene for the trait. They can be transmitted even though not visible in the parents.)
Black skin (partially dominant)	White skin
Non-red hair	Red hair
Curly hair (partially dominant)	Straight hair
Baldness in men	Baldness in women
Color blindness in men	Color blindness in women
Free ear lobes	Adherent ear lobes
Brown eyes	Blue or gray eyes
Hazel or green eyes	Blue or gray eyes
Farsightedness and nearsightedness	Normal vision
Short stature	Tall stature
Blood Types, A, B, AB	Blood type O
High blood pressure	Normal blood pressure
Allergy	No allergy
Susceptibility to tuberculosis	Resistance to tuberculosis

Uncertain inheritance pattern

Schizophrenia	Feeble-mindedness	Artistic talent
Manic depressive psychosis	Musical talent	Mathematical ability

Joseph L. Stone and Joseph Church, *Childhood and Adolescence* (New York: Random House, 1957), p. 44. [Adapted from E. C. Colin, *Elements of Genetics* (New York: Blakiston Division, McGraw-Hill Book Co., 1941), pp. 118 and 162], by permission.

The environment

Regardless of the natural potential with which a person is blessedly endowed or wretchedly cursed, he only realizes his possibilities within an environment—the total of all *external* conditions and influences affecting life and development. Heredity deals the cards but environment plays the hand.

A student may be born with a rugged physique and natural inclination to be a splendid Atlas of a man. But if he is not fed properly or protected from cold and bodily neglect, he will become undernourished, prone to disease, and a physically weak specimen. He may have the potentialities for high scholastic achievement; but if he is deprived of mental stimulation and confined to an environment where people provide him with no intellectual stimulation, he will rarely develop his gifts. A dramatic example is the story of a man who at an early age was committed to an institution for the mentally defective. Years later, he was discovered by a psychologist to be of superior but undeveloped native ability. The amazing thing was that he retained enough intelligence to show on a battery of tests, in spite of the tragic mistake that had been made.

Perhaps most prevalent in cases of undeveloped potential is the thwarting of the great, native capacity to express our feelings and emotions spontaneously and freely and to venture into new situations with the freedom to experiment and learn. Unless this capacity for self-expression is encouraged and fostered by an environment of people who are loving, accepting and warm, this greatest gift of all, *freedom to grow*, will be misdirected into the countless anxieties, fears, and defenses that mar so many lives.

The paradox of nature and nurture

And yet, there is sometimes a surging assertion of ability that somehow bursts forth from the most discouraging circumstances. Booker T. Washington, born a slave, founded Tuskegee Institute, and became one of the nation's most famous educators.[17] Conversely, there are those who seemingly have more love and care than others and still develop distorted selves, as in the case of Judd and Artie in *Compulsion.*[18] Most of the cases known to us in day-to-day dealings with students are more like that of the gifted boys in southern Italy.[19] Several boys in an obscure village were found to possess exceptional artistic talents; but because of the low level of aspiration and indifference to artistic success among their parents, these boys were curiously unmotivated to develop their talent. At sixteen they were still content to be behind the plow instead of the easel.

Research has contributed much to our understanding of the influence of environment in developing personality and abilities. And, since there is very little we can do about the inheritance with which we are endowed, it is important to understand the forces over which we can exert some control.

Influence of the home and family in self-development

The child is first introduced to his social environment through the home. A person's early contacts with parents, especially the mother, develop him into a growing, feeling, responding person.

The positive conditions that the home should provide for growing children are numerous. We have already indicated that the growing child needs love and warmth in order to build his inner security. A cold and indifferent home prepares the way for insecurity.

. . . . through a variety of adverse influences, a child may not be permitted to grow according to his individual needs and possibilities. . . . In simple words, [parents] may be dominating, overprotective, intimidating, irritable, overexacting, erratic, partial to other siblings, hypocritical, indifferent, etc. It is never a matter of just a single factor, but always the whole constellation that exerts the untoward influence on a child's growth.[20]

"Just as biological organisms have a ground plan from which the various parts arise, all in their proper time until all have become a functioning whole, so there are certain inner laws operative in personality development."[21]

Erikson sees the personality, or self, developing through eight stages:

In each of these stages, the inner laws of development create a succession of potentialities for significant interaction with those who tend him. While such interaction varies from culture to culture, it must remain the proper rate and the proper sequence which govern the growth of a personality as well as that of an organism . . . Personality can be said to develop according to steps predetermined in the human organism's readiness to be driven toward, to be aware of, and to interact with a widening social radius, beginning with the dim image of a mother and ending with mankind, or at any rate that segment of mankind which "counts" in the particular individual's life.[22]

Oral Sensory	Trust vs. Distrust							
Muscular Anal		Autonomy vs. Shame and Guilt						
Locomotive Genital			Initiative vs. Guilt					
Latency				Industry vs. Inferiority				
Puberty and Adolescence					Identity vs. Role Diffusion			
Young Adulthood						Intimacy vs. Isolation		
Adulthood							Generativity vs. Stagnation	
Maturity								Integrity vs. Disgust, Despair

Erik Erikson, *Childhood and Society* (New York: W. W. Norton & Company, Inc.), p. 234. Used by permission.

Fig. 1–2. Erikson's Eight Stages of Man.

Fig. 1-2 illustrates Erikson's stages of growth. The left-hand column describes ages in psychological terms. For our purposes we shall use age designations as substitutes. The first four stages roughly represent (1) birth to one year old; (2) one to three; (3) three to six; and (4) six to twelve. The next stages, beginning with puberty and adolescence, include (5) 12–16; (6) 16–20; and (7 and 8) 21 on into the rest of life.

The family, and particularly the parents, have an all-important role to play in launching the person into each successive stage. We speak now of the emotional as well as the physical environment. Beginning with the first stages of infancy, labeled by Erikson "Trust vs. Distrust," an infant first becomes aware of his environment in terms of the way it meets his physical and emotional needs. The mother, or a substitute, builds trust by providing for the child's needs. Since the infant must depend on others, the way in which parents answer the child's needs gives him a view of the world as being good, stable, safe and encouraging or frustrating and non-trustworthy. The satisfaction of needs lays the foundation of trust. If the infant is comforted and fondled and relieved when he is in distress, he grows to believe the world can be trusted. Deprivation of maternal love, lack of comfort and cuddling, produce distrustful, anxious children. Infants may actually die of the deprivation of love, of warm caresses, of tender loving care.

"Autonomy vs. Shame and Doubt" is the toddlers' problem area. The child at this age has already become aware of many of his abilities. If his parents have built a foundation of trust, he practices and exercises his new-found abilities. He learns to trust himself as previously he learned to trust others. The child learns to control his behavior, as in toilet training, at this age. Erikson indicates that overemphasis on toilet training exposes the child to shame and doubt. He may become aware that there are things about himself that are dirty and unpleasant and cause others to frown. Not only toilet training, but also control of other bodily functions draw parental responses that help him or shame him— clumsiness, meddling, crying, for example. As he learns to see himself through parents' eyes, the way in which they knock him around, scream at him, or cuddle him and accept his emotions aid him in accepting himself *as he is*. And the goal is to have him see himself as acceptable and constructive.

The next years—the pre-school years—are years of maximum spontaneity. Individual differences are beginning to emerge. Often parents complain that their children "run hot and cold"—so rapid are their emotional fluctuations. The child is mastering skills, concepts, values, and social relationships. The parents are still the crucial people in this age of development. First, they decide which experiences the child will have. These experiences may add color, give the child an expanded "life space," or limit his environment. Family members make it possible for the child to initiate projects and succeed in using his new-found skills. Often, during this stage, the child develops a sense of guilt over the acts he initiates which bring about the displeasure of adults. Second, as the child begins to expand his circle of friends, one can observe him behaving in a way that suggests that he has internalized his parents' code of "do's and don'ts," and has a system of control of his own. He has standards of good and bad. He now is capable of experiencing guilt. The worst parental influence at this age, according to Erikson, is to produce excessive guilt in a child. This may cause constriction of behavior and limit or erase spontaneity.

We see the influence of the family on the next stage of development when the child is in school. He learns to produce. He learns that rewards come from adults when he learns and gets good grades, or displays his talents. He senses their disappointment when he does not produce. Many parents, by nagging and disapproval, reinforce a sense of failure or inferiority in children who do not succeed academically. On the other hand, many parents help by rewarding a child's efforts and demanding industry in areas consistent with a child's ability and interest. Excessive demands cause a child to lose hope and see himself as not measuring up.

The central theme of adolescence is finding oneself. The adolescent is concerned with what he appears to be to others. He must come to terms with the demands of society, which dictate that he must begin now to identify himself with the institutions of work, marriage, home, and community. Somehow he has to fit his concept of self into a life plan that has direction and purpose. The danger of this stage of development is role diffusion—overidentification with other adolescents or with adult models to the point where there is complete loss of identity as an individual.

It is difficult to explain the influence of parents in aiding or abetting the development of identity. The average adolescent rebels against excessive parental authority. But the amount of parental authority is difficult to assess. Often parents feel that they are damned if they do, and damned if they don't. It is difficult for parents to be helpful to adolescents. But among those attitudes and methods of constructive treatment that help is knowing and accepting the idea that adolescents need something to rebel against—as a way of assuming responsible grown-up roles. When parents provide limits, when they say "Beyond this you cannot go," they offer security and also give the growing adolescent something tangible to fight. Guide lines laid down by parents provide this security. The parent has helped in this developmental stage if he has offered respect and encouragement to the growing adolescent. Parents help further when they provide flexibility within the guidelines. Increasing an adolescent's opportunity to become independent can aid in preparing for adult independence.

However, it is important to point out the limits of parental influence during adolescence:

. . . there are very real limits to what parents can do to influence the adolescent's development. Their work has to be done earlier, in infancy, in toddlerhood, in the pre-school years, in the school years. Now they can serve as bulwarks and as good examples, or as sparring partners, or they can make the adolescent's life miserable, but his fate is now decided largely outside the home.[23]

The other stages of man lie in the future for most college freshmen. But it may be helpful for students to look back at the quality of their own relationship with their parents. Not that one should be critical. No person has had perfect upbringing. But the influence of parents on current feelings of trust and distrust, being able and free to use one's talents or being doubtful about them, being able to initiate plans and projects without feeling the crushing pangs of guilt, feeling capable of learning instead of fearing inferiority, being able to assume identity in the world of people and work are all closely related to past childhood experiences. Students should look back not to blame, but to assess their good fortune and calculate what must be done to make up for misfortune. For the college freshman the hope lies in the future, though he must understand and even remedy the foundation built in the past.

Social class influence on self-development

For many years college was an experience available only to those who could afford it financially. Consequently, only the upper income groups, the upper-middle class and upper classes, enrolled. Mueller describes a basic formula which is currently operative, though rapidly changing in our society:

The upper social-economic levels (professional people, owners, managers) produce about 8 percent of all the children of this country, of whom about 90 percent complete high school and go on to college.

The middle classes (small businessmen, clerical and office workers, minor professional people, farmers, foremen, a few skilled workers) produce a little more than 30 percent of all the children, of whom 60 percent finish high school and 15 percent enter college.

The lower classes (skilled, semi-skilled, unskilled laborers, etc.) produce about 60 percent of the children, of whom 30 percent go through high school and only 5 percent enter college.[24]

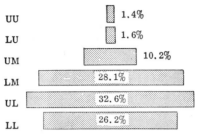

UU   1.4%

LU   1.6%

UM   10.2%

LM   28.1%

UL   32.6%

LL   26.2%

Crombach, *Educational Psychology* (New York: Harcourt, Brace and Company, Inc., 1954), p. 131. Data taken from W. Lloyd Warner and Paul S. Lunt, *The Social Life of a Modern Community* (New Haven, Conn.: Yale University Press, 1941), p. 203; and W. Lloyd Warner *et al., Democracy in Jonesville* (New York: Harper & Bros., 1949), p. 219. Used by permission.

Fig. 1–3.   The Social Structure. The social structure is a pyramid.

Fig. 1-3 describes the social structure of the country. It shows the upper-upper classes as having 1.4 percent of the population and the majority of the people categorized as upper-lower (32.6 percent) and lower-lower (25.2 percent).

We have to recognize class distinctions even though we don't necessarily like them. Social class patterns of child rearing and family expectations have their effect on personality development. In discussing this, however, it is important to point out that these are general tendencies, not rigid patterns.

There are certain factors in American life that have kept social classes from becoming rigid. The principle of equality, the idea that "all men are created equal," the respect for individuality, the tradition of equal opportunity, the ideal of the American melting pot have tended to work against a rigid class system. In the light of these ideals it is distasteful to admit that there are differences between classes in society. Still there is a class structure, which can be defined and studied. There are differences in the behavior and values of different classes.

Among people of college age, the most striking difference between upper and lower classes is that most people in the former expect to go to college, while in the latter they do not. Upper-class and middle-class parents expect and encourage their children to attend college. Lower-middle and lower-class parents seem to value education, but they either do not care or do not know how to give their children the extra push to go on to college.[25]

However, most parents expect their children to have a better life than they had. They encourage their children to improve their status and income. Social mobility, moving from one class to another, is characteristic of the American class system. "The American dream" is a dream of *upward* social mobility. It is a particularly vivid dream among middle-class parents and children. Education is regarded as a principal way to move upward in the social scale. As the need for people with higher levels of skill and ambition increases, the desire for social mobility plays an increasingly important part in American culture. There is now great interest in increasing this desire among lower-class families in order to increase the number of highly skilled people in society.

The last decade, in particular, has seen a concerted effort to encourage more and more students from the lower-middle and lower classes to enter college. One educator indicated that the percentage of youth from working class homes would increase from three percent in 1940 to 24 percent in the future. Such an effort is needed to help offset the fact that four out of ten in the top ten percent of students with intellectual ability to do college work now fail to enter college.[26]

Like the family, the social class in which we have been reared has also greatly influenced our personality. This aspect of our environment plays a major part in molding our concept of self.

Culture includes all behavior which the human being exhibits in conformity with his family, his play group, his school group, his social class, his church, and all his other human groups. The processes by which the individual learns his basic culture are subsumed under the concept socialization. Socialization includes not only social learning, but also those processes which help form the human personality itself, including both its emotional and its intellectual aspects.[27]

There are at least three social class considerations of importance: (1) In different classes there are strikingly different ways of rearing children and molding personality. In college, a student may for the first time get acquainted with people from social classes unfamiliar to him; and he may consider some of their behavior strange and uncouth. He may find them easier to understand if he avoids labelling strange behavior "good" or "bad" until he determines whether a moral or social judgment is appropriate.

(2) The typical American college is geared for students who have middle-class values, habits, and vocational expectations. Even though there are some colleges that attract most of their students from financially deprived families (where parents may or may not be college graduates), the college officials and professors expect and often demand that students display middle-class behavior. Even the janitor of

one such college, shaking his head after watching a student throw trash on the floor, commented: "And he's a college student. He should act like a college student! I know better than to do that and I never went to college!" The janitor expected neatness and a respect for cleanliness and orderliness. These traits are not the sole possession of middle and upper classes, but are more rigorously enforced among these classes than elsewhere.

(3) Society in general expects certain by-products of a college education that have little to do with accumulated intellectual skills and knowledge. These include manners and ways of behaving toward people in social situations. Often a student who has developed his intellectual side and neglected to participate in opportunities for educating the social and cultural side of the self will find himself uneducated according to most people.

Although social classes develop different manners and behavior patterns in children, there is increasing evidence indicating that social mobility is enhanced by education. The schools and the colleges are perhaps reaping the benefits of planning activities so that common social standards are introduced to all—regardless of class.[28] And the school and the college provide the education needed to move upward in the social scale through increased income, wider personal contacts, and mastery of good standards of manners and taste.

What are the possible influences of social class on the self? First, social class often provides the growing child with a sense of who he is— his relative position to others. Jane may have heard, "Remember, we may be poor, but we're as good as anybody else." Or Jill, "Don't dare bring that trash into our house again, what will the neighbors think?" Or "Pay no attention to those people, they're stuck up." The fact that a person feels that he comes from the wrong side of the tracks can place an additional burden on the self's efforts to feel worthy. Furthermore, the self is influenced by the perception of others. As soon as a child enters school, there are subtle as well as direct ways of communicating the fact that he (and others like him) is acceptable or unacceptable. Allison Davis believes it unfortunate that most teachers favor the middle-class child because they are "at home" with his way of acting.[29]

Furthermore, it is possible for a person to grow up believing that he is behaving properly, then to discover that his behavior is not acceptable to others. He may have been rewarded by his own class group with praise and warmth, only to be faced in college with having to alter the concept of how others view him. Such an experience can prove harmful

unless the person knows certain behavior is offensive to people who
have been reared differently.

"What's wrong with me?" asked Hank. "I walk into this class, I know
my homework. I'm ready to recite. I feel good—real good. Then all of
a sudden—bam! The prof. sails into me. All I was doing was eating a
sandwich. I've always done this when I have a class at noon. I'm not
bothering a soul. I'm just eating. Do you know the prof. yelled: 'This
class is supposed to be a feast of knowledge, not of lunch; eating during
lectures is rude!'? I was so embarrassed. Who does the prof. think he is
—God or something? All I was doing was eating!"

To Hank, there is considerable consternation! Eating when he is
hungry is acceptable to his parents. It did not make sense to him that he
must go without lunch when he could both eat and listen in class! He
had not been reared to consider how others would react to munching or
facial contortions while they were attempting to concentrate on the
lecture—to say nothing of the fact that they too were hungry! Eating
habits differ from social class to social class.

The influence of social class on the self may be damaging—depending on, of course, the individual. Some genuinely never care to be accepted by others, and are able to label Hank's experience as *superficial*.
For some, just to be bright is enough. But, for others, the humiliation
and feeling of unworthiness may take its toll. There is help for those
who do care. Social mobility is acceptable in this country and college
provides a major vehicle for achieving this. Simply understanding the
influence of social class or modes of behavior provides insight. And, if
after gaining understanding it seems advantageous to present oneself
in the manner which is expected of people one admires, countless experiences at the college—dinners, teas, receptions, dormitory programs,
charm-clinics, plus heart to heart talks with counselors and teachers—
can help build social skills. In other words, college experiences can
modify whatever unfavorable influences social class membership may
have on a person's concept of self.

2

Clearing the hurdles

*Major developmental tasks
of college students*

When a child suddenly shows a surprising new form of behavior, usually undesirable, his parents say, "He's going through a phase." They wait patiently and use a firm hand in appropriate places, confident that in time the child will learn to manage his new-found behavior in the right way at the right time. Learning how to control new forms of behavior that appear at different stages of growth is referred to among social scientists as a *developmental task*. At each stage of development, a person has to learn how to behave so that he can adjust to three important factors that vary with age: (1) bodily growth and physical maturation; (2) the expectations of important people in his life, partly affected by cultural pressures and social demands; (3) his own individual aspirations and values. Success in mastering each developmental task depends upon satisfactory adjustment of one's behavior to these three factors, at the appropriate time, and ". . . leads to his happiness and to success with later tasks, while failure leads to unhappiness in the

25

individual, disapproval by society, and difficulty with later tasks."[1]

New developmental tasks appear throughout life, from birth to death. For example, when physical growth is completed in late adolescence, accepting and using one's body becomes a task; but a child of eight to ten has the developmental task of controlling changes brought about by continuing growth. Retirement is a developmental task of old age, occupational choice a task of college age.

Developmental tasks form a regular series, mastery of one leading to mastery of another at a later stage. For example, the physiological development of sex organs and functions during puberty and adolescence paves the way for marrying and having children in adulthood. Mastery of social tasks prepares for more complex social relationships. For example, choice of an occupation during the college years opens the way to development of a career. The sequence of developmental tasks is continuous and irreversible. The adolescent may act childish, but cannot go back to being a child. Failure to master a task in one stage creates delays and difficulties in later stages. The college student must make an occupational choice; if he does not, he may float from job to job with no sense of accomplishment until he finally makes a firm commitment.

Developmental tasks at different ages have been defined by social scientists through the study of the behavior of many people of different personality types at all stages of development. Social scientists have depended largely on three methods: (1) observing the behavior of people at different ages to see what most of them want to do and what they can do; (2) getting people to describe their chief concerns and interests at different ages in questionnaires and interviews; (3) analyzing their own personal experiences, interests, problems, and goals at different ages.[2] The general pattern of most people's behavior seems to fall into a regular sequence with fairly clearly defined stages and developmental tasks.

Erikson's concept of eight stages of growth (see Chapter 1) is an example of such a developmental sequence, with typical problems at each stage. Another writer, Robert Havighurst, has been particularly interested in the stages of adolescence and young adulthood and in developmental tasks of the college age, which overlaps these two stages. He regards the *achieving of identity* as the characteristic problem of the college years. He suggests that six developmental tasks must be mastered in order to achieve identity as an adult:

(1) Learning a masculine or feminine social role.
(2) Accepting one's body.
(3) Achieving emotional independence of parents.

(4) Achieving new and more mature relations with age mates of both sexes.
(5) Selecting and preparing for an occupation.
(6) Achieving a scale of values and an ethical system to live by.[3]

The first three of these tasks are described in this chapter. The last three are discussed in other sections of this book. The six tasks form a developmental sequence in themselves; for achievement of the first three leads to success in the last three, the more complex combinations of tasks that require basic mastery of self-understanding.

ACHIEVING EMOTIONAL INDEPENDENCE OF PARENTS

This developmental task is the most immediate concern of college freshmen. Students in a residential college are separated from their parents physically, but must still achieve emotional independence. Commuting students live at home, but are on their own at college, and must achieve independence without separation. Colleges generally expect all students to be on their own, make their own decisions, and come to terms with college life and academic work without depending on their parents. In college, students must make the most important decisions on their own initiative: choice of courses and major, choice of organizational memberships, choice of an occupation, and choice of friends and dating companions.

Emotional independence is often equated by students with financial independence from parents. Eventually, of course, both will have to be achieved. But it is possible to get financed by parents without being emotionally dependent on them. Part of this developmental task is learning to distinguish between financial and emotional dependence.

It is not too much to expect that a student will solve his problems without "getting the word from home." Most parents are wise enough to listen to the anguished voice on the long-distance phone, say, "Well, dear, you seem (or ought, or have) to be able to figure that out for yourself," hang up, and pay the collect charges with a rueful grin. Most students have learned enough from their parents to have pretty clear standards to use in making decisions. Their standards are internalized, and have "soaked in" as the student grew up. They are the basis for the new standards he will develop to meet new situations in college. (These new standards and consequent changes in behavior and values, however, apparently must be consistent with some important established value to be acceptable to the individual.)[4]

Lolly, for example, had been accustomed to talking over her dates and her ideals of romance with her mother in late night chats after dates. There was nothing, absolutely nothing, that she couldn't talk over with her mother. She and her mother worked out difficult decisions about necking and petting during high school. Lolly felt very comfortable about her decisions, though some of her standards were different from those of some of her friends. In her first semester at college, she yearned for her mother to talk to about some of her problems with dating. She felt under pressure to do things that were unacceptable to her. Her roommate was no help, for she had her own problems. Having had her mother as an anchor for her emotions, Lolly felt cast adrift. Nobody seemed to care very much how far she went with Larry.

Lolly is typical of many freshmen who have to give up emotional dependence on parents. She had the advantage of a pretty good set of standards and some independence training by her mother. She found she could trust her feelings and her judgment, without having her mother there. She could be self-directed, not mother-directed.

The goal of emotional independence from parents is just such self-direction. The mature student wants to be self-directed, not other-directed, independent, not dependent.

Faulty efforts at emancipation

Some students attempt to avoid the developmental task of independence by *finding a substitute parent,* placing another person or persons in the parents' role.[5] A faculty member or faculty wife, a housemother or counselor, or another adult may be chosen. Counselors are trained to avoid playing the role, and most faculty members are aware of its difficulties for them and the student; but less well-informed adults may allow a student to become dependent upon them. Plenty of people are only too willing to dictate to green freshmen and assume the parental role. Upperclassmen will advise about the best or easiest "profs" and what courses to take or avoid. They are in the know about the best fraternity, the best boy to date. They take advantage of "the vulnerability of all adolescents to the seductive voice of the false leader."[6]

A student cannot become independent by transferring dependence from parents to friends or other adults. In the end, he may form the habit of dependence, never becoming self-directed. He may become "driven, but not the driver." The danger is that students who want to be dependent may find or be found by persons who want to dominate. One student who had fallen into this trap said: "So what? There are plenty of people who like to make decisions for you." Unfortunately, when the really crucial decisions come, most of these domineering types take to the woods, and the student has to face the decision all alone. If he has not mastered the developmental task of independence, he will have to master it right then, or else. Most dependent students are completely incapacitated and cannot make decisions on their own; or else they are so overcharged with anxiety that they make a quick decision, snatching at a straw to keep from drowning.

A second faulty effort is *devaluation of parents*.[7] Sooner or later, everyone sees his parents fail or make mistakes. He learns that parents are human, with faults, liable to error. It is a sign of health to accept human fallibility, including one's parents' and one's own. It is a sign of faulty judgment to be hypercritical, intolerant of parents because they are not perfect. Students who devalue their parents make the task more difficult for themselves. They "throw out the baby with the bath," abandoning sound standards just because their parents do not always live up to them. They annoy and irritate their parents, producing unnecessary conflict by criticizing them for trifles.

In a recent novel,[8] Richard, a Harvard student, has a heart-to-heart talk with his father about the family maid. She's a disgrace, impertinent, arrogant; his parents make too many allowances because she's a refugee. They should read Emily Post and brush up on how to make her behave. She wears an old brocaded gown she brought over from Germany, not a neat uniform, and "looks like Sitting Bull disguised as Queen Victoria." She calls him "the Richard" not "Mr. Richard." He can't understand his parents' tolerating that sort of stuff. Bill Hodges' parents would not stand for it.

Richard is an example of the students who try to change the family and make it conform to new ideas. They may criticize the home and the rearing of younger brothers and sisters. They may challenge parents on political and social ideas, especially on political parties and race relations. They may reject parental guidance and replace it with that secured from adults in authority outside the family unit.[9] ("We eat our artichokes *cold* at school!")

A wise student understands that his tastes and standards are changing. This does not mean that his parents must change their tastes and standards to conform to his. In fact, parents tend to be more tolerant of their adolescent's new ideas when they do not have to change their own opinions or habits. The effort to establish independence is a private task, best accomplished when one allows for the right of parents, as individuals, to their own ideas and life patterns. Commuting students, in particular, have a better chance to win independence when they remember this simple rule.

Deterrents to successful emancipation from home

One would think that a student would be glad to leave a home in which he was in continuous conflict with his parents. This is not necessarily the case. When the parents are left behind, the student may have a feeling of guilt over the way he has behaved. He may feel responsible for an unhappy home life, even though he really could do nothing about it. Home looks better from afar, and he may feel guilt because he didn't appreciate his happy home while he was there. He may feel jealous and think he has been cheated out of a nice home when other students brag about the fine, understanding parents they left behind. Such negative feelings or unresolved guilt may have to be resolved before the student can feel free to establish other emotional ties and develop happier personal relationships.[10]

Financial dependence on the parents is a fact of life for most students, and can lead to a good deal of confusion in achieving emotional independence. Sometimes parents do try to use financial controls to keep a student emotionally dependent or to enforce their demands for a particular choice of mate, occupation, or major field. Many students fear that their parents may do so, even though there is no evidence that their parents wish to dominate at all. Some students yield unnecessarily to parental suggestions, saying, "They're paying the bills, the least I can do is follow their advice."

But most parents feel that the best yield on their investment is a happy, socially useful, independent graduate. They may complain and threaten, but they do not often enforce the threat to dictate choices. Expressing an opinion and dictating are different; most parents reserve the right to the former, but not the latter.

Should parents try to keep students dependent on them, or try to dictate, by imposing financial conditions, it might be better for the students to cut loose from the parents, go to work and study part-time. Or a loan might be secured, especially now that the government, colleges, and industry are making loan funds so readily available.

Homesickness

An epidemic of homesickness usually hits a freshman dormitory in the fall. The disease is carried by discussion of the symptoms of nostalgia which almost everybody has upon separation from loved ones—parents, boy friends, girl friends, brothers and sisters. The homesick ones report feelings ranging all the way from "being all choked up inside" to stomach-ache or intestinal upsets. Many cry and mope. Some have fainting spells.[11] Most freshmen recover when classes start or they get an attractive date. Some are ashamed of being homesick. But it is a common form of emergency reaction that recurs throughout adult life. Nostalgia is said to be older than Nature itself—in classical mythology even the gods and heroes were homesick. Homer wrote that Ulysses wept and rolled on the floor when he thought of home—and Ulysses was no freshman!

Many factors precipitate homesickness. Physical discomfort is a factor, though most campuses are modern enough for few students to claim this excuse. Change in routine causes some homesickness; the college schedule is very irregular and a marked change from high school. Discouragement, perhaps from a low grade on a test, may be a factor. Not being as popular in college as in high school, or parting from a boy friend or girl friend back home, lead to homesickness. Uninteresting courses and monotony aggravate symptoms.[12]

Rose studied a group of Smith College students,[13] and found that personality factors were related to homesickness. The girl who was never homesick was usually one who made friends easily and tended to have a large number of acquaintances. Her emotional stability was above average, and she did not feel overdominated by or unusually close to her family. The girl repeatedly homesick showed a general lack of adjustment, felt inadequate, anxious, and socially inept. She showed inability to make contact with the opposite sex, and tended to feel dominated at home and disapproved of by her parents. She was unable to compete intellectually. Among the girls who reported that they had only been homesick once, there was a generally well-adjusted pattern; but they were accustomed primarily to be with a small intimate group. They tended to be more closely tied to home.

Homesickness can be further understood as a reaction to insecurity in new social relationships. It may be caused by the reluctance of established students to accept newcomers, or their insistence on behavior different from what the freshman previously found successful. For example, a southern Negro girl, one of only four or five Negroes in her class, became homesick because she felt the other students were reluctant to accept her. Her experience with whites had always been negative in the past, and she interpreted the natural reserve of older students as rejection.

Generally, the normally adjusted student, who is willing to get around and get acquainted, will find activities he enjoys and feel comfortable in his new social setting. Homesickness is supposed to fade. If it does not, a student should seek help from the residence hall director, dean, or counselor. For he may not be suffering so much from homesickness as from another problem masquerading as homesickness. Problems that masquerade may be so serious that they can't be faced directly. In such a case, the student had better get help quickly in finding out what the trouble is and in dealing with it.

Being on one's own should be a pleasure. It is what the student has been waiting for throughout the period of adolescence. As a young adult, he moves toward final separation and independence of his parents. Winning emotional independence prepares him for a life of his own.

ACCEPTING AND USING ONE'S BODY

The last of the series of physiological changes in human development is complete in most people by the ordinary age for college entrance. The sex organs mature and their functions become regular during the high school years. The secondary sex characteristics are established: the boys look and talk like men; the girls look and talk like women. Bodily growth is about complete; physiologically, the bodily functions are ready for adult life and biological reproduction.

Most students enter college with substantially the type of body that they will have and use throughout adult life. They can expect to be recognizably themselves, to have the same physical self, from now on. They cannot be shorter, and very little if any taller. They may gain weight; in fact, most freshmen gain weight noticeably, perhaps because of the combination of regular meals and heavy snacks.

Inevitably, some Joan will meet some Mrs. Doe on the street during Christmas vacation, and she will give the usual greeting: "Why, Joan! How you've grown! I hardly recognized you!" Joan may be slightly mortified, if she has gained some weight. Really, she hasn't changed to speak of. Mrs. Doe expects dramatic changes in people of Joan's age; and, therefore, she sees them. But Joan's pattern of physical change will no longer show dramatic spurts. What strikes Mrs. Doe, because she hasn't seen Joan for three months, is the gradual change produced by greater maturity and bodily poise, better taste in makeup and clothes, and other calculated rearrangements and improvements.

The stabilizing of physical development makes it possible for the student to have a fairly clear and accurate picture of himself. Psychologists call this impression of physical appearance the *body image*. It is made up of several elements: the image seen in a mirror; the image reflected in responses of family and friends; the kinesthetic image reflected in the feel of the body in movement and at rest. Adolescent awkwardness, for instance, is known to have passed, because the student can see that his posture is better; his parents tell him he is standing up straighter; and he can tell where his hands and feet are without paying much attention to them. The image and the feel of the body are certain and sure.

Influences affecting the body image

A person's body image may be affected by his own ideal picture of himself. This may differ from the way others see him. A particularly disliked feature may be left out of the image of the self. Bill, for instance, was convinced that his freckles were not noticeable and had a picture to prove that they did not show. His friends, on the other hand, could see his freckles, and some thought they were very attractive. Bill cringed when they admired his freckles, which he thought were horrible, and tried to convince himself that they could hardly be seen at all.

The body image may be colored by comparison with the appearance of others. This competitive feature is almost universal in American culture.

From an early age many girls are made aware of being pretty or not very pretty as compared with other girls. They also become aware of other particular physical features such as having pretty eyes or having curly or straight hair. Many boys become especially aware of their height, and to some extent of their weight, as features of their own self-evaluation and as features that influence the impression they make on others. For many boys the fact of being large or small as compared with others is very important, especially when they are exceptionally short or tall.[14]

The body image, consequently, is not merely a picture of oneself but also a value judgment of the worth of the self. It is an estimate of comparative physical attractiveness, of desirability, of ability to compete with others for admiration and acceptance.

Karen Horney speaks of the cultural standards of physical attractiveness as "the tyrannical shoulds": a woman *should* be five feet five, weigh 122 pounds, measure 34 inches in the bust! In one study[15] a group of college women were asked to compare their own bodies with these standards and others used as an ideal rating. Their responses indicated that their satisfaction with their bodies varied inversely with the magnitude of the deviation between their measured size and what they considered to be the ideal size. Since none had physical measurements identical with the ideal rating, none rated positively all their bodily features.

Studies like this seem to indicate the significance of the body image in personal development. Attitudes and feelings toward oneself, esti-

mates of one's worth, influence the body image. In turn, they are influenced by satisfaction or dissatisfaction with the body image.[16]

Faulty body image affects self-acceptance

Lack of acceptance of the body image may be related to lack of self-
acceptance in two ways. The body image may be faulty, as an effect of
a general feeling of worthlessness of the self. Or particular faults in the
body image may lead to a feeling of unworthiness or self-rejection.

There may be undue concern with pain, disease, or bodily injury.[17]
Likes and dislikes for the body or particular parts of it are often shown
in unnatural worries about health or injury. There may be fears of possible disfigurement of a pretty feature. "Oh, doctor, are you sure it won't
leave a scar?" one cries as the doctor puts in the stitches. Some students
overdose themselves with aspirin or other pain relievers, or take vita-
mins whether they need them or not. Some students are so oversolici-
tous of their bodies that they are always diagnosing mononucleosis
every time they catch a cold. One college physician used to refer to such
overanxious students as "those internes over in the dorm."

Overrating the importance of the body may appear in *feelings that
all one's wrongdoings are visited upon the body*. This feeling often results from parental warnings about various unacceptable practices. "If
you don't eat your carrots, your hair won't stay curly," is just a joke.
Really serious threats may be uttered about the awful physical consequences of masturbation, which persist in spite of evidence against such
results. For example, one bit of folklore regards pimples as punishment
for masturbation. The body does sustain a lot of damage from careless
abuse, but it does not pay the price for all transgressions, real or fancied.

A feeling of insecurity in social situations may often be related to
shame over some aspect of physical appearance. Tamara was finally
persuaded after many protestations and excuses to go to a night club
with her boy friend. After they were seated at their table, she looked
around the room, and gasped: "Oh, I'm so glad to see some other *fat*
women here! I always thought only skinny people went to night clubs."
Many examples could be given of students who choose or refuse to
enter certain social situations because of some aspect of the body image.

Some students adapt to disliked features of the body image by *calling
attention to the fault and making a joke of it*. Jimmy Durante has made
a fortune by poking fun at his nose, by accepting it and making an asset
of it. Ordinarily, joking does not show self-acceptance but displaced
hostility, the unhealthy rejection of a distasteful feature. Nicknames,

such as "Fatso" and "Jughead" may be accepted by a student and used derisively against himself, revealing his dislike of his waistline or "jug-ears."

Sometimes a faulty body image may be reflected in *habits of care of the person, in dress, or manners.* Both carelessness and meticulous habits may reflect self-rejection. An image of the self as slob may be expressed in sloppy dress, unwashed or unshaven appearance, and rudeness. An attempt may be made to falsify physical appearance, to look like somebody else, by dyeing the hair or using extravagant makeup.[18] Falsification indicates distaste or rejection of the body image since it is chosen as an alternative to genuine improvement in appearance. The high valuation of beauty in our culture is a problem for men as well as women. Short men may dress attractively and fashionably to compensate for lack of attainment of the masculine ideal of height, broad shoulders, and well-developed muscles. Those who sport blue jeans and black leather jackets, or flashy checkered coats and blue suede shoes are often showing rejection of themselves, as worthless types who needn't even try to approach the ideal, or who reject ideals of beauty and taste altogether.[19]

Strange as it may seem, beauty brings its problems, too. The very pretty woman and the handsome man may be exploited and shown off for their good looks at the expense of their feelings of personal worth.[20] Some have feelings of guilt or anxiety over excessive admiration which they feel they don't deserve, everything being considered. They are often objects of jealousy and carry the scars of rejection and cruel slander. Some of them have their heads turned, and regard their good looks as a mark of personal achievement. They overinvest emotionally in their good looks; and when they grow old and their beauty fades, the blow to their self-esteem is extremely painful. Experience in counseling seems to indicate that the body image of beauty is just as hard to accept and use effectively as the image of plainness or disfigurement.

Accepting and using one's body

"Lord, help us to hae a guid conceit o' oursel's," is an old Scottish prayer. To think well of ourselves is not to have undue pride, to overinvest emotionally in appearance or physical prowess as sources of self-esteem. "A guid conceit" is accepting oneself with pleasure, not pride. To be pleased with one's body image, to enjoy dancing, sports, singing, work, love, food, all the things a sound body enables one to do, is evidence of a healthy personality. A high school student at a forum once asked Karen Horney, "How can you tell you have good mental health?" She thought a moment, then replied: "When you go to brush your teeth in the morning, look at yourself in the mirror. If you like what you see, you probably have good mental health."

Asking, "Mirror, mirror on the wall, who is the fairest one of all?" is not such a healthy idea. It leaves one open to disappointment. Comparison with someone else leads only to wishing to be like someone else, not to self-acceptance. But if he can stand the shock, the mirror will tell one who he is and whether he likes himself.

The person with a sound body image can stand to look in the mirror first thing in the morning. He also generally looks good to other people. He lets them know who he is and that he likes himself by the way he dresses, moves, speaks. He has good taste, and is in good physical condition, neat, clean, well-groomed. He has style, that subtle individuality that makes him distinctive and enables people to remember him as a special person. He has charm, that indefinable quality that people recognize as characterizing a person who accepts himself and wants to share his pleasure with others.

A great deal can be done to cultivate physical attractiveness and an acceptable body image. Very often simply doing something to improve appearance or make the body more comfortable makes the body image more acceptable. The striking improvement in personality from having one's teeth straightened is familiar to many adolescents. Simple measures also have desirable effects on the sense of personal worth; just taking a bubble bath, for instance, seems to have marvelous effects on the self-esteem of some persons. Even people with physical handicaps can develop strikingly effective charm and style. One blind student was one of the best-dressed men on campus, and a very desirable date. He had a system of coding his clothes so he could always choose matching combinations. His manners were not merely good, but polished; a girl on a date with him felt like a queen when he took her into a room—he used a system he explained in advance by which she guided him while he appeared to guide her.

College physical education requirements are not so trivial as they seem. They are designed to give students different kinds of opportunities for cultivating an acceptable body image. Some students are mainly interested in learning new individual or team sports, in dancing, or otherwise extending their recreational skills. Others may get individual programs designed to improve vigor, posture, or bodily comfort; some body mechanics programs offer help in reducing tension, overcoming awkwardness, or compensating for physical weakness.

College health services also can help students with physical difficulties that are hard to accept and manage. Those who have not quite finished growing, or have some functions of the body that haven't settled down; those with chronic diseases or physical handicaps; and, of course, those with acute ailments, can get not only treatment but also useful guidance in the management of physical health from a good health service. Of course, many colleges with limited health facilities have little health service, and have to refer students to private physicians for guidance. Medical advice costs money, but it is worth it to a student to make whatever improvement he can in physical condition to back up the big changes and opportunities that confront him in college. One student with a heart condition, for example, got medical advice from a specialist to whom the college physician referred him. He learned how to follow a disciplined pattern of living and to do twice as much as he ever thought he could do in academic work and college activities.

There is a growing specialty called *ephebiatrics*, a medical practice with young adults and late adolescents. A few such specialists are beginning to be used as college physicians. But any good physician, acquainted with some of the conditions of student life, can give students valuable help. It remains for students to find the medical services that they may need, and use them to gain understanding and control of their bodies.

Anything that can be done to develop an acceptable body image is an asset to the student. "A guid conceit" and pleasure in using the body contribute to the general joy of living. Above all, acceptance and use of the body is necessary as a foundation for the next developmental tasks of the college years—establishing masculine and feminine roles and finding a mate. For being a real man or a real woman depends in large part on a clear sense of identity based on an acceptable image of how one looks and feels. Understanding the body is needed in order to be somebody.

ESTABLISHING APPROPRIATE MASCULINE AND FEMININE ROLES

Perhaps the most important feature of the body image is identification with the sex to which one biologically belongs. Being biologically determined, sex has to be accepted as part of the body image. Sex is also used as a basis for determining appropriate social roles. Society prescribes dominant sex roles—wife and mother, husband and father—and gives them social content over and above the biological functions necessary. For instance, the division of labor between husband and wife in the home is socially, not biologically determined. The added roles are secondary sex roles, set as part of the patterns of behavior that characterize a culture. Acceptance of one's sex as part of the body image does not necessarily mean acceptance of all the secondary roles prescribed for that sex. Some may be accepted, others rejected; some may be easy for a particular person to play, others distasteful.

A role is the enactment of a part in a social relationship or institution, the behavior and attitudes one shows in actualizing the self. It may be "the part an individual plays in the life of the family as indicated by the prerogatives he exercises and the obligations he assumes in carrying out his part."[21] It may be the part an individual plays in other institutions: school, church, business, government, and others. Every person plays several different roles in different institutions.

Individuals throughout life are handed scripts in which their appropriate parts are described in the drama of the society. In changing societies like our own, new scripts of behavior are added which offer new ways of acting. Since it takes more than one person or one role to produce a play, these new scripts often produce confusion in the members of the society.[22]

Society prescribes roles as a way of regulating the behavior of its members so that important tasks will be accomplished. For example, children have to have food, shelter, clothing, and discipline until they are able to care for themselves. Society prescribes the role of breadwinner for the father to assure the child's financial care; the intimate physical and emotional care of the children is the role assigned to the mother. On this division of labor, there is clear differentiation of roles in American society. Confusion may arise on secondary matters, such as who makes the decisions in the family, how kind or stern the father may be, the taste the mother uses in furnishing the home, or how firm or tender she may be.

Most roles are reciprocal: wives and husbands, workers and bosses, teachers and pupils, for example, cannot carry out their roles without each other. Each must not only understand his role, but also accept and understand the role of the other person.[23] Not only must the father accept the role of breadwinner and provide the family income, but he must also understand how the mother's role in keeping the home enables him to do so. The mother must not only care for the home and children but also appreciate the father's part in providing the necessary income.

Without mutual understanding of the reciprocal character of roles, confusion, disagreement, and inability to play an individual role successfully may result. Frustration also results when an individual is not permitted, in his culture, to play a role for which he is suited by temperament and competence. A certain amount of confusion and frustration is built into most cultures. Some permissible roles are not rigidly prescribed, but left to individuals or groups to work out within certain limits; confusion may result from the variation in patterns that develop. The number of possible roles for any individual is always greater than the number of roles permitted in his culture; frustration may result from social prohibition of the use of abilities and interests that he enjoys.

Confusion and frustration are particularly likely to develop in changing societies. American society today is in a period of transition marked by such confusion in roles, and particularly in roles traditionally prescribed according to sex. Cultural change cannot affect biology; it still takes a man to be a father and a woman to be a mother. The dominant sex roles in marriage and parenthood have not changed. But, beyond that point, there is no longer very much clarity about appropriate roles for men and for women.

Two things seem to be happening. First, a greater number and wider range of roles seem to be permitted for both men and women. *Without being considered less masculine,* men are entering many occupations traditionally regarded as women's work: elementary education, nursing, social work, for example. Fathers are beginning to help with the housework, care for children, and show more affection for them; but confusion and controversy still remain over whether there is a danger that they will thus become less manly. Similarly, women now are represented in every single category used in occupational analysis by the U.S. Department of Labor; but there is still some confusion and controversy over whether they become less feminine by entering occupations traditionally reserved for men, such as mechanics and railroad engineers. Yet, *without being considered less feminine,* women are permitted, even expected, to play multiple roles: to hold down a job while raising a family and doing volunteer community service.

Second, there seems to be a tendency to use something beside sex to define important social roles, especially those outside the family. Individual differences in ability, interest, and achievement increasingly are being used to determine appropriate occupational choice, with sex becoming a secondary, though still an important, factor.[24] For example, in the current manpower shortage, women are sought to fill needs in science, engineering, and college teaching, traditionally men's work. Apparently, there is a trend in American society to meet such crises as wars and manpower shortages by removing some sexually determined restrictions on occupational roles. Whether this represents a real tendency to replace sex by individual merit as a basis for defining roles in this area remains to be seen. And it is still not clear whether a similar shift may be taking place in the definition of other roles. But the development of this tendency to replace sex with another basis for definition of role has led to confusion. For an individual or group may find it difficult to know just when differentiation between sex roles is being made, or whether it is appropriate.[25]

One factor that adds to confusion of roles is the prescription in society of distinctive styles of life for men and women. These include patterns of behavior that symbolize sex: manners and mannerisms, attitudes and preferences, dress, interests, hobbies, and personality traits. Little girls, for instance, are expected to prefer dolls, little boys, trains. In our society the masculine style is characterized by adjectives such as independent, forthright, strong, assertive. The feminine style is described as soft, sympathetic, modest, devoted.[26] But both men and women temperamentally are very much alike, and able to develop some of both sets of characteristics. In fact, there is more variation between members of the same sex than between the two sexes taken as wholes. So there can be both confusion and frustration in members of either sex when they have to meet expectations that they will develop a style that does not permit expression of some emotions and requires other temperamental patterns. Every little boy and every little girl must repress some responses and strengthen others to show appropriate masculine or feminine style.

These styles are changing. For instance, it is considered acceptable for fathers to be soft and affectionate with children, so long as they maintain masculine strength. There are also occasions when exceptions are made. In time of trouble a woman is expected to be a tower of strength. She preferably should not show much business skill or interest herself unduly in her husband's affairs during his lifetime; but to act soft and modest while settling his affairs after his death will earn her little respect. Occupational patterns may allow for shifts in style; a physical education major may show more masculine types of mannerisms than a woman majoring in English. Fashion also affects distinctions in style, changing a man's shirt overnight into a "sexy," feminine outfit.

So society has not arranged for an orderly distribution of roles between men and women. The student can understand and accept masculinity or femininity only by recognizing the existing confusion of sex roles and the increasing range of roles and styles acceptable for both men and women.

What is masculine? What is feminine?

"Of course," said a delegate addressing the French National Assembly on the suffrage question, "there is a difference between men and women." With one voice, the Assembly responded, "Vive la différence!"

But what is the difference? Unquestionably it is biological. Without the difference between male and female, there would be no love, no children, no human race. There would certainly not be a France! All humanity might shout with one voice, "Vive la différence!"

But the enthusiasm is beset by controversy. What is gained, what is lost by replacing sex with other distinctions in determining social roles? What cultural changes threaten the existence of the human race by confusing or blurring the distinctions between male and female? Here unanimity ceases, conflict rages.

The biological point of view holds that identity and happiness depend upon clear distinctions between sex roles both in marriage and in other aspects of life. Masculine and feminine traits are considered to be related to sexual anatomy and physiology. For women, the very nature of the sexual act is considered receptive, submissive, passive. In men, aggressiveness and a degree of dominance are required. When either a man or a woman engages in activities that require marked deviation from these fundamental patterns of behavior, they are likely to confuse sex identity and head for unhappiness. To be masculine, a man must carry his assertiveness out of the nest into the world. To be feminine, a woman must follow passive and dependent roles.[27] Masculinity and femininity depend on selecting roles consistent with the roles determined by the distinctive part played in the sexual act.

The cultural point of view is based on the principle that, in order to understand differences between masculinity and femininity, one has to look not for biological reasons but for cultural ones. Cultural patterns press men into assertive roles, women into passive roles. Women are taught to be passive and retiring, men aggressive and outgoing. Horney accounts for Freud's concept of the emotionalism of women and their overdependence on love for happiness as resulting from the restricted roles women have had to play in our culture.[28] Their personal contacts were limited to the home and family, in which there was more emotionality and dependence on love, in contrast to the less personalized world of work. Women naturally cultivated, even overrated love.

Anthropological studies of both primitive and contemporary cultures support the cultural point of view. What is striking about them is the great variety of ways in which sex has been treated in the structure of different cultures. There may be no recognition of temperamental differences in the sexual act itself, or in relationships between parents and children, husband and wife. There may be no contrast between masculine and feminine roles; both may be expected to be aggressive, or both submissive. There may be a complete reversal of our sex attitudes, with the women playing the dominant role and the men a dependent one. Yet individuals show about the same range of temperamental differences in culture after culture.[29] So there is no reason to conclude that the biological difference must be used consistently to define social roles. Age, kinship, social class, talents, and other factors can be and have been used to differentiate roles. There is no reason to believe that clarity in masculine and feminine roles is necessary to either adequate biological or social functioning.

But anxiety over changes in distinctions between masculinity and femininity, and the resulting confusion in sex roles, exists in our culture. There is a fear that changes in distinctions between men's work and women's work may affect relations between sexes. Women's work has been centered in the home, men's work outside the family in fields, factories, offices. If women were employed, positions in the "nurturing and caring" professions were believed most appropriate because women's role in bearing and rearing children was considered consistent with such work. Changes in society have opened the way for women to work in almost every other field. And it is interesting to note that, as salaries have improved in women's fields, men have entered them in larger numbers. There is no evidence that these changes have made men or women feel less masculine or feminine, in spite of the anxiety expressed over confusion or loss of identity.

Some anxiety is also expressed over the possibility that women will identify with masculine roles to the extent of neglecting home and children. There is no evidence that the mother's employment in itself affects the development of children. Significant factors affecting the adjustment of children of working mothers seem rather to be the attitude of people in the neighborhood and other children at school toward women who work outside the home, and the extent to which adequate care is provided for the child while the mother is at work.[30]

Anxiety is felt that competition between men and women for employment will introduce undesirable tensions into marital relationships. This may present a problem, especially where the woman is more successful or has a higher salary. The problem is not insoluble; there is simply very little evidence in experience since women are at a salary disadvantage in so many fields.[31] Another fear is that the employed woman may develop aggressive behavior that may be a threat to male identity. A passive husband may become compliant, dependent, and, therefore, feminine.[32] Loss of male identity and confusion of sex roles is feared as a source of disturbance in sexual relations. So far, however, no evidence indicates that there are more serious sex problems in marriages in which both partners are employed, in which both share the housework, or in which one or both deviate from the presumed biological role. Many other factors seem to be more significant in sexual compatibility, including the expectation that husband and wife can solve marital problems.

Anxiety is further expressed over the possibility that children may fail to find a clear and consistent model to follow in the parent of their own sex, and, consequently, reject their proper sex identity. This possibility seems genuine, particularly if the parent of the same sex as the child is colorless, unattractive, or uninteresting. However, there would seem to be not loss but gain in increasing the permissible range of roles for both sexes. Children of both sexes are likely to be born into the same family. And they might all find identification with an appropriate parent easier and more rewarding if both parents had a good education, had done interesting work, and had developed individuality in style and the ability to fulfill a variety of roles.

A good marriage and successful parenthood, like so many human relationships, draw upon many human qualities that are not necessarily associated with sex. When students list qualities desirable in a mate, both sexes list the same qualities. The general human virtues common to both sexes provide a foundation for a healthy relationship between them: intelligence, initiative, compassion, judgment, talent, enthusiasm, capacity to master situations, generosity, to name a few.[33]

Faulty identification with masculine and feminine roles

Children learn masculine and feminine behavior from their parents. The mother introduces her daughter to feminine roles; the son is introduced by the father to masculine ways. Both parents reward children for showing behavior in keeping with their sex. In other subtle ways, they guide children into appropriate patterns. Adults who enjoy being male or female seem to afford the models with whom children can most readily identify. Happy relationships between the parents, and between the child and the parent of the same sex, make it easier for the child to accept being male or female. And the growing person who has the opportunity to appreciate both masculine and feminine roles played in the family has greater understanding and security in reciprocal roles that he plays with the opposite sex.

Of course, no parents have ideal relationships with each other or perfect relationships with their children. Both parents have problems of their own that affect the family. In terms of traditional distinctions, neither parent these days is likely to play a consistently masculine or feminine role. Apparently, conformity to tradition is not as significant as the individuality of the parents and the consistency of their behavior with the ideal patterns they try to teach their children. Individuality and consistency make it easier for the child to accept his parents as models. Consequently, they increase the likelihood that he will find in the parent of the same sex an acceptable model for his development of an appropriate sex role. *It is the way the child perceives his relationship with both parents and their relationship to each other that affects the patterns of behavior he learns.* Which parent plays what role is important, but only in relation to the way the child sees it.

Variations in behavior related to parental roles. In traditional distinctions between masculine and feminine styles, the male is conceived to be assertive, aggressive, and strong; the female warm, compassionate, and dependent. The male is the authority figure, the female the affectionate figure in the traditional pattern of parental roles. As roles have changed in modern American society, this pattern has changed, if, indeed, it ever generally existed. Parents share in different ways the affection-authority roles. These differences do affect their children's behavior. For example, in a recent study at Harvard[34] differences in students' reactions under pressure seemed to be related to their perception of their parents' roles. Students who thought of their fathers as strong and authoritative tended to react with anger and to blame other people for their difficulties. If they saw the mother in the strong authority role, they tended to react to pressure with anxiety, and to blame themselves. If they regarded the parents as sharing authority, and both were seen as warm and affectionate, the students tended to curb their anger, and try to see how they could change their own behavior, without being overanxious. But whether the students saw their fathers in the traditional aggressive, masculine role, or saw their mothers in the role, or viewed both parents as sharing the role of affection and authority, did not seem to make much difference in their ability to stand up to pressure and produce, in the long run.

Thus, people who do not conform consistently to masculine or feminine styles may still have adequate reactions to life situations. Without conforming to traditional patterns, they may still be adequate parental models of masculine or feminine behavior for their children.

Such variations in behavior do not necessarily lead to faulty identification with one's own sex. But they may lead to anxiety in students who do not conform to patterns acceptable among their associates. Students whose reactions are "different" may be teased unmercifully until they are so self-conscious that they can hardly respond comfortably. They may be the victims of idle gossip or slander about how effeminate or mannish they are. They may become misfits and outsiders, rejecting their fellow students because of their unfair criticism.

It is very difficult to decide for oneself whether different reactions that are considered unmanly or unwomanly really are faults in oneself. The fault may lie in lack of maturity and understanding among fellow students, or in stereotyped traditions and standards in the college. The student can usually work out such a decision best with the help of a skilled counselor. For of all the deadly weapons that students use on each other, accusations or fears of sexual inadequacy are the most deadly. A student who is the object of gossip about it can be badly hurt; and he can hurt others badly if he tries to fight back with this two-edged sword of sex.

Rejection of roles related to rejection of parents. An unhappy relationship between the parents, or between one or the other parent and the child, may lead to difficulty in finding an acceptable model of one's own sex. Inconsistency in the father's pattern of behavior may make a son see him as an undesirable model. If the mother is perceived as unfair and tyrannical, a daughter may reject her. Similarities and differences between themselves and their parents in interests and abilities may lead children to identify with a different parent in different roles. If these similarities and differences favor one parent over the other, a child may overidentify with the favored parent, or in some cases with the underdog. For instance, an intellectually gifted girl may model herself entirely on a brilliant, successful father if her mother is weak, ineffectual, and uninteresting. The selection of a good model depends on the child's response. In this instance, a daughter who was sympathetic and understanding might accept the mother as a feminine model without necessarily emulating her weakness and dependence.

There are some special hazards in the relationships between children and their parents that affect the development of masculinity and femininity:

a. A child who fears and hates a parent may reject the femininity or masculinity that his parent stands for and tend to pattern himself or herself after the other

parent. If John fears his father and dislikes him, he may very well identify with
his mother and try to be like her.

b. Fear and hatred of a parent may generalize to other individuals of the
same sex as the feared and hated parent. John may further dislike all men because he thinks they are like his own father.

c. Dominance of a masculine or feminine model in the child's environment
tends to produce a personality corresponding to the model. Since John's mother
is more attractive, in that she is warm, considerate and understanding, both he
and his sister have patterned themselves after her. This is good for his sister Lucy,
but John needs a strong male role to emulate.[35]

The inadequacy of parents is never an absolute limitation on a child's
development. Rejection of a feared and hated parent does not always
lead the child to reject the role that the parent represents. Other significant adults may be substituted as models for a missing or inadequate
parent. Fatherless boys may find a good model in an uncle or cousin,
grandfather, neighbor, or teacher. Motherless girls may model themselves on a grandmother, aunt, teacher. Or particular traits, lacking or
inadequate in a parent, may be emulated from other models. Sometimes
the parents themselves are sensitive and understanding enough to encourage a child to supplement his supply of models from outside the
family, to strengthen his development at points where they know they
are weak.

Problems of women. Studies consistently show that girls indicate
less preference for the feminine role than boys do for the masculine role.
Less than four percent of adult males, compared to nearly 31 percent
of adult females, in one study, indicated that at one time or other in life
they desired to be of the opposite sex.[36] It has been suggested that these
findings indicate a rejection by women of the entire biological and
social function of being female. A more reasonable explanation seems
to be that women's roles appear dull and restrictive in comparison with
men's activities. Little girls are in a position to hear their mothers complain about washing, ironing, cleaning, and doing dishes. They share
these duties and discover that they are dull and repetitive. They see
their fathers walk out of the house every morning and leave these chores
to their mothers. They hear less from their fathers of the routine aspects
of men's work, which consequently seems more glamorous. Mothers do
not seem to be paid for their work; fathers earn money.

This difference in the social valuation of men's and women's roles,
especially in the money value of work outside the home, seems to be a
real source of difficulty in identification of women with the feminine
role. It might not be so bad if woman's role were not taken for granted.
But both the biological function of childbearing and the social role of

homemaker seem to women to be underrated. They do not get paid, nor do they seem to get status for themselves.

The problem seems to be particularly difficult for college women, for confusion over the socially acceptable relation between marriage and intellectual interests in scholarly work has not been settled. Cultural standards have not caught up with the statistical finding that more than two thirds of women college graduates can now expect to be gainfully employed outside the home within six months of graduation, most of them in professional jobs.[37] The definition of acceptable roles for women has not given serious weight to their intellectual interests. Some people say that, consciously or unconsciously, the college woman diverts her energy away from academic work to the pursuit of a mate. Even some educators are not sure that women should strive for scholarly attainment, which may divert them from their major task of developing the entire feminine role of wife and mother. They are not sure that women college students can achieve intellectually, that they want to achieve intellectually, or that they can play the multiple roles that are necessary.

One social scientist developed an "educational typology" based on studies of women college graduates. He suggests that women students can be classified in five categories:[38]

(a) *The High Achievers:* These girls are headed in their thoughts and in reality for a pattern of life in which scholarly or professional activity will have an important place. These girls are not to be measured by the fact that they make high grades alone. These girls are committed to an intellectual life— to the exclusion of all else.
(b) *The Over-Achievers:* Those who work hard and earn good grades without acquiring any serious appreciation of the intellectual life.
(c) *The Under-Achievers:* Those who enjoy college and grow intellectually without becoming seriously involved in study.
(d) *The Social-Achievers:* Those whose life is marked primarily by social activity and peer group orientation.
(e) *The Seekers of Identity:* Their college experience is primarily one of radical adjustment to a social world quite different from the one from which they came.

According to Sanford,[39] the high achiever is exceptional among women. Not lack of ability or personality difficulties, but lack of motivation and conflicting interests seem to be responsible. The general American social pattern, which offers a woman many alternatives to academic achievement, encourages diffuseness in her interests and activities. It is difficult for her to focus sharply on scholarly work, particularly for such a highly concentrated program as study for the Ph.D. Two stereotypes in thinking about graduate study tend to discourage a woman from proceeding for a doctorate: Graduate faculties (primarily made up of men) think it best to proceed directly from the B.A. to graduate study; and they tend to assume that it is not intellectually or economically advisable to invest in doctoral study after age 30—which is just the age at which many women are ready to re-enter employment and might seriously consider getting an advanced degree.

A further deterrent, in the folklore about marriage, is that brains (in women) and marriage don't mix. Men are not thus deterred; the intelligent and well-educated male is considered quite marriageable, in spite of some oddities and intellectual mannerisms. A wife may work her husband's way through college (she gets a PhT, for "Putting Hubby Through"), but nobody will chide him if he does not see her through.

The emphasis on achievement of social status in the student culture is another deterrent to high intellectual achievement among women. If a woman student is to be a genuine intellectual, she must be prepared to be regarded as different or exceptional and, on many campuses, to lose status. Entire women's colleges have sometimes been downgraded in the status ratings of intercollegiate folklore because of real or fancied emphasis on intellectual interests among their students. But the intellectually gifted woman may find it difficult to maintain social status and honor her intellectual interests. "The most acute frustration . . . lies in failing to belong to the especially chosen group."[40]

There is some encouragement for high-achieving students, both men and women, especially in colleges where students not only tolerate but actively encourage achievement. Friends help each other a great deal; perhaps nothing can be so helpful to an intellectually gifted woman as encouragement from an understanding man. Women who combine intellectual attainment with happy marriage offer valuable models. Above all, the encouragement of parents is the most effective help a woman can have in intellectual attainment. There is a close relationship between the high value placed upon scholarly attainments by parents and the eventual scholarly achievement of a daughter.[41]

The problem of achievement, of course, is neuter gender. Both men and women need encouragement and support for high achievement. But women, in particular, need special help in striving for scholarly excellence. For men, women, and children—and the whole of society—have a considerable stake in enabling women to achieve higher levels of education and performance.

Children first. Nothing less than excellence is needed in their education. They need good teachers—more men of high intellectual interests, as well as women. But the most important educators in the most significant years of learning are parents. It is not enough for the father alone to be well educated, or for his education to be limited to the practice of his profession. He needs enough general knowledge of the liberal arts and sciences to recognize and encourage intellectual interests in his children—and to answer all those questions (with the help of the *World Book*). And the mother cannot leave it to him to provide the intellectual life of the family. She is in a key position in the critical, preschool years to recognize and stimulate intellect in children. In a recent lecture, Margaret Mead gave an amusing, but instructive example:

Mathematicians do their best work when they are young, usually before the age when most people finish college. We have to catch them young. This means that mothers are in the best position to catch them. Suppose a child is playing with his blocks. He takes one, puts another by it, and looks around him, apparently puzzled. A mother, with some degree of education, may come to help, and think, 'He's making a pattern. Is it colors or numbers?' She puts a third block down so it makes a row with the other two. The child laughs. She counts, 'One, two, three,' and the child crows and claps his hands. But what does the less educated mother do? She coos, 'Come, dear, let's build a nice house!'

Women second. Some women have the urge to go places, to try out their talents and abilities. There are individual differences among women, just as there are among men. And rigid limitation of women's roles makes many of them into square pegs that rattle around in round holes. Just as there are some men who refuse to drive themselves in order to keep up with the Joneses, there are some women who simply want to work for self-fulfillment. Among them are women who combine a marriage and a career, those who marry later in life after completing advanced education or beginning a career, and some who never marry —and they all are happy.

Some women want to begin work, or return to work, after the last child is in school—to add to the family income, finance the children's college education, or fulfill interests of their own. As Fig. 2-1 illustrates, women now get through with the job of rearing children and are free to return to the labor force at an earlier age than before. In 1890 the average woman had her last child when she was about 32; in 1950, when she was about 26. Now the projected age for getting the last child off to the first grade is 32. At least 40 more years of life are ahead of the average mother.[42] A college-educated woman can use her education, not only in teaching her children during the early formative years, but also in earning the income that is a return on her investment in college education.

Men third. Their stake in the education of women is greater than many of them realize. The modern equivalent of the dowry that the woman brings to the marriage is a college degree. It is the gift that the

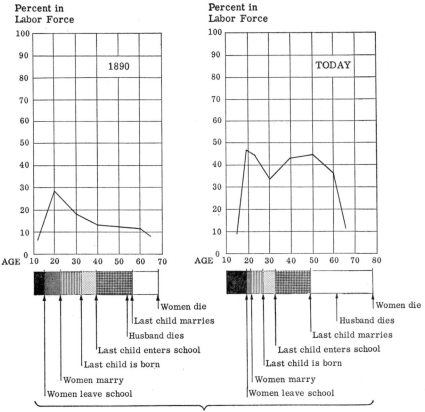

Fig. 2–1. Work in Relation to Significant Stages in the Lives of Women, 1890 and Today.

father of the bride makes to her husband, instead of linens, cattle, and gold pieces. It has the same financial function as a dowry: to insure the financial security of the children in the event of the father's death. The added income that a college degree represents provides a kind of insurance that the father could not afford to buy. Some of the financial pressure is taken off the man who does not have to press quite so hard for extra income to assure financial security. Any reduction in pressure makes life easier for him, and improves the chances that his marriage and family life will be happier. The gains in security increase the chances of durability of the marriage and the stability of the family.

Society last. There are not enough men to fill all the jobs requiring high-level intellectual capacity; women are needed to help meet the shortage. Some of the worst shortages are in fields traditionally supplied by women: teaching and nursing, for example. Yet the proportion of high-ability women continuing their education beyond the high school is lower than that of men. Only 37 percent of women students graduate from college, as compared to 55 percent of the men. Women earn 34 percent of the masters degrees and only ten percent of the doctorates.[43] The proportion of advanced degrees earned by women has declined since World War II. This loss of trained minds from the labor supply is a serious handicap to the nation. Manpower shortages are not only quantitative, but qualitative; we are short of excellence as well as of jobholders. To assure our nation of progress and productivity, women as well as men must be encouraged to achieve high levels of training and effective work.

Unresolved conflicts concerning sex. Despite improved sex education for adolescents in communities and schools, students still come to college with unresolved conflicts and uncertainties concerning sex. In one study, 40 percent of the college students in the sample reported that their attitudes toward sex had been affected by their first source of information; 40 percent were uncertain about the effects, and 18 percent felt that they had been unfavorably influenced.[44]

Many people have guilt feelings about sexual experiences they have had. Kinsey, for instance, reports that 92 percent of the men and 60 percent of the women in his studies had masturbated at some time.[45] Masturbation seems to be widely used in youth as a sexual outlet. And the higher the educational level the higher the incidence of masturbation.

Much fear surrounds masturbation. From the standpoint of mental health, there seems to be no deterioration, either physical or physiological, as a consequence. But if the act is accompanied by intense, prolonged feelings of guilt or fear, the practice may interfere with later sexual adjustment. Of course masturbation is not satisfactory as a means of sexual expression. As the individual matures and relationships with the opposite sex become more successful, it gives way to effective sexual outlets. One problem in sex education is that of diminishing fear and guilt in connection with masturbation.

Homosexuality is another source of feelings of fear and guilt. The blurring of distinctions between masculine and feminine roles has led to confusion over what is adequate behavior for men and women. Sometimes men are considered to be acting like women, or women like men, when both are simply responding to the demands of the role they have assumed, in accordance with individual temperament. This confusion of sex roles is frequently mistaken for rejection of the biological sex role

—for homosexuality. There is no reason to conclude that every person who rejects a sex role is homosexual, or that every person whose behavior resembles that traditionally associated with the opposite sex has homosexual tendencies.

Frequently, homosexuals have a history of a childhood in which they preferred to perceive themselves as belonging to the opposite sex consistently, not just occasionally. This tendency is often strengthened by some factor in the parental relationship that makes it difficult to identify with the parent of the same sex, or easy to form an excessively strong attachment for the parent of the opposite sex—for example, the death of the father or mother. This does not mean that children will become homosexuals if they act out in play or daydreams a role associated with the opposite sex. Nor does it mean that students who reject their parents will become homosexuals. Rather it indicates that the acceptance of their own sex and the roles associated with it is necessary if children are to accept a mature masculine or feminine role. Confusion or rejection may clear up with maturity, or may persist as factors that make a person vulnerable to homosexual practices.

Many people find it difficult to identify with their own sex. Some of them never engage in any homosexual act. Some of them probably do engage in homosexual practices at some point. But it is difficult to make clear distinctions between homosexuality and normal sexual behavior. There are endless gradations and the information available is difficult to evaluate. Kinsey, for instance, found that only four percent of white adult males are exclusively homosexual, following adolescence. Still, two out of five males studied reported some experience, regarded as homosexual, between adolescence and old age. One in six had more than incidental homosexual experience, for a period of three years or more, between the ages of 16 and 55. The largest number of college age males reported such experiences in the late teens (one in six); less than one in ten had such relations between 21 and 25.[46]

Similar findings appeared for women, although the data are not altogether comparable.[47]

Such statistical studies seem to indicate that the incidence of homosexual experiences is higher than most people assume. But whether this means that the number of homosexuals is greater than we might imagine cannot be concluded from the information available. Attitudes in society cloud the facts. A person may be branded for a single experience, or even the report of an experience, without consideration for age or habitual behavior patterns. Like masturbation, much homosexual behavior is not carried over into adult life. "For the group that will go to college, the chances are better than four to one that pre-adolescent activity will not be followed by later homosexual experience."[48] Usually, with increased frequency of acquaintance with the opposite sex as one enters college, it is easier for a person to develop a heterosexual pattern. But, like other forms of sexual outlet, homosexual experiences may produce guilt in the participants. The act is legally, socially, and religiously disapproved. Exposure can cost a person the acceptance he needs to get a job, make friends, and marry. Consequently, if failure to establish a biologically appropriate sex identity develops into homosexuality, only counseling or psychotherapy can be expected to handle the problem.

Relationships between men and women during the college years

Sooner or later most college students will marry, probably someone who is a college graduate, possibly someone met in college. The achievement of identity and independence, the establishment of masculine and feminine roles, lead to intimate friendships and relationships with the opposite sex. Eventually the student chooses a mate, and will be ready to marry either during, or soon after college.

Dating. As early as 1930, social scientists found the dating patterns of college students to be a subject for serious study. Willard Waller[49] contended that college dating in the 'twenties and 'thirties was poor preparation for marriage because it encouraged students to prize such superficial values as fraternity and sorority membership and competitive dating. He concluded that dating was "dalliance," and not marriage-oriented. Students placed a premium on good clothes, new cars, smooth manners, and popularity with members of the opposite sex. These campus standards were not good values to take into a healthy marriage.

By the 1950's, the "big man on campus," fraternity, car, clothes, money complex had been scrapped by college girls, and even the boys held more humanistic and less materialistic values as important in a dating relationship.[50] Most students today seem to prefer a date who (1) is pleasant and cheerful; (2) has a sense of humor; (3) is natural; (4) is a good sport; (5) is considerate; and (6) is neat in appearance.[51] Such values are considered by social scientists to be a sound foundation for marriage, and tend to make good human relationships in general.

Promiscuity. One of the stereotyped notions that non-college people have concerning college students is that they are promiscuous. Seeing them parked along a moonlit lane is apt to provoke an alarmed reaction from the public. A popular saying is that students are "free in their affection." "Going steady" is no excuse, so far as the strictures of public opinion are concerned. On the contrary, it seems to be the prevailing opinion that constant companionship with one person leads inevitably to sexual intercourse.

There is no evidence to support the idea that pre-marital sexual intercourse is more prevalent among college students than any other group. The biological pressures, which are very great during the college years, are handled as a rule in ways that generally stop short of sexual intercourse.

Petting. "Petting is the particular activity which has led many persons to conclude that college students are sexually wild and perverted."[52] According to Kinsey, contacts which are confined to latitudes not lower than the neck are referred to as "necking." Most college students neck at one time or other. Petting goes further. Heavy petting involves several techniques, such as "deliberate stimulation of the female breasts, or of the male or female genitalia."[53] College-bred men and women more or less accept petting as usual and proper in pre-marital behavior. Though some may have started after college, the vast majority studied by Kinsey had already established this pattern before they were 18.

About 92 percent of all college-bred males are involved in petting before marriage. Orgasm as a product of petting occurs in over 61 percent of the college-bred males who are married by the age of 30.[54]

Kinsey indicates that the frequency of pre-marital intercourse has not increased, but petting has. He suggests that petting is an outcome of the upper classes' attempt to avoid pre-marital intercourse. In fact, some students go to great pains to assure themselves that they are not breaking the moral code of virginity.

All kinds of folklore warn of the consequences of petting. One myth is that it inevitably leads to intercourse. This belief, according to Kinsey, is widespread among lower-class or uneducated groups, who cannot see how a person could go so far in erotic activity and still refrain from intercourse, unless he were abnormal. But apparently petting simply leads to more petting. Another myth is that it renders a person incapable of effecting satisfactory sexual relations in marriage. Again, there is no evidence to indicate that petting becomes a permanent adjustment to sex. Most couples make the transition to full sexual relations without undue difficulty.

Yet, there is a question as to whether this is a wholly satisfactory

adjustment to the biological pressures of youth. Petting occasions physical stress that must be recognized.

A portion of the males, perhaps as many as a third, indicated that extensive
petting which stopped short of orgasm left them in a state of nervous tension,
and some reported physical pain.[55]

Among women, at least one half indicated that they had been disturbed on some occasions, and a quarter stated that they had physical
pain after petting. Only 39 percent of the women reported a release
that left them in a relaxed state.[56]

Perhaps this problem is what students have in mind when they report, as did one group recently, that "willingness to pet" is not a
criterion for casual dating.[57] There may be growing awareness among
students of the stress and meaninglessness of simply going through an
act that does not lead to fulfillment.

There also is a moral question about the deviousness of the method,
and the self-deception involved in petting. From the point of view of
mental health, it arouses anxiety. For technical virginity is at best a
shoddy way of realizing one's concept of self. It resounds of Horney's
reference to the idealized self (see Chapter 1), something in the imagination that must be satisfied by devious ways. A student who enters
into a relationship knowing that he is only fulfilling the technical requirements, and is not committed to the personal responsibilities and
qualitative aspects involved, is deceiving himself. Many students treat
the moral values in petting as they do the moral values in cheating: It
is all right as long as it doesn't carry over into life after college. What
is done in petting is not related to sexual adjustment. The student can
still say, "I have not had pre-marital sex relations."

But despite the accusations of promiscuity among students, and the
tendency to ignore the moral problems concerned, students do seem
to take a fairly healthy attitude toward petting, and to have some sense
of moral standards about the practice. Studies show that most college
students feel that petting is acceptable only in relationships that are
seriously headed toward marriage, between partners that are going
steady.[58]

Going Steady. At least one observer of college student behavior[59] is
struck by the tendency toward monogamous relationships. Like many
faculty members who finished college in the 1930's, he is puzzled by
changes in dating and courtship patterns. The stag line has vanished
from dances. When students go steady, they "go out of circulation,"
exclusively dating each other. A student who "seeks to make friends

with a girl somebody else brings to a dance is liable to be called a 'bird-dog.'" Women collect only one fraternity pin at a time. Popularity is not determined by the number of dates. "Youth at present is almost completely monogamous in a thoroughly established fashion. And it is aggressively sure that its customs and ways are right."

Going steady is a high school term that persists in college. It refers to the next step after "just seeing each other." It means more than "often dating the same person." There must be a marked and preferably exclusive pattern of dating the same person, of preferring the same date, of dating no one else for the duration of the relationship. The steady relationship has to last long enough for other people to become aware of it and for the student group to give it recognition and encouragement. Going steady is a fairly formalized arrangement.[60]

There are pros and cons about going steady. Students and parents and faculty members note some of the advantages, as follows:

1. Less attractive students have a fair share of courting opportunities. The Scarlett O'Hara type is circumscribed in her operations, and less aggressive women can get out of the wallflower class. The less aggressive man has social opinion to back him in resisting the "bird-dog" who moves in on his girl.

2. Going steady is less expensive than casual dating. Once a date becomes steady, the man does not have to spend a lot of money entertaining the woman. They have a "kitty," go Dutch, or just lead a quiet life of study and coke dates.

3. It gives "social security." Students can count on a date for big social events. This idea implies that students now have little patience with competitive systems of dating and courtship.

4. It gives plenty of time for a mature relationship to develop. The years of steady dating give plenty of opportunity to talk things over, share hopes and dreams, understand each other—and to gain self-understanding.

5. The relationship goes deeper and develops more quality, while random dating leads to superficial relationships.

6. It makes for earlier marriage. Maturing together in ideas and interests make a more stable marriage. Children will come earlier while both parents are young and vigorous. And the children will enter school earlier, giving the mother earlier re-entry to her occupation, and thus increasing the family income available for college education for the children.

Dissenting opinions are equally vigorous.

1. Self-understanding is a personal quest for each individual alone.

Until personal identity is clearly established, marriage is risky. Early development of a stable, or presumably enduring, attachment to a partner may interfere with the development of identity. Acceptance of sex role, independence of parents, self-direction are developmental tasks that must precede the development of intimate relationships, if enduring attachments leading to marriage are to be satisfactory. A person must be himself before becoming part of a twosome. Erikson points out that individual identity cannot be achieved by going steady or getting married. As far as the best psychological findings indicate, identity must precede intimacy.[61]

2. Individual differences are not allowed for. Some students are ready for intimacy earlier than others. Some are slower to develop or need to delay the formation of an intimate relationship. Conformity to a single pattern of steady dating may force them into a relationship before they are ready for it, deprive them of any other acceptable dating pattern if they are not ready for going steady, or make them feel guilty or afraid they are sexually inadequate. Students need more freedom for individual differences in dating patterns. Big changes of personality structure, important shifts of direction in life plans, come for many students in the college years. These make steady dating undesirable, or postponement of choice of a mate advantageous, for many students.[62]

3. Women students in particular suffer from the pressure to go steady and the lack of tolerance for individual differences:

The most insistent pressure for the young woman in college today is to get married and get married young. It is the female who is marriage-oriented and marriage-conscious.[63]

Women suffer real conflict between pressures to marry and pressures to achieve intellectually. They need sexual fulfillment; postponement of it is a hardship both emotionally and intellectually.* But colleges—and American society in general—have not worked out any relation between intellectual achievement and sexual fulfillment that is not frustrating to students, and particularly to women students.

4. Dating several persons provides a wider range of acquaintance and experience that increases the chances for a better choice of mate.[65] But pressure to conform to the pattern of going steady prevents students from exercising a very wide range of choice. "Going out of circulation" upon going steady breaks off the formation of friendships. And

---

* David Tiedeman says: "The productive intellectual creativity of many women appears to be immobilized by the high level of diffuse anxiety generated by the partial or total lack of fulfillment of the complete feminine existence."[64]

when a steady relationship comes to an end—and people do fall out of love—there is no readily available group of friends of the opposite sex from whom a more suitable partner can be selected. Students who could profit from a wider range of friendships are prohibited by student mores from doing so.

The controversy over going steady cannot be easily resolved. On the whole, its advantages are very great, and it seems to be a rather mature way to deal with the necessity for postponing marriage until the end of the college years. It makes it possible to maintain consistent standards in intimate relationships, and puts the weight of student opinion behind strong attachments that do develop. Provided there is provision for other dating patterns, so that the late starters can do exploratory dating before going steady, the pattern should meet the needs of a great many students.

Marriage. Most students expect sooner or later to marry. The college years will come to an end, and marriage is expected to follow upon graduation. Many a college woman has received her degree in the morning and married in the evening. Some college chapels have a very crowded schedule of weddings around the time of commencement. When the wedding is postponed past commencement, it is usually set for some foreseeable date—when he, or she, has completed the bachelor's degree or an advanced degree or a professional certificate, or when the job question has been settled for him, or her, or both.

But between 15 and 20 percent of students in larger coeducational colleges are likely to be married before graduation. (Small colleges generally do not provide for married students.)[66] And the proportion of married students is rising each year. Students' marriages are more acceptable than they were a generation ago. So the possibility of marriage before graduation may be considered reasonably and realistically by many students at some time or other.

Many factors have to be considered in making the decision. Students for the most part are dependent on parents for financing a college education. Some parents can and will continue financial support after a student marries. Others prefer to terminate their contribution upon the student's marriage. Students who wish to marry and continue in college, consequently, have to leave an important part of the decision to their respective parents. This increases the difficulties in entering upon a happy marriage. The interests of parents as well as of the couple are involved, and even the most loving parents find such an emotional burden an undesirable and sometimes impossible responsibility.

The situation can be worse complicated when one family agrees to continue financial support, while the other will not or cannot make an equal contribution. A good deal of bitterness may be generated in the marriage under such circumstances, and in-law relationships are a problem anyway. If neither family continues support, the couple is thrown back on its own resources, which are usually negligible. College education may have to be given up by one or both.

A study of married students at Iowa State College found that "married students were less likely (13 percent) to receive financial help from parents than were single students (60 percent). . . . College marriages often result in an end of financial support."[67] Some couples try to make up the difference by part-time work for one or both partners. But this adds to the strain of academic work and a new marriage, both of which are great enough anyway. "The typical married couple lives under financial stress, either severe or mild. . . . Their first complaint is undue fatigue."[68] Forty percent of the married couples at Iowa State College worked part time. But the pressures of household work and part-time employment prevented most of them from participating in college activities. They tended to live in a world apart from other students because they had less time or lost interest in student life.[69]

Housing can be another deciding factor in student marriages. There is rarely enough good housing in a college community at a price young couples can afford to pay. Some housing for married students is provided by large universities and colleges, but the demand exceeds the supply. The cost of off-campus housing is a strain on the budget. And colleges do not provide the counseling personnel in housing units for married students that is ordinarily provided in residence halls; yet their needs for such help are even greater than those of single students.[70]

Marriage is expected to be the foundation of a family, and married couples usually want to have children. A considerable number, however, intend to put off having children. Various reasons, especially the severe financial burden and lack of settled occupation, seem to make the decision advisable. Of course, some couples, because of religious convictions, do not practice birth control. And a majority of married couples in college have children, either "intentionally (33 percent) or inadvertently (67 percent)."[71] The financial hazards and the burden of child rearing fall most heavily upon women students. "Truly, the campus marriage earns top priority as a hazard to women's education today. . . . Ninety percent or more of these rising numbers of campus wives are literally working their husband's way through college."[71] The first intention is for both husband and wife to finish college, and some carry it out. But only about three out of twenty couples finish the academic journey together. At the State College of Washington, marriage was found to be the most important reason for the academic mortality of women students.[72] When financial support is inadequate, or when a child is born, the woman rather than the man ceases college study, either to provide family income or to take care of the child and the home.

There are some signs that new educational approaches are being found to meet the trend toward young marriages and to help both partners complete college. Scholarship help, once terminated upon marriage, is more generously provided for married students. More liberal loan provisions help solve some financial problems. More housing units are being built for married students. Some additional counseling service is being provided. Public opinion is beginning to approve of parents who continue financial support for student marriages, and to frown upon cutting off support because of parental disapproval. An increasing number of activities of interest to married students is appearing on campuses: wives' clubs, couples' clubs, church activities, and volunteer service in community organizations.[73]

It has been suggested that the education of women who marry young may need to follow a different pattern from that of men. One program might be early marriage and child-rearing, with women staying in the home until the last child enters school, then entering college or work about 30 years of age.[74] Changes in the pattern of higher education will require variation in the traditional pattern based on the life cycle and career expectancy of men. College faculties will have to revise some of their thinking about the admission of students, and patterns of undergraduate student life will have to vary somewhat from traditional forms.

Not least important is the love, companionship, and assurance that are found in marriage. Happily married couples find a rich fulfillment that is the greatest reward of adult life. In considering whether to marry during the college years, students should size up the factors that affect the outcome of marriage. If the factors seem weighted on the side of success, happiness, and self-realization for both partners, marriage before graduation might be realistic. But personal fulfillment in marriage is so very great and so very desirable that it is only fair and wise to make sure that the person one loves most deeply will find it along with oneself.

Achievement of the developmental task of establishing masculine or feminine identity is not merely individual self-realization. Sex role identity leads to fulfillment in an intimate, loving, caring relationship with another person. For the man to care for his wife, for a woman to care for her husband, is the final fulfillment of the masculine or feminine role. Personal development in the college years leads to such intimacy. Personal development makes it possible for the student to accept gladly the responsibility for one of the great choices of life: the choice of a mate. And when that choice is made, it will be good and enduring if both a man and a woman help each other to continue personal development and gain personal fulfillment.

3

Strictly in self-defense

Emotional development and
self-understanding

We speak of feelings and emotions interchangeably. To the student who "feels lousy," the distinction, if any, between the two makes little difference. It won't matter a bit to him whether his feelings are labeled and classified. He just has the feelings, and that is enough for one day, thank you.

Yet it is sometimes useful, for purposes of self-understanding, to look back at experiences highly charged with feeling, or to look ahead to situations that may evoke strong emotions, just to see what emotion means in terms of self-expression, and what problems it poses in self-control. For expressing and controlling feelings are significant tasks of self-development.

Feelings are the conscious evidence we have of our inward state of being. They are perceptible reactions to persons, events, situations, or to our general state of being. They are the answer to the question, "How are you?" (Of course we are polite enough to reply, "And how are *you*?"

instead of giving a detailed account of our aching heart or hearty muscle tone.)

Emotion is a state of being "moved." There is an inward feeling or sensation that things are moving inside, that within the self there is turmoil or excitement. The sense of movement has different meanings, depending on the situation evoking the feeling of movement: anger, joy, fear, exultation, for example. There is an impulse to act, to move outwardly in keeping with the inward feeling: to run and jump for joy, to fight, to run away, to lean back and enjoy things. Emotion involves awareness of the agents, conditions, or circumstances evoking feeling; and we act in response to these agents, seeking rest, running away from them, holding on to them, or attacking them, depending on the feeling they evoke and the value we attach to the feeling.[1]

According to William James, emotions are the product of events and the feelings they induce. Bodily responses, he suggests, call forth emotions, not the other way around. We *feel* moved because we *are* moved.

. . . the bodily changes follow directly the perception of the exciting fact, and . . . our feeling of the same changes as they occur *is* the emotion. Common-sense says, we lose our fortune, are sorry and weep; we meet a bear, are frightened and run; we are insulted by a rival, are angry and strike. The hypothesis here to be defended is that this order of sequence is incorrect, that the one mental state is not immediately induced by the other, that the bodily manifestations must first be interposed between, and that the more rational statement is that we feel sorry because we cry, angry because we strike, afraid because we tremble. . . .[2]

Controlling emotions, consequently, involves controlling our bodily reactions. If we stand our ground, we will have feelings that differ from those we have when we run away. The emotional response will differ if the bodily reactions differ. The problem of emotional control is to choose the most appropriate response to the situation so that we can have the desired emotional reaction or express the feelings we have in a meaningful way. It is probably wise to run away from a large, angry bull who is clearly determined to run you out of the pasture; and the more frightened you are, the faster you are likely to run. On the other hand, it is foolish to run away from friends, or pleasure, or gainful employment. Yet some people do. Somehow the bodily reactions associated with fear get attached to situations that should evoke pleasure. Instead of feeling and expressing pleasure, some people feel pain, fear, anger.

This confusion of feelings and expression of unsuitable emotions is characteristic of many young adults. To some extent, they all seem "crazy mixed-up kids," and college students most of all. "You can't tell what they are going to do next," say parents, or teachers. And in fact, students themselves sometimes can't tell what emotional reaction they are going to have next. For one thing, they go into many new situations where they don't know what feelings to expect, or what emotions they are permitted to express. They are playing a lot of life by ear. For another, they have reached the age when many emotions previously expressed are no longer acceptable, or have to be expressed in different ways. As adults, for example, they are not expected to show affection so openly and freely as they did when, as little children, they hugged and kissed anyone they loved, of any age or sex, spontaneously and freely. As grownup men, students are not expected to shed tears when they are disappointed or grieved; yet the grief is there and has to be expressed somehow. The little girl could throw a temper tantrum when she could not wear her favorite dress to Sunday School; but as a grownup woman, she dares not throw herself on the bed weeping when she has nothing to wear to the party; instead she goes out and borrows a cocktail dress from one of the sorority sisters.

Part of the emotional turmoil of the college age, then, is due to the uncertainty over acceptable ways to express new-found feelings in new situations; and part is due to the persistence of childish emotional reactions that have not yet been replaced by adult forms of expression. But a much more important source of problems of emotional control stays with us throughout adult life. This is the need to protect ourselves, to defend the self and preserve the identity that we have developed as we grew up. To express some emotions may damage the self; to fail to express others may make us feel less than ourselves. The emotions that we have are usually given meaning by the feelings we have had in similar circumstances in the past. They are often increased in strength or intensity by force of habit. Past experience may also flood the senses with feeling, often without our having any conscious memory of the past or its meaning. Yet we react in each situation with all that we are or have been. And we try to be fully ourselves, to express the emotions that will strengthen the self or protect it from harm. Emotional expression and emotional control are exercised strictly in self-defense.

The task of self-defense, therefore, depends on self-understanding. To enjoy the feelings and express the emotions that will be to our advantage in self-development, we must understand ourselves and have some idea of what we are defending and developing through our responses to events, people, and situations.

To understand our emotions, we need to be aware of two important aspects of the human condition: anxiety and frustration. These are common elements of human life, which are almost always associated with any strong feelings, whether pleasurable or painful. They may be aroused whenever any strong emotion is present. They may serve either to strengthen or to weaken the force of the feeling. They are often responsible for the mixed emotions that we feel so often when we don't know whether to laugh or cry. To learn to control emotions, to express them in ways that will protect and develop the self, requires an understanding of anxiety and frustration. With understanding, we may learn to respond effectively to anxiety and frustration in self-defense.

ANXIETY

Everyone struggles with anxiety, perhaps the college freshman most of all. The developmental tasks of the college age produce stress and strain, and often constitute threats that arouse strong feelings. Anxiety is different from fear. Fear is attached to a specific, real object or event that poses a real threat in experience. Anxiety is generalized, unspecified fear without an object. We are afraid of—we know not what.

Anxiety is, therefore, hard to bear. So people usually deal with it by worrying—that is, by attaching the sense of vague threat to some object, and worrying about that. Studies of "worries" among college freshmen indicate that they worry about many things: not being as successful as they would like to be; hurting the feelings of others; making a bad impression upon others; and not working hard enough, for example.[3] Looking at these worries closely, we see nothing specific or immediately dangerous in them. There is just a vague, general apprehension, an uneasy "I can't put my finger on the problem" kind of feeling. This is anxiety in the pure state.

Anxiety can be distinguished from fear in that it is more anticipatory than actual; a dread of what might be, rather than a fear of what is; a feeling of impending doom, rather than a feeling of pending doom. However, fear and anxiety have similarities:

"There is kinship between the two. Both are emotional reactions to danger and both may be accompanied by physical sensations, such as trembling, perspiration, violent heart-beat, which may be so strong that a sudden, intense fear may lead to death."[4]

Many people find it difficult to admit to feelings of anxiety. It is much more common to hear a person say, "I am afraid" than "I am anxious"; and, of late, the tendency is to use the terms interchangeably, "anxious" meaning "worried," with some specific worry being mentioned. Anxiety, being subconscious and subjective, is hard to recognize. When anxiety causes uneasiness sufficiently strong for a person to become aware of it, he naturally attempts to find a cause in the environment that would account for the feeling that is so close to fear. Normally enough threats are present to make it easy to select some object that he could justifiably fear, and to attach his feelings to that object. Because feelings without an object or meaning are almost unendurable, a person naturally seeks relief from anxiety by finding a meaning for it. But the meaning is often a fraudulent or contrived one, not the real meaning or root cause of the anxiety.

Most of the time fear arises out of an external threat, but the vagueness of anxiety, its pervading, diffuse, and often long-term nature, its excessive or unreasonable strength and persistence, suggest an internal threat—a condition arising from thoughts, feelings, and impulses that threaten one's existence, that keep him from developing into the kind of self he would like to be. Anxiety arises out of disturbances within a person's inner life.

According to Horney, "the average person in our culture is little aware of the importance anxiety has in his life."[5] And it manifests itself in different ways.

Some neurotics are fully aware of being hounded by anxiety. Its manifestations vary immensely: it may appear as diffused anxiety, in the form of anxiety-attacks; it may be attached to definite situations or activities, such as heights, streets, public performances; it may have a definite content, such as apprehension about becoming insane. . . .[6]

Horney indicates that there are those who realize that they have anxiety now and then, with or without knowing the conditions that provoke it; and they probably attach little importance to it. We are aware of having depressions, or feelings of inadequacy, but are unaware of having anxiety. The degree of awareness of a feeling does not indicate its strength or importance. Anxiety may be a determining factor in our lives without our being conscious of it.

Certain elements of anxiety can be particularly frightening to a person who does not understand anxiety, or is not aware that it is a common human experience. These may include:[7]

(1) *Helplessness.* One can be active and courageous in facing danger, but most often in anxiety he simply feels helpless. Those who have a need for power, ascendancy and dominance, may take their anxiety to mean cowardice, inferiority, or incompetence.

(2) *Irrationality.* The irrational character of anxiety is betrayed by two things: the feeling is stronger than any real present threat will justify; and the object to which one attributes the feeling is often transparently specious, contrived, unrelated to the feeling. Those who accept the high cultural valuation placed on rational control of behavior are upset by the irrationality of anxiety, and

fear that they may be inferior or inadequate because they play irrational tricks of this sort on themselves.[8]

(3) *Something out of gear.* The fact that irrationality and helplessness exist indicates that something must be changed about us. We must overhaul a part of ourselves, and few of us are willing to do this. It takes great strength to admit that we may be out of kilter, and more strength to set this right.

Jersild[9] indicates the following conditions underlying anxiety:

(1) Stress and uncertainties tied to human existence that affect the lives of all people: These may include illness, death, accidents.

(2) Conditions linked to the college-age and the stresses arising from its developmental tasks (fear of being isolated from a key group of one's peers, for example, as in failing to make a fraternity).

(3) Difficulties associated with unresolved problems and conflicts in life, often dating from early childhood, and arising from failure to master early developmental tasks.

Other authorities indicate that anxiety is likely to occur under the following conditions: (1) physical flight is impossible; (2) punishment is strongly anticipated; (3) no opportunity is present to make rewarding responses; (4) loss of emotional support is actual or imminent.[10]

Physical flight is impossible

When we have to sit and take it without being able to do anything about it, or when we cannot run away, anxiety is sure to result.

Punishment is strongly anticipated

As we grow up, we learn that certain acts will provoke punishment from significant people in our lives. Even when these people are not present, acts that were punished in the past are likely to trigger the anticipation of punishment. When punishment does not ensue, the feeling of anxiety persists. Studies of children who masturbate show that actual physical harm is negligible. The anxiety which is aroused, however, from the anticipation of punishment "if caught," or punishment "through loss of sexual power" can be hazardous for the person.

No opportunity is present to make rewarding responses

College students often manifest anxiety as a result of tension that cannot be reduced because there is no opportunity to make responses that will satisfy needs or reduce tension. When sexual tension arises, often the individual has no direct way to satisfy it. He may become anxious, for example, because he feels he cannot control his needs and impulses. He may fear that he may satisfy his need in some forbidden or unacceptable way. Deprivation, or lack of opportunity to make a response that is rewarding, can also provoke feelings of impending doom.

Loss of emotional support is actual or imminent

We have all seen a lost child in a department store! The child is not screaming because he is physically threatened, but because he has lost a parent, a source of love and affection, of emotional support. As we mature, we are concerned about maintaining good human relations, keeping close to people who give emotional support. Anxiety may well occur when we feel a threat to these relationships. Many freshmen, for example, suffer from homesickness. They have seen their parents drive away from the residence hall; they have lost their emotional support. When they make new friends, the anxiety is reduced. Some colleges advise parents to put the student on the train, or even to say goodbye at the front door and put the student in a cab. Apparently it is easier to cope with the feeling of separation (leaving the folks at home and being sure that home is there and they are safe) than with the feeling of desertion (having the folks drive off and leave you alone).

FRUSTRATION

In the course of everyday events the college student, like other human beings, encounters frustration. In the process of satisfying his human needs—for affection, status, approval, and the like—he encounters blocks which stand in the way of his efforts toward satisfaction.

One student may say, for example, "I wish I were a student leader." He may feel disappointed because he isn't. But he is not frustrated because *he hasn't tried*. His buddy, Jack, is frustrated because he tried out for the debating team and was blocked by his lack of ability to think on his feet. He tried to join a fraternity, but he was blocked by a blackball. In trying to overcome blocks toward his goal as a student leader, he has made unsuccessful attempts, which resulted in frustration.

Table 3-1 indicates some sources of frustration. The first column indicates the type of obstacle causing frustration. The second column indicates the frequency with which obstacles stood in the way of students' efforts to achieve. The third column of the table shows the relative frequency with which obstacles in a given category were not overcome, but remained as frustrating conditions. Lack of compelling drive, and conflict with parents appear to be most difficult to overcome.

TABLE 3-1
The Most Frequent Obstacles to the Satisfaction of Goals
Encountered by a Group of 105 High School Students

Type of obstacle	Percent of total obstacles	Obstacles for which no resources were found
Health and physique	15.8	29.5
Lack of finance	15.2	21.5
Personality traits	12.3	3.3
Lack of mental ability	9.8	21.0
Conflict with parents	5.3	42.8
Lack of compelling drive	4.3	45.8
Lack of social techniques	4.0	18.5
Lack of stability in the home	3.8	2.9
Conflict with family standards	3.6	7.0

From Marian Brown and Vibella Martin, "The University High School Study of Adolescents," *University High School Journal*, Vol. XIX (1941), pp. 177–219, by permission.

The role of frustration in self-understanding is important. First, there must be recognition and acceptance of permanent limitations. Then, self-understanding further demands acting appropriately on the basis of this diagnosis: "self-improvement if this is possible; self-acceptance if it is not."[11]

Developing a variety of methods of overcoming frustration is a challenge since frustration is inevitable. Our college friend who wanted leadership experience should have started with club activity in a small group that needed members.

Another implication is the need to develop frustration tolerance.[12] This means "the ability to endure delay, thwarting, or conflict without resorting to ineffective, maladaptive responses."[13] Studies show that low frustration tolerance is related to susceptibility to maladjustive behavior.

WAYS IN WHICH WE DEFEND OURSELVES

Anxiety and frustration are emotional reactions with which everybody has to cope. Everybody has psychological and physiological needs that require satisfaction. These, of course, vary from person to person. From the outside, a need as perceived by a person may look ridiculous: "Why does he need to make an A? He is already an honor student!" What seems irrational to others is, nevertheless, a real need to the individual; it may be unreasonable, but there is a reason why he has the need. And he feels the need has to be satisfied; if it is not, he is frustrated and anxious. As an infant he needed his bottle, and soon learned that screaming would get it. Or, if he didn't get fed, he could expect to be cuddled and petted and played with instead—and that was almost the same as being fed. As a college student, he may still, sometimes, scream and cry to get what he wants. But in the years between, he has also learned many other ways to satisfy his needs—coaxing, fighting, holding on hard, competing, working, begging, borrowing or stealing, buying and trading, or just plain asking for it. The college student tries to satisfy his needs in many ways. Some of them are successful, reasonable, or appropriate; others are ineffective, irrational, or harmful to himself and others. Part of the process of growing up is learning effective ways to satisfy needs and avoid frustrations.

Many needs go unsatisfied, and much frustration is unavoidable. Some desirable things, when they are secured, turn out to be dust and ashes. The student who has won the election for the editorship of the college paper discovers that it involves more headaches than rewards, more work than prestige. "One man's meat is another man's poison," as a student may discover when she pledges a sorority that her best friend from high school simply adores, only to find that she cannot stand most of the other members of the pledge class. Some desires cannot be satisfied, and some needs cannot be fulfilled. The student who dreamed of being a great research chemist cannot go into a chemistry major because he could not pass college algebra. The beautiful blond freshman one wishes to date turns out to have a fraternity pin and a large "no trespassing" notice from the president of one's own fraternity. The student who expects to have everything his way is going to take his knocks and experience his frustrations, like everybody else. And it is no use crying "sour grapes," because he cannot get away from the fact that he wanted something he can't get. If he denies it outwardly, he still knows subconsciously that he has been frustrated.

So everybody is frustrated in some ways, and everybody seeks ways to avoid, reduce, or overcome frustration. A person tries to keep himself on an even keel, in spite of the knocks he gets. Psychologists refer to this reaction against frustration as expressing a need for maintaining emotional equilibrium. Apparently, it is related to a general need of all living things to maintain themselves as they are. "All living organisms tend to preserve a state of . . . internal consistency."[14]

In human beings, simple internal consistency is not enough. It is the whole self that must be kept in equilibrium. A person reacts to frustration with self-defense. He selects the reactions that bolster his concept of self. Even though the self-concept is idealized, unreal, or impossible to attain, he will try to defend it and develop it the best way he can.

The ways that a person selects for defending the self against frustration and anxiety are called *defense mechanisms*. These are habits of reacting in self-defense in situations that threaten, block, or interfere with the satisfaction of needs. These defense mechanisms may be rational or irrational, successful or unsuccessful, just as the threats and blocks may be real or fancied. People can devise elaborate schemes to handle the blocks that appear in their way. In the final analysis, however, these boil down to three types of defense: deception, redirection, and avoidance. Whatever type of defense a person puts up, he always tries to defend and develop the precious identity that he has won, the self that is the center of his existence.

Whole psychology courses could be given on defense mechanisms. Any individual probably has enough of them to fill a whole book. Only the most common ones can be described in a text like this. But any student can gain a great deal of self-understanding by trying to identify the defense mechanisms he uses, and the needs he satisfies with them. Although defense mechanisms are *unconscious*, through introspection and willingness to face himself, he can become aware of a good many. A good way to begin is by asking: "What am I after here? What do I seem to feel I need? What is the block here? Is it internal or external? Am I withdrawing, attacking, or avoiding the block? Am I trying to solve the problem this situation presents, banging my head against a stone wall, or running away? Is there another way to get more satisfaction?" The more we question ourselves in many different situations, the more personal needs we can identify, and the better we can understand ourselves. We can distinguish the successful from the unsuccessful defense mechanisms. We can understand ourselves better, and learn to react in ways that will assure greater satisfaction.

Mechanisms of deception

Self-defense may be based on principles of deception or camouflage. A person may attempt to deceive himself, or others, or both. He may pretend that a situation is fancied, not real, assuming the attitude of the ostrich with its head in the sand: "If I don't see it, it will go away." He may pretend that all his actions are consistent with his ideal self-image, by making ingenious excuses and alibis: "Everything will be all right, if I simply look at myself in the best possible light." He may pretend that he is perfect, without fault, and all his difficulties are caused by circumstances beyond his control, or by some other person: "It must have been two other fellows." Whatever his intentions are, it is always himself he deceives. Deceptive defense mechanisms, at bottom, are self-deceptive. For example, take two of the most common ones:

Rationalization. Carol can really alibi. She has to be good at it because she suffers from anxiety over a nagging fear that she is really irresponsible. This does not fit her ideal picture of herself as a thoroughly responsible person. She wants to enjoy herself, but feels that having fun means being irresponsible and immature. So, when the girls beg her to go to the movies though she has to study, she goes with them, saying to herself, "This picture is a *must*. It's a great classic that I have to see in order to be well-educated." While this is one good reason for going to the movies, it is not Carol's real reason, but an alibi. She is rationalizing, persuading herself into feeling that she is a responsible person. She is not facing up to two real questions that sooner or later she will have to confront: "Why do I feel irresponsible when I am enjoying myself?" "Am I really a responsible person?"

Projection. Clarence regards himself as a real liberal, tolerant and free from prejudice. But he has a deep-seated prejudice against Catholics that he cannot admit, since he would not be living up to his ideal picture of Clarence, the great liberal. Instead, he sees evidence of anti-Catholicism in people all around him. By deploring anti-Catholicism in others, he can protect his idea of himself as a liberal. He can recognize that prejudice is there, not in himself, but in those other fellows. He is projecting his feelings onto others.

Mechanisms of redirection

Self-defense may be based on a redirection of interest and purpose, either genuine or pretended. A goal that is unattainable may be replaced by one that is attainable: "A bird in the hand is worth two in the bush." A task that seems impossible may be performed in another way: "There is more than one way to skin a cat." A block that is insurmountable may be circumvented: "There is no law that says you have to beat your head against a stone wall." And sometimes: "The longest way 'round is the shortest way home." Mechanisms of redirection are ways of changing one's goals, one's concept of self, one's skills, or the situation itself, in order to attain satisfaction in spite of blocks. Some of the more successful defense mechanisms fall into this category, though none results in lasting satisfaction unless the basic problem of anxiety and frustration is solved in the process.

Substitution. Gladys hates her name, which is completely unglamorous, not at all like Renée or Sharon. And, being a brunette instead of a blonde, and with that name, she feels like a dowdy, unglamorous person! But she has a good mind, and by developing her intellectual capacity, she may win the admiration, status, and prestige that she pictures in her ideal image of herself. So she neglects her nails and hair, lets her clothes go unpressed, and concentrates on learning all she can about French drama. She dreams of going to Paris on a Fulbright. With luck, Gladys may become aware that Fulbright scholars must be not only intellectually superior, but also attractive representatives of American colleges; and she may take measures to make her appearance neat and tidy, if not glamorous. She may eventually have to face up to two other questions: "If I can't be a glamorous blonde, could I be satisfied with being an attractive brunette?" And, "Am I using my intellect as a real source of satisfaction or as a way of escape?"

Compensation. Instead of substituting one goal for another, achieving in an area of strength rather than weakness, a person may achieve a goal by compensating for a weakness or overcoming a handicap. He may take the "longest way 'round" and still reach his goal. For example, Napoleon, who was too short to meet the entrance requirements for officers' training, came up out of the enlisted ranks, as "The Little Corporal." He proved his manhood and his military genius in spite of his short stature and "unofficerlike" physique. Glenn Cunningham, the great miler, was so severely burned about the legs that the doctors said he would never walk again; but he overcame the handicap, and is still remembered as a great distance runner and a tremendous competitor. Theodore Roosevelt developed his rugged character in recovering from tuberculosis. The literature and folklore of heroes and great men is full of examples of compensation. And their stories also remind us that compensation is effective unless it goes too far. Napoleon, dying in exile on a remote island, is a reminder of what disasters lie in wait for the man who does not know when to stop compensating, who does not relieve his acute anxiety in dealing with his weakness.

Identification. Though identification is a help in building a healthy self-concept, it must not become a crutch. Just as one grows out of creeping into walking, he must grow from identification to self-realization, from imitating a model to being somebody in his own right. Norman, for example, cannot see himself apart from "my old man." He has a strong emotional tie with his father and achieves satisfaction by basking in his dad's reflected glory. He is content to be a satellite, rather than the earth. Identification may have positive value. We all enjoy the accomplishments of our friends and family and see in them an extension of ourselves. After all, we cannot do everything or be all things, so we must enjoy some things vicariously, in seeing them well done by people we admire. But when identification keeps one from becoming the person he is capable of being, it is harmful.

Sublimation. Freud's concept of sublimation is one of the monuments of psychological theory. He first recognized the tendency to channel unacceptable drives into socially useful channels. In particular, he used the term to describe the redirection of sexual energies, thwarted by social conventions and mores, into non-sexual activities. Sublimation is a word that college students like to throw around. Actually, many of them probably use this defense mechanism very effectively. Most students are mature sexually, and all are in the stage of rapid sexual development. The desire for sexual satisfaction is very strong. But the regulations of the college fix very narrow limits for its acceptable expression. Not that the limits are not transgressed! But most students tend to observe some limits, and turn some of their energies into writing and acting, athletics and music, even into study and research. A great deal of the drive that keeps academic work and extracurricular activity going comes from sublimation.

Mechanisms of avoidance

An easy way to deal with an obstacle is to run away. Flight consumes energy and increases stress, however. So it is even easier to avoid stress by avoiding any situation that might threaten—to move from the habit of running away into the habit of never going in the first place. "Nothing ventured, nothing gained," is converted into "nothing ventured, nothing lost." It is a relief to escape from a threatening situation or to withdraw from an obstacle. It is even more comfortable to avoid trying anything at all. For example, the following defense mechanisms are commonly practiced in avoiding threats.

Regression. Deans of Women could furnish many examples of this mechanism as a favorite among freshmen. They feel they are not quite up to facing the challenges of college, which say *change, change* so often. They don't want to change, they just want to go home. Or they have a frantic desire to return to a pleasant earlier period in life, such as those last days in high school when life was beautiful and there were lots of dates. Regression is often accompanied by tears and tantrums, just to show how far back into childhood one can go to escape the awful threat of college. Ordinarily, the freshman who can stick it out long enough gains confidence as the newness fades away and he makes new friends. But regression as an habitual way of coping with problems leads to nothing but trouble. Looking to the past is no adequate solution to the present. And once regression starts, there may be no stopping place short of becoming a completely dependent, infantile person.

Repression. Of all the defense mechanisms, this is the most dangerous. Painful thoughts or memories which are in conflict with a person's present standards are buried in the unconscious. The habit of repression may develop from over-attention to self-control. Many persons who see themselves ideally as never being afraid or angry, vindictive or jealous, boisterous or enthusiastic, simply sit on the lid when they feel these emotions. Those who repress feelings get themselves into serious trouble, for the feelings that are repressed are, nevertheless, there, building up tension that can grow only so much before the dam bursts. Repression is necessary for the deceptive mechanisms to work effectively, so it tends to be very much overworked. Finally, it is easy to get into the habit of repressing desirable as well as undesirable emotions. To feel nothing, neither joy nor sorrow, anger nor enthusiasm, destroys the self and prevents self-realization. Self-control is necessary, but to be a person means responding to experiences with feeling, not acting as if feelings shouldn't exist at all.

Daydreaming and fantasies. Everybody uses this mechanism. One study of college students' daydreams found that the favorite images were: (1) vocational success; (2) money and possessions; (3) sex.[15] How pleasant it is to leave the field of action altogether and fulfill one's desires in an imaginary world! Certainly it provides relief from frustrations. And some of the dreams may someday come true. But it can become troublesome, as in the case of Jack who wanted desperately to be a doctor, yet was blocked by a low I.Q. He coped with his frustration by daydreaming hours on end of himself as a famous surgeon. Certainly, from the standpoint of mental health, it would be better for him to spend time exploring vocations within his range of ability.

Flight behavior. There are several flights that students may take as avoidance mechanisms. One popular one is *flight into intellectualization,* or "beating about the bush." Here a person skirts away from the issue by weaving long verbal theories which take him further and further away from the emotions the issue arouses. All problems of life cannot be solved by brilliant mental work, especially if feelings are being avoided. Among the more important uses of the intellect is the control of emotions through understanding, imagination, and action. But control cannot be exercised by avoiding emotions or pretending they don't exist. The proper use of the intellect is in understanding one's emotions, relating them adequately to the issue at hand, and gaining emotional satisfaction through action on the issue. To accept and use emotional reactions effectively is a real challenge to our capacity to learn. As the very young Scottish curate prayed, "Lord, teach us to take our hearts and look them in the face, however difficult that may be."

It cannot be stressed enough that the defenses mentioned here are common to all people. They come to our aid when we need to deal with an obstacle. But the goal of mental health is not to defend the self, but to realize it. If one always tries to be safe, he may not always be sane. To be sure, the further one goes in college, the more he uses his abilities, the more likely he is to encounter frustration. But by becoming aware of his defense mechanisms, he is more likely to use them effectively in dealing with obstacles and frustrations.

CHARACTERISTICS OF SELF-UNDERSTANDING AND SELF-ACCEPTANCE

How does one know when he has gained self-understanding? Perhaps one never does have it completely. But there are some signs that he is gaining in insight and awareness of his needs and his ways of achieving satisfaction:

1. *Ability to realize the emotional significance as well as the intellectual significance of what one has discovered about himself.* Some call this *awareness*. A person must develop insight into what he is doing. He must also be sensitive to the emotional implication of his behavior and to its effect on others. For example, Jim knows that he is, at this moment, talking a great deal in class. He knows he annoys others. He also needs to be aware of the real reason of his garrulity. Is it a defense? Or does the situation call for it?

2. *Ability to localize specific sources of difficulties.* The self-understanding person is able to examine ideas and feelings of his own, despite the fear, shame, and guilt that may result. It is important to know what he is doing and feeling at the moment. This frees him to take the next step, changing his behavior.

3. *The capacity for changing behavior.* Many students rationalize and say, "I know what I am doing and why I do it, but I can't change." Such rationalization is illustrated in a dialogue from a counseling session:

Things are getting worse this term—I don't seem to be able to study—I know I'm lazy—it's getting worse. And it's so easy to turn on the T.V. set when I get home. I might as well because my sister will anyway. Then I can't study—the walls in my room are like paper.

I think my trouble is discipline—I never had enough at home. My father never encouraged or forced me to do a damn thing—He's always been like that.—I don't think he cares what I do—he just sits there and reads—doesn't even talk to my mother—but I guess he knows better—that would just end in a fight. And my mother—she keeps telling me: "You did O.K. in high school—why can't you pass now—what's the matter—you losing your brains?" (or else) "It's that girl you're going with—you see her too often." Then she looks over to my father to get him to agree—but he keeps right on reading. Well, maybe my mother is right about the girl business—but I've got to pay a lot of attention to her otherwise I'll lose her.

Well, they never made me study—everything has always been easy—I got through high school without cracking a book. I could get by on my ability—but now I'm in a real mess—being on probation. These professors in school don't help very much—they're dull and don't seem to care what happens—I lose all interest and can hardly keep my eyes open.

Well, why can't I study? You've got to help me. Maybe I shouldn't be in engineering—I don't really know why I'm in engineering—mother told me it's secure—I better sign up for those tests you give—so you can tell me what to major in if they throw me out of engineering.

This student's self-understanding rates *low*. He deals with problems as though they are all outside himself; he externalizes them. There is little sense of personal responsibility. It is as if he says, "Things should be different, and if they were, I'd be all right." He avoids the discussion of internal feelings, although the counselor caught feelings in voice and tone.

Now turn to another student's description and account of his trouble:

I used to wonder why I'd get into these fights with my mother—especially after my father died—why me? Why does she pick on me—she nags and nags—nearly drives me nuts—and I can sense it coming on.

It happened again Friday night—I talked about leaving home again—and renting a room—then she started in on me. "You're just like your father—never satisfied—no responsibility—just looking out for yourself—you don't give a God-damn for me—how I've suffered—sacrificed—to put you through school and you talk about moving out—leaving me all alone."

I knew where this would lead to—I didn't want to get into another fight—I was getting more and more tense—I ran into my room and slammed the door shut—but she came and pounded on the door—screaming and cursing. I couldn't stand it anymore—I pulled the door open—and I wanted to strangle her—to shut her up forever—I just screamed—shut up—shut up—and ran out of the house. As I walked along—I got to thinking about myself—what a miserable home—and how lonely I am—I don't think I've got one close friend—how easy it would be to end it all—just step in front of a passing car—no effort at all. I felt excited and scared—my heart was pounding—I was sweating—a million thoughts were running through my mind—then quite suddenly—everything seemed to change—I realized that I would never step in front of any car—what a sense of relief! I nearly *got* the wrong person—I just can't get my feelings out—toward mother—I hate her—she's driving me crazy—and you know—I'm beginning to see why I'm not close to anyone—I'm so afraid myself. How can I get close to anyone?

This shows a higher level of self-understanding. First, the student deals with his feelings even though some are violent. He knows what he does and how he feels about his actions. He has localized a fairly specific area of difficulty. There is a strong drive to examine impulses and ideas despite fear and guilt. There is a movement toward changing behavior and resolving problems.

SELF-ACCEPTANCE

When we speak of self-understanding we also indicate the need for self-acceptance. Jersild lists seven characteristics of self-acceptance:[16]

1. *The self-accepting person has a relatively realistic notion of how he looks or how he might look in the eyes of others . . . a person needs to know and accept his looks and body build and put both in the best favorable light.*

2. *The self-accepting [person] will be better able than the self-rejecting person to view his strengths and weaknesses in a realistic way. He is not misled by "what would be nice to do." He has amassed evidence from many sources and then comes to see his strengths and weaknesses.*

3. *The self-accepting [person] does not usually like to be criticized, but he also has the freedom to accept criticism and some capacity to profit from it.*

4. *The self-accepting [person] keeps his hopes and demands upon himself fairly well within the limit of what is possible.*

5. *Acceptance of self and acceptance of others tend to go together.*

6. *The self-accepting person is better able than the self-rejecting one to get joy from life.*

7. *The self-accepting person is not a self-righteous person, but there are strong moral undertones in his manner of life.*

Because demands on self are kept within reason, the self-accepting person is not likely to get into situations that cause him to compete unnecessarily or to prove his worth in an unhealthy way. He will have unpleasant tasks and hurdles to face, but he does not conclude that life is altogether unpleasant, or fall into despair. The more he learns about his abilities and capacities the more he puts them to use. There is a very great pleasure in the effective use of one's capacities, and the self-accepting person makes the most of this pleasure, even though he may have mediocre endowments.

The self-accepting person will be able to understand the struggles of others, to lend a hand, to make friends. And in helping others, he will not be self-righteous or a stuffy moralist. Self-acceptance makes it possible for him to accept responsibility, to control his behavior in keeping with sound values, and to assume his moral obligation to others. He will have a healthy moral attitude, distinguishing between the degrading and restricting limitations of society and standards that free and exalt the spirit of man.

No college freshman should now try to analyze himself, or say: "I haven't accomplished *all this*. Therefore, I am not self-understanding. I don't accept myself." Self-acceptance and self-understanding are never fully attained; they are recurring tasks throughout life. No student can make a check list to see if he knows himself. His business is to go on knowing himself. The direction of his mind should always be toward increasing self-understanding. As new experiences occur, new understandings should develop. But, it is most important at the threshold of college to assess one's powers, feelings, and goals, and to undertake the developmental task of self-understanding.

4

How do you measure up?

*Self-appraisal and
self-direction*

Never before in history have there been so many instruments for measuring various aspects of human character. Tests have been devised to measure individual abilities, interests, character traits, attitudes, and values. Surveys can be made of opinions, attitudes, abilities, and values in large groups of people. It would seem to be possible to know more than ever before about oneself and about human nature.

Nevertheless, the task of appraising one's personal strengths and weaknesses is a vexing one, and it is difficult to estimate human capacities with very great precision. Infinitely more difficult is the problem of predicting how human affairs will turn out, and deciding whether one's personal desires can ever be fulfilled. On the one hand, both individuals and groups may be excessively proud and self-centered, overestimating their capacities and striving for unattainable goals. On the other hand, they may be excessively meek, self-effacing, and dependent, relying on other people to determine their worth and direct their behavior. Somewhere between the extremes, people can seek for an honest, fair, realistic estimate of their worth and their powers.

Such sound self-appraisal is necessary in order to develop self-direction. In order to avoid being driven by an idealized self, a person has to choose goals that are reasonably attainable and satisfying. To know whether goals are attainable, he must have a fair estimate of his abilities. To know whether they may be satisfying, he must have a fair estimate of his interest and expectations. To become what he wishes to be, he must know what he is and what he can do.

The development of the self-image is, therefore, an important factor in self-appraisal and self-direction. Of many significant elements in the self-image, four seem to have particular bearing on the task of self-appraisal and self-direction.

The first is the level of expectation. It emerges out of the picture of the real self (who I am and what I can do) seen in relation to the ideal self (what I might become or achieve for myself). The difference between the real self and the ideal self represents the level of expectation. There is a tendency for the level of expectation to be higher than the present level of achievement, especially in healthy young people. In most students, the level of expectation seems gradually to rise with their skills and achievement. Without such a rising level of expectation, there would hardly be any point in self-direction. Smugness, complacency, and self-satisfaction would replace the desire for personal development.

For the student, a second important element is the image of the self as student, a picture of himself in a student's role. Most students have a pretty clear understanding of the role, and a fair estimate of the quality of their performance. They can tell just about where they stand, whether their grades reflect their real ability, and how they rank in relation to other students. Both in high school and in college, most students can tell pretty accurately who are the best students in the class. Many students can make surprisingly good distinctions between imaginative, creative performance and good routine work.

Third, the self-image must include some standards for judging performance and measuring progress toward desirable goals. Standards of value help the student to decide what goals are desirable, and should also include some way to measure progress toward them. Such standards are part of any adequate image of the ideal self. And to be realistic, personal standards must bear some reasonable relation to social and institutional standards. Students, for example, cannot get along very well without a clear understanding of the requirements of the faculty for academic work. But a person has a right to expect that social stand-

ards will be not only clear but reasonable and objective. Academic requirements, for instance, are expected to be related to the quality of
academic work, not to the color of a student's eyes or the social status
of his family. Standards also have to be generally applicable and free of
bias, not weighted in favor of a particular type of person or group of
people. For instance, "unwritten standards" holding that "a woman
must do twice as good work as a man to get the same grade" are neither
relevant to scholarship nor generally applicable, and tend to add to the
confusion, rather than clarify standards of achievement.

Fourth, the self-image should include a realistic relation between the
level of expectation and the opportunities available for realizing it.
Some students, for example, feel that the world is their oyster and the
sky's the limit. They often find that they have been over-optimistic and
must accept limitations of time, energy, financial resources, and general
background that reduce their level of expectation. Equally unrealistic
are the students at the other end of the scale, who pessimistically scale
down their expectations for fear that a hard and indifferent world will
keep its doors closed and force them to beat their heads against a stone
wall. The student who makes an honest, realistic self-appraisal will
probably come out somewhere between the two extremes—more hope-
ful than the pessimists and less smug than the optimists.

Self-appraisal and self-direction have a reciprocal relation; as one
develops, the other is strengthened. Success in achieving a purpose
sharpens the capacity to estimate one's powers. And the two tasks are
related reciprocally to the development of the self-image. As the accuracy of self-appraisal is proved in practice, the self-image is clarified.
But the process begins with the image of oneself as the kind of person
who can understand himself, who can have a realistic level of expectation, who can develop good standards and take advantage of opportunities. This is the foundation of self-direction, and opens up the possibility of reaching desirable goals.

AIDS TO SELF-APPRAISAL AND SELF-DIRECTION

Of course, everyone needs to make sure that his appraisal of himself
is realistic. Parents, brothers and sisters, friends, teachers, often without
being asked, provide the kind of advice, criticism, correction, approval,
reward, and punishment that help a person clarify his estimate of himself. A college student is expected to be able to secure on his own
initiative the help he needs to check his self-appraisal. His college provides some rules of the game, some check points, and some counseling
services for him to use. He can check his performance against the re-

quirements of his courses, and his behavior against the regulations of the college. He can seek the advice of teachers and counselors to help make sure he is realistic in the appraisal of his abilities and achievement.

A great many check points are built into the educational system, and function almost automatically. The sequence of courses leading to the degree moves from beginning to advanced work. A student who passes one course can be reasonably sure that he is ready to go on to the next, which should be more difficult or cover new material. The sequence of examinations in a course is similarly designed to lead from simpler to more difficult tests of performance. If a student passes one exam, he can realistically expect to be ready to prepare for the next.

THE USE OF STANDARDIZED TESTS

However, many students are not satisfied with the rough estimate of their capacities provided by such steady progress in academic work. They feel the need of more information about their abilities, more refined measures of their performance, more extensive information about their interests and personality. Students consequently are making increasing use of other kinds of tests, particularly of standardized tests of ability, achievement, interests and values, as aids in self-appraisal.

The present generation of college students has pretty much accepted standardized tests as a normal part of school and college education. But those of their professors who were in college before the 1940's, were admitted, chose majors, and planned their careers without much hullabaloo over standardized test scores. Of course, many such were then in use, but since World War II testing programs have become common in almost all parts of the country. It is said, only half in jest, that college students today have developed a special set of skills in blackening the spots on IBM score sheets, putting x's in boxes and writing words and figures in the proper blanks.

Standardized tests are more than a passing fad in American education. They have proved to be of great value in research, making it possible to measure behavior and define processes of learning that otherwise could not be so clearly understood or precisely measured. Of course, one major factor in the increased use of standardized tests is the advantage they offer school and college administrators, who have to make decisions affecting large numbers of students. These decisions are costly both to students and their families (in terms of tuition, fees, and other expenses) and to the taxpayers of the city, state, and nation (in terms of public funds spent on educational institutions). Plans based on standardized testing programs have proved fairly successful in cutting down the time spent in making decisions and reducing waste caused by costly trial-and-error planning. For example, the results of high school testing programs give an estimate of the number of graduates of college caliber coming up the educational ladder who must be taught and housed and fed. Achievement test scores of an entering freshman class provide a rough estimate of the distribution of students among types and levels of courses, so that plans can be made for organizing teaching loads and securing the right number of teachers in freshman English (including "bonehead" or remedial English), mathematics, or science.

Such help in administrative planning ultimately is to the advantage of the students. The quality of their college education is affected by administrative plans, and many administrative decisions directly affect the individual student: his placement in "bonehead" English or an advanced English course, for example. College administrations want all the help they can get in making decisions affecting individual students, and standardized test results afford additional information of great value. As two experts in tests and measurements wisely observe[1]

We assume that the more we know about a person that relates to our present decision, and the more accurately we know it, the more likely we are to arrive at a sound decision about him or a wise plan of action for him.

In practice, tests are rarely if ever relied upon as the sole basis for decision about college admissions or students' standing. Grades, observed behavior, interview records, personal references and recommendations as well as the students' own expressed ideas and interests, are taken into account. But test results carry a good deal of weight, although not as much as student folklore and popular legend might lead one to believe. For example, the "College Boards" (the Scholastic Aptitude and achievement tests in academic subjects, published and administered by the College Entrance Examination Board) are taken by hundreds of thousands of high school graduates each year as part of their application for admission to college. These tests are particularly helpful to admissions officers in comparing the level of achievement of students who come from different types and sizes of high schools, in all parts of the country. The scores help insure a fair comparison on a uniform scale in spite of variations in high school grading systems.

Over and above their value as an aid to fair evaluation of students by college officials, standardized tests offer aid to the individual student in self-appraisal. It has been said, with some truth, that these tests rarely tell the student very much about himself that he did not know already. But they afford a check on the accuracy of his self-appraisal, and give some guidance in self-direction. The very term *standardized* sums up pretty well the source of their advantages. Standardized tests must meet logical and mathematical standards designed to provide more objective measures than can be secured by personal judgment.

First, standardized tests must use clear and distinctive standards of adequate and inadequate responses. Some of these standards are set by the common culture. For example, a test of general intelligence assumes that a child in an American town would be expected by most people to distinguish different coins from each other and to have an idea of their value. Other standards are set by the educational system itself; the "College Boards" use the generally accepted content of freshman courses as the basis for entrance examinations. Some standards are based on general practices or traits in a particular group—vocational interest inventories use the pattern of preference for activities found among people in different occupations as a measure with which a student's pattern of interests may be compared.

Second, an effort is made to avoid premature moral judgments. The introduction of standards of good and bad into a test of vocational interest, for example, would serve to confuse rather than clarify the matter. While a student's own responses may be affected by his own sense of what is good and bad, the test itself may confuse him if it invites him to decide whether a forest ranger is good and a stockbroker bad. Even standardized tests of values do not assume that one moral judgment is better than another, but are designed to see what judgments are in fact made.

Third, standardized tests are checked by rigorous logical and statistical methods to insure that they really do measure what they are supposed to measure. The items are checked to make sure they are related to the subject, and that they are understandable and not ambiguous. Statistical measures are applied to make sure that the results do in fact show distinctive differences in individual or group performance—tests of masculinity and femininity would be checked to make sure that the items did relate to generally accepted differences in masculine and feminine behavior; the results would be checked statistically to make sure that patterns of response among men were significantly different from those among women.

Fourth, logical and statistical methods are also used to make sure that there is as little error and as much uniformity as possible in results. Directions for administering, scoring, and interpreting the test are given in precise detail. When speed is a factor being tested, timing is carefully worked out. Statistical methods are used to determine whether there is an excessive degree of error in measurement due to irrelevant factors such as variations in test administration, errors in scoring, variation in individual experience, and the like.

In order to standardize a test, it is administered to the kind of people who are supposed to take it. A random sample, representing a cross-section of the population is tested. It may be a rather small group or a very large number of people all over the country. Rigorous statistical standards are used for selecting an adequate sample regardless of the total number tested. Norms, or standards for scoring, are derived from the results. A check of standard error in measurement is made at the same time. In other words, the standards by which the test is constructed and the system of scoring are tested to make sure they are generally applicable and favor no particular type of person in the group to which the test is supposed to apply.

It is this final process of statistical standardization that gives the standardized test its distinctive value. The process increases the range of comparison. Comparisons, then, can show where an individual or class stands in relation to a very large group of people of widely varying background and experience. The student can see himself in a larger context. He can tell just about where he stands, not only in relation to students in his class but also in relation to college students all over the country. He can be reasonably sure that the results are affected as little as possible by accidents of fate or fortune, and, consequently, show him where he falls on a scale that is fair, unbiased, and uniform, so far as possible.

This is not to say that teacher-made tests are necessarily lacking in accuracy and objectivity. On the contrary, the principles of standardized test construction are derived from the best practice of teachers over the years, and refined by scientific study, statistical analysis, and experimentation. Teachers try to be fair and to use good standards in constructing their tests. Increasing numbers of them have some training in test construction and apply some of its principles in making up their own tests. The tests constructed by teachers give the student a check against the requirements of his courses at his college. Standardized tests make it possible for him to check his self-appraisal against the test results from people generally, or from students all over the country, or people of his own age, or members of a particular professional group. Teachers may also use standardized tests to make similar comparisons for the group of students they teach. Both types of tests give needed help in self-appraisal.

Finally, standardized tests have been devised to measure some traits which cannot be very accurately measured in other ways. A teacher working with a single class, for instance, has no effective or objective way of measuring the vocational interest of his students against the typical interests of people in various occupations, except by using one of the standardized vocational interest inventories. Standards for appraisal are made available to teachers and students through standardized tests that cannot be provided in any other way.

APPRAISING INTELLIGENCE

By intelligence we mean the ability to learn, to solve problems, to deal with abstract matters, to engage in complex thought processes.

Intelligence is the aggregate or global capacity of the individual to act purposefully, to think rationally and to deal effectively with his environment. We know intelligence by the things it enables us to do . . . such as making appropriate associations between events, drawing correct inferences from propositions, understanding the meaning of words, solving mathematical problems. . . .[2]

Human abilities have two characteristics that make it possible to test intelligence as a whole. On the one hand, these abilities are specific, appearing independently of each other. On the other hand, they are related to each other in such a way that they reinforce each other's effects. Each specific ability seems definitely related to all the rest. Superiority in one tends to be associated with superiority in certain others. For instance, a student who scores high on vocabulary tends to score high in remembering facts and in recognizing similarities. So specific abilities are tested, such as defining words, reproducing facts from memory, solving mathematical problems, and recognizing similarities and differences. Taken all together, the results of the specific tests are used as a measure of general intelligence.

Combinations of specific abilities, according to Wechsler,[3] form three main types of intelligence: "(1) Abstract or verbal intelligence, involving facility in the use of symbols; (2) practical intelligence, involving facility in manipulating objects; (3) social intelligence, involving facility in dealing with human beings."

THE I.Q.: EXPLODING THE MYTH

Myth 1: The I.Q. measures brain power

But what a student usually asks for is his I.Q. He seems to regard it as somewhat like the pulse rate. The I.Q. shows how fast his brain is working, just as the pulse rate shows how fast his heart is beating. But as the pulse rate is not all that is needed to determine the condition of the heart, so the I.Q. is only one bit of information needed to understand one's intellectual abilities. Knowing one's I.Q. contributes just about as much to self-appraisal as taking one's pulse.

The I.Q., the intelligence quotient, is a figure that serves as a ready index to intellectual maturation. It measures the extent of growth, rather than brain substance or mental capacity.

For school children, the I.Q. is calculated by dividing the mental age (M.A.), measured by a general intelligence test score, by his chronological age (C.A.) in years and months. The mental age scale represents progressive stages in the development of intellectual capacity. The intelligence test provides a graded series of intellectual tasks which the average child of a certain age is expected to be able to accomplish. Thus, the average child of 12 should have a mental age of 12, an I.Q. of 100. A child of 12 who can pass only the 9-year-old test and fails at higher age levels has a mental age of 9, an I.Q. of 75. Some 12-year-olds may sail through the tests the average 15-year-old is expected to pass, and their I.Q. is figured at 125.[4]

General intelligence tests for adults are scored in a different way. For example, on the *Wechsler-Bellevue Intelligence Scale* (an individual test of general intelligence), three formulae are used to figure a score for a verbal I.Q., a score for a performance I.Q., and a total I.Q. from the combined subtests. The standard score is set so that the average score of a normal sample of adults is 100, with a standard deviation of 15. This means that an individual scoring 100 on the combined scales may score 100 on all three or over 100 on some and below 100 on others. And the standard deviation also allows for errors of measurement, so the total score is to be understood as somewhere within a 15-point range around the figure given. Thus, an I.Q. of 100 should be understood as somewhere between 93 and 108, for example.

Myth 2: The I.Q. is an absolutely accurate measure

When a student gets his I.Q., he should interpret it as a score subject to a standard error of measurement, rather than a fixed, precise measure of his intellectual ability. He should also bear in mind that it shows where he stands in relation to the distribution of intelligence among people generally. It is not an absolute measure of his personal ability. For example, the distribution of intelligence in the general population as measured by tests of general intelligence is shown in Fig. 4-1.

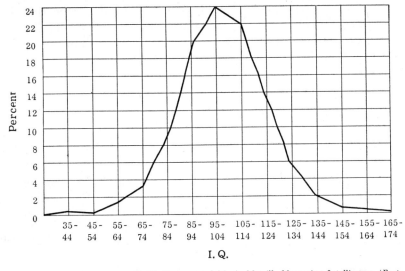

L. M. Terman and M. A. Merrill, *Measuring Intelligence* (Boston: Houghton Mifflin Company, 1937), p. 35. Used by permission.

Fig. 4–1.   Distribution of I.Q.'s of 2,904 Individuals, Ages Two to Eighteen.

Note the broad range of scores, the wide distribution of intelligence, and the concentration of most I.Q.'s between 95 and 105.

In Fig. 4-2, the I.Q. is given as a percentile score, the most commonly

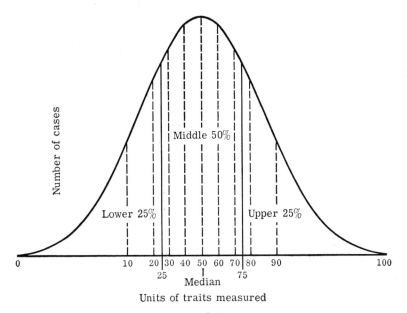

Fig. 4–2.   Distribution of I.Q.'s as a Percentile Score.

used form for reporting results on most types of standardized tests. A percentile score represents a person's standing in a representative group of 100. For example, if Jim's verbal I.Q. places him in the 90th percentile, he is in the highest group; the 50th percentile is an average position; at the 10th percentile, he would be in the lowest group, with the least ability in tasks requiring verbal skill. A percentile rank of 100 is the best possible score, while an I.Q. of 100 is average. The moral for students is, "Don't peep at the scores over the shoulder of the counselor; you may confuse an I.Q. with a percentile score!"

Myth 3: The I.Q. will tell whether you ought to go to college

In wanting to know his I.Q., a student really wants to know what it means in terms of his expectations for himself. He may ask a counselor, "How much of an I.Q. should I have to go to college?" Table 4-1 shows how I.Q.'s compare with percentiles, and in which percentile ranks students have the best chance to succeed in college. It shows that 99 per-

TABLE 4-1
Possible Success in College Achievement as Related to I.Q.
and Percentile Rating

I.Q.	Percentile	
140	99th	
130	96th	
120	87th	Likely to succeed in College
110	69th	Level of median college student
100	50th	Average of unselected population
90	23rd	Unlikely to complete traditional school program
80	8th	
70	3rd	

Adapted from Lee J. Cronbach, *Educational Psychology* (New York: Harcourt, Brace and Company, Inc., 1954), p. 192, © 1954 by Harcourt, Brace and Company, Inc.

cent of the population ranks below I.Q. 140. Most college students rank at or above the 69th percentile, with an I.Q. of 110 or above. An I.Q. of 100 or percentile rank of 50 indicates that success in college may be uncertain, and the chances of success decrease markedly below this level.

But the I.Q. alone will not tell a student whether he can expect to succeed in college. With the same I.Q., he may be average in one college and above average somewhere else. No college has students whose distribution of intelligence test scores exactly matches the national distribution among college students. Traxler[5] found that among 300 colleges the average (median) I.Q. of freshman classes ranged from 94 to 123. A student with an I.Q. of 125 would be superior in the former college, about average in the latter.

Furthermore, tests of general intelligence cover a broad spectrum of abilities, of which the abilities required to succeed in college are only a part. Also, individual intelligence tests, such as the Stanford-Binet or Wechsler-Bellevue, are expensive and time-consuming to administer, since they are based on an individual interview between a psychometrist and the subject. So the most commonly used tests are pencil-and-paper tests that can be administered to a group, and frequently are set up for machine scoring. These are for the most part tests of the special verbal and abstract intelligence needed to perform the tasks required in school and college. Most of them are explicitly referred to as tests of scholastic aptitude, rather than general intelligence. The "College Boards" include a Scholastic Aptitude Test, for example, which provides scores for verbal and mathematical aptitudes. Although individual intelligence tests cover a wider range of abilities, group scholastic aptitude test scores may yield information that may help the student more than the I.Q. in deciding whether to go to college, or which college to choose. The national norms tell where a student stands in the whole college population. But each college usually works out its own local norms, to use in predicting the probable success of students in its entering classes. A student can be fairly certain that if he is admitted to a particular college, the chances that he will do acceptable work there are pretty good.

A student can be misled in appraising his ability unless he knows the group with which he is compared. For example, a bright student (I.Q. 130) was enrolled in a college with a highly selected, extremely bright student body. She felt inferior, expected to do just average work, and came to believe her B's and C's were all her ability justified. During the summer, she took a series of individual tests in another city, and learned that her abilities indicated she could reasonably expect a level of achievement higher than 96 percent of college students throughout the country. The following excerpt from the letter she wrote the person administering the tests shows the change in her estimate of herself:

. . . even though you refuse to tell me about my extraordinary I.Q., I have taken heart at its possibilities, and have never worked so hard in my life.

A student can be misled in appraising his abilities unless he understands the specific things that a test measures. Scholastic aptitude tests cover the specific abilities needed for general college work. But other aptitudes—mechanical, artistic, social—are required for some specialized studies such as engineering or music. A student should be sure that his test scores provide a good measure of the particular abilities he needs to appraise.

Myth 4: The I.Q. remains constant throughout life

Though the early psychologists believed that the I.Q. remained fairly constant, now they usually assume that it is subject to change. Apparently the rate of intellectual growth, which is what the I.Q. measures, varies from time to time, like most other aspects of individual development. Changes in physical health, family situation, cultural opportunities, and motivation, may affect the I.Q. One study of the growth of intelligence between the ages of 16 and 21 indicated that the I.Q. increases through 21 years of age.[6] The evidence seems to indicate that the emotional climate affects the rate of intellectual growth. Encouragement or discouragement, reward or punishment, approval or disapproval of intellectual interests, drives toward intellectual activities or toward other competing activities, all affect the development of intelligence. Material factors also exert strong influence; the opportunity for reading books, the extent of travel, the kind of conversation with family and acquaintances, the availability of works of art, music, drama, all affect the growth of intelligence.

At best, intelligence tests measure what has been learned. Home environment, school opportunities, and individual motivation all set limits to what is learned. Some things are not learned because of lack of individual capacity or motivation; others are not learned because the environment and personal relationships available to the individual do not provide the necessary experience. One psychologist who believes that 88 percent of mental ability is attributable to inherited factors nevertheless recognizes that environmental factors affect test results.[7]

Some parents take care to provide books that stimulate curiosity, converse with children on intellectually stimulating subjects, and have music and paintings of quality in the home. Other homes have no books on the shelves and no paintings on the walls, and the conversation of parents is anything but intellectual. There are unusual cases of gifted students emerging from culturally impoverished homes, but they have usually supplied their intellectual needs from other sources. A college student who comes from such an environment, even with other resources available, still starts out at a disadvantage in comparison with students from homes rich in books, music, and ideas. The level of culture available to the student, as well as the use he makes of it, influence the growth of intelligence. Improvement in the availability and use of cultural resources can raise the level of intelligence.

Educational resources also have an important influence on intelligence. Some schools provide more intellectual resources than others. There are significant differences in quality related to length of time in school, classroom and laboratory facilities, library size and quality, the quality of teachers and their rate of pay, and class size, among other factors. Allison Davis[8] gives evidence that poor educational opportunity affects two groups in particular, Negroes and students from lower social and economic backgrounds. Social class and racial influences fix inferior cultural and psychological conditions for learning. However, thousands of Negro students succeed in college despite low test scores, apparently because their motivation is high and their objectives clear, and they get encouragement from teachers. Davis also reports that, at higher age levels, performance scores of both white and Negro people are related to the quality of the educational system in which the individuals were trained.

Myth 5: Intelligence is inborn and will always develop in spite of everything

Intelligence is not a measure of pure brain power, which will grow regardless of other factors such as culture and class. Motivation is also an important factor in intelligence. The rate of growth of intelligence is affected by many sources of motivation—the encouragement and affection of key people, pressures, rewards, and above all an individual's own desire to develop and improve. Even a modest capacity may produce a high level of intellectual performance when it is employed steadily, in diligent, accurate, speedy work.[9]

In Fig. 4-3, Still shows graphically how little of our capacities is actually employed. The failure curve is characteristic of the intellectual development of far too many people today. They cease growing and begin to decline early in adult life. In contrast, the upper curve indicates the optimum ages for championship performance in four general intellectual fields, the curve of intellectual development corresponding closely to the curve of physical development. Memorizing is at a peak in childhood, while creative imagination flowers from the late teens into the early thirties. In the forties, intellectual growth has proceeded to the stage of analysis and organization, and young poets or mathematical prodigies may become writers and editors, scientists, administrators and professional leaders. Finally, the fifties and sixties and beyond bring the age of philosophy and elder statesmanship, the fruit of intelligent reflection on rich experience. Motivation seems to be the key

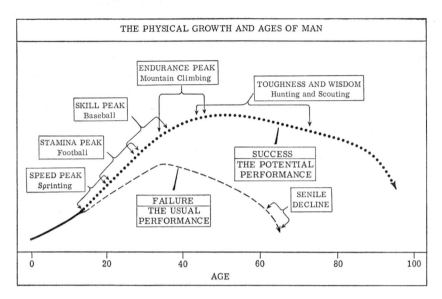

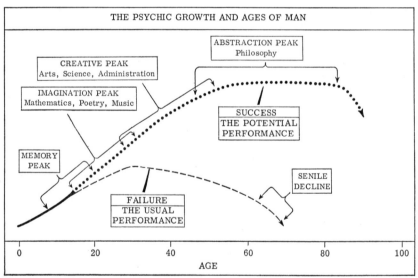

Joseph W. Still, "Man's Potential and His Performance," *New York Times Magazine*. Used by permission.

Fig. 4–3.   Possibility and Performance. This figure was devised to indicate the physical and psychological potentials of normal people. Note the wide gap between what is possible and what is achieved. Not more than five percent of the population follow the upper curves. The rest fail for lack of motivation and understanding of their abilities. Note also the peak periods for various age groups. At the age of 20 there is still great possibility for success, but the usual growth potential declines after 20.

to the progression, providing for shifts of interest and direction of ability into new fields.

Whatever motivation is, it appears to be controlled by the individual student and no one else. All the encouragement and opportunities in the world may not move one student to develop his abilities, while poverty, disease, disaster and discouragement seem only to stimulate another to increase his powers. Take Mary and Cyril, for example. She had very high entrance examination scores, he had only average scores. She is interested in getting a husband, he in becoming a lawyer. Her family has comfortable means, his is very poor. She produces a bare *C* average, he produces the *B*'s he needs to get into law school. A look at the following comparison suggests that Mary is poorly motivated, while Cyril's motivation is very high.

CYRIL	*MARY*
1. A clear goal (lawyer) related to academic work. He is *future-oriented.*	1. Real goal (marriage) not related to academic achievement. She is *immediacy-oriented,* having no plans beyond getting married, not even an idea of what marriage will mean.
2. Clear acceptance of the fact that he must produce in order to get into law school. Every good grade brings him closer to his goal. Real energies put into academic work.	2. Accepted the fact that she must pass courses. Good grades may interfere with her real goal. Result is poor work habits. Real energy directed toward social purposes.
3. Good work habits have been established because of his desire to achieve. He is able to study long hours and is not easily distracted. When in conflict between study and recreation, he is able to choose whatever will fit into his personal goals most effectively.	3. Since she is only interested in getting by, she is easily distracted. She cannot study very long at a time. She is easily interrupted, and interrupts others, for immediate recreation. She "goofs off."
4. Attitude toward work is that of interest. He anticipates interesting facts in each course. Asks questions, does independent reading.	4. Attitude toward work is that of indifference; any dull or difficult task bores her completely.
5. He receives rewards and approval from family all along the way.	5. Family attitude is indifferent; they just expect her to pass.

Students reviewing the five factors relating to Cyril's achievement can evaluate their own motivation. Few students have a perfect score. The best ones, at most, have a good batting average. The self-understanding student *at least* recognizes and assesses himself on each point. He counts his assets and then works on his weaknesses. For example, once a goal has been established, it is possible to develop more interest and use more opportunities to raise the level of achievement. Cyril, for example, listed all the skills he would need as a lawyer, and noted how each course contributed to his development. He visited courtrooms, observed trials, got a job in the probation office one summer, in a law firm another summer. Each course, each summer job, was an immediate goal related to his future goal. He felt he was achieving something at each step along the way.

In the long run, the most important aid to motivation is a clearcut vocational goal. This decision, with its effect on motivation, is just as important, if not more so, than the I.Q. score, for it can make the difference between success or failure.

ABILITY IN RELATION TO ACHIEVEMENT

Students apparently tend to form remarkably consistent patterns of achievement that seem to have almost the force of habit. In predicting college grades, for example, high school marks seem to be the best single measure that can be used. Correlations of college grades with high school grades are as high as or higher than correlations with scores on group intelligence tests. Of course, a combination of grades, intelligence test results, and achievement test scores gives an even higher correlation, and a better prediction of college grades. But there is striking consistency in achievement as measured by grades.

This gives some advantage to a student. He can get a fair estimate of his probable achievement in college from his achievement in high school. If he also uses other data, such as intelligence and achievement test ratings, he can make a rather accurate prediction of his probable performance in college. If he finds that his level of achievement is high enough to move him steadily toward his goals for personal and vocational development, he can be pretty sure that his appraisal of himself is realistic, and can have confidence in his ability to attain his expectations.

However, the student must also consider another factor, the relation of his achievement to his ability. There is often a discrepancy between students' aptitude and achievement test scores, and sometimes between both scores and college grades. Achievement may be either higher or lower than aptitude ratings would indicate; and both differences tend to be remarkably persistent throughout the college years.

While we need to know more about the factors that make for over-achievement or under-achievement, any student may well conclude that under-achievement is not a very desirable habit to form. The student whose level of achievement is in line with his level of expectation and intelligence, or a little higher, is doing fine, and can expect to maintain his level of performance as he goes on to more difficult work. But the student whose level of achievement is lower than his aptitude is in a rather dangerous position. For he cannot be certain that he can maintain even his present level of achievement, especially when his courses become more difficult as he advances in college. In order to succeed in meeting college requirements, he somehow has to close the gap between achievement and ability. But this requires changing his pattern of achievement, and it is almost as hard to improve achievement as to break a lifelong habit.

There is no simple set of directions that will help a student work up to capacity. All that can be offered are a few check points for self-appraisal that may help him decide where to begin.

First, he may check his work habits. A regular, well-organized schedule, attention to polish and detail, economy in use of time and material, and following through are habits to be cultivated. (Chapter 5 deals with habits that help control stress in order to improve the quality of work). Orderliness and system in the organization of ideas also seem to enable students to work with greater speed and accuracy; and most of the prizes in academic work, and in most other work, go to the person who "gits thar fustest with the mostest." Good form in writing, taking notes, making references, planning papers and experiments, helps a student get there quicker with more ideas, information, and evidence in hand.

Second, he may check his expectations of his academic performance. Students seem to perform close to their level of expectation. An image of the self as a good student seems to be related to good academic work and improvement in achievement. An image of the self as a mediocre or poor student is more likely than not to be confirmed in failure or work of poor quality. For example, some students of perfectly sound intellectual ability fail to make the grade in college because they aim to make "gentleman's C's" instead of the A's and B's of which they are capable; an illness, accident, or unforeseen difficulty that could happen to anybody becomes a disaster, bringing the C average quickly down to the point where they are disqualified. Students who shoot for B's seem to stand a better chance to make the required C average or better, with a surprise A here and there. The A students are likely to be those who have better than average ability and expect to do first-rate work. Bringing the level of expectation into better line with the level of ability may be one step needed to improve achievement.

Third, the student may check his reaction to what others expect of him. Deans and counselors can give many examples of students who lower their sights or do little more than average work because they take seriously a chance remark, a discouraging reaction, or a series of contemptuous comments from another person. Mary decides not to go to college because Aunt Susan says to her, "Why, Mary, you know very well that no woman in the family was ever bright enough to waste money on a college education." Ed gives up pre-law courses and decides to go into business because a lawyer tells him that it is hard for a Jew to get ahead in the profession, "unless you are a Brandeis or Frankfurter." The one girl in a family of five boys fails mathematics, in spite of good aptitude and interest; she has heard, "Oh, you're just an old dumb girl who can't do math" so often that she has come to believe it. The student who wishes to improve his achievement may wish to associate with people who value intellectual achievement and encourage his efforts to raise his sights. And he may need to improve his defenses against the belittling, discouragement, and contempt of others. At least, he should make sure that he does not let himself be over-persuaded to under-achieve.

Fourth, the student should set short-range as well as long-range goals, and the two should be related to each other. Waiting and working, hoping to become an astrophysicist, may postpone satisfaction too long for motivation to last. The student must also see some immediate goals, such as carrying out a special experiment, that will give him satisfaction in the feeling of success.

Whether in the end any student will decide to try to improve his performance is up to him. All that can be said is that the statistical chances are that he probably can if he goes at it right. For human beings have only begun to discover what their potential levels of achievement may be, and there is every indication that more students underestimate their potential achievement than overestimate their abilities.

Appraising special aptitudes

Intelligence, or I.Q., as it is measured by most standardized intelligence tests, is a measure of general ability or capacity to perform the tasks that people have to undertake. As we have suggested, intelligence alone is not an effective means of predicting performance or achievement. Neither does it measure ability to perform some highly specialized tasks that are not commonly required of people. In determining realistic expectations of achievement, or setting vocational goals, it is often helpful to have more precise measures of specific aptitudes in addition to a measure of general intelligence.

Intelligence tests, such as the Wechsler, often are made up of subtests designed to measure specific aptitudes. In school and college, aptitude tests are more frequently used than intelligence tests for assessing mental ability. What the school and college actually find more valuable for their purposes than a measure of general intelligence is a measure of the capacity to learn what is taught in school. Even though an I.Q. can be derived from some of the group intelligence tests, the standardized pencil-and-paper tests that are generally given in school are really tests of this scholastic aptitude. The term "aptitude test" is frequently used to distinguish these from tests of general intelligence. The *College Boards,* the examinations for college admission given by the College Entrance Examination Board, include a Scholastic Aptitude Test which is designed to measure capacity to learn from college study. This is a special aptitude, included in general intelligence, but measured more specifically by such a special test. There are many other tests of scholastic aptitude: the California Test of Mental Maturity, the Otis Test of Mental Ability, the American Council on Education Psychological Examination, to mention only a few.

Scholastic aptitude tests cover a wide range of ability to learn different subjects. The Scholastic Aptitude Test of the College Boards, for example, gives two scores, one for verbal, the other for mathematical aptitude. The verbal sections seems to be a good measure of ability to learn subjects requiring reading and writing—history, foreign language, social sciences, for instance. The mathematical section is related to learning not only in mathematics as such, but in subjects requiring logical and mathematical thinking, such as most of the sciences and music.

Other aptitude tests are more specific in the abilities they measure. Some of them may be extremely useful for a student who needs to appraise his aptitude to master some special skills, study particular subjects, or enter specifically related occupations. They measure specific factors in intelligence as they act independently of others; general aptitude or intelligence tests measure some of these factors as they act interdependently. In using these special aptitude tests in self-appraisal, the student should bear this distinction in mind. He should remember the dual nature of intelligence. He should be sure to use tests that will help him appraise both his special, independent aptitudes and the interdependent pattern into which his intelligence organizes them.

Some special aptitudes for which standardized tests are available are as follows:[10]

Perceptual speed and accuracy. These factors are related to the ability to make useful distinctions, to recognize similarities and differences, to perceive relationships between things. Reading skill is in part dependent upon rapid and accurate perception; spelling correctly may be partly related to accurate perception. Mathematical and logical reasoning seem to depend on accurate perception.

Manual dexterities. There are several different kinds of manual dexterities that can be distinguished from each other. It is fairly common knowledge that fine manual dexterity, using the small muscles of the hand and arm, is more common among women, while gross manual dexterity, using large muscles, is more common among men. The wife gets called to sew on the buttons; the husband gets the call when there is a jar top to be unscrewed, or the heavy punch bowl to be put back on the top shelf. These aptitudes for different kinds of manual work do not seem to be as significant as other factors in achievement, probably because practice seems to bring most people up to required levels of skill unless they are completely muscle-bound. There is a minimum level of dexterity required in most academic fields: science, medicine, home economics, engineering, art, and music require specific manual skills. Shorthand and typing require manual dexterity. And if faculty members could have one wish granted, they might very well wish for all their students to improve one skill requiring fine manual dexterity— handwriting! (Students, too, may share this wish!)

Spatial visualization. The aptitude for distinguishing forms and shapes and working out the relation between them is a special kind of perceptual ability. It is needed in such fields as art, architecture, and engineering.

Mechanical comprehension. The ability to figure how the wheels go round, how the apparatus works, how the instruments measure things, and how processes work out is a complex aptitude made up of several others, probably including perception, abstract reasoning, and manual dexterity. In point of fact, probably no occupation requires a higher degree of mechanical comprehension in greater variety than being a housewife, and there is none in which this skill is more neglected. People who understand machines and can master them and fix them are highly esteemed in our society and very necessary. Ask any husband who has tangled with the vacuum cleaner.

Art, music, and aesthetic judgment. Here we get into a vexed area of opinion and prejudices, and we do not know enough to have very useful estimates of aptitudes. The forms of art are exceptionally varied, and neither practicing artists nor expert students of art can agree on whether they have any elements in common. There are some tests of aesthetic judgment and talent, such as the Meier Art Judgment Test and the Seashore Musical Talent Test, on which performers tend to surpass teachers and students. But tests so far have added very little to our understanding and appraisal of artistic aptitudes. There seems to be an unknown factor, referred to as creativity, involved.* Certainly artistic ability adds to the enjoyment of living. It can be learned and improved through practice. And it is necessary for study or entry into occupations in many fields: literature, criticism, the performing arts, design, engineering, science, journalism, and advertising, to name only the most obvious. The student who is interested in such fields can best get an estimate of his artistic aptitudes by trying them out in practice.

Any student who has special aptitude could well consider entering a field of study or an occupation in which his talent could be employed. Lack of a special talent or aptitude, however, need not be a block to students interested in work involving these special abilities. These abilities can be measured independently, but in practice they are interdependent. Many of them can be learned, and all can be improved by practice. Successful work can be done with no more than the required minimum of aptitude, provided other intellectual abilities are applied to the maximum. For instance, limited skill in using apparatus in chemistry can be compensated for by practice, or by patience and taking extra time. Skill in abstract reasoning may eventually lead into work where theoretical and mathematical operations are needed, and someone else can handle the apparatus.

For satisfaction in the choice of academic work or an occupation, the student should be prepared to do some things which are not easy for him. No one is equally apt in all aspects of intelligence, or equally strong in all aptitudes. The requirements of a college education, like the requirements of any occupation, include work in fields where the student is weak as well as in fields where he has strong aptitudes. In self-appraisal, he consequently needs to estimate his weaknesses as carefully as his strengths. Because aptitudes are used all together rather than independently, he cannot succeed if he simply builds up his strengths. He must also overcome his weaknesses so far as he can. It is extremely helpful to get as precise an estimate as possible of all his aptitudes, so he can plan the kind of experience in college that will enable him to make the most of all his powers. Remedial study to overcome deficiencies in skill, courses that develop his strong abilities and interests and studies and activities that will develop a variety of skills will all help raise his level of achievement.

* The Institute of Personality Assessment and Research, University of California at Berkeley, is presently engaged in exploring the aptitudes and personality factors involved in creativity, and the findings may help to define it more clearly.

Appraising achievement

Measures of achievement, like measures of intelligence and aptitude, are not absolute, fixed, or constant. They have to be interpreted in relation to other factors. Grades, for instance, are not precise measures of the quality of a student's work, but rough indications of its quality in relation to the requirements of the course. Grades may also show the standing of the student in relation to the performance of other students in his class. One semester's grades tell the student only how he stands in relation to these two factors. If he compares them with grades for previous semesters, he can estimate his progress and improvement in achievement.

Ordinarily many students in most colleges may expect their grades for the freshman year to be about the same as in high school, or a little lower. Because college work is more difficult and the competition is stiffer, a drop of a whole letter grade below high school grades is not unusual. As long as the overall average is C or better, students need not be alarmed about this. As a rule, they may expect their grades to show a gradual upward trend after the first year, and to reach or sometimes surpass the level of high school grades.

Such an upward trend is what every student should try to establish during his college years. It is not enough to hold to a steady level of mediocrity; he should strive for excellence, or at least for continuous improvement. Of course, the gifted student cannot expect to show much of a gain in achievement as measured by grades. He is stuck under the ceiling set by A's, and has little room to move upward. But most students will find that there is plenty of room at the top.

Of course, grades are not the only measure of achievement. They tell the gifted student very little, for example. A monotonous string of A's gives him very little feeling of progress. And the meaning of grades for the average student is just as limited. They tell him only how his work is rated in relation to the requirements of a particular course, under a particular professor, in a particular college. From his grades alone, he cannot tell how he stands among students in his field all over the country, or how much he has learned about the subject as a whole, or how well he can apply his mastery of the subject to unfamiliar problems or fresh material.

Standardized achievement tests enable students and teachers to get some information about these important questions. They are designed to measure what students have learned about a particular subject, and to what extent they have mastered the skills and information needed to go on to more difficult studies. Achievement tests are usually graded so that they measure the student's achievement in relation to what is taught or what the requirements are at a particular grade or class in school. Some cover required achievement in high school subjects; others are designed for use by college freshmen; some are graded at the sophomore level; and still others are for senior or graduate students.

For example, at one college entering freshmen take California Achievement Tests in reading, language, and math. The scores are used to place students in sections of freshman English or math that start them off at different points, depending on how much they show they have learned in the many different high schools they attended. In the sophomore year, they are given the National Guidance Test for sophomores, using the Sequential Tests of Educational Progress in six different subjects. The results are used to evaluate the freshman and sophomore courses in these fields. Content may be changed, added to, or upgraded, to compensate for weaknesses in achievement, or to increase the range of learning, so that students will have the opportunity to keep their levels of achievement in line with, or better than, the performance of students all over the country. In the senior year, the Graduate Record Examination is given as a basis for comparing student achievement over four years with the best standards and requirements in colleges generally. This examination is also used by many graduate schools in considering admission for advanced study. There are many other standardized achievement tests that are widely used. The College Entrance Examination Board, for instance, offers achievement tests in several different subjects; these are required or advised for admission by many colleges and universities.

Achievement tests have many different uses. They are probably most commonly used in administrative decisions: admitting students, placing them in graded sections, waiving requirements, giving advanced credit, or requiring remedial work for subject-matter deficiencies. They are valuable for other purposes requiring evaluation or comparison of students' achievement. They can be used to evaluate the effectiveness of teaching as well as learning, and to guide curriculum planning or the development of local teacher-constructed tests.

For the individual student, achievement test scores give additional information that can be used in self-appraisal and in improving achievement. Some achievement tests can be used to diagnose his problems; they can be reviewed with the help of an expert adviser to spot specific weaknesses and errors that may be overcome. Standardized tests make it possible to compare his achievement with a larger population. For the gifted student, they are especially helpful, because most of them are so designed or graded that perfect scores are infrequently possible. He does not bump his head on the A ceiling, but has plenty of room in which to demonstrate his performance. The scale is great enough to give a more precise measure of his achievement in relation to the maximum score attainable. Students with above average grades are often delighted to find a test that they cannot finish, that pushes them to the limit of their performance. Because their score is on the scale, they often for the first time get a clear idea of their standing, a feeling of making progress, and a sense of progress that still can be made.

No test score alone should ever be taken by a student as evidence that he must give up or quit trying or shift to another field. Such decisions require the most careful and complete self-appraisal, based on a comprehensive set of measures of ability and achievement. And it is probably always wise for the student to get the help of an expert adviser before making any crucial decision involving appraisal of ability and achievement. The interpretation of standardized test scores of all types, and the relation of these measures to grades and other factors, is an extremely complex task. Rough estimates can be made safely on one's own. But amateur standing is not good enough for interpreting measures of individual capacity where precision and accuracy are required. Counseling is almost a necessity in making crucial decisions involving self-appraisal—choosing or changing a major, going to college or withdrawing from college, choosing an occupation, or getting a first job, for example.

Appraising interests, personality, and attitudes

Emotional factors are naturally involved in achievement, and they need to be considered in self-appraisal. Feelings and emotions can block effective performance in academic work. Or they can sustain a high level of achievement. Emotional resources can be appraised to determine their possible effect and to discover ways to control the effect of emotional factors. Likes and dislikes, preferences and aversions, add up to a pattern of feelings that defines interests, attitudes, and values—factors affecting satisfaction and dissatisfaction, achievement and disappointment in one's work. It is important to know one's abilities and the level of one's achievement, but it is also helpful to know something about one's interests, attitudes, personality, and other temperamental factors.

Particularly in occupational choice and career development, these factors play an important part. It is becoming increasingly desirable to make early and stable educational and occupational choices. Changes of occupational choice, for example, are becoming increasingly expensive in time and money for both individuals and institutions. The needs of society in a period of manpower shortage make trial-and-error occupational decisions hazardous to the entire nation as well as to the individual. While freedom of choice is still protected for the individual and shifts are always possible, they are costly and risky.* Consequently one should make the decision that leads to an occupational choice with as clear an estimate as possible of all the factors that may affect satisfaction in one's work. However, occupational choices never satisfy all of a student's interests. So many students who have made a choice, still feel they might be happier in another field, where the grass looks greener (see Fig. 4-4).

THE FIELD THEY MAJORED IN		PERCENT WHO WISH THEY HAD DONE OTHERWISE	THE FIELD THEY MOST FREQUENTLY MENTION AS A BETTER CHOICE
	PRE-MEDICAL	9	A DIFFERENT PROFESSION
	PRE-LAW	14	MEDICINE
	HOME ECONOMICS	14	THE HUMANITIES
	PRE-DENTAL	18	A DIFFERENT PROFESSION
	ENGINEERING	19	A DIFFERENT BRANCH OF ENGINEERING
	FINE ARTS, MUSIC	22	THE SOCIAL SCIENCES
	PHILOSOPHY, RELIGION	24	THE SOCIAL SCIENCES
	SCIENCE, MATHEMATICS	24	A DIFFERENT BRANCH OF SCIENCES
	AVERAGE FOR ALL GRADUATES	25	
	AGRICULTURE, FORESTRY	27	MEDICINE
	EDUCATION	28	BUSINESS ADMINISTRATION
	SOCIAL SCIENCES	30	BUSINESS ADMINISTRATION
	BUSINESS ADMINISTRATION	30	ENGINEERING
	HISTORY, LITERATURE, LANGUAGE, ETC.	33	MEDICINE
	PHARMACY	33	MEDICINE

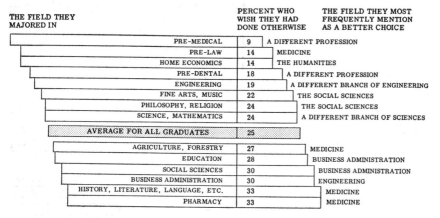

E. Havemann and P. S. West, *They Went to College* (New York: Harcourt, Brace and Company, Inc., 1952). Used by permission.

Fig. 4–4.   The Grass is Greener.

Personality factors such as interests, values, and attitudes, are not yet subject to very precise measurement. All of the cautions that must be issued about interpreting aptitude, intelligence, and achievement tests must be repeated about personality and interest tests and inven-

* H. D. Kitson and L. Culbertson[11] found that 16 percent of a large sample selected from persons listed in *Who's Who in America* had changed their occupation at least twice. This pattern may very well persist today; occupational reorientation is certainly possible. But, as Eli Ginzberg[12] indicates, one feature of occupational choice is its irreversibility.

tories—and the range of deviations that must be allowed for is even greater. As in the case of other standardized tests, instruments designed to assess these factors add something to the precision of one's information about oneself. Personality test instruments put the information into a form permitting reasonably good comparison with other people's records. They make it possible to test common-sense ideas about individual behavior or the characteristics of people in general by getting fairly objective evidence from a large population. Essentially, they tell a person little about himself that he did not know or suspect already. But they may correct some erroneous impressions or confirm correct conclusions. And they sometimes reveal information that is hard for a person to admit to himself in another way; they help him to observe behavior that he might otherwise overlook or discount.

Standardized tests are not necessarily the best way to appraise interests, personality, and attitudes. Although they can be used as an aid, there is no substitute for honest self-examination of one's habits, preferences, and desires and for awareness of the meaning of the patterns into which these habits, preferences, and desires fall.

Understanding interests. Sometimes we are not aware that our preferences and aversions form a pattern that can be studied objectively. We know, for instance, that we like being with people but dislike being in large crowds. We make immediate decisions on this awareness, refusing to go to a world premiere of a movie, for example, because the crush will be more than we can stand. But other implications of this like-dislike pattern may not dawn on us, and we may never even recognize it as a pattern. We are aware of being interested in people and wanting to avoid crowds, but not of a general pattern into which these feelings fit.

Interest inventories are a rather ingenious device for finding the pattern into which interests fall. They were constructed to test the impression that people engaged in the same occupation have a characteristic pattern of interests that are expressed in terms of likes and dislikes. The common-sense image or stereotype of occupational groups as having strong common characteristics was found to be true, so far as common interests are concerned. And the extent to which these interests are characteristic of people in particular occupations can be roughly estimated—and much more precisely than the common-sense impression that teachers have to be interested in people and research physicists prefer working alone, for instance.

Such inventories as the Kuder Preference Record or Strong Vocational Interest Test are constructed by surveying the likes and dislikes of a large number of people in different categories of occupation and then finding the likes and dislikes that are most frequently expressed by the greatest number. Different patterns of interest are found in different occupational groups, and the particular interests are indexed according to the occupational group in which they are most commonly expressed. Students record their likes and dislikes on a form that tabulates these interests at random, with slightly different forms being provided for men and women.[13] (One feature of the Strong Vocational Interest Test is a scale of masculinity-femininity which helps to assess the preferences sometimes attributable to sex that affect other interests or the way they are expressed in work.) A person is given an opportunity to indicate which of 100 occupations, ranging from actor to YMCA or YWCA work, he likes, dislikes, or is indifferent toward. Then he responds accordingly to school subjects, amusements, activities, peculiarities of people. Example:

People who are natural leaders	Like—Indifferent—Dislike
People who assume leadership	Like—Indifferent—Dislike
People easily led	Like—Indifferent—Dislike

He rates his *order of preference for activities.* Example: What are the three most important factors affecting work?

Salary received for work
Steadiness and permanence of work
Opportunity for promotion
Courtesy and respect for superiors
Opportunity to make use of all one's knowledge and experience.

Further questions deal with his own abilities and characteristics (Like —Indifferent—Dislike) as he sees them. Example:

Smooth out tangles and disagreements between people
Discuss my ideals with others.

A series of scores is obtained showing how closely the responses given correspond to those typically given by each specific occupational group. A score of A means that responses closely resemble responses of a lawyer. A score of C means that the score is not very close to the interests of an artist. The student is able to conclude that he seems to share the interests of more men and women in the law than in art.

A student with a low score in a certain interest pattern may not necessarily conclude that he should shift his choice to another occupation. If his score for the ministry, for example, is C—, he may still feel that other factors impel him to continue study for the ministry. He may have perfectly valid reasons for continuing, perhaps reasoning as follows:

(1) He may say: "I don't care. I feel the ministry needs revolutioniz-
ing anyway! I'm the man to do it! But I must calculate the possibility
that I will be up against long-established habits and interests. But I can
be patient and work it out, for I believe it will be worthwhile to me and
to the profession."

(2) He may say: "I really haven't been around ministers at all. I'll
spend a summer working in a rural church, or in the Council of
Churches' Office, and then see if I like the ideas and activities that they
are interested in."

There are, of course, other tests of interests. The important factor in
self-direction is to be absolutely fair. Certainly the tests given in an
academic setting are helpful only to the individual being tested. One
student who bragged that he gave the typical responses he felt an insurance salesman would give and scored A still has to answer the questions: "Do *I* like these activities? Am *I* really the man who sells insurance?"

Apparently, interest inventories, fairly and honestly taken, give more
stable and reliable information than can be got from the expression of
interests (what people say they like) or from interests manifested in
activities (hobbies, collections, and the like). But all three ways of
assessing interests are valuable. And they can be checked against each
other to improve the effectiveness of self-appraisal. Inventoried interests have fairly reliable connections with specific occupations. Consequently, they can be used to check tentative occupational choices to
see if there is a real fit. Seeing the characteristic pattern of interests in
a particular occupation may add to the information needed to make a
realistic choice; the student may discover things he did not know about
certain occupations and decide that he needs more information about
them in order to make a wise choice. The range of possible choice may
be either widened or narrowed when expressed or manifest interests
are compared with results of an inventory; the student may realize that
his interests are closely related to occupations that he had not considered but that might be worth further exploration.

Inventoried interests help the student crystallize his understanding
of himself. They give him a clearer picture than he can get in other
ways. Since inventoried interest patterns seem to be rather stable, they
give him a firmer impression of his preferences. They may suggest
specific relationships between his interests and specific occupations,
for they seem to have reliable relationships to entry into specific occupations. But they seem to have little relation to success or satisfaction
in most fields. Finally, many interests can be expressed outside of one's

work. And having a clear, stable pattern of interests in mind may make it possible to find recreation, community service, family activities, and group relationships, which are related to personal interests outside his occupations. Satisfaction of interests in these ways is just as necessary as satisfaction on the job. It is more likely to be secured if a person is aware of his whole pattern of interests, so that he can include in his life plan some way to increase the variety of interests that he expresses and enjoys throughout life.

Understanding attitudes and personality. Attitudes differ from interests principally in depth and persistence. Perhaps they are best understood as habits of attention, thought, and action. The term includes such things as tastes, prejudices, biases, and temperament. Attitudes may be reflected in patterns of *adjustment,* the way people habitually handle situations or fit into groups. Personality traits, identification with important social roles, tendencies to anxiety, aggression, conformity, independence, and tolerance are also elements of the attitude structure.

We are aware of attitudes, just as we are conscious of likes and dislikes. As in the case of interests, we are not likely to form an impression of the patterns into which our attitudes fit, except in a rather vague and imprecise fashion. For example, one may think of himself as an aggressive person who competes actively for desirable goals; and yet, in reality he competes only against people who are recognizably inferior to him. He may be aggressive, but only when competing for a sure thing; the bigger risks for greater rewards may be passed by. Self-deception is easy in appraising attitudes.

The aid of more objective measures would be most welcome in appraising attitude patterns. There are useful standardized tests. But the usual cautions must be issued; and tests in this area are less reliable than interest tests, just as the latter are subject to greater error than intelligence tests. Apparently, the deeper the instruments go into the inner self, the less reliable the results. Intelligence and scholastic achievement, and to some extent, interests, are aspects of the public self, which we customarily and rather easily display. Attitudes are characteristics of the deeper, inner self, which we are not so ready to disclose, even to ourselves. Thus, the measurement of these elements of the self is extremely delicate, and the results must be interpreted with the greatest of caution—preferably with expert assistance from a qualified counselor.

Many types of attitude tests and personality inventories are available. Some are administered individually in writing or in an interview, or by a combination of the two methods. Others are designed for use in groups. For instance, some colleges use group tests, such as the Bell Adjustment Inventory, California Personality Test, or Weston Personal Adjustment Inventory, as measures to determine the general level of adjustment among students or to provide a picture of the attitudes and common emotional problems in the student body. The results may also be used in counseling interviews, provided the student being counseled needs a general picture of his attitudes and level of adjustment. Individual results are rarely reported to all students routinely; they are useful if the student asks for them to help solve a personal problem, but they may just stir up problems that students do not need to have if they are reported generally to students who have no reason to use them.

For example, the Guilford-Zimmerman Temperament Survey sets up test items related to traits such as sociability, friendliness, thoughtfulness. Presumably, everybody should have these traits; but the results give some measure of the comparative degree of strength of these attitudes, and the pattern into which they form. A high score on sociability indicates that one has many friends and acquaintances, is not shy, seeks social contacts, likes social activities, likes the limelight. Sample test items in this category are:

You would dislike very much to work alone in some isolated place.
Shyness keeps you from being as popular as you should be.

On tests of temperament, attitudes, or adjustment, a cluster of items always relates to each attitude, not just one or two items. The sampling of each attitude is a rather generous one, taken from several different points. If the whole attitude were regarded as a barrel of apples, the items related to it would represent a dozen or so apples taken from different layers of fruit, to be compared for size, flavor, and color, giving a general idea of the quality of the whole barrel of apples.

Another type of personality test attempts to identify a number of distinct categories of abnormal behavior: hysteria, depression, hypochondria, paranoid tendencies. The items were tried out on a group of normal people and also on a group of people who were clinically determined to have personality disturbances that incapacitated them in some way. Comparison of response to selected items, which are related to various feelings of emotional distress and anxiety, show different patterns distinguishing normal from disturbed subjects. Results are scaled from a strong tendency toward abnormal reactions, at one end of the range, to normal levels of stress and anxiety at the other.

One example, from the Minnesota Multiphasic Personality Inventory, relates to the tendency to be chronically depressed, to feel useless and unable to face the future.

Sample Item

I am easily awakened by noise. Everything is turning out just like the prophets in the Bible say it would.

This test, and most others of its type, should only be used in a clinical situation where the results are used for counseling and guidance. It helps the counselor focus the interview on problem areas that might otherwise take hours of exploration to discover. Amateur interpretation, or attempts to interpret one's own results, can be misguiding at best, and at worst can do grave damage to a person.

RESOURCES OF COUNSELING AND GUIDANCE

The road through self-appraisal to self-understanding and self-direction need not be traveled alone. Over the years counseling and guidance facilities have developed in most colleges across the country. Students who need help or an understanding companion on the road may seek a counselor. Because self-appraisal is essential to self-development in the college years, college faculties and administrations have had to recognize the need for help in this task, and to provide the facilities that seemed most useful to students. As indicated in Table 4-2, these facilities have a variety of forms and offer different kinds of help.

TABLE 4-2
Mental Health Facilities of 728 Colleges

Program	Number	Percent of Total
No organized Program. Facilities include faculty advisers, deans, and psychology department.	322	45
Some organized Program, outside the health service, including such facilities as a dean who has had some experience in guidance, a guidance clinic, or a school psychologist.	220	30
Well organized Program, outside the health service, including those schools having an organized counseling service available.	56	7
Specific referral system, to clinics outside the school or to a medical school.	31	4
Special facilities, within the health service or closely related to it.	99	14

From Sigmund Gundle and Alan Kraft, "Mental Health Programs in American Colleges and Universities," *Bulletin of the Menninger Clinic,* Vol. XX (March, 1956), p. 62, by permission.

Often students confuse counseling with advising, although the two are not mutually exclusive. Often they confuse counseling with testing, although testing is only one of many professional skills the counselor offers. Counseling services are specialized programs aimed at helping students adjust or resolve problems that are more or less emotional in nature. Even if the problem is academic, the aims of counseling would be to get at the underlying factors, such as interest, motivation, and attitude, that make it difficult for the student to solve his problem. College advising is usually done by major professors or Deans; it is usually confined to academic matters, although many advisers can help in the area of personality problems.

Generally speaking, however, the kinds of problems and areas of interest discussed in Part I of this book are counseling areas. The resources differ from campus to campus, but at most colleges some of the college personnel listed below should be available to give help.

Dean of Students and Staff
Dean of Men or Dean of Women and Staff
Residence Hall Counselors
Vocational Guidance or Placement Service Staff
Counseling Center Personnel
Counselors
Psychologists
Physicians
Psychiatrists

Colleges organize their services differently. In any case, however, students must seek help on their own initiative and arrange appointments for themselves.

Tests are not the equivalent of counseling. So the student should not assume that, if he knows his test scores, the counselor has nothing more to tell him. Tests serve in diagnosis of problems, but they do not solve them. Tests tell where the student stands, but not where he is going. So in using test results to make choices and solve problems, counseling helps to make testing meaningful. It is up to the student to seek the expert help of counselors in deciding what the test scores tell him about himself and his decisions in life.

WHO SHOULD BE COUNSELED

It is usually thought that failing students and students who are having serious personality problems should seek counseling. Evidence shows that students who are confused with I.Q., percentiles, and other misinterpreted test scores also profit from counseling.[14] Though there never are enough counselors at any college to help everybody, good students profit from counseling too, and they can make effective use of it. At one college a group of alumni who had been out of college ten years were asked to respond to the question, "How might the university have prepared you better for the demands of the last ten years?" It is striking that the graduates *whose averages ranked highest* stated overwhelmingly that they felt a need for counseling in four areas: self-assessment, vocational information, human relations, and personal philosophy.[15] Scholastic and emotional problems are only two reasons for counseling. Good students can become better with the help of counseling. Certainly counseled students when matched with an equal number of noncounseled freshmen tend more frequently to persist in college and graduate.[16]

Thus, it does not seem either possible or wise to draw the line and say that one kind of student ought to have counseling while another kind should not. Most students probably could make effective use of counseling at some time during their college years. The student who can make effective use of counseling is the one who thinks he needs it and wants trained help in solving his problems or in assuming responsibility for self-appraisal and self-direction.

part two

The student's role

5

Standing the stress and strain

*The development of
scholarly disciplines*

THE ROLE OF THE STUDENT

Of all the differences between high school and college, perhaps none
has greater significance for the student than the change in his own role.
Under the education code of most states, up to the age of fourteen or
sixteen the boy or girl has little or no choice except to go to school. The
expectations of family, prospective employers, and community tend to
lead most adolescents to finish high school.*

From high school on, further education is voluntary. The decision to
go to college is certainly affected by attitudes of families and social
groups. But the final decision is made by the student.

---

* In the biennium 1952–1954, high school graduates exceeded dropouts for the first
time. Out of every 1,000 students enrolled in the fifth grade (taken as the base figure
representing maximum stable enrolment) in 1946–1947, 553 graduated from high
school in 1953–1954; 283 entered college.[1]

Furthermore, he is chosen to be a student. The faculty admits him to college on the basis of his past performance and requires him to maintain high standards of scholarship in order to remain a member of the college in good standing.

Being a college student is, therefore, a vocation, in the strict sense that one is called to take up a special kind of work. As a member of a college, the student takes on a full-time job. He must make a capital investment in the college by paying tuition and fees. He has a course of study representing a contract, with standards of production that he agrees to meet.*

The student whose function in school has been to be taught becomes in college the scholar whose function is to learn. There is a real difference between the two roles: *to be taught* is not the passive form of *to learn*. There is a transfer of responsibility for learning from teacher to student at the college level. Many tasks formerly assumed by teachers become the student's responsibility: defining his interests, relating them to the interests of others, planning a program of studies, directing his own work, evaluating his skills and performance.

And the student assumes a full-time job. His course of study commits him to a normal work week of 45 hours: 15 hours a week in class, 30 hours a week in self-directed study, based on the general rule of thumb of two hours out of class for every hour of class scheduled.

THE STRESS OF LEARNING

Academic work is subject to certain occupational hazards, and particularly to some sources of unusual physical and emotional stress, of which the student ought to be aware.

First, its basic workweek is somewhat longer than the standard in other occupations. According to some authorities,[2] mental activity can be sustained consistently for somewhat longer periods than physical activity, so there may be some physiological justification for this variation.

Second, the irregularity of the work schedule produces discomfort and irritation conducive to stress. Of course, the registrar sets up the college class schedule according to a carefully timed, rational plan; but

---

* From the cover of the registration book of Mills College: "By signing her name in this book the student acknowledges that she has read the regulations of the college as printed in the catalogue and agrees that she will endeavor to give intelligent and honest adherence to the letter and to the spirit of these rules." Students generally sign such a contract upon registration, and are well-advised to read and understand it before signing.

from the point of view of the student interested in the content of courses, the schedule works out according to the laws of chance. There is a story (probably apocryphal) of a Harvard student who beat the system by substituting one of his own, based on the principle of selecting only courses meeting after 10 A.M. below the third floor. His faculty advisor is reputed to have regarded the content of his program as rather exotic.

There is a devil, junior grade, in the registrar's office specifically charged with contriving that classes separated by the shortest interval of time shall meet at places most widely separated in space. Women students are his particular victims, since they can be faced with the delightful experience of emerging, with dripping hair, from Intermediate Swimming at 10:50, and arriving on foot, well-groomed and poised, at 11:00 in French Literature III, half a mile away.

Third, some types of mental activity are more fatiguing than others. Some subjects are more difficult and, therefore, more fatiguing for particular students. Some methods of learning, such as experimentation or field work, involve both physical and mental activity of a higher than normal level and induce more fatigue and stress.

Fourth, a particularly subtle hazard in scholarly work is cumulative fatigue. The signs of fatigue in mental activity being of relatively low intensity, the student easily becomes accustomed to ignoring them and can continue longer without pause in study than in physical activity.[3] People in intellectual work are extremely vulnerable to fatigue because of their habits of maintaining their bodies in a rigid posture of attention for long periods of time. But the demands on neuromuscular activity are light, the motivation is high, and the usual response to discomfort is to increase muscular tension and continue work. The student may push his body beyond the limits of its normal resistance to fatigue before he notices its signs. By the time conscious fatigue has been reached, its stress tends to produce a kind of intoxication, an excitement that makes the student want to go on working; hence fatigue feeds itself and carries him toward the point of exhaustion.[4]

Cumulative fatigue is particularly hazardous for students who have relatively low resistance to illness and become highly vulnerable to disease when tired. A college is subject to epidemics, like any other closely-knit community, and these have a way of coming at times when academic pressure is heavy. Certain diseases of the young adult, such as mononucleosis, have prolonged effects of lowered resistance to stress and of heavy tissue damage. Fatigue, added to these ordinary health hazards, creates a very dangerous condition of stress for the college student.

Fifth, learning itself is a process of repeated mental and emotional response to stress, through repeated demands to produce order out of disorder. The student barely gets his mind made up on a subject when he meets a new idea that upsets the whole system. Learning presents a series of problems that resolve themselves in part into new problems; it is a procedure of repeated mental discomfort and emotional stress, repeatedly but never finally resolved. Integrating ideas and techniques is deeply satisfying, but its permanent incompleteness is a source of repeated stress.

Finally, pressure on the student to improve his performance constitutes continual stress. Pressure from parents and faculty is accentuated as the student tries to develop his own standards, which may justifiably differ from theirs. He has to set his own standards of performance and evaluate his own work, for many of the things he deals with are quite new, unfamiliar, and outside the range of conventional standards. The stress of self-evaluation imposes serious demands upon the emotional strength and maturity of the undergraduate. In addition, he has to exert a good deal of energy and ingenuity in overcoming the dead weight set against effective scholarship by the patterns of conformity and mediocrity characterizing much of student life.

In gaining the very great satisfactions that come from learning, the student must, therefore, endure considerable stress. Successfully controlling stress increases pleasure in scholarship. The disciplines of the profession are determined in part by their usefulness in controlling stress and increasing comfort and success in academic work.

Stress as a means of adaptation

In recent years a new physiological concept of stress has emerged in research in medicine and biochemistry. The study of stress has led to a more comprehensive theory of disease; but perhaps more important is the light cast on patterns of healthful living. The concept of stress is particularly valuable in lending scientific support to the traditional wisdom of scholars in organizing their lives.

In common-sense terms, stress is defined as the general wear and tear of life, the physical cost of any activity to the organism. All human activity involves stress. The exercise of any bodily function, including the mind, requires the mobilization of energy and the organization of neuromuscular activity into appropriate patterns. Stress* may vary in intensity from the usual tired feeling to actual damage to tissues.[5]

Bodily reactions to any activity are defined as adaptation to stress. Stress may be caused by many agents: injury, disease, work, temperature changes, irritants, weather, fatigue, and many other factors. The stress reaction appears, for example, when a thorn scratches the skin. A little welt starts to form around it, setting up a wall of connective tissue and white blood cells; the skin itches and becomes inflamed. A chemical produced in the area is carried through the blood stream to the pituitary gland in the center of the brain, and it releases hormones which act directly or through the stimulation of adrenal hormones to limit inflammation to the immediate area of the scratch. In a few minutes, the pain, itching, and discomfort disappear, and one goes on undisturbed with the process of healing begun. "Stress reaction" refers to all of these bodily processes, taken as a whole.

Adaptation to stress develops in three phases:[6] First, there is an alarm reaction, characterized by the chemical signal and hormone production. Second, there is a stage of resistance in which the physical symptoms disappear; it is characterized by bodily reactions designed to limit the area of stress and reduce discomfort, as in the disappearance of itching and pain after a scratch. Third, after prolonged resistance to continuing stress, there is a stage of exhaustion, in which the organs resisting stress wear out, resistance is completely lost, and the organism breaks down. Most stress is limited to the first two stages; only severe, prolonged stress, such as serious illness or extensive physical injury, usually eventuates in exhaustion, and even then health can possibly be restored by proper treatment and rest.

Most stress of life is of low intensity and short duration. Every evening we feel the low-level alarm reaction of being tired; we resist by sleeping; and we wake next morning refreshed. The alarm reaction and the stage of resistance recur repeatedly in response to conditions of normal living. We get into a situation, get used to it, settle down, and continue comfortably in it.

---

* The clinical definition of stress is as follows: "Stress is the state manifested by a specific syndrome which consists of all the nonspecifically induced changes within a biologic system." The General Adaptation Syndrome (G.A.S.) is the term used for the complex of systems associated with stress, which form a syndrome, "a set of manifestations which appear together." These include "adrenal stimulation, shrinkage of lymphatic organs, gastrointestinal ulcers, loss of body-weight, alterations in the chemical composition of the body." The general result of these changes, so far as they are consciously felt, is that people feel tired, tense, under pressure, or sick. The acute stress reaction, manifested in the General Adaptation Syndrome, does not develop except in instances where stress is very severe or its early signals are disregarded.

In adapting to stress, the entire body is not maintained in a state of alarm, but resistance is limited as far as possible so that most of life goes on undisturbed.[7] Stress does not necessarily entail extensive physical wear and tear. One organ or system takes on the task of resistance, leaving the rest of the body to function normally.

Stress also has its emotional aspect. The "keying up" of the body in alarm reaction is associated with strong feelings, whose meaning ranges from anxiety or fear, anger or hatred, to pleasure, excitement, or enthusiasm, depending upon the circumstances. Both pleasurable and painful emotions are occasioned by stress; and strong drives of both pleasure and pain produce stress.[8] The "tuning down" of the body in the stage of resistance involves a reduction in emotional tone as well as physical reactions.

Conditions conducive to stress, consequently, are conducive to higher than normal emotional reaction. Stress is significantly involved in motivation, especially in "keying up" for high levels of performance. Examinations, for example, are in part tests of performance under stress; they challenge the scholar's capacity for adapting to unusual demands, meeting high standards of excellence, rising to an occasion.

However, physical and emotional "keying up" for peak performance is very costly, drawing heavily on the adaptive reserves of the body for additional energy.[9] In more than short bursts, stress exhausts one's resources to a damaging extent. And prolonged stress induces typical exhilaration and excitement, akin to intoxication. This drunkenness invariably is followed by a prolonged period depression in level of activity, a typical "stress hangover."

Adaptation to stress can be managed in three ways: "advance, retreat, and standing one's ground."[10] Advance or attack on the situation may remove some agents of stress and reduce the amount, duration, or intensity of stress to be endured. Retreat or withdrawal entails a deliberate shift into rest, recreation, or an activity involving different behavior. Standing one's ground and accepting stress may be advisable when there is no way out of the situation except through stress, or when the cost in wear and tear is outweighed by the values gained by enduring stress and "keying up" for high levels of performance.

Disciplines designed to reduce stress: the method of advance

The disciplines of scholarship are predominantly based on an *advance* or attack on stress to reduce its sources and intensity. The principal method used is the establishment of order out of disorder, regularity out of irregularity in patterns of life and work. The ordinary daily round can be kept below the level of severe stress by establishing regular routines. By foreseeing and preparing for unusual demands for peak performance, quality can be improved with little increase in stress; "keying up" a little bit in a regular schedule achieves as much improvement as "keying up" a lot in a disorderly schedule. Breaking large scale tasks up into small parts readily absorbed into a regular pattern of work keeps the pressure down to a tolerable level, leaving reserves available for unusual occasions.[11] Rewarding work by a change of pace, recreation, rest, food, or care of the person, both reinforces learning and restores energy. Scholars for centuries have formed habits of regularity, planning, piecemeal activity, and reward. The tradition of scholarly discipline is confirmed by some scientific principles of controlling stress.

Getting regularity into an irregular schedule. Freshmen working out their first college study schedules make two surprising discoveries. First, the random sequence of classes, without regard for space, time, or subject matter, is a shocking change from the similarity in the daily round of high-school classes. The unit of schedule planning is lengthened in college from the day to the week. Second, adding up the time demanded of them by all the activities in which they engage, many of them find they have committed themselves to putting anywhere from 180 to 200 hours into each week!

So freshmen, unless they are prepared to die of exhaustion, learn that they cannot do everything and that they have to work out their own personal schedules, based on their own habits. Each must choose for himself what he will do and when he will do it. Going to college may entail a few changes in habits, but it is the student's task to choose the adjustments to make. He may seek the advice of others but cannot delegate the task to them.

The basis of regularity in group and personal living. Like any community, the college falls into a fairly regular schedule for meeting the two essential demands of life for *food and sleep.* Everybody keeps to much the same schedule. Mealtime and bedtime recur pretty consistently. The family may have to change some meal hours, or accept a later bedtime, in the interest of the commuter student. The student in residence may find that the living unit settles on a bedtime that is too late or too early for him, and some ingenious adaptation may have to be made. A student purported to have been at Dartmouth slept from one to five each afternoon and from midnight to four each night. He got in on the after-dinner bridge games and bull sessions and woke before dawn to a perfectly quiet house, suitable for concentrated study. He stands as an heroic example of the fact that *it can be done*. The student can protect his individual needs in the pattern of group or family living.

Each student has to keep up his established habits of care of the person, and can schedule them at times when they may help reduce stress. A shower between an hour of French and an hour of History, cleaning the room between outlining and writing the freshman English paper, a shampoo and manicure between two hours of review for the biology exam, serve to break up large tasks of learning into smaller blocks. The change of activity and the self-esteem represented by attention to one's person add to the sense of well-being that reduces stress. But to achieve these effects, habits of personal care must be explicitly scheduled at regular times in the week, at points where they will serve the specific purpose of reward or variety.

Social and recreational activities, dependent on the common interests of many people, tend toward variability in scheduling. But some effort is made to coordinate the calendar: fraternities and other living units usually have a fixed meeting night; student activities, rehearsals, and performances are regularly scheduled. A regular date night has certain advantages, both in nailing down a desirable steady date and in avoiding less desirable ones. The college physical education requirement will provide more or less regular exercise. Such scheduled activities lend consistency to the pattern of college life.

Some students think that regularity is conducive to boredom. But it is regularity that makes the spontaneous bull sessions and the very special date stand out as memorable occasions. Only against a background of habit do special events take on their flavor of pleasure and surprise.

Organizing irregularly scheduled events. The random distribution of classes throughout the day and week gives the student an irregular schedule with which to start. Disorderliness is compounded by the irregularity with which term paper deadlines, midterm exams, finals, lab reports, and field trips are scheduled. Each professor follows a system of his own, and a familiar complaint of college students is that professors pay no attention to the requirements of other courses, and everything is due on the same day. The students are perfectly correct; but the professor is not expected to take account of anything but the requirements of his own course: it is the responsibility of the student to fit the work into some sort of schedule. A *study schedule* is indispensable to effective work; it gives the student control over the stress produced by irregularity.

Alarm reactions can be used to define appropriate periods of study. Upon settling down to work, the student can observe his pattern of response to stress. For the first two or three minutes, he will adjust his posture, wriggling and squirming until he gets comfortable. After he gets settled, he can hold his position and concentrate steadily for twenty or thirty minutes, until an alarm reaction of muscular discomfort, the symptom of fatigue, interrupts him. He wriggles about, trying to get comfortable. If he does so quickly, he can often continue for another twenty to thirty minutes without undue fatigue.

The period of concentration between the first and second "wriggle-squirm" periods is the attention span. This is the optimum period of learning, with negligible losses due to fatigue. The first alarm reaction is not strong enough to interfere very much with learning, and a slight shift in posture can start another attention span without interruption. The fifty-minute class has some physiological justification; it fits the effective attention span of most students and pushes none to the point of fatigue.

Beyond an hour, however, losses in learning increase rapidly. Research in memorization and rote learning indicates that short, spaced periods of study are more effective than long, sustained periods, and that once the period of optimum attention is passed, losses in learning are as great as the gains. In one experiment (see Fig. 5-1), three days

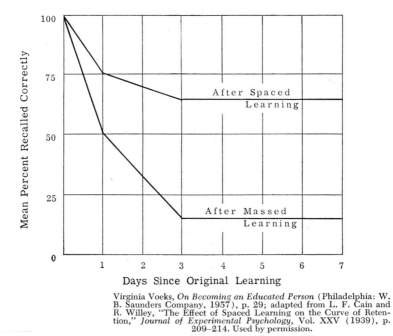

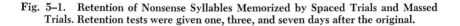

Virginia Voeks, *On Becoming an Educated Person* (Philadelphia: W. B. Saunders Company, 1957), p. 29; adapted from L. F. Cain and R. Willey, "The Effect of Spaced Learning on the Curve of Retention," *Journal of Experimental Psychology*, Vol. XXV (1939), p. 209–214. Used by permission.

Fig. 5–1. Retention of Nonsense Syllables Memorized by Spaced Trials and Massed Trials. Retention tests were given one, three, and seven days after the original.

after spaced study in short periods, over 60 percent of memorized material was recalled; but only 20 percent was retained after sustained study in long periods.[12] The attention span seems to define the period of maximum learning as well as the period of minimum fatigue.

The optimum attention span seems to vary somewhat with the subject matter.[13] Ten to fifteen-minute periods seem most suitable for material requiring motor skill or memorization. A brief period before lunch, an odd fifteen minutes waiting for an appointment, are suited for memorization.

Longer periods of an hour or more are required for material involving complex reasoning and integration of ideas. The same subject may require both types of learning. A language, for example, is mastered both through rote memory of some forms and inflections and through reading to learn the meaning of words in context.

Taking into account the type of subject matter and his own attention span, the student can base his regular weekly schedule on periods suited for different types of work. At the end of each study period, whatever its length, a definite change of activity will reinforce learning and reduce fatigue. The alarm signals of fatigue can be read as signs to shift subjects or techniques, or to interrupt study with a different activity altogether. By careful observation of his own behavior and selection of optimum periods of attention for different subjects, the student can work out a schedule in which periodic discomfort is anticipated, work is interrupted *shortly before* the alarm reaction appears, and fatigue is reduced to a minimum with no cumulative effects to speak of.

Long and short periods can be alternated to reduce stress. Once the class schedule is laid out and time is allowed for sleep, food, personal care, and recreation, the first step in setting up a schedule is setting aside a block of three or four consecutive hours daily for study. Residence halls frequently set "quiet hours" for study in the afternoon or evening. The commuter student will have to plan his study time with the cooperation of the family at the beginning of the college year. Perhaps the dinner hour will have to be later if a chemistry lab runs until five o'clock. His bedtime may have to be later. Chores may have to be redistributed to protect study time: the student may have to start study right after supper, rather than washing dishes; and weekend duties such as shopping, gardening, cleaning, and laundry may fit into the study pattern better than daily chores.

In selecting material to be studied in long periods, the student should choose subjects requiring complex analysis, problem-solving, generalization and organization of ideas, and reading or writing of substantial length. Then the block of time should be divided among tasks taking approximately one attention span. For example, in history, the student may read and summarize a chapter on the medieval universities in the first hour. After a five-minute break for a cup of coffee, he may spend half an hour reviewing his lecture notes on the medieval church. A quick stretch (or cleaning the room) to loosen up, and he may return for another half-hour outlining his term paper on the development of universities in the middle ages. Ten minutes for a phone call to confirm the Friday night date, and he is back for a final half to three-quarters of an hour of reading on the medieval guild system. The subject is the same, but the focus of interest varies sufficiently to sustain attention and reduce fatigue. Each step is complete in itself, but it carries him forward toward a finished block of work in the course.

The second step in planning is assigning smaller blocks of work to short periods. Hours between classes, intervals between long study periods, and unexpected intervals of time require more careful advance planning and selection of appropriate subject matter. Some periods can be regularly scheduled, others have to be used as they appear on the spur of the moment.

Study requiring rote memory is most suitable for very brief periods, but any small task will do. For example, the commuter student, who has to make full use of every minute on campus, has an hour free between French and Chemistry. The five-minute walk to the library is good exercise after an hour in class. The ten-minute wait for the art history book might be an irritant, producing tension that will keep him from concentrating when the library finally disgorges the volume. But reviewing the list of irregular verbs that are giving him such trouble in French, both prevents tension and improves the French. Forty minutes will see him through the article on Breughel that he has to read for art history, and the five-minute walk to chemistry class sets him up for another lecture. The period of reading is the kind of short study period that is easy to plan. It is the use of the ten-minute delay at the Loan Desk that may make or break him. For effective use of such unexpected intervals, the student may carry around with him a collection of appropriate short tasks: review of memorized material; lists of books to be checked in the card catalog; an outline for a paper; proofreading of a report.

Securing appropriate variety in patterns of work for a change of pace reinforces learning and reduces stress. Variety in the study schedule improves learning and reduces stress by lending meaning to irregularity in activity.[14] Changing from one activity to another also shifts the load of adaptation from one part of the organism to another. Fatigue, thus, does not come on all over, all at once.

Variety being practically inescapable, the problem is to make effective use of it to improve learning and reduce stress.

First, variation most effectively reinforces learning when sequences of subjects are arranged so that clearly similar or clearly contrasting content and methods follow each other. The student must be sure that there are clear differences on critical points of method, structure, or content. For example, studying two foreign languages, or a foreign language and English composition and grammar in sequence confuses cognate meanings from one language with precise meanings in the context of the other. Inappropriate use of grammar rules transferred from one language to another may produce confusion. Clear differentiation in either content or method is necessary: the history of Renaissance art coupled with Renaissance social and political history gives a good historical structure which the differing content of the art course fits like a glove. An hour of history followed by an hour of biology give clear contrast.

The gains in learning from similarity in consecutive subjects seem to be secured principally through the integration of ideas and principles in associated fields of study. These gains, however, involve some risk in increased stress through boredom and confusion. Contrasting sequences of subjects offer gains which are almost as great, and seem more effective in reducing the general level of stress through greater variety in the total pattern of activity. The choice between the two patterns of study might be reasonably based on the immediate aims of the student: If it is desirable or necessary to improve performance by integrating ideas, even at the expense of added stress, similarity in sequences might be used. If it is necessary to reduce stress to a minimum in order to maintain a steady level of performance, maximum contrast in sequences might be preferable. A good rule of thumb might be to use contrast while beginning new courses, similarity later on when they become more familiar.

One way of making gains through similarity, with minimum stress, is to follow classes with private study in the same course wherever possible. For example, a free hour between the freshmen English lecture and chemistry class yields maximum value at minimum cost in the study of English. Fatigue seems to be increased by using it to study chemistry, apparently in part through the additional stress induced by working to the deadline represented by the approaching class hour.

Contrasting sequences of subjects are relatively easy to set up. Suitable subjects for short, intensive study usually afford maximum contrast with subjects suitable for long integrative periods of work. A long period of review in science, followed by a short period of reading in French, provide contrast in both content and technique.

Some students secure contrast by starting with their favorite subjects, then going on to less favored ones. The approach is probably a good rule of thumb for securing contrast, but some advantage in reducing stress might be gained by reversing the sequence. There is some reward to be gained by starting on a distasteful task knowing that when it is finished something you like will be next in line.

The selection of varying techniques in one subject is a useful way to carve up large tasks of learning into smaller steps. For example, reviewing for exams can be broken up into periods of outlining the major topics in the course, testing how much one knows about each topic, reviewing unfamiliar topics in more detail, and quickly summarizing the material by reading a short book on the subject.* Preparation of a paper can proceed in similar short steps: Preparing a list of possible topics can be done in an unscheduled interval. Checking the available material on the chosen topic is a good occupation for waiting periods in the library. The student may jot down ideas for the outline as they occur to him, or produce a rough outline in a short period taken as contrast to sustained study. Reading or research must be allocated to some long periods of work. Preparation of a final detailed outline requires a long sustained period of work. Writing sections of the paper may begin as soon as preparatory research or reading is completed, in fairly long periods. When all sections have been written, a long period must be allocated to final organization and revision of the paper. Typing is suited to a series of brief periods for contrast with stretches of less active work.

Reward reduces stress and reinforces learning. The Law of Effect, stated by Thorndike and revised by others[15] states that behavior is learned—that is, it is more likely to be repeated—when it is followed by some reward. We train a dog to do tricks by making sure of two things: first, that the dog is hungry, and second, that there is a supply of puppy biscuits to reward him when he performs what we teach him. Human learning is a little more complicated than that. For one thing, there is not the clear distinction between punishment and reward in mature persons that animals or very young humans sometimes show.

---

* A short, "popular" account of the subject is sometimes available for summary reading at the end of review periods. Topical outlines of subjects, such as the *College Outline Series,* are very useful in the final stages of review, provided adequate study has been done during the term. The regrettable practice of using them as substitutes for regular course reading is not recommended.

Since most of us desire attention, and punishment generally means that some attention is being paid to us, there seems to be little difference between punishment and reward in the effect on learning. Man seems to be a learning animal, and about the only way to prevent him from learning something undesirable seems to be to ignore him altogether.

From the point of view of the theory of stress, however, clearly desirable rewards offer somewhat greater advantages than punishment in strengthening learning. Reward involves less wear and tear—on both student and teacher—than punishment.[16]

Rewards that strengthen learning are relatively simple in form and easy to secure by careful planning of a well-organized schedule. Food is an effective reward, and intensive periods of study before mealtime receive a substantial reward. Sleep is a substantial reward; scheduling a short period of memorization or review just before bedtime insures a good reward; and some authorities suggest that additional strengthening of learning is secured through subconscious rehearsal of the material during sleep.* Short rest periods after intensive study are a form of reward—provided the student doesn't drop off to sleep and tangle up the whole schedule. Smoking, drinking coffee and cokes, and eating between meals can be converted from vices into rewards if they are appropriately scheduled and properly controlled. Any pleasurable activity can be used as a reward for study if it is reserved for the end of a period of work. Cigarettes do not reward the chain smoker who reads with one in his hand and another in the ash tray, nor coffee the student who writes with a cup on the desk; these function as distractions rather than rewards. But a study break for a coke, cup of coffee, or cigarette is a reward; and even washing out a pair of socks can reward with a change of pace.

Change in activity is a reward in itself. Study sequences shifting from one subject or technique to another at the end of an attention span have the effect of reward; the effect may be enhanced when more difficult or disliked material is followed by easier or more enjoyable work. Five- or ten-minute periods of exercise between study periods reward through improvement in physical tone and reduction of tension.

The great intrinsic reward in learning lies in completing a significant task and feeling it has been done well. Change of pace becomes a greater reward when it comes after a unit of work has been completed. Both small units of work and substantial blocks give satisfaction upon their completion. Reward is just as certain for a chapter read as a paper

---

* A study by J. G. Jenkins and K. M. Dallenbach seems to indicate that people can recall more on the morning after than they could the night before.[17]

written, for a completed course as a published book or an earned degree. In breaking long-range study into smaller units, reward is increased if the small tasks are planned so that they are complete in themselves and compassable in a reasonable time. The weekly work schedule will then insure repeated daily satisfaction in study, strengthening learning through reward.

Reward is greatest when least tinged with anxiety, shame, or fear. Hence, intrinsic satisfaction in accomplishment is probably the most effective reward of scholarly work. It represents the kind of pleasure children get from the exercise of bodily skills as they mature, running, climbing, jumping, talking incessantly for sheer pleasure after they first learn how.[18] There is similar reward in the pleasure of using newly mastered intellectual skills and new techniques of scholarship.

The recognition and approval of others is a most pleasurable reward. Awards for scholarly merit, honor society membership, and other forms of recognition have great value in expressing to the scholar the benevolent attention and support of his colleagues. Competitive awards have somewhat less value because of the persistent uneasiness aroused by the feeling that someone just as good may have been left out, as well as by the anxiety involved in competition. One disadvantage of regarding grades as reward is the stress occasioned by the period of anxious waiting for reports, accentuated by disappointment over grades lower than expected—and sometimes by anxiety over maintaining grades higher than expected. No form of recognition or attention that increases stress through anxiety can be considered an altogether satisfactory form of reward. Those rewards are greatest which reduce stress and increase pleasure: pleasure in the use of newly mastered skills, food, affection, approval and encouragement of others, recreation, rest, exercise.

Patterns of living that strengthen learning by reducing stress can be planned by the student on the basis of his personal habits and interests. The regular patterns that establish themselves in eating, sleeping, personal care, and community living give a core of orderliness and regularity to academic disciplines. The stress of an irregular class schedule can be reduced by breaking work up into meaningful units, scheduling it in appropriate periods based on the individual attention span and suitable to different subjects, securing variety and change of pace in the schedule, and establishing a regular rhythm of work and reward. A schedule that attacks and removes factors causing stress and that establishes a comfortable and satisfying rhythm of life will sustain a consistent level of performance throughout the undergraduate years. Such a schedule will also form habits that will continue throughout a lifetime of productive scholarly work.

Disciplines designed to avoid stress: the method of retreat

If one cannot overcome stress or use it to his advantage, he had better run away. The *retreat* from stress lies in two directions: toward rest and toward recreation.

Rest restores the body after fatigue. It is the principal factor in recovering from exhaustion. Recreation is a way of moving from a stress situation toward pleasure. Rest and recreation are alternative ways of avoiding stress; one is not a substitute for the other. Eighteen holes of golf is an excellent relief from stress on a fine sunny afternoon in May after a week's work in the library. After four hours of strenuous field work in geology, rest rather than recreation may be a better choice; stretching out with a good book, listening to records, or taking a nap is more appropriate than a round of golf.[19]

Recovery from stress. Regular maintenance is the cheapest form of repair. Food and sleep, recurring daily with regularity, represent the inexpensive maintenance of the body. They repair the daily wear and tear of stress.

Sleep. The eleven-to-seven routine for sleep, hopefully mentioned in college handbooks, is for many students simply a pious hope. Two factors in student life seem to work against regular habits of adequate sleep. In the first place, the student is afraid he will miss something if he goes to sleep. The bull session just gets started by eleven; the bridge game works itself into a deadlock, both sides vulnerable, around midnight; the term paper all of a sudden crystallizes, after hours of struggle, just at bedtime. In the second place, the student regards staying up late as evidence of freedom from parental authority, and forming regular habits of sleep appears to be a surrender of the newly-won freedom of adulthood. He would rather drop in his tracks than admit he needs seven or eight hours of sleep regularly, like any other adult.

In fact, these two deterrents to sleep are signs of stress and signals that sleep is urgently needed. In the first instance, excitement after a long day of classes and study is not a sign of stimulation but a symptom of the hazardous cumulative fatigue producing auto-intoxication. The bull session, when it hits a high pitch of excitement, is on the verge, not of inspiration but of intoxication; it will produce nothing from that point forward but a "stress hangover," and the student will not miss a thing by going to bed. The bridge players stand game-and-game in the fifth rubber, each side repeatedly going down, not from scintillating defensive play, but strictly from hunger. The excitement of night life in the residential college offers a spurious promise of productivity that vanishes with morning, and the really sophisticated student will see through it and stop before it grips him. Its intoxication is the most insidious form of stress, pushing the mind and body toward the threshold of exhaustion and obstructing scholarly disciplines.

The use of drugs such as Benzedrine and other amphetamine derivatives is a habit that is becoming altogether too common among college students. Using such aids to key up for study interferes with the basic task of establishing effective disciplines. They may be appropriately used under careful direction of a physician to control specific deficiencies. But precise control and timing is necessary since stimulation wears off after a short time, usually in about an hour, and is succeeded by depression. There are side effects, also, which interfere with judgment and resemble in this respect the intoxication of stress.*

Two horror stories of the effects of Benzedrine intoxication, well-authenticated, may be instructive. One student, who worked long hours late at night, using Benzedrine, to cram for a preliminary examination for the doctorate, wrote a brilliant paper; the only trouble was, he never wrote below the first line of the blue book and turned in a heavy black bar. Another stayed up all night to cram for a crucial final examination, taking Benzedrine, and turned in six blue books, which she said "creamed the exam"; but they were simply filled with wavy, squiggly lines. The feeling of the students that they were highly stimulated and keyed up for the exam, even their feeling that they turned in a peak performance, probably gave an accurate picture of their physical condition; but their papers were a little difficult for the instructor to read and evaluate.

Self-assertion against parental control by staying up late is just as deceptive in its effects. The resident student is not with his parents, and staying up late will not show them a thing. Forming the habit of staying up late amounts to indulgence in auto-intoxication; the habit and its attendant hangover will interfere with progress in college and send the student right back to the bosom of the family.

The commuter student has to deal with two forms of parental pressure, neither of which is successfully managed by stubbornly staying up

* E. M. F. Weaver and Kenneth G. Bergin, who have written on the American and British Air Forces' experience in the use of Benzedrine to control stress, both found that such stimulants could be safely used only under direction of the flight surgeon, following careful observation of the pilot's reaction to the drugs, and then only by experienced and dependable pilots.[20]

late. Parents may continue to regard him as a high-school student and set a fixed bedtime, nagging him to go to bed just when he needs peace to finish his work. In such a case, his best strategy is to set his own regular bedtime, late enough to get his study done, early enough to get enough sleep, and ask his parents to help him hold to it by leaving him uninterrupted time for study. On the other hand, some parents themselves regard staying up late as a mark of maturity, and show the student that they accept him as an adult by insisting that he take part in all the usual family social activities of the evening: visiting with neighbors and relatives who drop in; attending the church social; going to the high school play in which Sis appears; staying up with the folks to watch the late, late show on TV. Here again, advance planning may help the parents understand how to support the student's scholarly disciplines and how to give the student freedom to plan his own activities, including when to join in family parties.

Learning to recognize the excitement of auto-intoxication and distinguish it from the true stimulation of pleasure and the enjoyment of using skills will help the student avoid stress by withdrawing from activity before cumulative fatigue becomes too great. And he can test his maturity, not by exercising his freedom to induce stress, but by accepting his adult needs for rest and recovery from the wear and tear of the day.

Food. There is no need to make a case for regular meals in an academic community. A mild admonition against skipping meals may be in order, not so much as a nutritional guide, but as a warning of its interference with regularity in the schedule. There seems to be a correlation between sleeping and eating habits, and regularity in one is conducive to regularity in the other. Both food and sleep being recuperative, the tendency is to make up deficiencies in one by excesses in the other as a means of recovering energy. This sort of deficit financing puts the adaptive budget out of balance, producing as much stress as is relieved.

Adapting to college food is a problem for some students; it is difficult to change the habits set at home. Natural differences in individual preference are accentuated by the regional food preferences represented in a student body coming from different parts of the country and all sorts of national and economic backgrounds. The dietitians and cooks are faced with an insoluble problem: they cannot, under any circumstances, satisfy everybody, but everybody wants to be satisfied. A steady diet of meat and potatoes will please the men and the midwesterners; a variety of salads and green vegetables, from artichokes to zucchini, will please the women and the Californians; a mixture of the two will produce mixed feelings in everybody. Griping about the food is the great collegiate indoor sport, and there is nothing much the kitchen crew can do about it.

However, there are some things the student can do about it. First, he can allow for the fact that college cooking cannot be like Mother's; prepared in quantity with minimum seasoning, representing more variety than the family diet, it cannot meet her standards or conform to his established habits. Second, before casting aspersions upon the asparagus, the student should examine his between-meals intake of food and tobacco, remembering that snacks dull the appetite and cigarettes dull the taste. Food is most rewarding when there is a keen edge on taste and appetite; and criticism, if warranted, is sounder if it is based on a fresh, sharp taste rather than a flat and jaded palate. Third, there is much to be said for: minding one's manners; remembering that finicky eaters are particularly hard on themselves, as well as nuisances in society; braving the unknown seas of broccoli, kohlrabi, and squash in hope of developing a gourmet's taste; and registering justifiable complaints, special personal needs and problems privately with the dietitian.

The commuter student does not have to change his food habits very much, but he has special problems. Family meal hours may be subject to slight adjustments, which can be planned in advance. But his major difficulty is lunch. He has a limited set of alternatives: given the money, to buck the cafeteria line; given more money and less taste, to eat at Joe's; to bring lunch from home; or to skip it altogether. Aside from starving, settling for one alternative and sticking to it is preferable to mixing the alternatives. The sack lunch trade have been known to sit down with college faculty and staff to work out a comfortable way for them to meet and eat. The sociability of mealtime contributes to their reward, and it is not sensible or necessary for any group of students to feel left out of the college community.

Atmosphere, as well as consistency of pattern and quality of food, contributes a great deal to the effect of meals in overcoming stress. And atmosphere is only one part oaken beams and candlelight to four parts good manners, good taste, cleanliness, and good order. Whether in residence or commuting, the student should exercise his responsibility for securing all the advantages he can in making food habits an effective part of his scholarly disciplines.

Withdrawal from stress. There are two aspects of withdrawal from stress, both of which should appear in the pattern of scholarly disciplines. First, brief periods of withdrawal for rest or reward should appear frequently—at the end of two or three spans of attention, if practicable. Second, longer periods of an hour or more should appear after long intervals, at least once a day, if practicable; and free weekends and holidays should be fitted into the schedule during the month and throughout the year, as needed.

The effective use of phased withdrawal is determined by one's comfort and efficiency upon returning to work. Efficiency has to be judged by the actual output of work, not by feelings of tension or excitement. If the student feels keyed up after a period of withdrawal, he may not be making effective use of free time in reducing stress. The person who comes back from vacation exhausted has induced stress, not withdrawn from it. Withdrawal is effective if study is resumed at a steady, comfortable level of production without tension.

Study breaks. An adequate study schedule includes five- or ten-minute intervals after each hour or so of work, with a selection of appropriate activity for removing fatigue and reducing stress. Food and rest are good restoratives and rewards during study breaks. Stretching out on the bed for ten minutes is a good idea. Coffee or snacks are good rewards.

Exercise both reduces tension and helps the student keep awake. Rhythmic exercise is conducive to relaxation; it relieves tension by loosening up some of the muscles held rigid in the posture of attention. During a long lab, just sitting on the edge of a table and swinging one's legs and arms help loosen things up a bit.[21] Cleaning the room or taking a turn around the patio for a cigarette loosens up some muscles. Exercise is probably preferable to food or sleep during a study break. Most students need more than they get anyway; and it has the advantage of reducing stress effectively in a very short time.

Recreation. In longer periods of withdrawal, good hard exercise is about the best choice for the sedentary student; a nap, recreational reading, or snack is preferable after more strenuous study such as laboratory work, practice teaching, or field work.

The important thing about recreation, whether active or sedentary, is that it be fun. Sociability adds to the fun, and social events should be scheduled so as to break up long weekly or monthly cycles of academic work. If they involve exercise, they are doubly rewarding; intramural athletics, dances, picnics, hiking, and mountaineering provide both exercise and emotional satisfactions that are exceptionally rewarding. Student government, interest and discussion groups, art, drama, and musical groups, debate teams, professional societies, volunteer service and religious organizations provide for expression of ideas, interests, and feelings in a rewarding way. Use of one's developing physical and intellectual powers in cooperation with others is a satisfying source of intrinsic reward.

There will be special social occasions of exceptional pleasure; their value is heightened when they appear as climaxes or surprises against an orderly well-planned background. A well-established rhythm of scholarly disciplines will include withdrawal from stress into rest and recreation that will keep the student's mind and his body comfortable for a sustained level of performance, consistent from day to day and year to year.

Disciplines designed for effective use of stress: the method of standing one's ground

Stress cannot always be reduced or avoided. There are also times when it is desirable, when the student needs to be "keyed up" for peak performance, to accept stress and go through alarm reaction and resistance, in the interest of values that can be attained only under stress. Scholarly disciplines are not designed to avoid stress altogether or to make life easy. They are intended to control stress and put it in the places where it will contribute to the advancement of learning.

In adapting to stress and using it for valuable purposes, two conditions must be met. First, stress must not be prolonged to the period of exhaustion, but must be accepted at the precise point at which extra effort will count most. The timing must be right, so that stress will be of relatively short duration just at the climax of the task. Second, there must be a plan allowing considerable time after the period of stress to recover from the "hangover," the depression and reduction in energy that always follow stress. (The old family doctor's rule, "A day in bed for every day of fever," is the best rule of thumb for recovery from stress.)

"Keying up" for exceptional stress should, therefore, be planned at fairly long intervals, and on those occasions when it will be of greatest value. Examinations, for example, are in part designed to test performance under stress. The performance of plays and music, athletic competition, student body elections, special projects, all require students to "key up" both physically and emotionally for top performance.

But the timing must be right. Placing maximum stress on preparation or anticipation rather than performance is anticlimactic. Anxiety, worry, or excitement before an anticipated period of high-level activity puts the alarm reaction so far ahead of the event that the student reaches the late stages of resistance with reduced energy reserves, just at the time that peak performance is required. The student should "key up" for just one thing at a time, and that thing the performance of the task or the enjoyment of the event itself.

Cramming for exams is poor timing. The student gears himself up the night before the exam, pours his energy into study and raises his level of resistance considerably. Next morning, when he should be keyed up to go all out on the exam, the "hangover" has set in, and physical and emotional depression reduce his level of performance. * He may be able to muster his remaining reserves and "key up" all over again, but then he must resist both the stress of fatigue and the stress of the exam, and he is asking for an even worse "hangover."[23]

Judicious planning for review periods in every course every week, with a brief, intensive general review shortly before the examination, reduces stress in periods of preparation. Stress then falls appropriately into place at the beginning of the examination itself. The length of time under stress being reduced to the time required for the examination rather than the whole period of review, the "hangover" period is short, and energy is rapidly restored in preparation for the next exam. After a series of exams, a long weekend or semester break very quickly overcomes the cumulative effects of repeated stress reactions.

The student who says, "I perform best under pressure," is perfectly correct. But nine times out of ten he misapplies his insight by putting the pressure in the wrong place. Many students deliberately induce stress to try to make up for deficiencies in scholarly discipline. By writing the term paper the night before the deadline, rushing the experiment through two days before it is due, postponing intensive practice to the week before the concert, they feel that they are really putting out the work. But this impression of high-level performance is spurious. Performance is judged on the quality of the final product, not the energy consumed in its production. Useful stress goes into production, not preparation, performance, not worry.

Studies of the effect of anxiety upon learning indicate that performance is strengthened by heightened emotional drive. But if complex material is being studied, an increase in drive tends to reinforce errors

---

* Some of the symptoms of chronic fatigue in flight crews are similar to those experienced by students who cram for examinations. For example, "gauche, coarse, imprecise work" is produced. Visual fatigue results in malfunction of eye movements, especially reduction of powers of convergence and fixation, so that written material appears blurred and it is hard to focus on the page. "Positional awareness" or acute sensitivity to posture and bodily movements, irritability, lack of judgment, and slow reaction time are all familiar symptoms in students who cram. Ask any roommate.[22]

as well as correct responses, with adverse effects on learning. Reduction of drive in the early stages of learning and increase in stress after the correct responses have become fairly familiar seem to be necessary to keep from learning errors. Students showing high levels of anxiety perform better than those showing low anxiety on simple tasks of learning; but in mastering complex tasks, the "high-anxious" students are inferior in performance and make more errors. Fig. 5-2 shows the error curves for both types of students in learning a complex skill.[24]

Effective use of stress depends upon following a consistent pattern of scholarly discipline, leading up to a final all-out performance. The

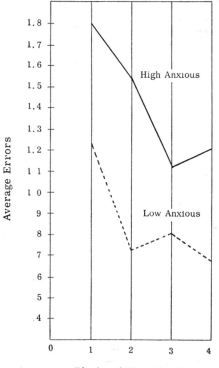

Blocks of Four Trials

David S. Palermo, Alfred Castaneda, and Boyd R. McCandless, "The Relationship of Anxiety in Children to Performance in a Complex Learning Task," *Child Development*, Vol. XXVII (1956), p. 335. Used by permission.

Fig. 5–2. **Error Curves for Anxious and Nonanxious Subjects.** The effect of increasing motivation (higher anxiety) upon performance depends upon the relative strength of the correct and incorrect responses aroused by the experimental situation; that is, the tendency of correct responses to predominate over competing tendencies to respond to the situation. The more complex the task of learning, the more errors are presented as competing tendencies to respond; the effect of increasing motivation is, consequently, offset by the tendency to select incorrect responses.

distinctive feeling of being "keyed up," ready to accept stress as a stimulant to exceptional achievement, then falls into the right place, into the climax, into the performance where quality and distinction have value.

LONG-RANGE PLANNING IN SCHOLARLY DISCIPLINES

The cycles of the college year

The basic workweek has to be set up in such a way that it fits into longer cycles of work, play, and rest in the academic year. The rhythms of the year fall into long cycles of stress and recovery which the student can use to his advantage.

First, it is extremely important to get into stride at the very beginning of classes. As soon as registration is completed, the student should work out a tentative weekly schedule. Some students like to do this with the help of the faculty adviser if time is available during registration. This tentative schedule can be adjusted as things shake down during the first couple of weeks of school; courses can be dropped, added, or re-scheduled, and periods of study, recreation, and rest shuffled around into a comfortable sequence. But once he gets behind, it is almost impossible for the student to catch up; the academic year has an inexorable rhythm that leaves him farther behind the more he struggles.

Second, after a weekly pattern is established, long-range planning can proceed. Preparation for exams, writing papers and reports, experiments and field trips, rehearsals and performances, and special projects and activities can be anticipated with periods of preparation and peak performance scheduled for them. Vacations, weekends, social events, and high occasions can be anticipated as periods of peak reward.

It is a good idea to *leave a block of unallocated time* in each week to accommodate spur-of-the-moment or unexpected events, the surprises that lend flavor to academic life. Saving two or three hours for catching up on study over the weekend makes it possible to relax and enjoy a special Wednesday night date, knowing that the review for the biology exam can be shifted to Saturday morning when there is time free for it.

It is a good idea to *anticipate deadlines*, rather than to wait for them. If the freshman English paper due Friday is finished on Wednesday, the student can be free to enjoy the big game on Saturday. But if he sits up all night Thursday writing the paper and types furiously all day Friday, he will have to struggle to keep awake during the game and be inexplicably morose at the dance afterward. Fun's fun, but only when one is free from worry or fatigue.

On most campuses, the calendar of events is planned as far as possible to set *a rhythm of work and play.* The fall formal may appear to have been scheduled in the midst of mid-terms and term paper deadlines in order to disorganize and harass students; it is much more likely to have been set at that time as a major restorative in a period of stress. Selecting the things one wants to do, putting them into the semester schedule well in advance, and working up to them as periods of reward have to be done on the student's initiative.

Fourth, *vacations should be firmly protected from invasion by other interests* because they represent prolonged periods of recuperation from cumulative fatigue. The faculty member who assigns a term paper over the Christmas vacation is just as reprehensible as the student who pays overweight charges to the airline for the dubious privilege of loading his luggage with textbooks needed to catch up on neglected work over the holidays. There is an irreducible amount of cumulative fatigue in the cycles of the college year, rising to certain high points of stress: in the round of social affairs before Christmas and commencement; in the hectic rush week schedule; in the excitement of spring weekend; in the recurrent stress of winter and spring final examinations.* After each of these periods, time is wisely reserved for recuperation in the Christmas and Easter holidays, the semester break, and summer vacation. For the cumulative fatigue of college life is genuine; to the amazement of their families and friends, students find themselves sleeping through a substantial part of the first few days of vacation, recuperating from residual fatigue of which they may not even have been aware.

The long cycles of the college year differ from the weekly schedule only in the length of time involved. The basic rhythm is the same, with cycles of stress and relaxation succeeding each other in regular rise and fall from week to week or month to month rather than from hour to hour. Using the cycles of the year to set up a long-range program, the student can get the proper timing into long periods of work, play, and rest so that he gets the least possible interference with learning and the greatest possible advantage from stress.

The cycles of integration and exploration

Beside the succession of the seasons, exams, social events, athletics, and vacations, there are other basic rhythms in college life which have

* Flanders Dunbar points out that seasonal variations in cultural climate, such as the social round of the Christmas season, are weighted with emotional reactions of pain and disturbance as well as pleasure, occasioned by changes in social behavior that produce stress.[25]

phases of a semester, an academic year, or longer. There is a basic
rhythm in the integration of ideas developing in phases from a semester
to a year in length, characterized by cycles of stress. It is partly responsible for the familiar phenomena of the sophomore and senior
"slumps," and for some of the stress associated with examinations,
papers, and choice of major.[26]

*First, the degree program itself determines certain cycles of integra-
tion in the undergraduate years.* Progress toward the degree requires
exploration of several broad fields of scholarly work combined with
intensive study in one specialty, around which interests and skills in
all fields are to be integrated. There are two common patterns in American colleges for integrating general education with the major field. In
the liberal arts colleges, the most common pattern provides maximum
breadth and variety in subject matter during the freshman and sophomore years, delaying the choice of major to the beginning of the junior
year, with heavy concentration in the major and minimum variety during the last two years. In the professional and technical colleges, the
most common practice requires declaration of major at the beginning
of the freshman year; the program combines specialized studies with
a couple of electives each year; both general and specialized studies
move along together in just about a constant proportion throughout
four years' work. The two patterns of integration may be diagrammed
(see Fig. 5-3).

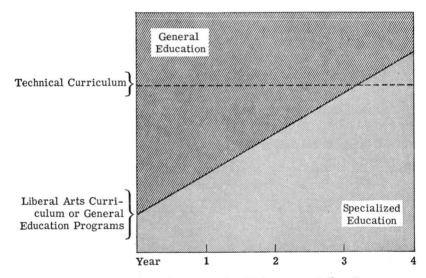

Fig. 5–3. **Proportions of General and Specialized Education in College Programs.**

Stress in both types of program tends to center around the "point of no return," after which a major cannot ordinarily be changed without extending the length of time required to complete the degree. By the end of the sophomore year, the choice of major becomes practically irrevocable. Uncertainty about this choice, plus a certain amount of fatigue, largely account for the "sophomore slump."

In any degree program, the sequences of courses are arranged so that a student first explores, then organizes the subject matter and techniques involved. In principle, the student who successfully organized his skills and ideas in each course and began to pull together some of the ideas about relations between fields of study would begin to find his interests focusing around a suitable major in plenty of time to confirm his choice. In practice, firm decisions are relatively rare, and when they are finally made, always involve some element of frustration in giving up some interests in order to concentrate in a specialized field.

The "sophomore slump" is, therefore, a pretty normal symptom, and it need not baffle or frustrate the student who recognizes it as a sign of the stress involved in making a significant decision. Taking some time to evaluate his progress and confirm his choice, perhaps with the help of a counselor, is an effective way to deal with the "slump," and to come through the period of decision with comfort and confidence.

The "senior slump" is a repeat of the sophomore symptoms, with the imminent choice of a job and development of a career replacing the choice of major as a crucial decision, and with the level of residual fatigue and frustration raised even higher. The only relief is as much careful planning and counseling as can be managed in charting the course of a prospective career. In the process, the integration of an entire degree program into a pattern of meaning becomes most important. The pattern of the degree program should suggest possible occupational interests outside of college, confirm intellectual activities that will lend meaning to one's work and play, and raise some unsettled questions that will keep scholarly interests active after college.

Second, as a student progresses through college, he assumes increasing responsibility for self-directed study. Guided initially by the degree requirements, he becomes increasingly skilled in working out other patterns of integration around his own interests and abilities, and an increasing amount of his study is planned around his own interests and undertaken on his own initiative.

In formal course work, the range of alternatives in method and content for term papers, research projects, experiments, and observation enlarges with each year in college. More options are given; a more flexible set of requirements is set; a greater range of material and more experience are at the student's disposal. The proportion of independent study increases as he advances in his major field, enabling him to focus more intensively on his own interests. A diagram of this trend (see Fig. 5-4) is very similar to that showing the trend toward specialization.

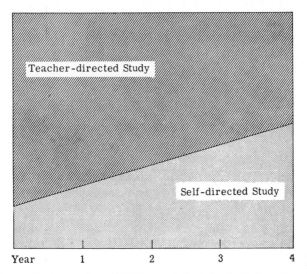

Fig. 5–4.   Increasing Proportion of Self-directed Study in the College Program.

In addition to affording more scope for student initiative in regular courses, many colleges make formal provision for self-directed study outside of formal course offerings. Frequently this technique is used to encourage interdisciplinary studies, independent research, and creative work. Two or three patterns of self-directed study are fairly common. First, tutorial or honors courses are offered, in which a student works out a plan for study of a particular subject in consultation with a faculty member, makes regular appointments with him to discuss reading or research, and produces a final report or demonstration.[27] Such programs are usually reserved for the students showing high levels of intellectual aptitude or academic achievement.

Second, the term independent study in the strict sense is often used to describe the procedures available for setting up a program equivalent to a standard course and carrying it out on one's own. In this form, independent study differs from the honors or tutorial program by being available to any student who can demonstrate the necessary experience and competence and secure permission from the appropriate faculty; it is not necessarily reserved for the gifted student, but is used to accelerate the progress or enlarge the experience of any qualified student.

The University of Buffalo, for example, is typical of many colleges which allow students to study independently following the syllabus of a standard course, and to receive standard course credit by passing an examination. One feature of its program is the opportunity offered to gifted high school students to add such independent study to some of their regular academic courses, and to enter college with some credit already established.[28]

Mills College offers two types of self-directed study to students who secure proper faculty permission and are well qualified.[29] The "independent problem" is an additional block of work for extra credit added to a course that the student is taking, or has recently completed. The results are presented in a special paper or demonstration, or a special examination is added to the final in the course. "Independent study" permits the student to set up the equivalent of a semester or year course, representing a standard course not currently offered, or material not covered in regular courses. The student works out a plan for self-directed study in consultation with the instructor, including scheduled conferences and material to be submitted for examination, criticism, and evaluation.

Whether the curriculum makes special provision for such methods of independent study, the student will find he must rely increasingly on his own initiative and interests as he progresses in his college work. Stress is increased by the sense of being on his own; the security of daily class attendance and regular recitation and examination is decreased; and evaluation of his progress becomes his responsibility—in a word, the pressure is on him. If the student has adequate scholarly disciplines, he should be able to accept it and use it as a step toward the day when he will be an independent scholar, when all of his work will be independent study.

Stress attends such periods of integration and exploration, for ideas are pretty tough and recalcitrant material, and a good deal of effort is required to fit them into meaningful systems. They also have a way of generating problems which irritate the scholar and practically demand to be put into some sort of order. The senior year has a high concentration of all the elements of physical and emotional stress: fear of the future; habits of study that have reached the point of boredom; a backlog of cumulative fatigue; grief and indignation at being forced to leave a warm and familiar community; and a major effort to bring some kind of order out of four years' work. The student has only the disciplines of scholarship to bring him through and "key him up" for the new adventure of finding gainful employment and beginning a career. He must prepare for graduation from the beginning of his freshman year, by beginning on the day he first attends a college class to establish the disciplines that control stress, generate ideas, and organize learning into well-integrated patterns.

The cycles of evaluation

As the student progresses through college, he assumes an increasing proportion of responsibility for evaluating his own work. The curve of increasing self-evaluation follows the trend in specialization and integration (see Fig. 5-5).

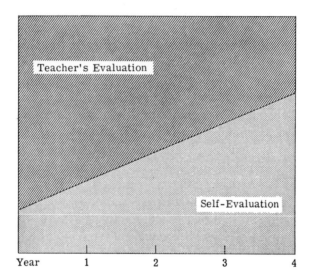

Fig. 5–5. Increase in Self-evaluation with Progress in College. The limits of self-evaluation are narrower than the scope of self-direction; the scholar is always dependent on outside criticism.

Criticism, however positive it may be, is a strain on self-esteem. One of the developmental tasks of scholarship is learning to control and direct the emotions aroused by criticism, and the stress of self-evaluation is the price of successful maturation.

The cycles of self-evaluation in college are of considerable length. The student has become accustomed in school to having his progress reported at frequent intervals, every six weeks or so. In college, grades are reported at the end of each semester or quarter, covering a longer span of activity. More frequent evaluation has to be secured directly from the instructor in a conference initiated by the student. The measuring of day-to-day progress during most of the year falls upon the student.

Here again the establishment of a regular pattern of work gives the check points needed for the student to determine his progress. If his work is done on time and meets the standards he has set for himself, he can be relatively sure that he is making adequate progress. In addition, however, he has to assume other tasks of evaluation.

First, *the college student assumes a great deal of the responsibility for recognition and correction of errors in his work,* in advance of the teacher's criticism. A well-organized method of review improves skill in recognizing and correcting errors.[30] For example, in reviewing, questions that cannot be answered in reading may be improperly framed and need to be recast. Or an answer that sharply contrasts with one's previous opinion must be tested against supporting data, and a better conclusion formed; or the results, being inconclusive, may suggest a more careful study.

The second task of self-evaluation is review and organization. Having committed himself to conclusions, opinions, and facts, the student owes it to himself to review and edit his work. In taking examinations, a good habit is to save ten minutes at the end of the period to check answers. Directions for many of the standardized short-answer tests advise the student to be very careful about changing answers to multiple-choice, true-false, completion and matching questions. These types of tests are designed to measure speed and accuracy of immediate response, and an increased number of responses will increase the likelihood of a good score more than the meticulous correction of errors. Furthermore, there is a little time for careful reasoning, and the risk of changing a correct answer to an error is rather substantial. It is usually suggested that the student pass over items about which he is uncertain, and return to them after he has come to the end of the exam, if there is time. In particular, essay answers need to be checked for adequate proof; *the reason why* is the key to good standards. In reviewing multiple-choice or completion questions, the basic pattern of such tests gives a clue to proper fit; right answers must supply the right reason. In the multiple-choice form, there is a pattern of alternatives which can serve as a guide for reasoning out the proper response: they are right for the right reason; right for the wrong reason; wrong for the right reason; clearly wrong; and, sometimes, just plain irrelevant. A perfectly legitimate method of answering unfamiliar questions of this type is to check the question and the data supplied against this pattern, establishing the clearly right answers by a process of elimination. Such tests are designed in part to teach just such a process of reasoning. Whatever the type of test, allowing time to check teaches the student to evaluate his work, helps him learn to recognize errors, and compensates for carelessness and confusion caused by the stress of working against time.

The third task in self-evaluation is criticism of form and style. It is poor manners to allow sloppy spelling, punctuation, and construction, typographical and mathematical errors, and errors of reasoning to slip through in a finished paper or examination. In some colleges, faculties have adopted the policy of grading in part on correct English usage and style in all courses, and the student may improve his grade as well as his general scholarly reputation by careful proofreading. Some students, particularly faster readers, tend to be blind to such errors. Reading the final copy with another person following the original draft helps focus attention on form and style.

In this process, *the fourth task in self-evaluation, criticism of content,* can also be carried out. The student assisting in proofreading may also be asked to make suggestions and criticisms about form and content. Such suggestions may or may not be used to improve the work before submission, but they are valuable in sharpening ideas and pointing to new interests in continuing study. The important thing is for the scholar to evaluate his own work, to see whether it meets the requirements of the assignment, provides adequate supporting data, has a logically organized pattern that helps the reader follow and understand the train of thought, and comes to some clear conclusion—preferably one that bears some relation to the purpose announced in the introduction. The only way to test work against these criteria is to put oneself in the place of the reader, and perhaps to discuss it with another reader.

Some students also try to estimate a grade in advance of the teacher's report; it is hard to see any objection to the practice, provided it is an educated guess made on the basis of some clear standards, with as much objectivity and as little pride as possible. Such an estimate is not acceptable as grounds for arguing with the instructor about the grade. The teacher expresses his evaluation, not in the grade, but in his critical comments in the body of the paper. The grade is not a goal but a guide in evaluation. A lower grade than anticipated is a sign to the student to confer with the teacher on ways to improve the quality of his performance; perhaps an unexpectedly high grade might even lead him to confer with the instructor to figure out how he did it so the performance can be repeated. Evaluation of one's work should be made in some detail and kept in mind to be checked against the teacher's criticism so that improvement in skill in self-evaluation may be made.

THE RESOURCES OF COUNSELING IN ESTABLISHING SCHOLARLY DISCIPLINES

The student is not expected to transform himself into a scholar unaided. The college makes other resources available to him in the task of establishing scholarly disciplines. From the instructor in the course, who will help him identify his special interests for term papers, research, or observation, correct his errors, and improve his performance; to the faculty adviser, who will help him set up a well-organized program giving him the education he wants; and the counselor, who will help him improve his scholarly disciplines for greater enjoyment and better performance in college—there is no lack of members of the college who will take an appropriate interest in the student's task of self-development.

Many colleges offer special services to students who wish to upgrade their basic intellectual skills. Members of the faculty or specially trained counselors are available for consultation and training in reading faster and more accurately, writing more clearly and concisely, concentrating better, organizing work schedules more effectively. English departments very often try to identify students who need to improve in reading and writing, and they assign these students to special classes giving intensive training in the basic scholarly skills. (They may call it "bonehead" English, but it is only the boneheads who cannot profit from it.) Deficiencies in other fields, such as mathematics, can also be identified early in the college career, and students can secure extra training to improve performance.

Failure to perform reasonably close to one's level of aptitude and failure to establish comfortable habits of scholarly work present somewhat more complicated problems for the student. Skilled counselors are available in most colleges to help the student determine exactly what is interfering with his performance and to decide how to deal with the difficulty.

Stress is an important source of interference with academic performance. First, the discrepancy between ability and performance often arises out of some uncontrolled stress in the student's scholarly disciplines. Second, the process of analyzing one's interests, purposes, and performance produces emotional stress. Third, both physical and emotional stress is induced by developing new patterns of behavior and control. It is hard for the student to work out such problems by himself, for he is reluctant to face the additional acute stress he must endure in identifying and controlling the agents that caused the stress in the first place.

The counselor does not take responsibility for solving problems, but he helps the student reduce stress in three ways: First, he can help him keep his attention focused on the major problem, without wasting time on irrelevant matters. Such concentration confines stress to the important task of adaptation and keeps it from becoming generalized. The counselor thus helps the student conserve his energy and keep his successful disciplines functioning while he works out a special problem.

Second, the counselor can suggest ways to establish successful scholarly disciplines with the greatest economy in time and energy. Third, the counselor can help the student determine how to evaluate his own behavior and performance more accurately, thus preparing him for self-direction in his academic work.

It is not necessary to have an agonizing personal problem to make it worthwhile to consult a counselor. A great deal of counseling is relatively routine, but it deals with matters on which the assistance of someone familiar with the patterns of college life is indispensable. A faculty adviser or counselor can help the student make sure that his program will, in fact, meet degree requirements and that his academic performance is moving him along toward the degree; it is a good plan for the student to check annually, or in each semester or quarter, on his progress. Checking over a tentative study schedule with a counselor or faculty adviser may produce some refinements that will improve performance; the student could discover them by experience, but spotting them in the planning stage will help him avoid some possible stress and gain needed time. Reviewing one's academic interests and prospective choice of major with a counselor may reduce the possibility of disappointment in the final choice. None of these things represent major problems; they are simply routine tasks of planning. Consultation in the process of planning helps to insure that routine tasks will not become problems.

Initiating counseling is the responsibility of the student. He can get maximum assistance from advisers and counselors by thinking out in advance the kind of help he thinks will be most useful, and by selecting the person who seems most competent to help him explore the questions he has in mind. He is free to select the person with whom he feels most comfortable in counseling, but he should be prepared to accept referral to someone else who may be better qualified on a special task.

And, finally, the student should bear in mind the highly individualized character of scholarly disciplines and the highly specialized assistance he secures in developing them. In discussing his work with other students, he should remember that his interests are different from theirs; and if he simply dishes out to them the advice he had from an adviser, he may actually interfere with their own disciplines and interests. He must bear in mind that all students have the same responsibility for developing their own scholarly disciplines; and while he can encourage them to seek the help that he has found, he cannot assume the responsibility for seeing that they get it.

Students can do a great deal, however, in helping each other establish effective scholarly disciplines. Encouragement of high levels of achievement is tremendously important, but the great need is not so much to extend the systems of awards and prizes from Phi Beta Kappa and Mortar Board, as to put the experience and insight of older students into service for the younger ones. Simply maintaining quiet hours for study in living units puts the support of a group behind good scholarly disciplines. Experienced students can set patterns of regularity in scholarly disciplines and can encourage freshmen to seek counseling in planning their own disciplines early in their college career.

Above all, students are confronted with a problem in academic attitudes with which they alone can deal. On many campuses, it is common understanding that excellence in scholarship, an active interest in study, or friendly relationships with faculty members mark a student as something of an oddity. In effect, those students who seriously accept scholarship as a vocation and recognize faculty members as colleagues rather than opponents must do so almost in defiance of student standards and attitudes.[31] Students who take the initiative in working with faculty members or seeking their advice, who are frankly conscientious in performing academic tasks, who admit that they enjoy college work, are regarded as misfits, deviating from normal patterns of student behavior.[32]

Such attitudes are an unjustifiable source of stress for students and an active deterrent to productive scholarship. Furthermore, they are not accessible to control by the faculty. If student mores are to support the establishment of sound scholarly disciplines, students will have to take the responsibility for reorganizing patterns of college life.

In spite of the stress of life in the community of scholars, the satisfactions of academic work are very great. There is enjoyment, excitement, and pleasure in membership in the goodly company of scholars.

It is the privilege and responsibility of those students and faculty members who have found their place in it to deepen its roots and enlarge its fellowship. Helping others establish sound scholarly disciplines and increase their pleasure in college life is their obligation, as part of their vocation.

6

Who's teaching whom?

*Resources for learning
in college and
community*

THE MEMBERS OF THE COLLEGE

A college is a group of individuals differing in function, but bound together by a common purpose—man as student, man as teacher, man as administrator, but in every case man thinking, not so much about how to sustain life as how to live it.

> Gerald W. Johnson, "Emerson's Scholar: A New Chapter of His Biography," *The Key Reporter*, Vol. XXIII, No. 4 (July, 1958), p. 2.

The most important resource for scholarship is a college—and the faculty and students who are its members. As permanent members of the college, the faculty have responsibility for maintaining continuity in the college program and the traditions of the community of scholars. As transient members, the students provide the supply of new blood, fresh ideas and questions, changing expectations and purposes that sustain the development of the scholarly enterprise. The classroom, laboratory, library, theatre, office, residence hall, and the broader community in which the college is set provide the context and materials for learning.

The response of scholars to each other is the fundamental requirement for learning. What they are working with, what their conversation is about is provided by the supporting materials in campus and community. But what keeps the process going and reinforces the ideas and techniques that are learned is the interest that members of the college show in each other's work. The teacher and student make learning possible by responding to each other and helping each other keep on with their work.

There is a kind of ritual, a code of academic manners, which defines acceptable ways of showing attention, appreciation, and regard for members of the college. Faculty and students keep regular academic appointments with each other in classes, laboratories, offices, studios, and meetings. They keep a schedule which insures regularity in scholarly disciplines and guarantees some privacy for individual work. They provide special rewards for exceptional performance in prizes, awards, ceremonials, or simple private expressions of appreciation.

Members of the college help each other to refine learning and improve its quality. They correct each other's work and criticise it. They exchange ideas out of different perspectives and backgrounds. They extend the range of interest by cultivating a variety of fields of study and cherishing individual differences in background and interest. The interest of the faculty in students is particularly important in providing an atmosphere in which students can master scholarly disciplines, define their purposes, extend their interests, and refine their abilities and techniques, without fear of reprisal, repression, or ridicule.

Such attention, regard, and acceptance of differences constitute what is called academic freedom. Within the framework of resources and standards that the college provides, the scholar can expect to feel free to pursue his own interests, ask for the assistance of others in his work, and give service to others. The student expects such assistance from faculty; he is also expected to give it to members of the faculty and to other students in return. To the best of their ability, all scholars must discharge a common obligation toward one another for showing attention, respect, criticism, and appreciation. As their scholarly resources improve with experience, the responsibility of students for supporting the work of others correspondingly enlarges.

THE ROLE OF THE TEACHER IN COLLEGE

Just as the role of the student changes between high school and college, so the role of the teacher differs significantly. As the student becomes progressively an associate in a common scholarly enterprise, the teacher becomes less a director of learning and more a colleague. The teacher's relation to the student is increasingly determined by the student; his services are available on the occasions and for the purposes that the student requests.

The relation between faculty and students is one of the most significant influences on the intellectual development and aspirations of students. In a recent study,[1] National Merit Scholarship candidates served as student observers. The faculties of schools producing comparatively large numbers of Ph.D. candidates in natural sciences were distinguished from "less productive" colleges by the following traits described by student observers:

First, their contacts with students are characterized by informality and warmth: open displays of emotion are not likely to embarrass them; in talking with students they frequently refer to colleagues by their first names; they are not as likely to be described as practical and efficient in dealing with students; students do not feel obliged to address them as *professor* or *doctor*. Second, they emphasize high academic standards: according to student reports their standards are exacting; they see through the pretenses and bluffs of students; they push students to the limits of their capacities; and they give examinations which are genuine measures of the student's achievement and understanding. Third, they have high standards for evaluating faculty productivity and selecting new faculty members: the faculty values pure scholarship and basic research, and the course offerings and faculty in the natural sciences are outstanding. Fourth, the faculty does not play the role of Big Brother: students need not sit in assigned seats and attendance is not taken; student organizations are not closely supervised to guard against mistakes; faculty members are tolerant and understanding in dealing with violations of rules. Finally, they tend to be more nondirective in teaching methods: students find it relatively hard to predict examination questions and to take clear notes in class; instructors less frequently outline explicit goals and purposes for courses; students are not required to submit outlines before writing term papers and reports.[2]

Faculties producing comparatively large numbers of candidates in arts, humanities, and social sciences shared some of the same traits, notably insistence on high standards and freedom from close supervision. But there was a group of strikingly different traits described by students, as follows: (i) excellent social science faculty and resources, (ii) a high degree of energy and controversy in instruction, (iii) broad intellectual emphasis, (iv) frequent contacts with students outside the classroom, (v) a flexible, or somewhat unstructured, curriculum, (vi) emphasis upon independent study and the development of a critical attitude, (vii) excellent offerings in the arts and drama, and (viii) relatively infrequent appraisals of student performance.[3]

The extent to which faculties "reproduce themselves" by stimulating gifted students to continue for graduate study is one useful index to the quality of a college faculty. But the quality of faculty-student relations

affects not only the gifted, the degree candidates and prospective graduate students, but all students—whether they finish college or not. The
behavior on which gifted students rated faculty members in the study
seems to distinguish "productive" colleges from "less productive" ones.
But there are many other factors, including the behavior and attitudes
of students themselves, that affect faculty-student relationships and
determine the quality of the college. Not all effective teachers show all
the forms of behavior rated as "productive," and not all students respond enthusiastically to even the best of instructors.

The roles played by student and teacher in college are reciprocal.
Each must understand and accept the other's role in order to play his
own part effectively. Fortunately, student and teacher roles are pretty
well defined in tradition and practice. There is no question about the
faculty's role in grading, curriculum planning, setting academic standards, and awarding degrees. There is no question about the students'
role in earning grades, following the course of study, meeting the requirements, and qualifying for the degree. The major theme of college
education is the development of the student into a mature, qualified
scholar. The role of the teacher is to support students' development and
set the tasks to be mastered in different stages. One way to look at college education is to view it as a rehearsal. The faculty members write
the script and direct the production; the student plays the role of a
scholar, under the direction and criticism of the faculty, improving his
performance and his conception of the role as he goes along.

Faulty conceptions of the roles of student and teacher

Social roles are never defined with complete clarity. Roles involving
unfamiliar experience are particularly likely to be confused because
they have to be learned as they go along. The student is not always
clear about his proper role, or what he can expect of the teachers' role.
If he knew what to do or what to expect, he need not be in college.

One assumption that has to be made, if there is to be a college at all,
is that both students and faculty members are adults acting adult roles.
Independence is expected of both, each being responsible for his own
ideas, opinions, work, personal affairs, and debts. The capacity for continued growth and improvement in performance is expected of both.
The capacity for self-understanding and understanding of others is
expected to be developed. Students are expected to develop self-direction through practice under the guidance and criticism of the faculty.
Teachers are expected to give guidance and criticism without inter-

fering with students' self-direction. Teachers must be willing to let students play an adult role; and students must be willing to accept it.

Misconceptions about the nature of adult roles, consequently, interfere with the understanding of student and teacher roles in college education.

First, some students fail to understand or accept an independent role. They see themselves as dependent on the teacher. They regard him as a person who does something to them or is responsible for directing their work. Teachers try to resist the efforts of students to shift responsibility to them. They restrain themselves when tempted to give unnecessary help. They try to make clear what is expected but try to make the student do it himself.

Some students have firmly entrenched habits of dependence that are skillfully defended. They cannot understand or accept a role in which they respond to a teacher who encourages independence. For instance, students commonly talk about grades that *teachers have given them,* rarely about grades they have *earned.* Their academic performance is spoken of as something the teacher does to them. The wiles with which they try to persuade an instructor to change a grade are sometimes a clue to their dependence. "I was coming down with the flu, and you know I deserve a better grade than C on the exam." "I didn't understand exactly what you wanted, but I was right about what I did answer." "You ought to give me some credit because you wrote a question I couldn't understand." Sometimes the requests are outright childishness, asking the teacher, in effect, to buy something the student wants. "If you don't change my grade to a C instead of a D, I can't be initiated into my sorority." Sometimes a childish threat is added: "It will just *kill* my mother."

To the over-dependent student, the teacher's role may be taken for that of an indulgent parent. The teacher is expected to give the student what is good for him—information, advice, grades. To such a student, a teacher who puts the responsibility back on his students, who holds firmly to clear standards, who expects independent thinking, will appear unfair, unjust, harsh. Much of the campus gossip about the severity and unfairness of teachers originates in just such misconceptions of the teacher's role. In rare instances, a faculty member may be too hard on students or too rigid in his treatment of them. But students need to understand that excessive severity may, sometimes, be invited by their own over-dependence. The teacher may not be able to find any way to correct over-dependence except to be excessively firm and resistant to students' efforts to make him take responsibility for directing their work.

A second immature reaction of students is to conceive of learning as a contest between students and teachers, to see who can outwit the other. To some students, being adult means being free to outwit others in order to gain some advantage. For instance, under the guise of seeking help in course work, some students "pump" a teacher to get advance information about the content of an exam.

Cheating, in all its forms, is the commonest device used by students to gain an advantage. Copying papers from a book or from another student, carrying "crib" notes into an exam, stealing advance copies of an exam, all sorts of devices are used in order to pass without doing honest work in a course. Cheating continues, and is widespread, in many colleges despite all efforts of students and faculty to cope with it. The difficulty in dealing with cheating may in part lie in the significance of deceptiveness in the self-image of some students. They may feel it is necessary to deceive or outwit the teacher in order to prove that they are grown up. This is a childish notion. People can learn that adult behavior is deceptive and fraudulent, through childhood experiences or perceptions of adults who deceive children. "When I become a man, I, too, can outwit and hoodwink people," may be the conclusion. Some students may have come to depend almost wholly on defense mechanisms involving deception, and to them cheating almost comes naturally.

Many students may cheat once, or deceive a teacher once, out of acute anxiety or some overpowering desire to succeed at any cost. But they often feel remorse, and whether they are caught, or confess, they are likely to reform and thereafter do honest work. It is the habit of cheating and the preference for deception that represent a faulty conception of the roles of student and teacher. The most reprehensible of all are students who take advantage of the anxiety of others by offering to sell advance copies of exams or write papers for a fee. A sensible student will resist their offers, and he should report them to college authorities for the protection of others.

Deception and cheating are not very successful. In the first place, the teacher is on guard against the highly competitive, hostile student. There is a real competitive factor in student-teacher relationships, to which teachers are sensitive. They are helping younger scholars develop the skills which will one day enable them to replace their teachers. But teachers are very much concerned with playing by the rules. There is enough integrity in the teaching profession, and enough pressure from other faculty members, to enable an instructor to restrain himself from being unfair or ruthless in his criticism and evaluation of students. But it is extremely unlikely that a teacher will be blind to evasiveness, deception, or cheating. Faculty members are pretty wise and experienced. They have had to protect themselves and the profession from deceptive tricks many times. The older men have seen it all before; the younger men have heard their anecdotes, and they also feel that they have to prove their own ability to recognize frauds. So if a student takes on a teacher as antagonist, he is very likely to lose the contest.

Attempts to outwit teachers usually fail just because they are so obvious. In a college where as a rule people are responsible for their own work, the dependent or deceptive student and the cheat are noticeably different. Their behavior and attitudes deviate from the norm enough to draw attention. Cheating is particularly likely to be detected because it follows a pattern that repeats itself. Thus, it can be anticipated and the culprit identified. Plagiarism is particularly easy to detect because passages copied from another source are usually strikingly different from a student's own style. Or the sources are well enough known to be readily identified. One student, for example, copied a passage from a widely used high school history text in which a well-known error was included. The classic story, of course, is about the student who turned in a term paper that he found in the fraternity files. It was returned with an *A* grade, and a note from the instructor: "This was an *A* paper in 1928 when I wrote it for Professor Blessingfellow. In my opinion, it is still an *A* paper today." His high opinion of the work did not prevent him from reporting the student to the discipline committee.

Whatever needs deception may satisfy, it is a faulty conception of the roles of student and teacher. To try to understand and play the role of student straight, taking responsibility for one's own work, is much more effective than to try to win in a contest that is not really taking place at all.

This misconception of the teacher as antagonist possibly is related to a third misconception of student-teacher roles. *Students often have a faulty notion of the teacher's authority.* The teacher does have authority. Part of his role is to administer regulations of the college, maintain order and decorum in the classroom, administer standards of grading, give honors, or record failure. He may determine who shall be admitted to his classes and who shall be excluded from them; in many colleges, not even the dean or president may enter a classroom without permission or invitation of the instructor. The teacher is also spoken of as an authority in his field. Because of his expert knowledge of his subject, his statements must be taken seriously and subjected to careful study and criticism. To accept the teacher as the person in charge of a class, and to accept him as an expert whose statements about a subject are important and worth knowing lead to a proper acceptance of the role of the teacher.

But students have some mistaken conceptions of authority. In viewing the teacher as *an authority figure,* they make mistakes about the teacher's role and about their own. Students who try to outwit the teacher may be trying to deceive a person who is regarded as an unfriendly authority. An authority figure to them is an antagonist, a hostile person. Encountering authority arouses anxiety, and they try to escape anxiety by evasion or deception.

Students who fear authority may try to placate the teacher, to "apple-polish." They try to cater to his special interests, to wheedle a good grade by spotting his pet ideas and prejudices, which they repeat in their papers.

Or, if he presents unfamiliar material and expects them to form ideas of their own about it, they will hang back and wait for him to assert an opinion before venturing one of their own. If they forget themselves and express an opinion of their own, they are distressed and anxious. A classic example is the oft-told story of the student in English literature who boldly advanced the opinion that Thomas Hardy was a better poet than Browning. The instructor said that was fine, and could he give any reasons to support his opinion. "Oh, no," said the student, "I take it all back, I didn't mean it at all."

Students who see the role of the teacher as a *feared* authority try to defend themselves by trying to get "the right" answers. Since the answers cannot be looked up in the back of the book, they try to get them from the teacher. The teacher, on the other hand, is trying to help students learn how to check their answers, to weigh the evidence for and against their ideas, to correct their own errors. His role is to help students find "right answers," or form sound opinions, on their own. If he gave them the "right answers" or the "best opinions," he would not be playing his own role effectively. Students need to accept their role in self-correction, self-direction and independent study to make the process of learning work. Fear of authority interferes with the development of effective adult roles in both students and teachers.

A fourth misconception of the roles of student and teacher appears in the faulty use of the teacher as a model. College teachers are good models for students to follow in establishing patterns of adult behavior. Many students use them in just this way. In the studies of Vassar students,[4] Freedman concluded that many of them tried to reconstitute in their relations with faculty members the "adult-oriented" relationships they had with parents. They came to teachers with many of the needs for advice, assurance, and encouragement that parents had answered. They observed the behavior of teachers and modeled their behavior on it, as they once followed patterns they saw in their parents. Freedman felt that teachers might turn the strength of this relationship to the support of academic goals, helping students find the way through mature scholarship to mature adult relationships.

Furthermore, college teachers are mostly pretty good citizens. They often win respect and admiration in the community. They often have some influence on public opinion and public policy. They have fairly solid status, in spite of the fact that many of the factors used in determining social class or status do not apply very well to them. For example, many faculty members are good examples of social mobility. They have risen in the class structure above the level of their families. They have come from humble origins and won a solid position by their own ability and effective work. For the ambitious student who is using a college education as a way to improve himself and win higher status, a college teacher may be a good model.

But there are two faulty conceptions of the student's role in using the teacher as a model. The first, against which teachers try to guard, is *slavish imitation*. Trying to imitate a teacher's style prevents the student from developing a style of his own. Trying to remember everything a teacher says and feed it back to him in papers and exams prevents the student from developing independence of mind and destroys imagination. A much more unfortunate result may be the adoption by the student of his image of the teacher as a kind of idealized self. The idealized self, as described in Chapter 1, is a tyrant. Its demands can never be satisfied. Many are completely unreasonable, they do not fit the natural endowment or temperament of the student. A student who feels he must be an exact copy of an admired teacher is courting disaster. He cannot really know what the teacher is like, so he can never be satisfied with himself. He is likely to suffer anxiety and frustration at his failure to become an exact copy of his model. He is driven, not the driver. He has no goals of his own, just those he fancies the professor to have for him. He has no real understanding of himself, just a constant awareness that he has failed to become a good copy of the model.

Furthermore, such idealization of the teacher by a student interferes with the teacher's own job. He cannot carry out his obligations or play his proper role with such a student. His job is to help the student develop an effective personal style; all he gets is a carbon copy of his own, rather smudged. He is supposed to invite students to criticize his ideas, and he often needs their individual responses and criticism to help him refine and clarify his ideas; but all he gets is a slightly garbled transcription of his own statements. A student's role requires him to fulfill certain obligations toward his teachers. He should have a speaking acquaintance with their published work and keep adequate notes of their lectures. If the teachers have a distinctive point of view, he should try to get a clear understanding of it. And he is expected to challenge, to criticize, to improve, to confirm the teachers' work, either by arriving at the same conclusions in his own way or by spotting errors and making effective criticisms. Any attempt of the student to imitate the teacher deprives the teacher of help he desires. And it prevents the student from playing his role in a way that will make the teacher's role effective.

A second and more serious fault is *rejection of teachers as models,* in favor of other models of adult behavior. Sometimes this rejection amounts to outright anti-intellectualism. A student who does not wish to think, who has a positive dislike for intellectual interest, who regards scholarly work as infantile, effete, or dangerous, may nevertheless find himself in college. He does not belong there. He has no place in the intellectual enterprise. But some pressure from parents, or some attraction such as a gay social life, or sheer lack of anything else to do, may bring him to college. He usually does not last very long if he cannot bring himself to play a student's real role.

But there are degrees of rejection. Sometimes it is selective. Students may accept certain aspects of teachers' character and behavior as worthwhile, but openly reject others. For instance, on many campuses there is a fascinating group of "Bohemians," or "beatniks," who wholeheartedly accept some scholarly disciplines but reject others. They cultivate independence of mind. They develop passionate interest in various subjects, many of them quite solid and respectable, such as art, history, quantum theory, finite mathematics, seventeenth-century literature, or American philosophy. But they are short on haircuts, baths, meals, and dress. And they often are sadly irregular and disorganized in their habits of study and unable to produce consistent work.

At the other end of the scale from the campus "Bohemians" are the students who reject faculty members as models because they do not understand or accept the status that teachers have. One student said to a professor, "Frankly, I am not interested in going into teaching because you do not live in the kind of neighborhood I want to live in." Another, who was considering graduate study and entry into college teaching, regretfully decided against it, because his income would be so much less than that of the rest of his family that he could not see how he could associate socially with them and their friends.

There are many status groups on and off campus that compete for students' allegiance and offer attractive models. Many of the standard status symbols are not of prime importance in a college. When it comes to clothes, cars, a home in a fashionable neighborhood, country-club membership, and other such status symbols, college teachers often can take it or leave it. To be sure, most of them do not have the kind of income that would buy such things. But even when they have the choice, they may prefer living on campus to living in a fashionable neighborhood. Membership in a professional society, travel for professional meetings, or financing a piece of research (some teachers still do pay for their own) may be more important than membership in a fashionable club. It may be hard for students to understand how a person could have the choice of status symbols and still prefer to wear an old tweed suit and go without a television set. Or they may understand only too well, and decide it is not for them.

On the campus itself, there is competition from other interests that lend more status in the student body than academic interests. The social structure of the student body in many colleges is actually divorced from academic life. The roles that students play in social clubs, the student union, student politics, athletics are sometimes unrelated to the social and intellectual roles of adults played by the faculty. The cost of these aspects of student life is often so much greater than the cost of things like books and concert tickets that it becomes a mark of social distinction, a status symbol. To buy books and concert tickets may be regarded as a confession of poverty and low status. The investment in student social life brings immediate rewards in status and esteem; investment in academic work pays off in the long run and uncertainly. Students may reject teachers as models because they prefer immediate to postponed rewards. Or they may value the expensive, sophisticated status symbols current in the community and widely advertised over the more sober and less ostentatious patterns offered by the faculty. Social sophistication may be preferred to intellectual sophistication.

In rejecting faculty members as models on grounds of status, students are in part reflecting some of the social changes that have affected the status of the college teacher in recent years. There are anti-intellectual factors in American society. Faculty members have been labeled "radical," "subversive," "egg-headed," both individually and collectively. The income of college teachers has not kept pace either with inflation or with the positions of esteem, influence, and status which they have traditionally held, and still hold. The effect of such changes has been to confuse the status of college teachers, to confuse still further the immature perceptions that students have of their roles, and to call in question the desirability of teachers as role models.

Actually, selectivity in use of the teacher as a model is desirable. The college professor is no plaster saint, and he has a lot of traits that he would rather not have students imitate. If they model themselves on his strengths and reject his shortcomings, students will make his role much more comfortable. And their own role will be easier to play if they see him as a human being from whom they can learn, not as an idealized self that drives and demands. What they do select should be chosen on the basis of some solid standards related to the scholarly enterprise in which both students and faculty are engaged.

Preference for social sophistication over intellectual sophistication may lead to a fifth faulty conception of the teachers' role. *Students often tend to see the teacher as an entertainer,* and to expect to be amused or diverted in class. A good lecture, demonstration, or performance is exciting and stimulating. An effective teacher often infuses learning with a dramatic quality. Students also find intense delight in using their own intellectual powers. Bringing off a successful experiment, writing an effective term paper, composing a dance, and *knowing that the work is good,* gives a tremendous lift to the student, "a real ego-booster," in student terms. These are the genuine satisfactions to be found in college. But some students settle for spurious enjoyments, treating the teacher's lectures as an entertainment, responding only to shocking or exciting ideas, trying to identify the professor's pet ideas and opinions instead of drawing their own conclusions. Genuine pleasures come only when students have personal interests or develop clear ideas of their own; these lead to the surprise and pleasure of recognition of common interests or divergent opinions or to the excitement of following the dramatic development of chains of ideas and events. The teacher cannot provide these elements of the joy of learning by his own unaided effort. Learning is not a spectator sport.

Some colleges have experimented with methods of evaluation of faculty by students. Since students are going to offer evaluations anyway and gratuitously advance opinions on the effectiveness of particular teachers, certainly no harm is done in making the process more systematic. Faculty members naturally object to using student evaluation as a basis for employment or promotion; students lack the technical background, experience, and above all, the long-range involvement in the college to make adequate judgments of this kind. But many faculty members feel that student evaluation is useful in improving their teaching, revising their course outlines, or trying to improve some of their techniques. Students, too, feel that it is helpful to them. They feel more a part of the common task of improving teaching and learning. They find that systematic evaluation of their experience with particular teachers tends to make them think more seriously about the process of teaching and learning rather than the personalities involved. They feel that the process of evaluation clarifies their own standards of intellectual achievement and improves their understanding of both the teacher's role and their own. It helps them correct some faulty conceptions of teachers' roles and of their own role in college.

Realistic conceptions of faculty roles

The student can expect the college teacher to play three important roles: those of expert, critic, and counselor. These roles are traditionally part of the responsibility of teacher toward students. Seeing his teachers in these roles helps the student understand and accept his own role as student more effectively.

The teacher as expert. The college teacher is, first of all, an expert in his field. He has demonstrated to his colleagues his mastery of the content and techniques of his specialty and his recognition of significant problems and issues in it. As expert, the teacher cannot give students all the answers. But he can help them put their questions in such a way that answers can be found by sound methods of reasoning to valid conclusions. The answers do not have to be identical with his own, but they do have to meet the standards of scholarship in the subject; and the teacher as expert can help students understand these standards and measure their work against them.

The course outline, for example, represents the advice of an expert on the best way for students to develop their study. But the teacher tries to set up this framework for study in such a way as to allow considerable flexibility so that students can explore subjects of special interest to them. Laboratory work, observation, term papers, artistic performance and production can allow quite a broad range for the pursuit of individual interests.

Students sometimes richly reward teachers by developing lines of work that enrich the entire course and broaden the scope of the entire class. One fortunate teacher, who mentioned that much seventeenth-century literature was written in the expectation that it would be read to or performed by groups of people, was approached by a drama major who wanted to produce Milton's *Comus* as a term project. It took the cooperation of the dance, music, and drama departments, with considerable expert advice from the English teacher on matters of seventeenth-century style; but the final production was of such exceptional quality that it was presented for the entire college. Part of the expert skill of teachers lies in using the special skills of various students. Consequently, no subject need be dull nor any study drudgery if the student contributes his special interests to the work of the class.

Faculty members have to undertake continuous independent study to sustain their expert skills. Dullness in teaching may result from poor disciplines in the teacher, but lack of responsiveness in students is a contributing factor. Lectures rapidly get out of date without continuing study; and the teacher has little to stimulate him to revise them if he is not forced to keep ahead of the class—and freshmen and sophomore classes in particular do little to force the pace. But students can help to make it worthwhile for teachers to keep up their research interests by showing some awareness of their importance and by relating their work to the special interests of teachers.

First, the student can seek out teachers who bring independent study into class discussion. The appropriate basis for selection is not the volume of research or years of experience offered by teachers but their active introduction of research problems and findings into their courses, both out of their own work and from the research of others. Such teachers often are hard on students because they may demand much more active engagement in the course while offering less formal structure within which to work; but they are worth seeking out because they give the student more opportunity to get out on the growing edge of the subject.

Second, the student can try to get acquainted with the interests of his teachers. A little library work will locate any of his teachers' publications; these indicate their interests and strengths. Study of those works that are pertinent to the student's courses will give him more useful insight into the teacher's resources than the information gathered from idle gossip. He can begin to develop some ideas of possible relationships between his interests and those of his teachers. He should get some leads for his own work—term paper topics, reading, experiments, and problems—out of the areas where he finds clear differences or similarities between his interests and those of his teachers.

Third, the student can then try to center his work on aspects of his courses that are of mutual interest to him and his teachers—not just those already dealt with in published work, but also the unsettled problems that define areas in which further study is useful. A teacher gains needed stimulation from students who bring in questions of their own. Scholarly legend includes many stories about students who ask foolish questions that illuminate the whole question. "What would happen if you connected this little wire over there?" is reputed to have solved a complicated problem in electronics through the question of an art student who got lost in a physics lab.[5]

The way in which students can make the most significant contribution to the academic enterprise is by asking more significant questions. The teacher is frequently discouraged in going beyond the routine presentation of known facts. For example, a young professor of chemistry, who had just published an excellent textbook, was roundly criticized by his students because he didn't lecture on anything in his text but insisted on introducing new material.

The response that students make to faculty as colleagues in the enterprise of learning makes or breaks them both. The interest, curiosity, and stimulation of students can feed the scholarly work of the teacher. The responsibility of students for maintaining the continuity of the scholarly enterprise is profoundly serious; and frivolity, apathy, or resistance are unforgivable failures to support the work of the faculty in the process of teaching and learning.

The teacher as critic. Self-criticism, being subject to the limitations of personal bias and self-esteem, is a very difficult skill to master. Yet it is essential to effective scholarship. The teacher as critic supports the development of self-direction in learning by providing two kinds of services: First, he offers expert criticism, from an objective point of view, based on his acquaintance with generally accepted scholarly standards in the field. Second, he helps students understand standards of scholarly excellence and apply them in self-criticism.

In the first year or so of college, the teacher's criticism is focused principally on the identification of errors in student work. The student is responsible for correction, but the teacher calls attention to mistakes. After the student receives the teacher's criticism, he can refer to the available readings, notes, and papers to find correct answers. Then he should practice the correct form in order to strengthen it and overcome the pattern of error that he has established.

The earlier the student corrects his errors, the easier it will be to establish correct patterns of information and judgment. Persistent errors tend to compound themselves, dislocating larger and larger sections of subject matter, and tending ultimately to produce serious shortcomings in the integration of ideas. Any criticism that cannot be understood, any error which the student cannot correct for himself is a signal for consultation with the teacher for assistance in establishing correct patterns of response.

The horror story of Jessica and the course in English novels may serve as a case in point. She entered the novel course with every sign of incipient incomprehensibility, a disorder characterized by exciting ideas having no apparent connection with each other. She had achieved junior standing without learning how to support her conclusions by adequate evidence or to give her work a form logical enough to enable others to understand it. Her first critical essay was returned with the comment, "Not clear," sprinkled in the margins. The second paper bore a more pointed criticism, "I am unable to see that you make any connection between these two statements." The third carried a developmental analysis of her difficulty, "Your work to date has moved from a lack of clarity through a failure to develop your ideas logically toward complete disorganization and lack of form. Your ideas are stimulating, your style pleasing, your diction fluent and felicitous. But the form does not convey the meaning to the reader."

By then Jessica began to feel abused, particularly since her grades had declined from C to D to F. The teacher was obviously incompetent, since plain English was not clear to him, and clearly stupid, since connections clear to her should be plain to him if he wanted to see them. She decided to take these complaints to the top, but the president of the college was in a board meeting, so she blew into the dean's office, furious at the entire English department for employing an incompetent. Why, she asked the dean, if she had such a serious problem, didn't the teacher ask her to talk to him about it? The dean sent her back to the English instructor, suggesting that she take her papers along as a subject for consultation, and tactfully reminding Jessica that a student, not the teacher, has the initiative in taking up academic problems. In the end she arrived, two papers and several grade points late, where she should have gone earlier in the semester.

It would be good to report that Jessica overcame her difficulties, made an A in the English novel course, and became editor of the college literary quarterly. Unfortunately, she had delayed too long to do more than scrape by with a D in the course. She had waited so long that a simple problem in diction had developed into a major problem in logical organization. The teacher helped Jessica see how scholarly writing must proceed from idea to idea by small logical steps that can be followed even by the uninitiated. He showed her examples of clearly demonstrated relationships between ideas. Jessica then worked out, with his help, a plan for a series of short summaries of papers that she had written in several courses. She wrote one such précis every day, and took it in for review and criticism with the teacher. She learned to improve her outlines, make her writing briefer and more concise, and lead the reader through logical sequences of ideas.

What the teacher did for Jessica was to perform his proper function as critic. He showed how one fault led to another so that Jessica could get at the root of the matter rather than giving it superficial treatment. He helped her understand the standards of scholarly performance that she needed to meet: clarity, logical development, and elegance, as well as adequate documentation. The exercise in précis writing was designed to help her practice these standards in her own work until they were no longer abstract generalizations, but principles she could use in distinguishing between correct and incorrect patterns of organization in her writing. She began to master the needed skill in self-evaluation, becoming less dependent on the teacher's criticism.

Some students may be puzzled at the failure of teachers to call them in for consultation on such obvious errors. But there are pretty sound reasons for it. In the first place, the teacher's time is limited, especially in large introductory classes, and follow-up conferences with every student are quite impracticable. In the second place, the teacher who initiated such consultation or made corrections for the student would tend to make a student dependent on him, interfering with development of self-direction. It is preferable for the teacher to rely, instead, on the student's initiative in asking for consultation after the student has tried to correct his own mistakes without special assistance. The student should also take the initiative in planning measures for improving his own work in consultation with the teacher.

The teacher as counselor. The student can expect the teacher to allow for individual interests only to a limited extent, within the disciplines and standards of the subject. Criticism is aimed at helping the student improve his mastery of the basic content and techniques in the course and his ability to meet commonly held standards of excellence in the subject. The teacher is valuable as a critic only insofar as he applies these standards consistently, without regard for the desires of a particular student.

However, provided these standards are met, there are ways in which students can reasonably expect teachers to allow for special individual interests and adapt course requirements to special purposes. Here again the initiative rests with the student. Faculty members customarily re-view requirements at the beginning of a course, and students are ex-pected to meet these as a minimum. Over and above these, there are ways in which the student can relate his personal interests to his plan for study in the course.

In such a process of adaptation, the teacher functions in his third proper role, as counselor. Individual interests are not very effective in guiding learning when they are introduced into the process at random. They have to be pertinent to the course. Teachers try to take account of the range of individual interests in their classes by including in course outlines and requirements a variety of alternatives for selection of term paper topics, laboratory work, observation, additional reading, and performances. Personal interests that fall within the range of suggested procedures are perfectly acceptable, and the student can proceed with-out further consultation. But there are certain points at which the stu-dent should consult the teacher in the process of planning the introduc-tion of special personal interests into his work.

First, the student who thinks a special interest of his own may con-tribute something of value to the rest of the class should confer with the instructor about its possible use. Some instructors anticipate stu-dent contributions to the course and inquire into individual interests at the beginning of the semester. The seminar method, used in many ad-vanced and graduate courses, depends mainly on the presentation of material by students for the criticism of the entire class, and the course is based from the outset on the interests of its members. Discussion methods of teaching, increasingly used in a variety of fields, are ad-dressed to the interests of the members of the class.

The range of material in a given subject is always greater than the topics covered in the course, and teachers can often draw on the in-terests and skills of students to enrich the course. The production of *Comus*, previously mentioned, is a case in point; related material in music, dance, and drama could be introduced into the course in seven-teenth-century literature in a way that would not otherwise have been possible. Instructors who make use of student contributions in courses report that they help the entire class become more involved in learning by adding variety, with a new voice, a novel point of view, a different manner of presentation replacing the same old lecturer with the same old notes.

Second, the student who is looking for ways of integrating his work in two or more different subjects can get valuable help in planning by consulting the teacher about key ideas around which his work can be organized.

One possible plan of integration is to set up a course of study for a semester or year centered on a key idea or general concept. For example, a music major, with the help of her faculty adviser, centered her work for a semester on the Romantic period. She selected courses in nineteenth-century philosophy, the Romantic period in English literature, and the Romantic period in music history, and in her courses in vocal music and piano she worked on the Schubert song cycle and the Chopin Etudes and Nocturnes. "It was the most wonderful semester I had in college," she says.

Another plan is to set up a single comprehensive term project covering requirements in two or more courses. For example, one student wrote a single report instead of separate term papers for courses in American history and community organization. She studied her home town, from both the historical and sociological point of view, analyzing the patterns of political, social, and economic organization, the class structure, and the social problems of the community and tracing their historical development as examples of the influence of these factors in American community life. Where such a procedure is used, the faculty members concerned must be consulted in planning. They will make sure that the proposed project meets all course requirements, that the general principles and methods used are based on valid relations between the subjects, and that the project is compassable in the time available.

One cautionary note should be added: the purpose of such interdisciplinary studies is to integrate learning, not to find ways to avoid work. The scope of study combining different fields and methods is necessarily broader than that of the usual term paper or project in a departmental course; the effort required is greater; the product has to meet the combined requirements and standards of two or more fields of study. The integration of learning is not achieved by simply changing the title page on an English paper and turning it in for history.

Third, the teacher as counselor can help the student try out some of his personal interests that may lead to professional interests in career planning—both the most attractive and the least interesting. A group of engineering students, looking forward with little pleasure to presenting technical studies to lay groups, got a public speaking class to act the role of members of the university board of regents, to whom they presented a plan for campus development worked out as a term project in engineering. In such processes of rehearsal, the counsel of the teacher assists the student in selecting a significant focus of practical interest, planning a project that tests his ability in it, and evaluating his experience in relation to future professional work.

Rehearsal of the basic techniques in various fields of scholarly work is one of the most effective forms of vocational guidance. Whether or not specialized vocational counseling is available, the student who makes wise and careful use of his teachers as counselors can get a solid foundation for choice of a vocation and development of a career plan.

One student who made effective use of teachers as counselors attended a college which had no specialized vocational counseling service. She created her own vocational guidance bureau by judicious use of faculty resources. She entered college with the expectation of going into medicine. But she had mediocre grades in chemistry and discovered that she enjoyed art much more than science. Upon consultation with the chemistry instructor, she realized her difficulties were due to a lack of mathematical aptitude, and the prospects of improving her math did not seem very good. Since her interest in science was fairly high, she explored some possibilities of combining her skills in art and science. Switching to biology in her sophomore year, she found that science much more suited to her aptitudes and interests. She also took a course in critical writing to develop an interest in scientific writing. At the end of that year, she asked the instructors in art, biology, and English to meet with her to discuss a choice of major and plans for a career. Together they helped her work out a program in art, biology, and English, with a major in the science, designed to lead to work in scientific writing or illustration. At the end of the junior year, the biology instructor helped her select schools offering a program in medical illustration, and by the end of her senior year she had worked out plans for specialized training for a career as a medical and scientific illustrator. Although she had no access to a vocational counselor, she made effective use of the counseling resources in the faculty, and she successfully managed the problem of changing her vocational aims and making realistic career plans.

The teacher, of course, is under no obligation to offer more than instruction and criticism in his subject. But there are usually teachers who are willing to help students make more effective use of their college experience through counseling and advice. It is the responsibility of the student to seek such help, and the resources available in the faculty are usually greater than he may expect.

INFORMAL STUDENT-TEACHER RELATIONSHIPS

The basic student-faculty relationship is centered in the classroom. If the academic relationship is productive and rewarding, there need be little concern about student-faculty relations. Adequate access to the services of faculty as experts, critics, and counselors is essential for student development. The interest of teachers in students is appropriately expressed in their courses; the respect and appreciation of students for teachers are appropriately expressed in the productive work they do in their courses. Out of such response to each other in the process of teaching and learning grow the warmth, respect, admiration, even enduring friendship, that students and faculty value.

Those discussions of student-faculty relations that begin with social relationships—student-faculty teas, faculty patrons at dances, the cost of entertaining students in faculty homes—are usually not very productive, since they approach the problem from the wrong end. Of course, it is desirable for students and faculty to like being together and to enjoy special occasions of entertainment and celebration. There are mature social skills that students can learn from the faculty, not the least of these being the art of pure fun. But the atmosphere of the classroom determines the social atmosphere of the college, not the other way round. If it is a pleasure for students and faculty to share scholarly work, the extension of this pleasure into the social life of the college takes a natural and comfortable course. Students who have discovered common interests with faculty in class feel more comfortable in conversation with them at teas and dinners or during the intermissions of concerts and dances. Scholars who are good company in class are more likely to be good company outside of class.

Part of the folk wisdom of the faculty warns against excessive involvement in student social activities. Social relationships with students that impose a sense of social obligation upon teachers are justifiably avoided since they may interfere with the objectivity of the teachers' judgment as critics. A certain social distinction between students and faculty protects the resources of the teacher for students by preserving the privacy the teacher needs for his own independent study and the energy he needs to meet a rigorous schedule. Teachers need time to talk to each other, exchanging essential advice and criticism. They devote time to their families and accept obligations for community service outside the college. Their resources have to be renewed by rest, reflection, and recreation if they are going to have anything to offer students. To add to the requirements of scholarly work demands for active participation in student social activities is to sap the vitality of the teacher and drain off his resources into unproductive affairs.

Both teachers and students need exclusive areas of social life to meet their special interests. But there need to be areas of common experience, too. No faculty member should be expected to endure the noise, confusion, and high jinks of the ordinary student living unit; but there are dinners, parties, and informal occasions which faculty guests may enjoy, to which they may be invited by individuals or groups of students. No student should be exposed to the acrimonious debate, private jokes, idle gossip, and political machinations of the ordinary faculty club; but there are informal discussions and social events in which students can participate with pleasure. Students and faculty can best leave each other's housekeeping alone; but they need to cultivate forms of social activity in which they find common interest.

Some of these social occasions have taken on the character of ritual observance; commencement, for example, is an occasion for all members of the college to honor degree candidates and scholars of distinction. Other occasions are designed for enrichment of the intellectual, artistic, and spiritual life of the community of scholars: assemblies, chapel services, lecture and concert series, and the like can be centers of social interest rather than dull obligations, provided the plans capitalize on the social possibilities they afford. And there are common organizational interests and programs: honor societies, interest groups, religious organizations, publications, athletics, clubs. Some include both faculty and student members; others have faculty advisers for a student membership. The social values to be gained depend, again, on deliberate planning for a program that will give satisfaction to students and faculty alike. There is nothing so deadly, from the teacher's point of view, as serving as faculty adviser to a student group that has not thought of anything useful the adviser can do.

Informal conversation with students and faculty members bears cultivation, provided the general college atmosphere is congenial and the ideas sufficiently stimulating to keep the conversation going. The invention of instant coffee has done a good deal to lubricate student-faculty relations by opening up offices and seminar rooms as coffee houses. But the essential requirement is the desire of students and faculty to keep the conversation going. If faculty give all the answers, if students conceal their interests, the talk degenerates into idle gossip, recrimination, and griping for want of ideas on which to feed. In such an atmosphere, friendships cannot flourish between students and faculty.

The student can reasonably expect his teachers to serve as experts, critics, and counselors. If he uses their resources effectively, he must do so on his own initiative in support of sound academic interests and excellence in performance. If out of this working relationship grow warm appreciation and deep respect, he is richly rewarded by unexpected gifts of friendship and by opportunity for enjoying the goodly company of scholars. These are not to be claimed or demanded; they will grow and develop as the student contributes out of his own resources of interest and enthusiasm to the life of the college.

7

What's in it for me?

The resources of
scholarship

THE RESOURCES OF SCHOLARLY SKILLS

Just as the roles of teacher and student change between high school and college, so the techniques of scholarship take on a new character in a new way of work. Some scholarly skills, such as reading and writing, are themselves among the subjects taught in the school years. In college, their mastery is assumed; they become, not subjects, but instruments in the mastery of other subjects. Moreover, they become the principal way in which students and teachers play their roles and respond to each other. Technical mastery of skills becomes the first step toward the exchange of ideas, the communication between scholars that is the process of learning.

Viewed as ways in which scholars respond to each other, the techniques of intellectual work take on much more significance as ways of enlarging interests and achieving excellence in performance. Some

176

problems in the adequate use of basic skills become easier to manage from this point of view. The handicap of deficiencies in skill appears even more serious, however, for such a handicap becomes an obstacle to learning and a source of interference with the student's role. Students who need help to overcome deficiencies are advised to seek help from specialists. But even the good student can get more out of college resources by using scholarly skills that he has successfully mastered.

Reading

In doing college reading, a student needs to keep in mind his role as a participant in a conversation. Reading is one form of listening. The book is a kind of frozen conversation, an invention for recording ideas so they can be communicated to others across the barriers of space and time. Speaking of a great philosopher with whom he had studied, a college teacher once told his class, "I often visit X—, but we rarely discuss philosophy. When I need to talk philosophy with him, I turn to his books. He is much clearer and more consistent in them. And talking to him about the ideas that he has already settled bores him." A book is its author's thinking, and the reader can respond to his printed ideas almost as actively as if the author were present. He needs to bear in mind that he is responding to the author as a person; part of his study is directed toward understanding the mind of the author.

If any one characteristic of reading skill is essential, it is *flexibility* in technique. Slower rates of reading with careful attention to detail may be required by some material; rapid reading with attention to the development of content and chains of ideas is appropriate for others. The student will have to set his own appropriate pace on the basis of his purposes and the author's method of presentation.[1]

The student approaching the reading for a particular course needs to have some purposes and questions clearly in mind to get the maximum possible value out of his reading. Lectures and class discussions point to key ideas in the subject, and reading is suggested to develop these ideas further. The student will, first of all, be attentive to the author's point of view on these key ideas. Second, he will respond to the author's ideas, agreeing or disagreeing with them. Third, he will compare the author's ideas with his own opinions and the ideas of the teacher. Differences in point of view may point to questions on which other evidence can be found as he reads other works, or listens to additional lectures, or performs experiments. Points of agreement will enlarge the evidence supporting settled conclusions of his own.

In addition to flexibility, *accuracy* in reading is a necessary element of skill. In the first place, it is only fair to get a clear idea of the author's meaning before comparing it with other points of view or criticizing it from one's own standpoint. In the second place, the student needs to read with care to protect himself from possible errors in understanding which may compound themselves into errors in interpretation and judgment. In reading, as in a conversation, it is important to be clear on what is being said.

What is worth reading is settled in part by the suggestions of the instructor, but the student does not have to limit himself to the assigned reading list. Independent investigation in the library may uncover other books and articles of interest. The student should also try to use primary sources as far as possible; reports written by the person observing an event or carrying out an experiment and contemporary personal records and critiques are much more reliable than secondhand reports or criticism. He should be acquainted also with *authoritative* works on the subject: criticism that opens up new lines of inquiry, classics that have stood the test of time, critical experiments that confirm key principles and concepts.

A word should also be said about the valuable help of the library staff. They are acquainted with systems of classifying and indexing material and skilled in locating useful books and articles. A good reference librarian is worth her weight in gold to the scholar, and the alert student will get acquainted with her early in his college career. She can help him learn how to find what he wants, how to identify authors and establish their qualifications, and how to trace ideas back to original sources.

Scholarly reading is designed to do more than register facts. It goes beyond the casual review of events in the daily paper or weekly magazine. The student reads to develop his ideas, to find the source of things, to carry his thinking forward with continuity and system to a settled conclusion. He reads for evidence, for questions, for opinions, for criticism, and for new purposes and issues toward which his work can be addressed. Reading is a means of scholarly discourse, a way of listening to the ideas of other scholars and responding to them with one's own thinking.

Writing

In writing the student responds in his turn to the ideas, the authors, the teachers he has encountered in the process of learning. Writing is the way his ideas are presented for further use and development: writing extends the range of memory beyond what can be held in the conscious mind. It is the form in which the student presents his work for evaluation by the instructor.

It may seem strange to regard a student's lecture and laboratory notes as having the same value as books of classic quality. Yet they have equal importance to the student in the advancement of learning. In the first place, a student's notes can record the important content of the subject that is not found in books: the teacher's lectures, the sequence of events in experiments, behavior, reactions to works of art, measurements obtained, criteria used in judgment. The taking of notes is of value in recording material from many different sources beside the traditional professorial lecture; notes may include material from reading, observation, experiments, artistic performance, even idle musing. The skillful student may develop a whole repertory of notes from different sources, which will vary according to the nature of the material.

Second, notes should record sources and circumstances under which the content was recorded. Accurate dating, bibliographical data, and identification of teacher or speaker help locate material for future reference. Brief descriptions of environmental conditions add to the value of notes of observation. Apparatus and techniques have to be fully described in experimental records.

Third, and perhaps most important, notes should include the student's own response to the ideas recorded and the method of presentation. A lecture has been defined as a way of transferring words from the teacher's to the student's notebook without going through the head of either. But notes cannot be merely a stenographic process. The student needs a record of his reactions to give him clues to ideas worth further development. His notes should, therefore, include his own thinking and provide a running record of the development of his views. Some students set up their notes in such a way as to distinguish their ideas from the content of the material on which they are working (see Fig. 7-1).

The student's performance cannot be evaluated on the basis of his notes, however. The ideas they suggest have to be developed into a form that can be criticized by the teacher, into reports, papers, and examinations. The examination customarily is designed to measure the student's mastery of content, his grasp of the facts, principles, theories, opinions, and standards that must be used in communicating with other scholars in the field. The paper (or report) may be a further test of mastery of basic material in the subject. More frequently, the paper is

OBSERVATION:

Nursery school   March 2, 1960

Observed behavior   My impression

George: Whatcha doing?   :
Helen: Building a house.   :
G: I live in a house.   :
H: You can't live in this house.   :   H. being matter-of-fact again.
G: Why?   :
H: It's a play house.   :
G: I could play living in it.   :
H: It's my house.   :
G: I wuv you. (Moves toward house.)   :   G. "Wuvs" everybody who has
H: Go away. (Pushes G.)   :   what he wants.

LABORATORY:

Phillips, Physics 1   November 1, 1959
Experiment: Magnetism
Hypothesis: Magnetized objects distribute themselves in a field according
            to the pattern of forces exerted upon them.

Apparatus   Operation   Observation
2 bar magnets   1. Magnets arranged in   See blueprint #1.
Iron filings   parallel
Blueprint paper

LECTURES:

Harris, Soc. 195   April 15, 1960

Teacher's Ideas   :   My Ideas

1. Social classes   :
   A. Basis of distinction   :
      1. Income and financial resources : The Country Club crowd at
      2. Patterns of association   :   home

READING:

Bibliography: Kemeny, John G., J. Laurie Snell, and Gerald L. Thompson, Introduction to Finite Mathematics (Englewood Cliffs, N. J.: Prentice-Hall, Inc.,
1957).

1. Theoretical distinctions:
   a. Simple statements (declarative sentences)
   b. Compound statements (combinations of two or more simple statements)
2. Problems:
   a. Forms of compound statements
   b. Confirming the truth of compound statements from the truth of the
      elements
(N.B.: Apply this to paper on Public Opinion.)

PERFORMANCE:

Hamlet, with Lawrence Olivier   The Cinema, January 5, 1960

Duel scene: Set like Elizabethan stage. Perspective from position of
   audience. Pan in; closeup of king has dramatic possibilities, but
   impresses me as merely busy, not nervous or anxious. How much did
   the king know? Maybe he was just preoccupied. How much do we know
   of other people's intentions? Where do the clues come from?

Fig. 7–1. Examples of Notes Suited to Various Purposes.

designed to measure the ability of the student to develop ideas of his own and work them out in relation to the course content. Scholarly writing is based on the assumption that the reader will be a reasonably intelligent and informed person, capable of following a train of thought and recognizing relations between ideas. The student has to write in the expectation that the reader is interested in following his lead and testing his ideas. He cannot simply say that such-and-such is so, but he must also demonstrate the reason why.

Writing an examination requires skill in making clear distinctions and establishing valid relationships between facts, events, or concepts. The examination may further test the speed of a student's response by measuring the extent to which the organization of ideas has become an established habit, done with a minimum of reflection. Some types of examinations, such as true-false tests, are deliberately designed to measure habitual responses to critical distinctions. Multiple-choice, matching, completion, and similar short-answer tests measure the capacity of the student to make quick, accurate distinctions, valid generalizations, or correct applications of principles. Short-answer tests should, therefore, be written as quickly as possible, almost by reflex action, with questions about which the student is uncertain reserved for more careful consideration at the end of the test period.

Essay and problem-solving tests measure skills in more extensive integration, criticism, or invention. Questions should, therefore, be thought through more carefully before answers are written; sometimes even a scratch outline may be needed since these examinations are very much like papers.

Thus, the student must write, as he must read, with attention to the material that is presented and to the questions and conclusions that he derives from his reflection on the subject. Flexibility in writing is required just as it is in reading. Sometimes his writing will be concise, reflex action, "thinking on his feet"; sometimes it will require the careful construction of ideas and relationships. Versatility in writing is desirable in scholarship, and the student can follow the lead of the teacher in learning to choose the form of writing that best suits the material with which he is working and the purposes he has in mind.

Writing is more than a means of self-expression for the scholar. It is a way of responding to others. It is an invitation to others to evaluate, criticize, improve upon his work. Reading and writing complement each other as means of understanding and being understood. They are the principal ways that scholars play their roles, both in the academic life of the college and across the centuries in the continuing scholarly enterprise.

Speaking

Students and faculty must also talk to each other. A great deal of learning is direct discourse, hammering out clear and distinct ideas on the anvil of conversation. Discussion does not replace reading and writing, but it carries the process of learning forward from the basic ideas and concepts found in reading and writing. Discussion is based on thorough acquaintance with the content and technique of the subject and with one's own interests in it. One must know something to talk about. Recognition of the interests and purposes of others is necessary so that common interests and agreement and clear differences of opinion and point of view can come out of the discussion.

The forms of scholarly discourse range from the most highly conventionalized to the most free and informal patterns. Debate and parliamentary procedure, on the one hand, are highly conventional forms in which manners and courtesy, logical forms of argument, and appropriate forms of conclusions are defined according to a very strict pattern. At the other end of the scale, the free exchange of ideas and feelings in ordinary conversation is a type of scholarly discourse that allows great variety in form and mood of contributions and great informality in organization of the group.

The conventions and rules of the game in formal procedures such as debate as well as in informal discussion specify principally the order in which the discussion shall proceed. There is an orderly sequence in which different kinds of statements shall be made. The subject has to be specified at the outset, for example, in the statement of a proposition in positive form for debate: "Resolved: that the United States recognize Red China." Informal discussions must stick to a general subject.

A second rule is that terms must be defined. Words cannot just mean what one says they mean; they must be used in a way clearly understood by others. A dictionary is an indispensable arbiter; a thesaurus helps a student discover words that convey meaning with more precision or greater weight.

A third rule is that facts must be distinguished from theories and presuppositions must be clearly expressed. All three must be brought into the open. Facts represent the hard reality that has to be accepted by everybody. Theories represent the possibilities for developing new facts or new interests. Presuppositions or assumptions underlie differences of interest or perspective, and stating them clearly as such insures against misunderstanding people or confusing untested assumptions with tested facts.

A fourth rule is that the discussion must get somewhere. Conclusions must be reached; decisions must be made; participants must make up their minds. Scholarly discourse differs from conversation or bull sessions in this respect; academic work has to lead to something of value while other talk can be less purposeful and just talk. Debates are supposed to clarify and support propositions; parliamentary processes lead to decisions on general policies or a program of action; academic discussion leads to conclusions, agreements (including agreement to disagree), problems or issues for further study.

A fifth rule calls for distinguishing judgments of fact from judgments of value. Participants in discussion are tempted to present personal value judgments as if they were facts, and sometimes they do not even clearly distinguish between them in their own minds. The effect is to require the rest of the group to concentrate on one participant's personal preferences, giving them greater weight than the facts and the realities of the situation. The place for introducing value judgments is at the point of making a decision or expressing preferences for action. But introducing them as matters of fact is an attempt to gain a personal advantage and to turn the discussion to oneself, not the objective issue, as the main subject.

A sixth rule is that judgment of personal character is not an appropriate subject. Discussion is a useful way of learning when it is centered on ideas not persons, presuppositions not character, conclusions not personal preferences. Students need to protect the freedom of their colleagues to introduce facts, opinions, and value judgments without fear of reprisal or exclusion from the discussion. Thus, the etiquette of discourse provides expressions of respect—"sir," or "miss," "the gentleman from Virginia," "the honorable opponents." Statements are addressed, in parliamentary form, to the chair, in a detached way, indicating that personalities are not involved in the discussion. Scholarly relationships are protected by the freedom with which ideas are exposed to searching criticism without passing judgment on the character of the person presenting them.

Manners and courtesy, suspension of judgment on character, and clarity in distinctions between different forms of statements help to improve the quality of discussion. Over and above manners, however, the student can lubricate discussion and encourage others to participate

freely by responding attentively to the contributions of others, by helping others make their ideas clear, and by trying to identify common
interests or points of agreement that may lead to firm, well-supported
conclusions.

Classroom discussion, whether formal or informal, is considered valuable for three reasons. It increases the range of ideas and interests that
can be opened up for study. At the same time, it tends to heighten the
attention of students, which has to be very actively engaged in following a pattern of discussion that is less well-organized than the usual
lecture. And it increases the motivation of students and reinforces learning because it offers the rewards of attention and responsiveness from
other people.

But these advantages hold good only where there is positive effort on
the part of both students and teachers to make effective use of discussion in learning. The teacher who uses seminar, debate, or discussion
methods should take some responsibility for helping students improve
their skill in using these methods. And students also must be sensitive
to the effects of their participation on others in the class and make sure
that they contribute to the advantages desired for everybody.

Speech is one of the things which separates man from the brutes. It
opens up possibilities of relationships to others, of responses that advance knowledge, of procedures that improve control of both judgment
and practice. Bull sessions, class discussions, seminars, debates, and
parliamentary decisions are not the fount of wisdom. But they do afford
resources in the cultivation of imagination, the development of judgment, and the control of processes of reasoning. Skill in their use en-
hances the capacity of the student for developing his own scholarship
and contributing to the work of his fellow scholars.

GENERAL INTELLECTUAL METHODS

An intellectual method, as distinct from a skill, has three elements.
It is applicable to a particular body of subject matter or set of problems.
It employs a set of skills or procedures appropriate to the content. It
employs certain standards of adequacy for determining when a particular judgment has been made correctly. The scholar selects an appropriate method according to the content of his subject, the skills he can
apply, and the objectives he wishes to achieve.

Scholarly methods are designed to handle questions, problems and
unsettled issues of doubt or disbelief. Answers to questions, beliefs,
opinions and tastes have to hold good for other scholars, as well as for

oneself, if doubts are to be satisfactorily resolved. The adequacy of scholarly methods, consequently, depends upon agreement among scholars on the conclusions to which the methods lead. This consensus of the people concerned is referred to by Raup[2] as "the common persuasion"; and the college, in his sense, is a "community of persuasion." So long as no questions are asked about a matter, the common persuasion holds that it is true, at least so far as it fits the experience of members of the community of persuasion. But as soon as doubt arises, or a question is asked, the matter becomes a subject for inquiry, which is not settled again until the people who are interested in it accept some conclusion as adequate for their needs and cease asking questions about it. The scholar wants not merely to resolve his own doubts or to be sure of his own results but also to have others resolve their similar doubts in the same way, to find his results adequate, or to help him correct his errors and find a more satisfactory way to settle the matter.

When we consider the kind of approval and acceptance that is appropriate between scholars, the kind that helps students learn, we are, therefore, going beyond ordinary personal acceptance and regard. The approval that is useful in scholarship goes beyond the ordinary everyday assurance, "Yes, it's OK if you say so," which leaves one wondering whether things *really* are OK, regardless of who says so. The assurance and approval that are effective in scholarship amount to saying, "Yes, I find it's OK by working the thing out the way you did." And equally reassuring is the response: "No, it didn't work out that way for me, but I think I have spotted a mistake in your method. Let's try it again." The formation of a community of persuasion in this way requires not only acceptance of the scholar as a person, but confirmation of his work in the experience of others. As Peirce puts it, "Unless we make ourselves hermits, we shall necessarily influence each other's opinions; so that the problem becomes how to fix belief, not in the individual merely, but in the community."[3]

Four principal methods are described below. They are not distinctions between subjects taught in college or between departments and divisions of the faculty. In choosing a major, or planning a career, or devising a plan for research, the student will have to make much finer distinctions. The four methods described here are distinguished from each other in the most general terms. The student will want to bear in mind that what is described in each instance is more a habit of mind, a purpose in thinking, a pattern of personal response than a particular course of study or major field. In using each method, the student will have to play a role that will fit the subject and the technique.

Mathematics and logic

Mathematics and logic are methods of choice when a scholar plays the role of organizer, clarifier, classifier. When a student wants to put ideas into systematic form, he uses some sort of mathematical or logical method. If he wishes to calculate or figure out the results of a process, mathematics is the most likely method. If he wishes to give a picture of his line of thought, he is most likely to use some form of logic. Mathematics and logic are alike in at least one respect; they are both useful in enabling one person to follow the line of reasoning of another. Another way of putting it is to say that mathematics and logic are methods of notation, a kind of shorthand that makes it possible to record rather briefly long chains of complex ideas.

For example, in writing a lecture or in taking notes, both teachers and students generally use an *outline.* There are several types of outlines. All are *logical forms.* They usually start with a statement of the topic, then give some assumptions about it, follow with a detailed description of the evidence for and against the assumptions, and end with some conclusions about the topic.

There are several different logical forms in which logical chains of reasoning can be followed. But they all have the same sequence: a beginning, a middle, and an end. They begin where the process of reasoning began, go on through the evidence, and end with a conclusion. Different forms usually are used for different types of evidence. The logical sequence enables one person to begin where another began, follow his line of reasoning, and see how he came out in the end. The *form* has to be clearly followed, regardless of the content, for this process of following the line of thought to be possible.

This is why so much time is spent in high school making outlines of readings or preparing outlines for written work. Students have to learn the *logical form* itself in order to use it effectively. If a student has not learned to use an outline before he enters college, he can ask an English instructor to give him some help in its use. Otherwise he will have a great deal of difficulty in writing term papers and reports—just as Jessica did in the course in English novels.

Learning to outline is not just a matter of learning to number major headings with Roman numerals and subheadings with capitals or Arabic numerals. It is not the index numbers that are important but the logical relationships in the sequence of topics. The student who has learned to make a good outline will probably find it easier to learn other logical forms in which to present his ideas and support his conclusions. Following is a sample of a logical outline:

I. Introduction
  A. The subject
    1⎫
    2⎬ Parts of the general subject
    3⎭
  B. Assumptions about the subject
    1⎫
    2⎬ Various assumptions
    3⎭
  C. Purpose of the paper
II. Evidence for the assumptions
  A.⎫
  B.⎬ Facts and opinions of others
  C.⎭
III. Evidence against the assumptions
  A.⎫
  B.⎬ Facts and opinions of others
  C.⎭
IV. Conclusion
  A. What the facts show
  B. What opinions I agree with or disagree with
  C. What I now believe about the subject

Most students probably know many more forms of logic than they realize. Like the man in the Molière comedy who suddenly realized he had been speaking prose all his life, students have been using logical forms all their lives without knowing it. For example, grammar is a form of logic, and diagramming sentences makes use of a kind of *symbolic* logic by drawing a picture of the relations between various parts of a sentence. The diagram (see Fig. 7-2) helps to show whether the parts of the sentence fit together properly. In this example one can easily see whether all the parts of the sentence are there. It is a complete sentence; it has a subject and predicate for both parts of the main line are filled. It is easy to check to see if the number of the subject and verb agree.

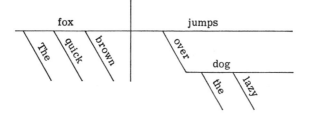

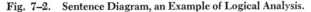

Fig. 7–2. Sentence Diagram, an Example of Logical Analysis.

Fox is a singular form and so is *jumps*, the related verb. One advantage of various forms of symbolic logic is the ease with which a student can see whether different ideas fit together. Some forms of symbolic logic make it possible to check, in quite simple diagrammatic form, exceedingly complex relationships of ideas. Even when the student is not exactly sure about the precise meaning of ideas, or is using unknown factors, he can record them and use them in reasoning out their relationships by using some symbolic form.[4]

Mathematics, like logic, offers many different systems of notation, including numerals and various signs representing relationships of different sorts: $x + y$, for instance, stands for one quantity added to another. The relation is clear, although both quantities are unknown. The relation of being added is the same when both quantities are known: $4 + 3$ stands for the same relation. It is easier to write $x + y = z$ than "The sum of any two whole numbers is a third whole number." It is easier to write $4 + 3 = 7$ than to write "If I have four horses and buy three more, I have seven horses."

In both examples, another relation, that of equality, is introduced, and the form is an equation, in which everything on one side must balance everything on the other. The form of the equation makes it possible to check the results obtained by making sure it balances. This checking feature is another advantage of mathematics, which is designed to be self-correcting; mathematics makes it possible to recognize and correct errors easily.

Mathematics and logic are not given by the world or nature. They are not present in everybody's experience. They are inventions of the human mind, which make it possible to have certain kinds of ideas and to communicate them to other people clearly. The forms have to be learned; they are not caught or inborn. Some kinds of mathematics, for instance, do not even fit the kind of world we live in but are invented to describe a very different kind of universe.[5] Such a universe may or may not exist. But by checking the way ideas about it fit the logical or mathematical forms prescribed for it, a scholar can follow the ideas expressed about it. The forms make sense, whether the content is nonsense or common sense.

For example, in ordinary arithmetic, $a + b$ and $b + a$ express the same relations. But in certain kinds of mathematics dealing with topology, $a + b$ and $b + a$ are quite different relations. These forms may describe the sequence in which things are related to each other or the position of things in space. So when a comes before b, the relation is different from b coming before a. This looks like nonsense, from the point of view of third-grade arithmetic. But from the point of view of a rocket guidance system, the sequence in which a and b are added to each other makes a lot of difference. The rocket will follow a different track depending on whether its guidance system gets the information $a + b$ or $b + a$.

The forms of mathematics and logic can convey many different kinds of meaning. The student cannot assume that they mean anything he wants them to mean. Each form conveys just the meaning it is designed to convey, and nothing more. For instance, logical systems of classification tell a great deal about the relation of classes and their members. They make it possible to distinguish between categories or classes of things on the basis of the common qualities or characteristics of their members. The classic form of the logic of classes is the syllogism: "All A is B; this is an A; therefore this is B." "All human beings are capable of speech; all students are human beings; therefore all students are capable of speech." It is a way of saying, "Things belonging to the same class have the same characteristic."

The logic of classes is used in subjects requiring identification of things on the basis of their qualities: chemistry, biology, art history, archaeology, geology, for example. But the logic of classes has no forms in which other relations can be put. "X is greater than y," for instance, or "Charles is the son of James," do not fit into a system of classification that is based on classes and their qualities.

So if a student finds that one form of logic or mathematics does not fit the meaning he is trying to convey, he must try another. For example, in recent years, a logic of relations has been developed with some mathematical systems of computation to go along with it. These systems, plus the introduction of electronic computation, make it possible to handle very complex chains of ideas or to calculate variable or unknown quantities, which cannot be handled just by classification. "X is greater than y; y is less than z; therefore x is either greater or less than z," may not seem to get you anywhere. But it does indicate that the relation of x to z is *variable* and cannot be used as a constant, a fixed element in further calculations. The logic of relations makes it possible to work out chains of ideas including relations of constancy and variability, direction, sequence, and other quite complex relations. For example, the logic of relations and the statistical treatment of probability (the odds for and against something happening) make it possible to analyze such complex forms of human behavior as voting, purchasing, marriage, economic development, to name only a few. In pre-election polls, for instance, the number of undecided voters questioned has to be treated as a variable, an element of uncertainty that affects the accuracy of the prediction of the election results.

Mathematical and logical information can be mastered just by rote memory, as we learn the multiplication table. But there are two shortcomings to the use of memory: It is difficult to recognize errors, especially if the information has been incorrectly memorized. And it is difficult to introduce new information or identify unknown factors. If mathematical and logical material are learned by studying the general form in which it is organized, the student will gain two advantages. He can use the methods more readily to correct his own errors. And he can fit new material into the system more accurately and easily.

For example, Jessica's problem in the English novel course may be regarded as a failure to understand the logic of relations. Her ideas were just strung together like wash on a line, without any relation to her conclusions. She learned to criticize and improve her own work by studying the forms of logical relations so that she could see whether one of her ideas really led to another. Just memorizing the proper form of outline did not help her see whether her ideas were logically related, because she had never understood what the parts of an outline meant.

Most courses include some introduction to the forms used in communicating ideas. In the study of languages, grammar is introduced as a method of understanding the relations that determine the meaning of words. A student who understands the forms of grammar in English can grasp more quickly the form of other languages. And if he understands grammatical relations, he can often grasp the meaning of words with which he is not very familiar by figuring out the meaning they must have to complete the sense of other words in a sentence. In courses using systems of classification, such as biological sciences, the student can often classify an unfamiliar plant or animal, figuring out its genus and species by matching its characteristics with those of different classes to see which it fits.

One advantage of mathematical and logical methods is that they are designed to be self-correcting, to show whether or not things fit together. Addition can be checked by subtraction, division by multiplication in mathematical forms that are reversible. Logical forms also make it possible to check results for "fit." One rule, for instance, holds that only things belonging to the same class can be compared with each other. So a student in statistics, for example, may check to make sure he has compared percentages with percentages, not percentages with whole numbers. In elementary arithmetic, this principle is learned by solving problems requiring accurate reading. "If John has two bushels of apples and five bushels of potatoes, and buys fourteen bushels of wheat, five bushels of apples, and six bushels of potatoes, how many bushels of apples does he have?" is the type of question that has trapped many an unwary student into answering 32. Apples cannot be added to potatoes, and a check of the logic of the problem shows the error and the correct answer, "7 bushels of apples." But the student cannot learn to recognize and correct such errors on his own without understanding the principles on which logical and mathematical forms are based.

Another advantage of mathematical and logical methods is that the forms used are designed to hold good, regardless of the person using them. What fits the forms for the teacher also fits the forms for the student. If they use the same forms, they can be sure they are talking about the same thing, and it is easier to understand one another. "All creatures having one eye and one horn and eating purple people are purple people-eaters; this creature has one eye and one horn and eats purple people; therefore it is a purple people-eater," follows a valid form of the syllogism, and both student and teacher can see that it is logically adequate, regardless of whether they like each other, believe in purple people-eaters, or prefer pink to purple people. Whether the ideas fit the forms correctly, whether the sequence of ideas leads to a conclusion is not a matter of personalities. Self-esteem or friendship are not involved in deciding whether an assumption is proved by the evidence or whether an equation balances. On the contrary, self-esteem can be bolstered or friendship strengthened by testing the adequacy of conclusions, the proof of assumptions, the accuracy of definitions and calculations. If his work proves adequate, the student feels like and is treated like a competent, worthwhile sort of person.

This does not mean that disagreements between scholars or unpleasant personal relationships can be resolved by simple calculation. Personal relationships, tastes, preferences are suspended in the course of logical and mathematical analysis. Some have, therefore, hoped that machine computation could take over the task of resolving disputed questions, leaving scholars' opinions and reputations out of it. Such hopes are probably excessive.[6] Logical and mathematical analysis is only one step in the whole process of scholarly work. It *leads* to conclusions, but scholars have to *draw* those conclusions. Then an important step must be taken: that of sharing the process of study and the conclusions with other scholars. The criticism, agreement, and disagreement of other scholars builds a community of persuasion that supports the whole set of ideas and brings it into the common body of knowledge. These tasks cannot be performed by machine alone.

Furthermore, during the college years, the student begins to build a reputation for himself as a scholar. His reputation for logical thinking, mathematical accuracy, and clarity of expression depends on his ability to use proper forms for analyzing and communicating ideas. If he tries to share his work, if he puts it in understandable form, he shows the personal regard for other scholars that is required in the intellectual professions. One great mark of personal regard is honesty among friends. And one advantage of mathematics and logic as intellectual methods is the assurance they can give the student that he is being honest with himself and frank and fair in his relations with his teachers and fellow students. If he understands the forms he is using, he can check his results for himself and be sure of their logical adequacy and mathematical accuracy. Then he can present his work in such a form that others can repeat it to see if they get the results to confirm or correct his conclusions.

Science

The forms of logic and mathematics are sometimes called "empty" forms. That is, they can hold any meaning that is put into them, sense or nonsense, reality or fantasy. *Alice in Wonderland* and *Through the Looking-Glass*, for instance, are wonderfully precise and accurate logical exercises although the content is pure nonsense. But if it is assumed that a grin exists in itself independent of any face to wear it, there can be a grin without a cat, as well as a cat without a grin, as the Cheshire Cat patiently explains to Alice. As Lewis Carroll points out in another work, logic simply insures that the shorthand is properly transcribed, that the conclusions follow the assumptions and the evidence; it doesn't have anything to do with whether the assumptions, evidence, and conclusions are sense or nonsense.[7]

So when a student is sure that the forms in which his ideas are expressed are logically and mathematically sound, he still does not know whether his ideas make any sense in relation to the world in which he lives. If he is trying to find out whether his ideas can be regarded as facts, or have any basis in reality, he has to use another method. It is the method of science that deals with the kind of sense ideas make in relation to hard reality. Science has been developed for the purpose of determining the nature of things as they are, or were, or can be. Science is used to tell whether things are what we believe them to be, regardless of our personal preferences or feelings about them.

Of course, it is probably too much to expect that what science tells us exists independent of the involvement of the human mind in it. The facts of science are determined in relation to the scientist and his apparatus, which affect the results. For example, in intelligence testing, the standard deviation allows for errors due to the process of testing itself. Even so, what science tells us is probably a good deal closer to reality than vague feelings and untested notions about the world we live in. At least, scientific facts have stood up better under the test of experience in the production of goods and services and in the practice of medicine. And the facts are established in such a way that they can be checked by other scientists using the same process and apparatus. A community of persuasion thus forms around scientific facts and helps to support, correct, or refine them.

Students use scientific methods when they are playing the role of investigator. Exploring, observing, experimenting, testing, all are roles in which science is the method of choice. When facts are needed, the student uses scientific method.

Scientific inquiry begins with an image of the way things will work out provided certain processes are followed. This is called an hypothesis. Sometimes scientists just invent an hypothesis and try to find evidence for it; sometimes they work back from evidence in experience or experimentation and devise an hypothesis that looks as if it would fit the evidence. In working out his general theory of relativity, for example, Einstein was trying to devise a new hypothesis that would cover some observations that did not fit Newton's theories about time and space relations in the universe as well as those that did fit.

Next the evidence for and against the hypothesis is found. Different techniques are used, depending on the subject matter. In history, for instance, events that are presumed to have occurred are checked by *documentation*. That is, if William Jennings Bryan is supposed to have made a speech in Ottumwa on July 16, 1896, the local papers are checked to see if they report the speech. The discovery of the ruins of Troy and the study of the trash heaps left by people successively occupying the site confirmed the historical fact that Troy existed and suggested that certain parts of Homer's and Virgil's writings may be regarded as historical. The evidence was there to confirm the story they told.

Different subjects require different kinds of evidence. In sociology, analysis of voting requires not only suitable statistical measurements, but also evidence that the people studied actually do vote—voting lists from polling places, for example. In chemistry or physics, experimental evidence is needed; the processes covered by the hypothesis are carried out in the laboratory, and the results are observed and measured to see whether the facts support the hypothesis, whether things worked out as it suggested they would.

Logical and mathematical forms are essential parts of scientific inquiry. The process of reasoning from the hypothesis to the results has to fit a proper logical or mathematical form. The hypothesis is a kind of assumption; if it is true, certain characteristic events will be observed; if they appear, then the conclusion may be drawn that it is a confirmed fact. For instance, it can be assumed that unicorns did exist. Other animals that once existed left their fossil remains in the rocks. The remains of unicorns should also be found—skeletons with one horn and equine form. So far no such remains have been found. So it is still concluded that the unicorn is a mythical beast. The evidence that should be there has not been found, so the hypothesis is not proved.

Scientific inquiry thus proceeds from an hypothesis through the evidence to a conclusion. The outline of steps is something like that following:

   I. Hypothesis
       A. Assumptions
       B. Evidence predicted
       C. Statement of theory to be tested
  II. Evidence
       A. Procedures followed
       B. Results obtained
           1. Positive
           2. Negative
 III. Conclusions
       A. Assumptions proved and disproved
       B. Conclusions
           1. Proved
           2. Disproved
           3. Doubtful
       C. Further hypotheses suggested by results

The development of new, complex systems of logic and mathematics has been speeded by the need of methods for systematically describing conditions under which complex hypotheses would be true. For example, the field of meteorology covers numerous complex factors, involving the use of both chemistry and physics. The hypothesis that it will rain under certain conditions can be checked by observation of air and cloud conditions, temperature and pressure changes, and the like. The meteorologist uses a very ingenious kind of mathematical logic, the mathematics of probability, to predict rain. He is working on a system of logic that is like laying odds in gambling. Frequent observation of the weather indicates that a rise in temperature or barometric pressure changes the odds, that is, increases or reduces the probability that it will rain, by a certain amount. Some weather bureaus issue predictions giving the odds: "Probability of rain: 90 percent." (This does not mean that if you go out in the rain you will only get 90 percent wet.) But this is still a hypothesis, a prediction. It can never be anything else. Only if it does rain is the hypothesis proved and rain a fact. The meteorologist cannot use his method to prove facts, but only to improve the odds on his predictions. He cannot be 100 percent accurate, for he is not trying for complete proof. His kind of science yields, not proven facts, but better knowledge of probabilities.

Thus, some kinds of scientific inquiry do not result in hard facts. They just help people improve their predictions and make better guesses. Even such limited gains are worthwhile. Modern weather forecasts are something of an improvement over the inspection of chicken gizzards and the pains in Grandpa's knee. In economics, the prediction of supply and demand, consumer preferences, and price movements is based on hypothetical principles, but it is still an improvement on uninformed hunches and guesses. Modern logic and mathematics have made it possible to apply scientific method to many new fields. They have been particularly useful in making it possible to know something about previously unknown matters. And methods of probability make it possible to know within pretty narrow limits just how much error has to be allowed for in what is known.

The student needs to be familiar with scientific method since one of his principal tasks in learning is to distinguish between facts and theories, between evidence and gossip, between experience and imagination. This is not just part of his work as a scholar. Familiarity with scientific method is essential to self-understanding. For the self exists in relation to reality. And the better his understanding of reality, the better understanding the student will have of his relation to it. So unicorns are mythical beasts; he can still enjoy the image of the gentle, proud beast and understand what it means to poets and mythologists as a symbol, not of fact, but of dreams and feelings and hopes. So there is 20 percent probability of rain; he will get wet if he is caught out in it, but there are four chances out of five that he will not need his umbrella today so he will leave it at home. So the Russians say the moons of Mars are artificial satellites; he would like to check the theory as a project in astronomy. His pleasure, his practical decisions, his interests can be understood and used more effectively as they are sharpened by scientific knowledge.

But this does not mean that the student should just memorize all the facts he possibly can. This is no way to learn the method of science. And it is the method, not just the facts it produces, that he must learn if he is to be an educated person. Mastering the method of science enables him to figure out the facts for himself. If he just accepts the facts that he gets from authorities on the subject, he is still subject to their authority. He can get some authority for himself if he learns the method. If he learns to figure out the facts and understand reality for himself, he becomes the driver, not the driven.

His independence is increased. He has direct access to reality and can understand it for himself without relying altogether on what some-one else tells him. He does not have to depend on memory alone; he can figure out the conclusions from the facts that are given. He can use his own experience more effectively as a source of information that can be used to test his view of reality and to guide his plans and behavior.

In the second place, the use of scientific method gives the student something to do with his failures. If the evidence in favor of his hypothe-sis is not found, he at least knows one thing that is not a fact. And if he is acquainted with logical and mathematical analysis, he can make use of negative results to see if they suggest a better hypothesis. His failures can be used to turn from unproductive toward more promising ideas.

In the third place, scientific inquiry can open up a wide range of interests and ideas. We have just begun the scientific study of the uni-verse and human life. The student who is prepared to use scientific methods of inquiry has a magnificent opportunity to find exciting and useful work. The student today stands on the shoulders of generations of men of science who have devised some methods and suggested some theories. But above him there is no apparent limit to the work to be done. This holds as true for the student of history, literature, psy-chology, or government as for the chemist, physicist, or biologist. Scholars have just begun to see what scientific inquiry will do. The student today has a magnificent chance to apply it to problems and questions that will make a vast amount of difference in the understand-ing that people have of themselves and their world. Even if he does not become a scientist, he can use the method of science to enrich his life and that of others.

Finally, the attitude of mind required by the method of science is significant in a student's self-development. To face the facts as they are and to accept reality bring one a long step toward maturity as a person. To deal honestly and logically with the facts makes him less likely to depend on self-deception to get along in the world. For the defense mechanisms of deception are essentially self-deceiving; and the habit of recognizing and accepting the realities is a more effective way of dealing with life than self-deception, blind faith, or submissive "adjustment." A student who employs the scientific method can adjust to the realities with some knowledge of the consequences for himself and others. He can foresee more of the probable consequences of his behavior and can accept or avoid them as seems best for him. He can submit his beliefs and opinions to the test of experience, experiment and observation and strengthen them as an effective defense against anxieties, threats, and fears. He knows more about where he stands. This kind of knowledge of self-in-relation-to-reality appears to be a great need of students.

In counseling interviews, many students say, "the worst part of it all is *not knowing*." The unknown does occasion a great deal of anxiety. Some things, of course, people cannot know. But science offers a very promising way of finding out about some aspects of the unknown. It can help a person to push back some of the dark. Even in the dark one can go along with less fear, for science provides a way of knowing what one is doing, even when dealing with the unknown. It offers a way of going ahead and trying to work things out in spite of anxiety. It identifies the things that are really to be feared, and knowing what to fear is better than being anxious about the unknown. To know what is there helps a student figure out where he is, where he is going, what he can do. As the motto of Phi Beta Kappa has it, "The love of wisdom is the guide of life."

Art

Logical analysis, mathematical calculation, and scientific inquiry are not the only ways of knowing. We know, for instance, that we enjoy something. The intellectual method that applies to enjoyment is the method of art. It is a way of understanding how things come to be beautiful, satisfying, pleasing. And it is a way of creating things that are enjoyable, beautiful, full of feeling and meaning that cannot be put into logical or factual form.

The role of the student in using the method of art is different from his role in logical or scientific judgment. In the first place, when he uses the method of art, his role is more active and he is more fully engaged in the work. He creates a work of art; he makes or performs or creates something. He enjoys a work of art created or performed by someone else. In either instance, he is involved in the experience and responsible for the meaning that emerges. Instead of working with forms of analysis and inquiry that yield meaning regardless of the person who carries out the process, he is working with a method that is personal. In this method the meaning that emerges depends on him as a self in relation to the work of art. The method will not work and works of art will have no meaning for him unless he becomes personally involved.

The student, in creating or appreciating art, must know what he is doing. By being aware of his role, understanding and accepting it, and playing it effectively, he employs art as an intellectual method. In this way, he participates in art through his own works or the works of others. Unfortunately no word in English to use for the role of the person who is enjoying a work of art compares to the word artist or creator. Audience, public, observer and the like are not adequate; for what is important is active participation in experience, putting oneself into it, which is not necessarily true of all members of the audience or public. Participant will be used here to indicate the role; though it does not quite convey the whole idea.

Both roles are very important in the method of art. The artist creates a work and endows it with meaning. The participant enjoys the work by finding meaning in it for himself. Whether the artist's own idea can be found in the work is a matter for the art critic to decide. The artist and the participant do not have to agree on the meaning of the work; in this respect, artistic judgment is different from logical or scientific judgment. But the participant must confirm the artist's feeling that the work has meaning; he must find some meaning in it for himself. In this respect, art forms, like logical forms, are ways in which one person can enable other persons to follow the way his mind went; the difference is that it is both possible and desirable for one to come out at a slightly different point from the other. The participant may find something in the work that the artist was not aware of; in fact, the artist may rather hope he will. So the participant to some extent shares the creative function of the artist and adds to the meaning of the work.

There are two roles that a student can play in relation to a work of art. He may create it and endow it with a meaning of his own. Or he may enjoy it and add to the artists' idea some meaning from his own experience. (There is a third role required of some art forms, that of performer of someone else's work in music, drama, or dance.) All require knowledge of the method of art. And all require a high degree of personal involvement. The student must really feel something, he must really *care*, if art is to mean anything to him.

In the second place, the meaning of the work of art does not have to be nearly so precisely or clearly expressed as the ideas conveyed in scientific inquiry. As a matter of fact, a certain amount of vagueness and ambiguity may be desirable to permit the participant to enter into the experience without feeling constrained to make his ideas conform to those of the artist. The degree of personal involvement required for enjoyment reduces the degree of precision that can be achieved.

This lack of precise meanings or clear limits to ideas makes some people feel uneasy about art. "There is no telling what it means!" "There is no telling what might happen if artists go on doing that sort of thing!" they say. This uneasiness may be related to the fear of the unknown. Sometimes quite unnecessary and ridiculous constraints are placed on the meaning people are allowed to see in works of art, apparently for no reason but the fear of something that is not quite clear. Statues of Venus are no longer draped in decent Victorian skirts as they were in the days when our grandparents were altogether too clear about what they *feared* to know. Censors are quite firm about the kind of ideas that have to be cut out of movies and plays. But one mother tells the story of the museum guard who angrily forbade her children to close their eyes and run their fingers over the Brancusi piece plainly labeled "Sculpture for the Blind"; she herself narrowly escaped arrest for suggesting that they touch it. And the furor over the American paintings sent to the 1959 Moscow exhibition was occasioned, apparently, by fear of what the painters thought about politics as well as fear of what the Russians might think about Americans. Nobody seemed much concerned about what the Russians would think about the paintings.

Latitude in interpretation is particularly apparent in the performing arts. The actor, dancer, or musician is an intermediary between the creator of the work and the audiences. Music, for instance, is not performed as a transcription of a code, but as a reproduction of the composer's idea as it is conceived by the performer. The performer's idea is not the same as that of the composer in all respects. Differences in interpretation lend the freshness and variety that make repeated performances of music vivid and exciting rather than mechanical and boring.* What is required is some knowledge of the composer's intention and sufficient faithfulness to his meaning to enable the audience to grasp it. What the audience hears and the varied meanings they find in the work will differ somewhat from the ideas of both composer and performer. But the work is the same for all of them; they have a common experience with it although its meanings are not limited to those per-

---

* I am indebted to Mr. Alexander Liberman of Mills College for the opportunity to see how this principle can be applied to the teaching of music, both in music appreciation and in instrumental instruction.

ceived by any one person involved. There is no right and wrong meaning to be found in it; there is a range of meanings expressed and understood. Short of complete misunderstanding, such as taking a waltz for a funeral dirge, there is plenty of room for differences in conception of meaning and for differences in feeling and enjoyment.

For art is made to be enjoyed, and enjoyment is highly personalized. Works of art endure in time as they are incorporated in the experience of participants. They have a kind of developmental history, in which their qualities and meanings enlarge and change with the response of participants.

Learning in art as in science, therefore, requires direct experience. To learn how to create works of art, the student must master some technique, some art form, and some material or medium. He must create his own works. He has to produce paintings, drawings, engravings, sculpture, pottery, poems, stories, novels of his own. To learn how to perform, he has to play an instrument or sing, act in plays, or dance. To learn how to enjoy art, he has to see it, hear it, and find his own meaning in it.

The student who is producing or performing works of art needs to improve his skill. He needs to learn to see the participants' point of view to determine how his idea comes through for them. Thus teachers and fellow students play a very important part in improving his techniques and bringing his ideas off in better form. They give expert advice. And they function as participants who can give a response directly to the artist—something which, outside the college, is not always so readily available. He can use their reactions to find ways to improve his works or his performance, to bring out his ideas so that the participants can see them more clearly in his work.

Techniques in art are varied and materials almost unlimited in variety. But form, technique, and material have to be suited to the idea and fit together properly. Sounds can be used in ways that wood, stone, paper, paint, and canvas cannot. Bodily movement can be put into patterns that words cannot assume. Words can convey ideas that pictures cannot. Complex art forms—dance, drama, opera, for example—combine several forms, many different techniques and materials to extend greatly the range of ideas that can be communicated in the work. The artist organizes his ideas around the form (music, painting, poetry, dance). He chooses materials that fit his form (sound, pigments, words, movements) and applies his technique (his way of working with the material) to express his individual ideas.

There is no substitute in art for experience with materials and practice of technique. Art is hard work, and practice is the key to effective use of the method. And it must be informed, intelligent, critical practice. Musicians, for example, have to know the theory of harmony (essentially a kind of mathematics) in order to get a clear idea of the nature of sounds, the relations between tones, the permutations of chords. Given some clarity of understanding of the harmonic relationships in music, musicians develop more sense of its dynamics and can develop better techniques for moving the audience into the meaning of the works they perform. The potter who knows enough chemistry to mix materials for body and glazes can come nearer getting the effects he wants and expressing the image in his mind than the one who just uses whatever he can get. Watching a musician, painter, or potter with highly developed technique is beautiful in itself. The grace, precision, smoothness, and economy of movement is lovely, almost a dance. One way a skillful artist can tell his work is good is that he feels good doing it. But the good feeling comes only with understanding of the theory of the art form, long experience and experimentation with the materials, and constant practice of the technique.

Of course, one essential element in art is talent, a gift for the work. Talent seems to be distributed among the human race at random; most people seem to have a gift for something; and many have talent who do not cultivate it. Artists of great talent seem to be born, not made, and in the most unlikely places, although there appears to be some tendency for talent to run in families—whether by heredity or contagion we cannot say: look at all the Bachs and Breughels, for example! To judge from recent studies of creativity, artists, like mathematicians, have to be caught young. (Perhaps good participants also are caught young.) At least, the signs of creative ability appear very early in childhood, and this ability continues to develop if encouraged by parents and teachers. There are artistic geniuses who just cannot be stopped, like Giotto or Leonardo da Vinci. Given half a chance, the talented student will practice, study, and master his medium and technique long before he enters college.

Of course, there are students of mediocre talent or of no talent at all, but with an intense interest in art. For them, art is still a valuable way of knowing. For art gives access to the experience of beauty, which can be had even if it is not made for oneself. This experience in itself is something of value, for it extends the range of knowledge and enlarges the self.

There is, of course, no reason at all why students of modest talent should not cultivate it for their own pleasure if for no other reason. But sometimes college art teachers are unhappy about having such students; for various reasons, both acceptable and questionable, they prefer to work with more gifted and experienced students. One faculty adviser, who urged all his students to meet the art requirement by taking a course in which they produced or performed works of art, was practically mobbed by irate colleagues for "forcing all those nincompoops with no talent into our classes." The outcry died down a little the following spring when some of the "nincompoops" turned in some pretty creditable work. His stock even went up a little in the drama department, where one shy little "nincompoop" was discovered to have a gift for playing comic roles, and in the art department, where one boy who had never touched a brush before turned out some beautiful canvases and went on to be an art major. Naturally, college is a little late to start if a student expects to develop effective technique and really outstanding skill. But there is no reason not to try something one has always wanted to do. Any talent is worth cultivating. There is a pleasure in creating one's own works that is like nothing else on earth, and students who want it can get it if they try.

The plain untalented student can learn to enjoy art even though he cannot create it. Ways of enjoying art and participating in it can be learned. Indeed, many have to be learned. The more abstract the art form, the more the participant must contribute to its meaning; but he can only play his part if he has learned something about the way to see what the artist has in mind. And what the artist presents may or may not resemble anything in experience. So in understanding music, the participant has to listen for the changes and shifts in the sequences of tones, not just for a tune he can whistle. In understanding painting, he has to look for the relationships, movement, and changes of shapes, lines, and colors in space, not just for a photographic copy of something. For art, like logic and mathematics, employs "elegance," the harmony and beauty of relationships, as one of the standards of adequacy. It is a short step from *logical* elegance to "elegance" in art. The participant just has to know what to look for. The pattern of the painting, the harmonic structure of the music, has to be understood, even to get maximum meaning out of works, whether abstract or realistic, familiar or novel in form.

The student can learn by practice—by listening, seeing, reading. And he can improve his understanding by study of theory and technique— by learning something about the form of art, about aesthetic standards such as harmony and dissonance, elegance, symmetry and asymmetry, color, tone, and the like. He can learn something about the artists themselves, their personal style, the relation of their works to the ideas characteristic of the times in which they lived. Art history, for instance, may give him an understanding of the works of a period that helps him see more in the paintings and sculpture, that gives him the "feel" of the people and their lives as the artist put them into his work. Music history likewise adds meaning to music: The cannon in the *1812 Overture* are not just blasts, but Napoleon at the gates of Moscow—connoting invasion, terror, impending doom.

What art, both in creation and in enjoyment, can do is to open to a student a part of the world rich in ideas and feelings. Some ideas he cannot put into words can be realized in music, painting, or dance. Some feelings he could never understand may become quite clear and vivid as he participates in a work of art. The warmth and light and color of a summer day, for instance, may all come together at once in a single feeling of what summer is, as he sees, really *sees* a painting, such as Monet's *Water Lilies*. He may become fully aware of aspects of his own feelings and experience that were vague and unfocused before. His image of himself is enlarged and developed in the enjoyment of art. So even though his talents be small, or his tastes crude and uncouth, he can give himself a chance to develop in self-awareness by learning something about art. And if he has gifts, he can cultivate his capacity for creating works of art that can be shared by others and can open for himself and others a world of ideas that would otherwise remain unknown, private, inaccessible.

The value of art as an intellectual method is precisely this possibility of opening up a world, and a rich lovely one, wider than the world of logic and facts, more understandable than the world of random feelings. Art makes it possible for the sense of beauty, of deep and moving experience underlying the surface of reality, to become more than a private experience. Through the method and forms of art beauty can be opened up and shared with others.

Practical judgment

When it comes to putting knowledge into practice, the role that has to be played requires planning, decision, and action. Of course, someone else can do the planning, make decisions, and take the action. Most people probably prefer just to go along smoothly following instructions and obeying orders. However, in the occupations which most college students enter, doing a competent job requires self-direction and active engagement in planning. Even being a cog in an administrative machine requires some initiative and personal responsibility, not just submissive, routine work. The teacher, lawyer, engineer, physician, administrator must be the driver and not the driven. Effective practical judgment requires some clear conception of where one is going and what he is doing.

Consequently, it is extremely important for the student to see himself as an active participant in practical affairs, as a driver and director, not a mere cog in the machine. This image of himself as an active participant can emerge most readily out of some experience in making practical judgments. And his chances for effective self-direction in practical affairs are improved by familiarity with the intellectual method of practical judgment. If he has some familiarity with this method, he has a better chance to use his experience in college and at work to improve his performance and make more effective judgments of practice.

Learning the method of practical judgment is not as easy as it may seem. In the first place, mature practical judgments depend upon maturity of judgment in other intellectual methods. Practical decisions are better when they are based upon established fact; so skill in fact-finding and scientific method has to be developed. In practical affairs, a person commits himself and his interests to his course of action, as an artist reveals himself in art and commits himself to his work. The development of the capacity for self-expression may be improved by experience with the method of art and the cultivation of the habit of personal commitment that it involves. The ability to make plans that can be followed step by step is increased by skill in logical analysis and systematic organization of complex patterns of ideas. Students usually begin the study of practical methods while they are still developing skill in these other intellectual methods. As they improve their mastery of other methods, it becomes easier to master the necessary method of practical judgment.

Second, mistakes are inevitable in practical judgment. Even experienced people make a lot of errors. In practical affairs, a great many decisions have to be based on calculations of probability, rather than solely on established facts. The odds can be improved in favor of the decision, but there is rarely any absolute certainty that it will work out. In undertaking an operation, for example, there is a statistical possibility of failure in the patient's recovery which the surgeon simply has to accept. The probability is in favor of recovery, of course. But the risk has to be run, in the interest of the patient, if there are greater odds against the patient's survival without surgery. Practical judgments always involve some risk and some possibility of error. A student who is afraid of taking risks, who has to know the answer before he starts to work, will have great difficulty in mastering the method of practical judgment. A student who has not developed the capacity for self-correction will find it difficult to recognize and correct his mistakes in judgment. But skill in self-correction is essential, not only because errors are inevitable, but also because there are some aspects of practical judgment that can be learned only by making and correcting mistakes. For example, the ability to foresee and avoid undesirable outcomes can probably only be learned by failing at some practical task and then going back over the course of action to see where the failure could have been avoided. Thus, in working out designs of bridges that will withstand stress, engineers build scale models which are deliberately destroyed by subjecting them to excessive weights and strains; then they go back over the design to see where it can be changed and the structure strengthened.

Third, these inevitable mistakes make it hard for many students to accept their role in practical affairs. They are reluctant to try to learn the method of practical judgment because they do not like to fail or cannot see themselves as failing and learning from failure. Practical judgments are irreversible. Their consequences are inescapable. "What's done cannot be undone." Whether the consequences are desirable or undesirable, they are had in the end. And they belong to the student; he produced them. Usually the consequences are mixed, both good and bad. But a student whose self-image will not include the possibility of failure along with success may stop trying to learn. He may give up the attempt to learn how to make practical judgments because he cannot bear to take the bad consequences along with the good.

An average, run-of-the-mill student with a fairly healthy ego can usually master the method of practical judgment. The college provides a learning situation that makes it easier for him. Some of its advantages also protect those students with a less well-developed sense of identity. Under the protected conditions of college study, some of these students can also manage to take the risks and succeed quite well. But learning to make practical judgments requires either the ability or the willingness to take the knocks and keep on trying. Mastery of the method of practical judgment includes mastery of the self and development of mature strength, patience, and endurance in carrying out plans and decisions.

In college, the student has the advantage of some protection against the hard knocks of practical action. Since he is usually studying both practical and theoretical subjects at the same time, he can more easily correct practical errors due to faulty logic or fact-finding by concentrating on these weak spots in his study of other courses. Working back and forth between pure and applied intellectual methods can give him more skill and confidence in relating knowledge and practice. He cannot always expect to have this advantage when he is on the job.

In college study, too, the student has the advantage of working in a model situation where practice is reduced to the scale of his present capacity. Since the tasks undertaken are not all beyond his strength, his chances of success are increased. The practical effects of his errors are also reduced. He can see where he has succeeded and where he has failed. But the failures do not ordinarily have irrevocable effects on his future career. They are just plowed back into the process of learning as material for further study and improvement.*

College provides a way to experience the results of practical judgment in such a way as to support learning rather than interfere with it. Although very much involved in practice and closely identified with it, the student's personal identity, his selfhood, is not at stake in the process. He lives to try another day, rather than having his career wrecked by the outcome.

There are several ways in which the results can be learned without being suffered. The process may be suspended at the point of application: for instance, in moot court proceedings in the study of law, a decision is made and sentence pronounced, but the matter ends there. The consequences may be reduced to nominal cost, as in the case of the engineer's scale models which break under stress without much cost in material and with no loss of life. The consequences may be accepted by a small group willing to undertake the experiment but postponed so far as the rest of the college and community is concerned. For example, for over thirty years college YMCA and YWCA's and church-related student groups have worked with various plans to improve interracial relations and move toward integration. The program has affected only the student groups involved. But as colleges and communities have moved toward integration, many people who had experience with it in college have given useful leadership in working out the practical problems involved in communities, schools, and businesses.

Another protection for the student is afforded by practice in groups rather than individually. The group forms a kind of protective shield for its members, resisting attempts to interfere with the study of practi-

---

* The college is not the only institution in which such model situations are set up. They are used in other institutions providing training and education as a standard technique. In business, industry, and government, for example, they are frequently used, and they have the added advantage of being even closer to the actual practice being mastered.[8]

cal problems. For many judgments of practice are highly controversial; otherwise nothing could be learned from them. And the college has to protect its members from ill-considered reprisals or interference by people who fear or dislike controversy.

Group study of practical judgment is important for its own sake, however. A great many of the plans, decisions, and actions in practical affairs are carried out in groups. So the student has to learn how to participate in group processes of practical judgment as well as how to use the method individually. Furthermore, group judgments can be used to extend the range of practical judgment. They are not a substitute for individual judgment or a different kind of judgment altogether but a way of enlarging the scope and complexity of matters on which practical judgment can be made. The effective group extends, rather than limits, the resources of the self, and it improves the chances of its members to discover and achieve common purposes.

Six phases of the method of practical judgment appear in both group and individual judgment. First, *initiation* is the phase in which a problem or issue is presented. Second, *mediation* leads to clearer definition by enlarging or focusing the question on its principal elements. Third, *fact-finding* uses scientific method or common-sense observation to assess the reality of the situation, to see what is really the problem or what really can be done. Fourth, in the phase of *decision,* proposals for action are presented and thought through; consequences are foreseen; proposals are developed into plans. Fifth, *action* is taken; plans are carried out. Sixth, in the phase of *contemplation,* the action, plan, or problem is checked against personal interests and values to see if what is possible to achieve practically is actually desirable or valuable.[9]

Individual and group decision-making does not proceed systematically from the first through the sixth phase. Practical judgments are made by working back and forth among various phases. Facts may change the definition of a problem; contemplation may affect the decision on a plan. The phases are a logical analysis of a very complex method. They are described principally to help students check the adequacy of their use of the method by making sure that needed elements are present.

Learning the method of practical judgment requires a kind of courage in the student. He has to be strong enough to accept disappointing consequences of his judgment and still keep on trying to correct his errors and improve his chances of success. He has to be brave enough to submit novel ideas, serious problems, or cherished ambitions to the judgment of others, without fear of reprisal. He has to be firm enough to hold to his considered standards of value while making them available for the consideration of others. He must have the courage to be himself, to express himself freely, with honesty and integrity, on matters that are of intense personal interest. But if he can muster the courage to make his decisions, carry them out, and accept the consequences and if he can contribute his resources to others in achieving significant common purposes, he stands to gain increased support and encouragement from others and a broader range of experiences in the process of learning.

INTELLECTUAL METHODS AND
ACADEMIC SPECIALIZATION

The distinctions made among four methods of learning are purely logical distinctions. Science and art, logic and practical judgment differ in certain logically describable ways. But they are abstractions; that is, they do not represent in any direct way the operation of the mind. They are ways of confirming or validating learning after we have engaged ourselves in it. They do not describe any courses taught in college but are used in learning all kinds of subjects classified in many different ways. Colleges use much more detailed classifications in curriculum, major fields, and professional specialization.

Such detailed classification and specialization are necessary in scholarship. As a high school student explained after preparing an exhibit of ciliates in pond water for a science fair, "There is enough material in a drop of pond water to keep me busy for the rest of my life." Specialization is where you find it, and can be as narrowly or broadly conceived in relation to the range of possible knowledge as one desires. Sometimes new insights are gained by narrowing the field, sometimes by broadening it. Every shift in focus requires a shift in the method used; subject matter will have to be added or eliminated; techniques of handling the material will have to be selected or invented; criteria of adequacy will have to be selected to fit the purposes of the study.

No subject matter can be exclusively claimed for any particular course of study. Psychoanalysis and anthropology have contributed to each other with an exchange of concepts, subject matter, and techniques; so have biology and chemistry. The development of ideas and skills has often been aided by the application of one discipline to the subject matter of another.

No standards of value can be exclusively claimed for any method of knowledge. Some are common to more than one method or can be transferred from one to another. The aesthetic principle of beauty and harmony of form applies in mathematics and science as the principle of "elegance"; theories are refined in part by organizing their elements into a more elegant form, tidying them up, pulling in the loose ends, and making recalcitrant parts fit more neatly. The mathematics of probability is similarly applied to practical judgment in calculating the risks of a course of action.

One task of learning, therefore, is mastery of skill in selecting the subject matter, techniques, procedures, and criteria of adequacy (standards of value) that will fit the immediate task of learning. It stands to reason that the broader the acquaintance of the student with different intellectual methods the better his selection of methods will be. This does not mean that all students should have a liberal arts education, for these methods are learned in professional and technical curricula as well as liberal arts courses. The study of almost any subject can be taken up by more than one intellectual method, and probably should be, if the student is to gain any freedom at all in the cultivation of new material and new ideas. And he has to know enough about each method to tell when it is appropriate to the subject he is working on.

This does not mean that the student needs to be master of every possible method. He has the resources of other members of the college, both students and faculty, at his disposal. If he finds himself needing material from an unfamiliar field, he can usually find someone who can give him some assistance in using it appropriately and effectively—a member of the faculty or a student majoring in the subject. The librarian presides over a collection of expert works and can help him find useful material, even in fields where the college offers no instruction. The student is not bound by his own limited knowledge, but can extend it by talking to an expert or consulting the important writing in the field.

THE RESOURCES OF THE CAMPUS

The campus affords other resources beyond the skills of its members and its library collections. There are usually opportunities to perform or attend performances of drama, dance, and music; there are traveling art exhibits available even when there is no art gallery. There are visiting lecturers and consultants to be heard and, frequently, questioned by members of the college. Student initiative can increase the resources available. Learning the methods of practical judgment is made easier by participation in student governing bodies for residence halls, fraternities, classes, or the whole campus. Interest groups, literary socie-

ties, language clubs, departmental organizations extend learning beyond the classroom and allow the expression and strengthening of
special individual or group interests.

THE RESOURCES OF THE COMMUNITY

No member of the college should for a moment forget that there is a
real community, full of resources for learning, just outside the college
walls. Student government need not be the only political experience
available for students interested in studying political science; there are
elections and political parties in the community of which the college is
a part, and the student can find opportunities to do precinct work,
public opinion surveys, speech writing or reporting, office management, and a variety of other work that will keep his general political
ideas in firm contact with the realities.

Community churches welcome active members. There are also community cultural and service organizations in need of student support.
The whole field of voluntary civic service is open for students to gain
practical experience, enlarge their range of knowledge, and contribute
valuable skills to the life and development of the community. Many
colleges have a volunteer service bureau which assists students in finding valuable community experience and informs them of the programs
and needs of local agencies.

Commuter students are in a somewhat more favorable position than
students in residence for making adequate use of the resources of the
community. The former are familiar with their city and its resources,
they have continuing relationships to activities and do not have to learn
the ropes before they can make effective contact with the services they
need. They also may help students in residence get acquainted with
the community and its resources, thereby performing a valuable service
by enlarging opportunities for learning.

Whatever the resources needed for learning may be, the college student can make effective use of them only on his own initiative and in
relation to his own interests. His awareness of personal interests,
strengths, and limitations determines the subjects, techniques, and
standards of achievement that shape his work and direct his attention.
It is his responsibility to select the courses, teachers, activities, and
community services that relate to his important interests and purposes.

part three

Choices and values

8

And so to work

*Vocational Development
and the life plan*

CHOICE OF VOCATION

During his college years, a student makes three great choices that shape his adult life and give meaning to his life plan. He chooses his work and lays the foundation of a career. He chooses his mate and lays the foundation of a home and family. He chooses a way of life and lays the foundation of values that he will serve in his community.

These three choices are interrelated. Each affects, and in turn is affected by, the other two. These choices are regarded as decisive; each makes a profound difference in the self and way it is realized in adult life. They are regarded as irreversible; once done, they cannot be undone, even though they may be changed. Stability, security, continuity in self-development in adult life are supposed to be won by making adequate choices.

In our time, work has taken on increasing importance as a source of self-realization. Personal identity is partly based on work. Yet at the same time, personal relationships in work have become less intimate and less enduring. A person is identified by the work he does; yet in his work he may find less and less support for his personal dignity and worth. Work is more important in the life of the individual, yet he may gain less satisfaction from it.

Under these conditions, the churches have felt themselves faced with the task of restoring the sense of self-realization in work and the respect for the work of others, that have been part of the Jewish-Christian tradition. An effort has been made to recapture the sense of *vocation*, the feeling of being "called" to work. This concept recaptures an important aspect of vocational choice. To find work really satisfying, a person must not only want to do it, but also feel that he is wanted as a worker. He must choose his work and also be chosen to do it. His choice is confirmed by its acceptance in society. This doctrine of vocation holds that all useful work contributes to the meaning of life; that in work a person serves God as well as his fellow men and himself; and that in work he "witnesses" to the values he serves—that is, he communicates something of life's meaning to others.

The questions usually raised in the choice of work are those of ability and opportunity: "Can I do this kind of work?" "Can I find a job in which I can use my ability?" To these questions, the Jewish-Christian tradition adds two other considerations: social need, and the meaning of work: "Will this kind of work help others?" "Will it enrich and enlarge their lives and mine?"

This effort to recapture the sense of vocation has been particularly significant for many people in colleges and universities. The sense of scholarship as a productive enterprise in its own right has been recaptured. College study is recognized as real work, not just preparation for some other kind of occupation. Ideas, theories, and thinking are affirmed as the results of real productive work; they do not depend for their value purely on their application to some other kind of enterprise, such as a business or industry or war. The productivity of teachers has been reaffirmed. The importance of the student as a worker and of his contribution to the effectiveness of the teacher has been rediscovered.

In this view of vocational choice there is a distinction between vocation and occupation. The student may think of his vocational choice as having been made when he decided to go to college. Recognizing his special abilities, he decided to use them in scholarship and was accepted as a student by the faculty of his college. His occupational choice is made when he selects, from the available jobs, the particular kind of work he will do to earn a living. The occupation, as a way of earning a living, is the outward form of the vocation. The vocation is the student's inward commitment to producing something of value for himself and others.

For the student, perhaps the most important implication of the idea of vocation is the recognition that scholarship is a vocation. He works at it in his college years. He continues to work at it after college, whatever his occupation may be. When the faculty admitted him to college, he became part of the scholarly enterprise. Now the task of occupational choice remains. He must find an occupation in which he can carry out his commitment to the scholarly enterprise and use his scholarly skills to earn a living.

The developmental stages of occupational choice

Vocational development is, therefore, not complete upon entering college. It has just begun. Occupational choice remains a major task. The process of higher education is designed to move toward final occupational choice, deliberately and inexorably. There is a series of steps and decisions that the student must take sooner or later. In each step, he must make a decision, and his decision must be accepted by others concerned in the scholarly enterprise. At each stage, there is this dual pattern of choice and acceptance. The student decides to enter college and is accepted by the faculty. He decides to specialize in a particular field, and his choice of major is accepted by the faculty in that field. In securing a job after college, he decides to enter a particular occupation and is accepted by an employer (or accepted by a graduate school, if he goes on for professional preparation).

Ginzberg and his associates describe three stages of occupational choice in college:[1] "exploration," "crystallization," and "specification." The choice of the vocation of scholarship and entrance into college opens the stage of "exploration." In it the student tries out his interests and abilities. He tries to decide what occupations they are related to. He tries to see himself as working at that occupation. The choice of occupation is tentatively made in the period of "crystallization." Then the major field is chosen, and the student is pretty well decided to enter an occupation related to it. This is not a final choice since most majors have many different occupations open to students completing a degree in the field. Securing a job or deciding to secure graduate or professional training is the final decision, made in the period of "specification."

The time spent in each stage is limited by the educational system.

The student is not going to live forever, and the point of decision cannot be indefinitely postponed. Formal degree requirements mark the points at which definite decisions have to be made, but these points are perhaps not so significant in moving the student toward a final decision as the reactions of other students. The student gets a more favorable response from others by saying, "I am a pre-law student" than by saying that he hasn't settled on a major yet but is considering philosophy or perhaps math and trying to keep as many occupational possibilities open for as long as he can and going into law, maybe. The identity of the student is communicated through his choice of major. The student who has not decided is something of an unknown quantity; his place in the occupational system is not readily definable; his identity is vague and indeterminate, he becomes an oddity.

Consciously or unconsciously, students have some conception of the relation between the phases of vocational development and mature self-development, which they apply to their judgments of others as well as to themselves. The weight of student opinion is on the side of early, specific, and irreversible occupational choice. In this respect, students are no different from their families, friends, and other people in the community. They expect both themselves and others to demonstrate what kind of people they are through the occupational choices they make.

A recent conversation between two freshmen may be a case in point. "Why do you want to be a social worker, of all things?" he asked. "Because I want to do something in my lifetime to help other people, and to make life better and happier," she replied. "Nonsense!" he retorted, "That doesn't matter to me at all. I want to do something permanent and enduring. I want to be remembered." "Well, if what you want is to be remembered," she said, "why don't you just build yourself a pyramid!"

In each stage of occupational choice personal values and purposes are involved. The student must choose; the pressures of parents, faculty, other students, society generally require him to make a specific occupational choice. His occupational choice should express his ambitions and hopes. He must choose, but he must determine the choice that is best for him.

The following analysis is presented as a check list for students who wish to check the adequacy of their career planning. It is not an exhaustive list; each individual will have special factors to consider in his own case. Such an analysis is necessarily very general while the student's interests are highly specific. He wants to be accepted as a scholar and as an employee, on his own terms. He wants to serve others out of his own good will rather than out of fear, obligation, or pressure. The acceptance he desires must come from particular people, in a specific college, in a limited geographic area, in a certain kind of enterprise. No general analysis can deliver this kind of assurance. The student has to find his own work and follow his own career for himself. All that this chapter can offer is a description of the general factors that others have found helpful and some suggestions of ways to plan in his own best interest.

Factors affecting the stage of exploration

College curricula. The stage of exploration is characterized by two major tasks: the exploration of aptitudes and interests, and the assessment of their relation to occupational choice. Increasingly, colleges provide for broader exploration of fields of study in the curriculum. Declaration of major no longer is regarded as ending the stage of exploration. The distinction between liberal arts and professional courses of study no longer implies a difference in breadth of exploration or focus of specialization; both programs provide breadth of interest, flexibility in occupational choice, and cultivation of personal interests.

From the purely practical point of view, college study offers the opportunity to get direct experience as a test of occupational choice. Course work, in particular, is a valuable rehearsal of occupational roles. Whatever the pattern of general and specialized education may be in his particular college, the student finds some opportunity for trying out different roles. The example, previously cited, of the frustrated pre-med student, who found a happy occupational choice in medical illustration, shows how the student can use course work to test and guide his occupational choice.

The value of course work as a test of occupational interest depends upon the student's approach to it. He can take courses as he would a dose of medicine, unhappily, but for his own good. He can take them as necessary steps toward the degree, required by the faculty. In either case, the experience will have little value in his occupational choice. But if the student wishes, he can approach his course work as a rehearsal of an occupational role. He can study sociology, or engineering, or French, or almost any subject as if he were using it in professional practice. He may try himself out in the role of scholar in the field and see how the experience fits his image of himself.

This is not to say that a student is interested in only those courses related to his occupational interests, or that he should limit himself to courses having occupational value. On the contrary, courses are as important for sheer enjoyment as for the light they cast on occupational decisions. The amateur has a place in scholarship, and the monopoly of study by a professionalized group is the death of learning. It is important for engineers to study sociology, for musicians to study astronomy, for journalists to study mathematics, out of personal interest, as a scholarly privilege and responsibility. The compelling reason for choosing any field of scholarship is the enjoyment one finds in it. College courses can add to the enjoyment of living, over and above the enjoyment of work.

What the student can keep in mind, however, is the possibility of using course work to test the realism of his occupational choice. Scholarly work is real work, and it gives a realistic test of the student's powers and prospects in a possible occupation. If a student enjoys reading, writing, and experimentation in psychology for nine hours a week for sixteen weeks, he may have good reason to feel that a forty-hour week in psychological testing, research, or counseling might be an enjoyable occupation. If he is happy in physics lab nine hours a week for sixteen weeks, he has reason to believe that he may be happy working in a scientific occupation involving physics.

The student eventually has to come to terms with the world of work, and that step is made easier if he asks himself, "Do I enjoy studying this subject? Do I find my skills in it adequate? Is my performance good? Would I be happy to work at such tasks all day, five days a week, the rest of my life?"

Intelligence. A student can probably safely assume that if he has shown enough intelligence to be admitted to college, he has the minimum capacity needed for entry into one of the occupations requiring scholarly skills. Intelligence is an important factor in choosing the vocation of scholarship, but occupational choice requires more careful analysis of particular aptitudes required by various kinds of work.

Super concludes[2] that intelligence does have some effect on vocational development, however. First, he finds that: "People tend to gravitate toward occupational levels and toward jobs appropriate to the level of their intellectual ability." Apparently, this is due both to the better capacity for intelligent judgment in brighter individuals and to the social pressures brought to bear on them in many instances to choose occupations requiring higher levels of capacity. Also more intelligent people probably get more satisfaction by moving into a new job, or a higher-level job, requiring different skills, than by improving their performance in a settled position. Second, provided the individual has the minimum level of intelligence necessary for entry into an occupation, his success is not influenced to any great extent by additional intellectual capacity. Third, in routine work, the effect of intelligence may appear in the speed of adjustment to the performance required and more rapid advancement; but there seems to be little effect on success once the person has settled into the job.

Specific aptitudes seem to have more direct bearing on occupational development. The student can get help from a counselor in using tests, grades, and other evidence of aptitude to determine whether he has the ability to do the work required in the occupation he is considering.

Interests, values, and attitudes. Interests are considered to be likes and dislikes, at least so far as the interest inventories are concerned. Attitudes represent established habits of preferring things of a certain quality, or of following certain fixed lines of reasoning, or of giving consistent emotional responses to repeated situations or ideas. And values have to do with the underlying structures of beliefs, knowledge, and purposes that influence long-range goals and directions of development. The three factors differ in the dimensions of depth and time, with attitudes representing the deeper habits underlying interests, and values representing the endurance of attitudes and interests in time and the projection of goals and purposes into the future.

Super distinguishes four ways of identifying interests.[3] *Expressed interests* are the things people say they are interested in or wish they could do. *Manifest interests* are those interests expressed by activity. A student may manifest an interest in ornithology by making and classifying a collection of birds' eggs or nests. "*Tested interests* are manifest interests but interests manifested under controlled rather than life situations." Tests of the information retained after reading, movies, or class discussion about occupations would be a measure of the effect of individual interests on the material remembered. *Inventoried interests* are those identified by comparison of preferences of an individual with the inventory of likes and dislikes expressed by people in different occupations.

When students talk about vocational tests or interest tests, they usually mean vocational *inventories* such as the Kuder Preference Record or Strong Vocational Interest Tests. Inventories seem to yield the most stable and useful information available about interests in relation to vocational development. For one thing, they give the student two kinds of information that he cannot get by himself. He knows his likes and dislikes, but the inventory gives him a picture of the similarity of his interests to those of people at work. He also gets information about the interests that differentiate one occupational group from another; and he gets a picture of the relation of his interests to those of several occupational groups.

There are useful tests of values and attitudes.[4] However, these have been used to assess student attitudes on a variety of other issues, and little information is available on their relation to personal vocational development except by inference from other findings. Only the most general applications can be made to individual decisions. But there is nothing to prevent the student from reflecting on the findings available and considering the relation of his values to his occupational choice. Tests seem to be of little immediate practical use in confirming his values or relating them to his occupational choice. But consideration of his basic values will be necessary at some point in his career planning, and the earlier he comes to it, the more effective his choice will be.

Personality traits. The systematic analysis of one's strengths and weaknesses in personality may yield unsuspected information about underdeveloped assets. It may influence the range of occupational choice through discovery of capacities for playing various roles. There are various techniques of measuring personality, and the student who wants something more precise and valid than the *Readers' Digest* check lists should seek competent advice from a counselor or psychologist. There are many personality inventories available, based on different conceptions of personality; and the services of an expert are needed both to administer the test and to help the student interpret the results properly.* However, the way in which he can apply this information to occupational choice is limited by some practical factors. As Super[5] sums these up, the relation of personality to vocational development is not clear-cut enough to serve as a principal determining factor in occupational choice. So far, personality traits show "no practical differential relationship to vocational preference, entry, success, or satisfaction." Any occupation involves many roles, and each role many traits, so that it is not possible to construct typical personality sketches for various occupational groups.

If he is aware of these limitations, and does not try to get more out of the results than is justifiable, the student can get a general idea of his abilities, interests, values, a profile of his traits or preferred roles, from

* Such inventories as the Minnesota Multiphasic Personality Inventory and the California Personality Inventory, used among college students, provide a comparison of individual scores on a questionnaire with patterns of response indicating such personality traits as dominance, dependence, aggression, masculinity, femininity, capacity for status, and the like. The Strong Vocational Interest Blank has a masculinity—femininity scale, which is useful in relation to the interest inventory results.

standardized tests of intelligence, interests, and personality. But the relation of test results to vocational development and occupational choice is not conclusively established. The results fill in the background and provide part of the context within which plans and choices can be marked out. But most of the tests tell the student nothing he did not know; they primarily put the information in more systematic and useful form. What the student makes out of his abilities, interests, and attitudes is up to him.

Family patterns. Students are sometimes a little reluctant or ashamed to consider family background, social contacts, income, or status in making career plans or to draw on the resources of the family in gaining entry to a desirable occupation. They feel they ought to choose an occupation and get a job on their own, without "using influence" or "pulling strings." On the other hand, some students do not bother to make a calculated occupational choice or career plan of their own; they depend on the family to give the decision, the means, and the entry to an occupation. Realistically speaking, family interests and resources have a practical effect on vocational development, and the student will do a better job of planning if he takes them into account.

Successful entry into a job seems to be related to independence and the ease with which one makes decisions about handling money, buying clothes, or going places on one's own. The family pattern of independence training for children, providing allowances, putting them on a budget, sending them on important errands, having them make decisions, affects the chances of children for successful entry into an occupation with a shorter trial period. The earlier and more consistent the independence training, the better.[6]

The socio-economic class of the family also affects vocational development. The student's range of interest is affected by the number of different occupations represented in the family's circle of acquaintance that are known or talked about in terms of the acquaintances' roles, status, abilities, and the like. Family income, an important factor in social status, also partly determines the amount of capital and credit available for entering an occupation; and therefore, it limits the range of possible choices. The social status of the family and its range of acquaintance with people in different occupations determines the accessibility of occupations, for entry is made easier by knowing people who can help find a job.

The influence of the family on vocational development, while very great, need not restrict the student to a narrow range of occupational choices. On the contrary, the vocational orientation of the family seems to put a kind of floor under the student's vocational development. The level of interest and the status attained by sons do not seem to drop below the status and interest levels of their fathers, especially in occupations requiring substantial education. Rather, the tendency is for sons to move upward in status although two-thirds to three-quarters of them go no more than one step upward in the scale.[7] The student can make effective use of support, encouragement, interests, and contacts that come from his family without reducing his independence. It is up to him to decide what to do with them, but he can plan more realistically and effectively if he knows what the family's resources and interests can contribute to his vocational development and what help he wishes to have from them.

Education. The amount, type, and length of education required for most occupations is not clearly defined. The more highly specialized the occupation, the more specific the educational requirements become. The longer the time required in education, the later the entry into the occupation; incomes during the working years tend to be higher under such circumstances, offsetting some of the costs of prolonged education and delay in financial returns.

The college record can be an extremely valuable asset in getting into a first job. College grades are a good index of intelligence and achievement, perhaps the best single piece of evidence for estimating ability to do productive work. The major field will not necessarily have a point-to-point relationship to the job, but it will define the range of interests, skills, and aptitude that a student can bring to his work. Entry into an occupation may be easier because of quite unexpected aspects of education: an unusual combination of courses, a special project in a class or student organization, a special interest outside the major field. Both breadth and specialization in college education have value in occupational choice and advancement.

College students gravitate toward the professions, women even more so than men. A little more than half the men and three-quarters of the women go into the professions; the rest principally go into business and industrial management.[8] Students who drop out of college are more frequently found in non-professional jobs than are college graduates. A recent survey of the first jobs of women college graduates showed 80 percent in professional positions, 16 percent in clerical, and 4 percent in various other business, industrial and government jobs.[9]

The student will want to appraise his educational program with a view to identifying the possible occupations to which it may give him access and the possibility of using his scholarly skills on the job. He can get some notion of the satisfaction to be found in possible occupations from his satisfaction in related academic work. And through the job information service available in most college placement offices, he can find out about the relation of education to opportunities to enter and advance in particular occupations of interest to him.

Status factors. There is a tendency to assign superior and inferior ratings to occupations and to attribute these ratings to people in them. The stratification of occupations seems to be based on some unexamined assumptions about the superiority and inferiority of different types of work, levels of responsibility, and income.

Caplow[10] lists five assumptions on which prestige and status values commonly held in American culture seem to be based:

1. White collar work is superior to manual work.
2. Self-employment is superior to working for others.
3. Clean occupations are superior to dirty occupations.
4. Larger enterprises are superior to smaller enterprises in the business field but not necessarily in farming.
5. Personal service is degrading, hence it is better to work for an enterprise than to do the same work for an individual.

Centers[11] found that values and beliefs, education, and wealth were the criteria most frequently mentioned in public opinion surveys as the basis for estimating one's own status. The Index of Social Characteristics developed by Warner and his associates[12] combines ratings of occupation, source of income, type of house, and residential area in the study of status. Occupational ratings seem to be more significant than any other factor in status judgments, according to these findings.

In determining his occupational choice, the student can hardly help being aware of status ratings. Status is part of his self-image; it is derived from family attitudes and represents an important part of the expectations he has absorbed from them. He sees himself as the kind of person who lives in a certain part of town, who associates comfortably with a particular kind of people, and above all, who can do a particular kind of work.

In the student body, status and prestige ratings are assigned on the basis of many different factors that vary from campus to campus. The status ratings of students by faculty seem to have less force than the status ratings of students by students because of the barriers to student-faculty relations erected by college mores. Since students see more of each other in a greater variety of roles, their judgments probably are based on greater breadth of experience. But there is probably more value in faculty ratings in terms of maturity and objectivity. Faculty ratings are also more closely related to status factors in the community, to which student ratings sometimes have little relation.

For example, the status judgments of student groups commonly include distinctions between major fields of study, reflecting in part the opinions current in the college about the strength of different departments and in part the assumptions current in the wider community about the status attributed to related occupations. Different status ratings of superiority and inferiority are assigned to majors on different campuses. Law rates high on one, low on another. Students may refer to English as "the major you choose if you can't decide on a profession," or education as "the major for people who can't do anything else." Engineers may be rated lower or higher than physics or chemistry majors. Some majors, such as theology or philosophy, may be regarded as a little odd. Their relations to occupations and the ratings of those occupations in the community are vague and uncertain, or just plain irrelevant.

Students' status ratings of majors and occupations have to be recognized as relatively immature and unreliable. Some status ratings in the student mores are irrelevant to occupational choice. Attaining high status in the student body may actually interfere with vocational development. The student may try to meet expectations that directly interfere with scholarly performance and preparation for a career. "Partying it up," for instance, may establish his prestige in the fraternity but reduce his level of academic achievement and limit his chances for entry into occupations with high educational requirements. The student may make an early choice of major or occupation in response to the expectations of others, thus cutting off the process of exploration prematurely and eliminating some interesting possibilities without adequate consideration.

The student needs to interpret status ratings from two points of view. Rather than concentrate exclusively on what they tell him about himself and the kind of person he wants to be, he should also pay some attention to what status ratings tell him about the attitudes and values of the people making such judgments. Just as his choice of a major is in part based on a preference for association with faculty members and students whom he enjoys, so his choice of an occupation is in part based on anticipated association in a common enterprise with people he enjoys and respects. He can interpret the status judgments of students who expect to enter the field he is considering as conveying some of their basic beliefs and aspirations. He can compare their attitudes with his own to see if he would feel comfortable at the prospect of working with them.

Status ratings are, consequently, more valuable as a means of understanding oneself and others than as criteria for occupational choice. They are evidence of what is regarded as valuable; they afford a way to find associates who may increase enjoyment and reward in an occupation. They cannot tell the student what occupation is best for him. But status ratings can give some notion, however vague and imprecise, about the quality of response he may expect from other people to the work he does.

Factors affecting the stage of crystallization

The end of the stage of exploration is marked by choice of a major and entrance upon a concentrated course of study related to a limited occupational field. Some students have a more rapid pace of vocational development and are in the stage of crystallization upon entrance to college. Others crystallize their choices more slowly. But as the college years pass, the inexorable demand for occupational choice practically forces a student to crystallize his choice.

The choice of a major. The choice of a major field of study does not represent a final occupational choice; occupational choice is a second crucial decision made when taking the first job after college. Choice of a major does not even determine the final occupational choice. One common error in students' vocational expectations is to look for a job which fits the major. Occupations use some of the specialized methods mastered in various major fields, but generally they require a great many more skills and more varied experience over and above the scholarly specialty. The choice of occupation has to fit the career plan as a whole if it is to be satisfactory, and the major field is only a part of the career plan.*

The student should differentiate in his own thinking between majors which require full identification with a highly specialized profession and those which only require identification of general occupational interests that may later crystallize into one of several highly specialized kinds of work. For example, the student who chooses to major in engineering must accept the implicit decision that he will further specialize

---

* In Eleanor Metheny and James E. Peterson's *The Trouble with Women*, a collection of case histories, the trouble with Lynn is an unrealistic conception of the relation among her interests, her major, her career, and her life plan. Her unwillingness to learn the intermediate skills, and take the intermediate steps between college study and an occupation leaves her frustrated, feeding on dreams without enjoying performance. There is something of Lynn in all of us. Many students, and some teachers, count too heavily on the choice of major to settle the choice of occupation. There is a lot of work between these two steps.[13]

in one field of engineering, and that he will begin from that point forward to see himself as an electrical or mechanical engineer and limit his occupational choice to that field. The student who chooses to major in sociology, on the other hand, may preserve in his planning a wide variety of possible occupations. He may still think of himself as a journalist, social worker, manager of a business, or teacher—even conceivably as a physician or lawyer, given wise management of his electives to meet basic requirements for admission to professional study.

There is no particular reason to regard early commitment to a particular occupation as preferable to consideration of a broad range of occupational choice as long as possible, or vice versa. The student simply needs to know *what his choice of major means in terms of occupational choice.* He should make sure that he is ready and able to accept either clear specialization or continued diffuseness in his expectations. He should be prepared to adapt his career plan to the specialized pattern implied in the choice of a major. The important thing is for the student to feel comfortable in his ultimate professional role and to commit himself at the time when he is ready finally to focus his interests and skills around a particular occupation. There are individual differences in timing of occupational choice as well as in preferences and aptitudes, and no student should expect his choice of major or choice of occupation to be made in the same way as everybody else's. He need only be sure that his choice fits the career plan he has in mind and makes it possible for him to grow into the kind of person he wants to be.

Work experience. In securing part-time or summer employment related to his occupational interests, the student needs more specific information about the particular jobs available and the opportunities they afford for learning something about the occupation. Jobs vary in terms of the opportunities for learning they present. One laboratory job may simply be a routine activity, confined to one laboratory and one type of operation; another may take the technician into different parts of a plant and require a variety of laboratory procedures, which gives the student a broader view of the whole enterprise and the place of laboratory work in it.

If the student is able to make a choice of jobs on some basis besides the income, he can well afford to take a little time to find out which job will put him in a position most favorable to getting the occupational information and experience he needs. Sometimes the placement officer or vocational counselor handling part-time and summer employment may know something about the possibilities for learning afforded by various jobs; sometimes students who have held the job previously can give some information about the opportunity it affords; sometimes the student can figure it out for himself on the basis of the information the employer gives him. Work-study programs, such as the Antioch College or Carnegie Tech programs, offer work experience designed to give the student a comprehensive view of the enterprise and the occupation. Supervisors are trained to give students the information and training that will be of greatest value to them.

Where major fields are not directly related to a specialty but apply to a variety of occupations, work experience is especially important in helping the student crystallize his choice. For example, the engineer may work in an oil field to see if petroleum engineering is the kind of occupation he likes, or in a highway construction crew, or an electronics plant, depending on the specialization he thinks he prefers. The sociology major will have to depend more on work than on courses to differentiate among such fields as social work, city planning, and personnel management. Work experience assumes greater importance with the greater number of occupations related to the major field.

Counseling. In crystallizing occupational choice, the teacher as counselor offers valuable help to the student. The choice of a major usually has to be approved by the faculty of the appropriate department. In considering his choice, the student can make effective use of faculty members, not just sounding them out on his chances of approval, but also getting information and advice that can be helpful in coming to a decision.

Faculty members ordinarily have fairly up-to-date information about the occupations related to their fields of study. They may inform the student of new types of jobs in the field, about shortages or surpluses of workers that affect his entry into certain occupations and about courses that are particularly pertinent to the jobs he wishes to consider. They may suggest work experience or conferences and professional meetings that may give a clearer picture of the occupations he is considering.

Students may also get help in deciding what occupations are appropriate to their aptitudes and interests. A counselor or teacher can review their plans, help assess their realism, and suggest steps to carry them out.

Specialized vocational counselors, where they are employed by the college, offer all of these services. In addition, they often offer testing services to assist the student in estimating his abilities and weighing his interests more realistically. Some of them are also specially qualified to help the student recognize and deal with individual problems that may handicap him or to make more effective and complete use of his abilities and assets in entering upon his occupation.

The stage of crystallization does not involve final commitment to a chosen occupation. But the student does limit the range of his planning and narrow his choice of occupation to a limited set of possibilities. Such focusing of his expectations need not mean the loss of certain cherished interests and ambitions. A broad range of interests can be preserved in those activities of adult life lying outside one's job. Careful planning and wise counseling can help the student make sure that his college studies lead to both satisfying work and rich personal interests.

Factors affecting the stage of specification

After graduation, when entering employment, the student reaches the stage of specification in occupational choice. In the phases of exploration and crystallization, the most important factors to be considered are those of aptitude, interest, personal preferences, and background. In the period of specification, the most important factors affecting choice are concrete, immediate questions of individual opportunity, social need, and economic conditions. The questions to be settled are less personal and inward, more social and objective in character. The student's attention is turned from himself toward society, from the college toward the community, from assessment of his interests toward relating those interests to an employer's desires.

This shift of attention outward to society holds true whether the student plans to continue graduate and professional study or to enter employment. After choice of occupation has been made by the student, the crucial choice determining entry into an occupation is no longer his. An employer, a professional accrediting body, a graduate faculty approve him for admission to a job or professional study. A physicist applies for admission to a graduate school to move into research in his field. A law student must be accepted by a school of law, a medical student by a school of medicine. Both in graduate study and in employment, the college graduate can only offer himself as a candidate; entry into his preferred occupation rests upon his acceptance by people already engaged in it.

Job information. Finding out about the qualifications for entry and advancement in various occupations is necessary in specific occupational choice. There are at least forty thousand different kinds of jobs in our society, and getting information about them all is an impossibility. The broad categories of field, level, and type of activity used in lists such as the *Dictionary of Occupational Titles* provide a classification system for occupations. General information can be found about the education, work experience, responsibilities and types of activity characterizing each one. Within these categories, specific information has to be secured from other sources. Special requirements and conditions of employment differ from one occupation to another, and from one enterprise to another within the occupation. So the amount and specificity of occupational information available will vary from one occupation to another and from one firm, institution, or enterprise to another.[14]

In considering a job after college, the student needs quite specific and detailed information. General descriptions of occupational fields give little help in deciding which job to take or which employers to approach. The student has to have a very clear idea of the kind of work he wants to do, the opportunity for stable employment it should afford, the chances for advancement it should offer, and the income and fringe benefits (health insurance, vacations, recreational service, expense allowance, and the like) it should offer. The number of employees in the classification he will enter; the practices relating to pay increases; the geographical location and possible moves from place to place with advancement on the job; opportunities for advanced study on the job; all will have a bearing on his final decision.

The placement officer or vocational counselor can help the student check the realism of his expectations on such points as salary scale, level of responsibility, and opportunities for advancement. Sometimes a teacher or counselor can help the student make a detailed check list of the information he needs to get. He may secure some counseling on the type of questions to ask to get good information, the advisability of visiting the firm or institution, the things to observe on a visit, and some criteria to use in evaluating the job or comparing it with others.

His expectations probably ought to be kept to himself, unless the employer inquires into them directly. The student's expectations will be most useful if they are expressed to the employer in terms of ranges of income, duties, and advancement that the student is willing to consider, rather than flat requirements. It is, naturally, foolish to walk into a personnel office and say, "I hold a B.A. degree in Investment Counseling from Polonius Institute, and I want a job as investment analyst paying ten thousand dollars a year, with Social Security, retirement annuity, medical insurance, three months' vacation a year, and expenses paid to the annual meeting of the American Economics Association."

Most colleges provide some kind of placement service for alumni.

The faculty members pool information they have about occupational developments and available jobs in a central office, which may also offer vocational counseling. In addition to information about openings, the placement office usually keeps information on occupations, graduate fellowships, local employment trends, and new vocational opportunities. The advantage of such a central service is substantial, for the student can get a more comprehensive view of the occupations and employment opportunities in which he is interested, at one sitting, without having to canvass several different departments and faculty members for the information.

However, in getting information about job openings, the student has to do his own work. Public and private employment agencies keep current openings on file. Faculty members can suggest ways to find leads in seeking a first job. Professional societies, such as the engineering societies and teachers' associations, frequently carry a file of available jobs. Family friends who are in the student's desired field can give useful suggestions. And there is always the want ad section of the paper.

Personnel representatives of various enterprises, especially in fields where there are shortages of manpower, have formed the habit of visiting colleges to recruit workers. Some of them are also willing to talk to students who are seeking not immediate employment but information about jobs in the field. Many students, in the years of manpower shortage, have formed a habit of sitting back and waiting for employers' representatives to make them a big offer. But one cannot expect such conditions always to prevail; and it is wise for students to take the initiative in seeking interviews with prospective employers or their representatives. Common-sense planning requires forming the habits of both seeking employment and being sought after. In the course of his career, the student can probably expect to do both, and thus he needs some idea of how to go about gaining entry to a new job.

Initiative and ingenuity in getting job information and leads on openings are probably the most important factors in securing a good beginning job. One woman college graduate wanted to design kitchens. No one on the faculty or in the placement office had ever heard of such an occupation. But she went through the yellow pages of the telephone directory in the city where she wished to work and made a list of manufacturers of household equipment, architects, and contractors. About the twelfth call or so brought results; a manufacturer of stoves and kitchen equipment was in the market for a designer, and she landed the job.

Economic conditions. At all stages of occupational choice, the student can use information about economic and social conditions affecting his prospective occupation. Manpower shortages and surpluses in the field will affect his chances of entry and the level at which he may expect to begin. In times of shortage opportunities for entry are increased and advancement is speeded up. On the other hand, satisfaction may be reduced by the pressure for output in an enterprise running short-handed and working overtime. For example, beginning engineers in an electronics firm report great satisfaction from the sense of accomplishment in meeting high-priority government contracts, and they like the rapid rate of promotion, as employees with relatively little experience are advanced in rank when new departments are organized for new products. On the other hand, they are dissatisfied with the constant pressure, the manpower and materials shortages that create bottlenecks, and the delay and confusion occasioned by a hastily organized management system.

Changes in economic structure and the organization of enterprises affect the level at which the entering job may be found. Changes in the organization of business, industry, and government may increase the numbers and importance of managerial positions. Some jobs at the managerial level may be open to college graduates on their first job. For example, considerable numbers of administrative assistantships and administrative trainees are sought for Federal Civil Service positions; some college graduates can go into government service at the middle administrative level without having to work up from a clerical or technical grade.

Automation seems to exercise two influences on job opportunities. Some skilled operators' jobs are reduced to machine-watching while others are upgraded to repair and maintenance. New jobs in quality control, process and data analysis, organization and control of production appear at managerial levels. A great many managerial jobs, particularly those requiring planning of processes, allocation of functions to people and machines, scheduling, programming, and analysis, require high-level intellectual skills. The net effect of automation seems to be a rise in the educational requirements for an increased number of positions involving supervision, control, and planning.

Recessions, depressions, booms, inflation and deflation, changes in public policy, shifts in fashion and taste, wars, disasters, acts of God, and depletion or development of natural resources affect employment. The student cannot foresee these, or calculate their effects on his career, with any great degree of accuracy. But he can make some allowance in his planning for chance events, and he can try to think of what he might do if they occur. For example, one of the side effects of the 1957–1958 recession was the elimination of management training programs by industries and businesses in some parts of the country. This reduced the number of opportunities for college graduates to gain entry to certain occupations, particularly at the lower and middle management levels through management training. But there were still clerical, technical, and low-level management and supervisory openings, which gave access to these occupations. Graduates had to adapt their expectations of beginning salary and rank to changed conditions.

The student needs to take economic conditions and trends into account in entering an occupation. Economics being a science of probability, the student need not expect to get any information that will enable him to act with absolute certainty or complete confidence. But he can get some help in estimating the risks he may run, the chances of advancement, the possibilities of expansion and development in the occupations he is considering in his choice of a beginning job. He can calculate these probabilities in the career plan he makes for himself and be prepared to adapt to change, opportunities, and risks that may appear in his occupation with changing economic conditions.

Social needs. The student naturally has to interpret the general information he can get about social needs in the light of his own skills, interests, and purposes. He is the only person who can say what these things mean for him. But his decisions will have some effect on his society, and he should act with some awareness of what these effects may be. He cannot solve the problems of society all by himself. But his decisions will have some effect on the finding of solutions.

Social needs may be expected to change. But for the time being, the following four areas are suggested for careful consideration.

The allocation of manpower. [15] In the foreseeable future, there seems to be no end to the shortage of manpower. The problem is now centered on the question of having enough people in the right geographic areas and in the occupations which need workers. The problem is allocation, rather than supply.

In other words, the student cannot think of just one general manpower shortage. A few years ago, there was much public discussion and interest in the shortage of teachers for the elementary grades. Now more is being heard about the shortage of high school and college teachers. But the concern about shortages in teaching has been rather overshadowed in the public mind by the shortage of scientists, mathematicians, and engineers. There is some talk about a shortage of doctors and psychiatrists, too. The teacher shortage has not been overcome; public attention has simply been drawn to another field in which there has been a manpower shortage for some time, even before Russian satellites shed some light on it. There are several other shortages, both occupationally and geographically defined—in social work, in nursing, in the ministry, in small towns and villages, in certain industries.

The student cannot adapt his occupational choice to the public concerns of the moment. It would be foolish as well as impracticable for him to change in the sophomore year from foreign languages to prenursing, in the junior year to mathematics, and in the senior year to sociology just because the newspapers and magazines at the time were full of articles about shortages in nursing, mathematics and social work. What he can better do is to estimate his chances of employment in his chosen field by ascertaining where the shortages are: in what occupations, in which enterprises, and in what geographical areas.

Certain elements in the manpower picture particularly affect the prospects of students. First, the general shortage of manpower means that there are more chances for people in minority groups to enter the work force and more freedom of choice of occupation for them. In periods of manpower shortage, gains can be made in opening up new fields of work for people who ordinarily are not considered suitable kinds of employees. Women can enter fields previously closed to them. Negroes find occupations opened to them where they were formerly unwelcome. Employers try to find ways of using the physically handicapped. People who can work only part-time find more jobs and sometimes more interesting jobs available. But they must have the necessary skills and must take the initiative in entering new occupations if the opportunities are to be consolidated in the long run.

This is not to say that the best thing to be at the present time is a physically handicapped, Negro woman mathematician. Minority status always presents hazards to a person seeking entry into an occupation. He is usually at the bottom of the barrel. But in a shortage period, the bottom of the barrel is constantly being scraped. Entry into an occupation even under these conditions gives him a chance to establish himself in it on his merits. And one side effect is to make it easier for people like him to receive consideration in the future if his performance on the job is adequate.

The student will want to bear in mind that his interests and abilities are always the primary basis for his occupational choice. Minority status may mean that he may expect to encounter discrimination at any time. It is probably never wise for him to limit his range of choice and preparation because of possible discrimination; he is entitled as a citizen to the fullest possible personal development, and he should realize this so far as he is able without anticipating any more hazards than there are. It is just as unrealistic to limit development for fear of discrimination as to disregard the fact of minority status, and perhaps more damaging to personal development in the end. The realistic approach is for the student to develop his own interests and abilities, to make his own occupational choice, and to look over the employment field for the opportunities that may open up for him and the advantages that he may secure, rather than to confine his development and restrict his choice within the limits of discriminatory practices.

A second general element in the manpower shortage is its appearance in all fields of work as a shortage in quality. This is particularly true in many occupations requiring college preparation. The college cannot secure enough qualified candidates to select and train only the best and still provide the number demanded by employers. So the student can pretty well anticipate that in almost any occupation related to a college major, there will be a shortage of good people, even though there may be an adequate supply of candidates.

The student will find a good college record to his advantage. If there is an adequate supply or oversupply of applicants, he may find it reasonable to take an entering job at a lower level than he might otherwise consider, with a fairly realistic expectation that *if* he makes good, his advancement may be more rapid than might otherwise be expected. A good educational record, confirmed by good performance at work, may give him a competitive advantage where quality is at a premium. If there is an acute shortage of candidates, a good educational record may make it possible for him to enter at a higher level of responsibility and income than he might otherwise expect. This likelihood is increased by good work experience in the field on a part-time or summer job. Any qualitative advantage he can gain, in his academic work or job experience, will give him a competitive advantage in entry or advancement.

A third aspect of the manpower shortage is the increased pressure on people at work. This effect is most pronounced in the occupations, industries, and geographic areas where there are shortages. The stress occasioned by pressure for production is unusually difficult to manage. It is more or less continuous. It is produced both by the extraordinary effort required to keep things moving and by the frustration of being unable fully to cope with the demands regardless of how hard one works.

The effects of stress are apparent in many ways. Managers of enterprises that are running short-handed report more curt and abrupt orders, less time for planning and detailed instructions, and breakdown of communications so that important orders do not get through. These are minor stress reactions compared with what looks like a general trend toward earlier incidence of gastric ulcers, high blood pressure, and heart attacks. On the opposite side of the ledger, however, are schools and plants and offices operating under pressure, but with high morale and good production records, indicative of successful adaptation to stress.

So one factor the student might consider is his capacity for adapting to stress. He may wish to avoid enterprises running short-handed, in order to avoid stress. Or he may find it challenging to work under pressure in an expanding enterprise, accepting stress in order to achieve high levels of performance and achievement. He may be wise, in any case, to try to form habits that will reduce stress so that he can work comfortably under pressure. In making his career plan and choosing his occupation, he should consider the stress factors in the occupation and on the job and then make realistic plans to adapt to them.

Personal preferences must also be taken into account in career planning. The student cannot simply decide on his preferred occupation and then get a beginning job in it, letting advancement, geographic location, and income fall where they may. If he is interested in advancement, he needs to prepare himself and his family for changes of residence and for increased stress. The college years can afford experience in adapting easily to different patterns of community living and new groups of people. The cycles of college life, with gradually increased self-direction and responsibility for working with others, afford experience that can prepare him to advance to new levels of responsibility on the job.

The student should avoid getting on an escalator he does not want to ride, or accepting stress in excess of his adaptive capacities, or sacrificing stable home and community relationships to the demands of the job. The pressure is on, the demands for productivity in most occupations are very great, and people of quality are sorely needed. The student should act in full awareness of these pressures and these needs. Whatever he does will be of value if he has any competence at all.

New patterns of organization and management. The student graduating from college in the last half of the twentieth century will be seeking employment in enterprises generally characterized by enormous size, complexity, and geographic range. The population of the United States will be more urban than rural and will require services for a tremendous number of people on a highly individualized basis. Enterprises are tending to become national, rather than local, in scope of operation. The number of centers of operation is increasing, the number of employees and types of jobs are growing rapidly, and the different services offered are becoming more numerous and highly specialized.

The first result of such growth and expansion is that many new jobs are opening, which require new combinations of skills and interests to fill them. The student in almost all academic fields may find a growing range of choice in final selection of a job. For example, industrial libraries, a relatively recent development, require a special combination of interests in business administration, technology, and economics, as well as skill in library science. Data analysis, systems control, and personnel analysis have opened up with the rapid increase in automation. The student can enlarge his field of occupational choice far beyond the traditional occupations of his parents and their friends.

Second, with specialization, automation, and expansion, the organization of enterprises has become extremely complex. Society has a great need for organization and management suited to complex operations. The problems of coordination with decentralization of control, of efficiency with flexibility of procedure, of expansion with individualized services are only a few of the management problems requiring solution. One overriding problem which has vexed large organizations is that of communication, of developing real understanding of the enterprise among its employees, clients, and publics. To achieve vast size while keeping the common touch with individuals; to operate economically while maintaining quality in products and services; to serve a whole nation full of cantankerous people with varied tastes and decided preferences, while keeping some semblance of uniformity in policy, product, and processes—these are problems in engineering, organization, economics, and human relations that remain to be solved. The student who aspires to executive levels will be confronted with them. The powers of imagination, invention, political insight, and technical mastery that are required are very great.

College resources to help students develop such managerial skills are rather limited. Even the big publications and cultural programs of the college, with budgets on the order of tens of thousands of dollars, are peanuts compared with the budget of a large corporation, or even of the college itself. The membership of student groups is very small, compared with the number of employees supervised on a job. The big national student organizations begin to approach the complexity of large national enterprises. But the scale of things in college is too small to yield very effective experience related to the management of large enterprises.

Third, the phenomenon of the "organization man" presents a real problem for students entering an occupation. There is a danger of loss of identity in the impersonal relationships of modern enterprises.[16] The pressure for conformity tends to stereotype employees and mark them with the brand of the firm. The student needs to be aware of these pressures, to come to terms with them, to find ways to maintain his own identity in spite of them. He may wish to avoid them if he can by finding employment in an enterprise that is less demanding and rigid and that offers more opportunities for individualization. Some enterprises have been more successful than others in coping with the problem of conformity; some have tried harder than others to develop techniques of human relations in management. The student, in his own interest, may wish to use discriminating judgment upon entering his first job by selecting the kind of organization in which he feels he can work comfortably, without sacrificing his identity and his interests.

Scientific and cultural development. Though little needs to be added to the volume of material on needs for scientific development and the enlargement of cultural life, there are three areas of special need which students may wish to consider in vocational planning.

First is the need for scientific and cultural leadership in the development of certain areas of the world. Underdeveloped areas exist in many parts of the globe, including the United States. The introduction of scientific techniques into industry and agriculture, the improvement of production, the enlargement of educational opportunities, the improvement of community services, and the improvement of health amount to a social revolution. If it is to be reasonable, conservative, and productive, rather than disruptive or violent, extremely skilled leadership will be needed. As a matter of national policy, the United States has undertaken to provide leadership as well as financial aid in the development of various areas. The jobs are not those which a fresh young college graduate can step into right after graduation; they require breadth of experience as well as education. They require persons who have some intimate acquaintance with another country, with its language and culture, as well as some technical skill. In charting the course of vocational development, this area of social need should be kept in mind by students who can present both breadth of interest and specialized skill.

Second, effective leadership is needed in the development of community life in this country as well as abroad. City planning and community organization are new fields of work which may command the interest of students. A whole new set of occupations in social welfare have grown up, diversified far beyond the traditional kinds of social work. Such programs require skill in planning, organization, and human relations of a very high quality. Here again both specialized education and mature experience are needed. But some students must move toward such work in their careers if the development of community life is to keep pace with scientific techniques.

Third, the cultural life of the nation needs constant replenishing. Music, art, drama, literature nourish and enrich family and community life. The enjoyment and understanding of life are as much a human right as food and shelter. Above all, a new view of the new world, through art, literature, and religion, is desperately needed in modern life. Some students with abilities and interests in the arts and religion will be needed in communities that have suddenly grown to the point where museums, libraries, orchestras, theaters, and churches are needed where none were before.

This does not mean that every college graduate is needed in overseas development, community welfare services, the church, or the theatre. It does mean, rather, that students who concentrate in languages, area studies, anthropology, the arts, religion, or similar fields have new occupations that may be open to them at some point in their lives. The scientist or engineer who also cultivates an interest in another country or another culture may be prepared and available for an acutely important service. The artists and religious workers who address themselves to the enlargement of cultural opportunities and the exploration of the meaning of a confused and changing world will be on the growing edge of their occupations. And it is at the points of growth, change, and development that scholarship of high quality is always needed, in any occupation.

Personal and family resources. Entry into any occupation requires some capital. Even if it is only enough money to buy a "little black dress" for the office or to live on cereal and fruit until the first pay check, the capital has to be there. The capital investment in a business of one's own, of course, is very substantial. The practice of professions such as medicine or law requires investment in an office and equipment and also something to live on until income builds up. A college education itself is a tremendous capital investment, often amounting to tens of thousands of dollars. The financial resources for entry into an occupation also have to be provided over and above college costs.

The family is the primary source of capital. Relatives, friends, the old family banker also help. But more and more ways are opening up for students from families of moderate means to get a start in their occupation. Scholarships and fellowships for advanced study, management training programs, junior partnerships, and residencies or group practice open up possibilities for entry into occupations that would otherwise be closed to many graduates.

Of course, where they go from there is a different matter. Once entered upon an occupation, the accumulation of capital is their own concern. And if they wish to start new enterprises or enter independent practice, they have to plan for the systematic saving and investment that will produce the necessary capital.

Families and family acquaintances also yield the personal contacts needed for occupational entry. The college graduate can, of course, look for a job all on his own and make his own contacts, through classmates, alumni, the college placement office, and teachers. But the resources of his family and its place in the community offer introductions that he can use effectively.*

Frequently students express reluctance to use family resources in entering their chosen occupation. Realistically, however, it is impossible to enter an occupation without help from somebody at some point. The student who really exercises mature judgment in vocational planning will try to determine the resources he needs and get them in the best way he can. Both capital and contacts available through the family can be used in the manner and to the extent he wishes. On the other hand, if his family has little capital and few contacts, he can look elsewhere for help.

Take the case of Jim Sawyer, for example. His widowed mother, unable to work, lived on a small pension. He arrived at college with a hundred dollars in his wallet, with no family resources whatever behind him except an introduction from a high school teacher to the Dean of Men. The placement officer helped him to find a room in return for doing odd jobs, yard work, and household repairs, ten days a month, and a job in a restaurant for meals and some spending money. He made his own way the first year with the help of loans for fees, which he paid back out of income from a summer job. His grades were good enough to qualify him for a tuition scholarship the next year. By borrowing in the fall and paying off the loans in the summer, he got through college.

---

* It is of interest to note that only 30 percent of the women college graduates in the 1956 placement survey got their job leads through college placement services. Family contacts, friends, public and private employment agencies, and old-fashioned pavement-pounding accounted for most of the effective leads.

He qualified for a graduate fellowship in sociology and got a start toward college teaching in his field of interest.

Ralph Eberhart, in the same college class, had a ten thousand-dollar trust fund left to him by his father. When he decided in his freshman year to study medicine, he revised his financial plan with the help of his faculty adviser. He found a part-time job to pay part of his expenses. He worked in the summers in the chemical laboratory of an oil company for experience and additional income. He and his mother arranged to borrow additional money for his medical education to supplement his remaining funds.

Neither student had unlimited assets and contacts. Both made wise use of what they had: family funds, family friends, college loan and scholarship funds, faculty and staff counseling services, placement services, and their own earning power. Perhaps the most important factor in their success was careful planning through the use of counseling services in the college. People are always willing to help, but they want to give the kind of assistance that will be most useful. The student himself must decide what that will be and ask for what he most needs.

ECONOMIC INDEPENDENCE

The college years are a time of transition from family support to self-support, leading ultimately to economic independence and a separate financial base for one's own career and family. The student's progress toward economic independence proceeds upon a base provided by the capital investment of the family. His parents may be able to provide little or nothing to cover college costs, or they may be able to provide everything. But their contribution to a college education and entry into a profession is the first factor to take into consideration.

The contribution of the student out of his own earnings is a second factor. Working one's way through college is a classic American tradition. From Booker T. Washington tending the furnace at Hampton Institute on up to the student entrepreneur running a travel agency or delivery service, the success stories have been notable.

However, the student must consider his own resources and interests in determining his contribution to college costs. His principal obligation is to his academic work, which is a full-time job. His earnings must come from work that will not interfere with study. And the student should bear in mind the added stress occasioned by adding part-time employment to an academic load. Added hours mean increased fatigue. Allotment of additional time to employment makes it both more difficult and more important to maintain adequate recreation and rest in the weekly schedule. Measures must be taken to deal with the stress of work as well as the stress of study. And there is no accordion-pleated week, allowing time to be stretched at will.

Third, the student must weigh the relative advantages of part-time and summer work. If he must work his way through college, his greater opportunities for employment and income are probably in summer employment rather than part-time work. Summer employment also can relieve the work load during the academic year. When making financial plans, therefore, summer employment should probably come first, with part-time work as a source of supplementary income.

Fourth, the student must bear in mind that his earning power is relatively low during the college years, and his income expectations are much greater after entering his chosen occupation. Loans against future income represent a much more substantial source of financial support than earnings in college. Students make effective use of loans in two ways. They may borrow money at the beginning of a college year and pay it off with summer earnings. Or they may borrow funds to be paid back after college. This measure is particularly effective in the junior and senior years when larger loans are often allowed under college regulations and the period of interest accumulation is shorter before a full-time salary makes repayment possible.

Students should not depend on loans alone to finance a college education. A good rule of thumb in determining a reasonable limit is to borrow up to the total amount of the anticipated income in the first year after graduation. Since college loans are usually made at relatively low interest on a fairly long-term basis (four to ten years), the annual payments will then be fairly reasonable in proportion to annual income.

Finally, a certain amount of earning power is represented by a student's academic performance. Scholarships and grants-in-aid are now generally awarded principally on the basis of personal need, but students still must maintain a better-than-average record to qualify. Colleges use part of their funds to purchase brains and excellence by relieving superior students of some of their financial burdens. Scholarships and grants buy time for the student to devote to academic work.

Neither a scholarship award nor outside work can be taken lightly by the student. These things have to be taken seriously as ways of showing the mature responsibility that will qualify him for future employment. The advantages to be gained in competition for beginning jobs after college are very great if the student can show that he really earned his pay check or his scholarship by reliable, consistent, and productive work.

Getting enough money to pay one's way through college is only half the task of attaining economic independence. The habits of spending developed in the college years are an important part of vocational development. Take Ralph Richardson's work sheet (Fig. 8-1), for example. Ralph can choose to spend his money on two different kinds of college education. He is in a position to choose the college he thinks offers the greatest advantage to him. He can choose on the basis of cost alone. Or he has a way of making up the difference in cost if the private college offers him more advantages. If the public college offers more of what he wants, he has the opportunity of earning money in the summer to save, to spend on additional education, to invest, to use for entry into a job; he has the alternative of putting in less time on employment and more time on study; he also may choose to take additional employment to reduce the financial load on the family. All of these factors must be considered, not only in choosing a college but in making a budget from year to year.

FINANCIAL WORK SHEET

Annual Costs	Public College	Private College
Tuition	$ 100.00	$ 800.00
Room & Board	630.00	750.00
Travel	50.00	150.00
Personal expense	350.00	350.00
	$1130.00	$2050.00

Sources of income		
Family	$1000.00	$1000.00
Grant-in-aid		750.00
Summer job		400.00
Part-time work	150.00	
	$1150.00	$2150.00

Fig. 8–1. Financial Work Sheet of Ralph Richardson. If Ralph is a better-than-average student and the private college affords advantages that he desires to gain, he may use such a work sheet to decide whether he can get the necessary resources to consider the private rather than the public college. He may choose the college which gives him some things he desires and plan to pay the increased costs out of summer work and scholarship-level grades. Or he may decide to spend less on his college education and save his summer earnings to provide capital for occupational entry, personal investment, or marriage. **All the alternatives are good; the choice is his.**

Even on the most limited budget, the student has to learn to spend wisely. He must get the things he needs to live: adequate food, housing, clothing, and personal services. He must pay the cost of education: fees, tuition, books. He must have some funds for participation in student life: for dates, memberships, entertainment, contributions, travel. He must plan to have some money at the end of the senior year for job hunting, to cover clothes, travel, correspondence, long distance calls, and the like. He will want some luxuries, and if he has income over and above his basic needs, he will have to decide whether to buy luxury or additional education. If he lives at home, he will have to pay commuting costs; if he goes to a residential college, the costs of travel must be covered. He should make some provision for emergencies: illness, accident, loss of family support.

Basic living and educational costs are subject to very little individual variation between students in the same college. But in other areas, a wide range of choice is possible and expenditures can be astronomical for things both educational and gastronomical. Competition for a desirable date can run into considerable money. Coffee, cigarettes, alcohol, and automobiles represent substantial cost items in a student budget. Oddly, though students seem to go through an incredible amount of money in nothing flat, the amount spent on books, conferences, concerts, and other educational resources seems to represent a very small part of the budget.

Budgeting for wise expenditures is not an easy matter. College towns are expensive places to live. Shopkeepers, boarding house proprietors, restaurateurs, and hotel managers have been accused of gouging students ever since there were colleges. Some quotations from Helen Waddell's book, *The Wandering Scholars*, indicate that student finances have always left something to be desired. "Paris eats money," is the plaint of one of the earliest extant student letters home, dating from the thirteenth century. "Help me, gracious parent, for I am sick for home and ill," runs another, "I have no books, no shoes, and hardly a decent robe to my back."[18] There are always more things to buy than one can afford. To get himself through college, the student has to face the same pressures that his parents have faced in getting the family budget under control and finding the capital to invest in his education.

There are no general rules for proper budgeting. The student's own interests and values will have to dictate what things come first. For the serious student, indeed for any student, getting himself to and from college, paying tuition and fees, eating and sleeping comfortably, keeping clean and personally attractive come first. If he has no money for

anything else, he can get through college creditably, comfortably, and
happily.

There are only three things that can be done with money: spend it,
save it, and give it away. The student who develops financial competence will learn to do all three things. What he gives away, of course,
must come from his surplus, over and above basic needs. College will
probably give him an opportunity to contribute to causes that need his
support. Scholarship funds are supported by students. World University Service, The Asia Foundation, the churches and Student Christian
Associations will come to him for money, books, and clothing that are
needed by students abroad, whose resources are pitifully meager and
whose financial problems are astronomically greater than his own. The
Community Fund and the health and welfare agencies in the community will give him a chance to contribute to the general welfare of
his fellow citizens. His gifts may not seem great. But the act of giving
will gain him two important advantages: First, he will learn to allocate
part of his income for gifts to important social purposes. Second, he will
be actively associating himself as a person with the welfare of his community and the development of colleges and universities here and
abroad.

These are hard lessons for anyone to learn. It is safe to say that at
some point in the college years, any student, even with ample family
support, is likely to face a financial crisis, to find his means acutely inadequate to his needs and desires. He will face a deficit that has to be
covered somehow. At this point, it will become important to learn how
to use credit. The process of borrowing can be used to his advantage,
or it can produce grave difficulties for him and his friends.

Most students borrow casually, unsystematically. Clothes go out on
various backs; the roommates' wardrobe is regarded as a ready source.
Small sums of money go back and forth among friends. Cigarettes are
practically communal property.

Student mores usually indicate the appropriate limits to casual borrowing and lending. Toothbrushes, fountain pens, and other highly
individualized property are usually "off limits." It is generally assumed,
too, that the attitude "what is thine, is mine" is inappropriate in college
as in other adult societies. Private property rights can be protected by
the student, and it is his responsibility to draw the line at which use of
his personal property by others becomes unacceptable. But there are
very strong traditions on many campuses of openhandedness and
casualness in borrowing and lending.

When it comes to large sums of money, other factors must be considered by students. All students must be assumed to be operating on a limited budget. Any loan, therefore, reduces the margin of the lender and limits his opportunities to satisfy his personal interests. In view of this fact, colleges generally make funds available for short-term loans—five or ten dollars to tide a student over to the next allowance or pay-check or to enable him to take advantage of an unexpected educational opportunity for which he had not budgeted. On the whole, both one's own interests and those of other students are better served by borrowing from official college sources than from fellow-students. Furthermore, systematic borrowing of this type establishes a credit record which can be useful to the student after college.

In the long run, the habits of controlling a personal budget in college can contribute much to successful income management after college. Realistic expectations of income, careful budget planning, living within one's means, judicious sacrifices and savings for long-range plans, contributing to community welfare, and maintaining a credit rating are all developmental tasks related to economic independence that have to be mastered in the college years.

Finally, successful financial management can form a sound basis for the long-range planning of vocational development, marriage, and family support after college. Any margin for saving or investment during the college years increases the capital available for such purposes at graduation. Students need to achieve financial responsibility during the college years as a step toward economic independence in the rest of their adult lives.

MARRIAGE IN THE CAREER PLAN

Marriage presents needs for a sound financial base and some capital investment. Being married while in college requires adequate provision of financial support both for the new family and for education. Husband and wife must work together in securing the financial resources needed for entry into an occupation by either one or both.

Sharing the tasks of planning their vocational development and their family can be a deeply satisfying experience for students. It is often pointed out that marriage may reduce or control many sources of stress and add to the resources of emotional strength and support for both husband and wife. On the other hand, there are additional stresses at the beginning of married life which must be controlled. In determining the appropriate timing of marriage in relation to education, students are wise to consider all the stresses involved, both in academic work and in marriage, and to insure that they can be adequately handled.[19]

The decision on the appropriate time of marriage is, therefore, a highly individual matter, to be settled by the two people involved. On the whole, colleges are disposed to accept whatever decisions students make about the timing of marriage and to offer counseling services for students to use in making the decision. College chaplains, deans, counselors, all are able to help if asked. There are, of course, regulations governing residence and student status which must be taken into account. Consultation on such matters in advance of marriage is always in order as a means of protecting one's status as a student and securing any services that may be provided for married students. Regulations and services vary so much from college to college, however, that each student must get the necessary information and guidance on his own initiative.

Marriage is an important part of the total life plan. It is a fulfillment of the developmental task of intimacy in personal relationships. In the vicissitudes of occupational choice and advancement, the love and understanding of a husband or wife sustains the sense of selfhood and individual meaning as nothing else can.

There are also changes in social patterns and personal expectations affecting both men and women of which they need to be aware.

First, paid employment outside the home is increasingly part of the life pattern of women. The typical cycle of work in the life of women seems to be employment up to the arrival of the first child; a lapse of time until the last child is in school (usually around the mother's 30th to 35th year); and resumption of employment until retirement.[20] Such a cycle may very well be included in long-range plans for marriage and career development. The major factor in successful planning for the wife's employment is the understanding and acceptance of the husband. He must share in plans for her vocational development and in relating her employment to family life if her work is to be a family asset, rather than a source of stress.

Second, employment for both men and women is almost exclusively outside the home. Employment can no longer be related directly to life in the family. New tasks, consequently, are posed for parents in finding ways of introducing and interpreting their work outside the home to their children. It is now particularly important for the mother's work to be understood by children, for two reasons. The girls need to be acquainted with the mother's work as a way of beginning to think of themselves as having a job of their own. They expect to become wives and mothers, but more needs to be done to develop their expectations that they will also work.[21]

The occupational interests of girls seem to follow similar developmental trends to those of boys. But at the stage of crystallization, they seem to become vague and general in focus.[22] Their work expectations may be sharpened and more clearly differentiated by knowing that women work and they, too, may expect to work.

In the second place, little boys need to know and understand their mother's occupation as a means of developing some expectations of what their wives may do when they are grown up and married. The chances of successful occupational adjustment on the part of both men and women can be enhanced by early childhood understanding of the occupation of both mother and father.

Where both husband and wife are college graduates and both expect to be employed outside the home for considerable periods of time, the problem of differences in income may become really serious. Men still expect to be the principal breadwinners for their families. Their position as fathers, their status in the community, their conceptions of themselves require them to be the major source of support. Where the wife's income is actually needed to meet deficiencies in the family budget, the question of the self-respect of the husband may arise. There may be a sense of inadequacy on his part, a feeling that if he were just a little bit better, if he could manage to earn a little more, things would be all right. There may be some embarrassment at allowing the wife to assume part of the financial load. The situation is aggravated further if the woman's income turns out to be higher than the man's, if she is a higher-paid worker than he, and thus appears to be more successful. Competition is not a very easy factor to deal with in marriage. It is hardly compatible with happiness, mutual trust and appreciation, and cooperation that an enduring relationship requires.[23]

Such questions cannot be resolved on a superficial or haphazard basis. Accepting and understanding the legitimate personal needs of both partners requires depth of understanding and consideration for the personalities involved. Self-esteem is a tremendously important effect of work and of the income from an occupation. Superficial resolution of the problems of work in the lives of married people is not enough to protect the sense of selfhood in both parties.

There are very few well-established guidelines for people to follow in resolving problems of this kind. About all that can be said is that some couples have successfully faced such situations and have worked them out to their mutual satisfaction. As each couple faces these questions and resolves them, more is added to the experience that can be made available to guide others.

Another problem is the difference in life expectancy of men and women. In the United States today, actuarial calculations indicate that the surviving partner is more likely than not to be the wife. Some people react to this fact with a great deal of anxiety. Some parents even put pressure on their daughters to go to college and prepare for an occupation so that they can support themselves in widowhood. Often, they urge their daughters to prepare to teach since preparation for teaching is completed in college and the occupation is one which can be entered and left with relative ease and frequency. It is also regarded as a profession in which women are more acceptable than in others. Some of these generalizations are true, to some degree. But there are other skills which may be more durable than skill in teaching, and other occupations which afford much more opportunity for re-entry after a lapse of time. Furthermore, teaching requires a skill that some women do not have.

We are living in an era when women need to plan for self-support at various times during their lives. But occupational choice for women is best guided by the same considerations that men follow: personal interest, aptitude, income, geographic mobility, marriage and family responsibilities. The dictates of prudence require foresight and planning to use one's best abilities in meeting the vicissitudes of life. The development of skill and adaptability go a lot further in plans for self-support than any stereotyped notions about occupations which are good for a widow to follow.

A college education is equally important for both partners as a capital investment that will support their marriage. For a man, it is a source of increased income, amounting in the course of his working years to between $100,000 and $150,000 more than he could expect to earn without a Bachelor's degree (see Fig. 8-2). For a woman, the difference in income expectancy is not so great, since her working years are somewhat fewer. But the Bachelor's degree is the modern equivalent of a dowry, providing potential capital and family income and insuring the support of children in the event of the father's death.

Hence, it seems highly desirable for students to finish college, from a purely economic point of view. If they feel it best to marry before completing the degree, it seems advisable for them to be sure in advance that both can finish college. If both sets of parents are willing to continue support after marriage, or if scholarship or loan assistance

YEARS
EDUCATION

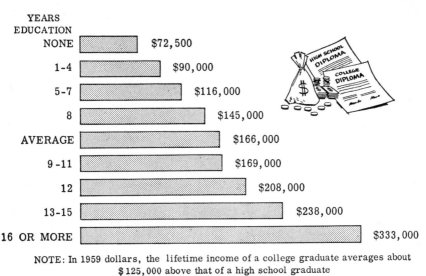

NONE	$72,500
1-4	$90,000
5-7	$116,000
8	$145,000
AVERAGE	$166,000
9-11	$169,000
12	$208,000
13-15	$238,000
16 OR MORE	$333,000

NOTE: In 1959 dollars, the lifetime income of a college graduate averages about $125,000 above that of a high school graduate

From *Investing in People* (Atlanta: Southern Regional Educational Board).

Fig. 8–2.   Estimated Lifetime Income For Men by Amount of Education, 1959.

is adequate, there seems to be no particular reason to postpone marriage in favor of an education.

Both college education and marriage should be adequately financed, however. If either student has to earn part of or all the costs of college, the odds seem to be in favor of postponing marriage. For one thing, the stress of combining study, work, and marriage reaches the point of hazard. The time requirements are almost impossible to honor. Either academic work or income must suffer if the marriage is to get a good start. The stress is most often relieved by having one partner drop out of college and work to support the other. This is most often the wife. But her economic contribution is reduced in value if she goes to work before receiving the degree. Her income is never as great as it could be. And the future income she could expect to earn, as insurance for the family in the event of the husband's death, is similarly reduced. As a result, the financial burden on the husband after graduation is actually increased; he has to make up the difference in income and insurance in order to protect his family. The short-run gains of marriage in the college years never quite come up to the long-term losses. They are paid for many times over in both economic risks and emotional strain, neither of which is good for a marriage.

Postponing marriage until completion of college education offers many advantages. More capital investment is made in both partners before marriage. Income expectancy is much better for both. If the wife works to support the husband's graduate study, her income will be more substantial, and he stands a better chance either to finish graduate study or get started in business with more help from her earnings. On the personal side, there are also some gains. Under present student mores, marriage tends to end the period of forming friendships; married people tend to "go out of circulation" and reduce their personal contacts. There are advantages to "staying in circulation" and continuing to make a lot of new friends, who are a needed source of practical and emotional support in later years. A postponed marriage may get off to a better start with more emotional and financial resources on both sides.

But students sometimes feel they can't wait. Men say it's the women who are frantic to get a mate, and women say the men won't wait. Perhaps the women have a shade more responsibility for the rush; they outnumber men in the general population, and college men don't have to marry college women, so the competition is stiff. It probably ought to be the woman who sets the time for marriage. It is her education, her future income, her ability to face the future's risks that are at stake. If she is in a good position to contribute to family income, now or in the future, her marriage has better prospects. But many college women fear the best men will be snapped up before they are ready to marry. Their fears may not be very realistic. On the whole, the best men—the ones with the most brains, the highest ambitions, and good income expectancies—have the longest period of education ahead. The men who have the most to gain from postponing marriage are those who plan to enter high-level scientific and professional fields: physicists, engineers, physicians, military officers, college teachers, ministers, lawyers. Generally speaking, from the point of view of status, prestige, and intellectual gifts, these men have a great deal to offer their wives. They are likely to be worth waiting for.

These general considerations are only guidelines. The decision to marry and the time of marriage are individual matters. But there is much to be gained by considering marriage as part of a total career plan for both partners. Marriage should enrich, not interfere with, their careers. And marriage should be planned so both students' college education will strengthen it, not increase its risks and difficulties.

VOCATIONAL DEVELOPMENT AND THE LIFE PLAN

A great deal has been written about the problem of aging. However, this problem is not an immediate concern of students and does not deserve very much treatment here. Suffice it to say that eventually students may expect to grow old and should look forward to the kind of activity which is appropriate in advanced years.

First, the life plan should anticipate retirement. Leaving one's occupation and giving up regular employment does not, of course, mean giving up activity. Plans for retirement should, therefore, include things which one would enjoy doing that were not permitted in the busy years of employment. What students can do now to prepare for the retirement years is to cultivate as many interests as possible. Studies of the interest patterns of older people indicate that interests cultivated in one's youth can be renewed after a lapse of years,* while it is rarely possible in one's mature years to cultivate interests that have not at least been tried in one's youth.

Second, plans need to be made for retirement income. Investment officers in insurance firms, banks, and other financial institutions can offer much better advice than can be given briefly in a textbook. But the plans must be balanced with immediate needs for vocational development, family support, and the enjoyment of living while one is alive.

Third, a great deal of work needs to be done in the world for which people are not paid. No job claims all of one's interest, so that in making a life plan, satisfaction can be increased by planning to include voluntary service in the community to satisfy some personal interests. Such voluntary civic service has often been suggested to women as a substitute for the satisfaction in gainful employment. Civic service has been represented frequently to men as a way of increasing contacts and influence, in the interest of success. But there are even more desirable effects to be gained from unpaid work. Self-development need not be limited to the job, but it can be greatly extended to interests expressed in many different forms of service.

Fourth, with increasing maturity and increased experience in one's occupation comes increasing responsibility as a worker and a citizen. The patterns of responsible scholarship developed by the student in the college years sustain the development of increased responsibility and success in a career. The same patterns of responsibility also sustain the development of responsible citizenship.

The life plan is an intensely individual matter. Essentially, the satisfactions to be gained in an occupation and in the community come first from the satisfaction of individual needs and the pleasure of self-realiza-

* Gardiner Murphy suggests that "canalized interests" are never extinguished, but return in later years.[24]

tion. There are rewards of popularity, income, and success to which people need to aspire. But the life pattern is not a continuously rising curve of success and reward. It has its ups and downs. Fortunes can be made and lost overnight. Success may be attained, but the student should be prepared also to recognize that success sometimes may require him to make unpleasant decisions or take action to which people may respond with disfavor or downright hostility.

Perhaps the life of a scholar is easier to plan than some other patterns of living. The experienced scholar knows that things will not always go well, and he accepts the fact that he will make mistakes and fail, perhaps more often than he will succeed. But he knows what to do with his mistakes; he recognizes them as a very important part of his personal development. So perhaps more than some other people, he is prepared for the ups and downs of life. Above all, whatever happens to him, his basic vocational goal can be attained: he can learn something, and he can put it into such form that others can learn too. And this is a very great gain. There are not very many occupations in which something can be attained regardless of success or failure, approbation or disapproval. In this sense, perhaps, the student can count himself fortunate to have chosen the vocation of scholarship.

9

The give-and-take of student life

*Human relations
in college*

SELF-REALIZATION IN A COMMUNITY

One way in which we experience self-consciousness is the feeling of a distinction between what is inward, personal, private and what is outward, public, revealed. In the course of growing up, all of us feel in various ways both enjoyable and uncomfortable the sense of uniqueness, distinctiveness and separateness that confirms individual identity. Sometimes it comes as a sense of almost unbearable loneliness or isolation of the precious inward self from everything and everybody else in the world. Sometimes there may be a feeling of happy recognition of things or persons outside as having a special meaning for the inward self.[1]

Self-realization involves both an awareness of inward, uniquely personal qualities and a relationship to things outside the self. Successfully managed, self-realization leads to integrity—the sense that the inward self is consistent with the outward self that is revealed to others.

For self-realization we require a community in which to live and act. We have to live with people who upon close acquaintance can help us make sure that our actions are consistent with our inner wishes, that we are known to others as the persons we would like to be. Such a community must be more than a collection of people in a given area. Its members have to be bound to each other by settled relationships and patterns of living that can be learned and understood. Consistent meaning in human relationships is needed if we are to be able to assess the meaning of our behavior.

The college is not like every other community. It has limited membership. It does not offer all of the services or require all of the responsibilities found in other communities. But these limitations enable the college to satisfy to an unusual degree the requirements of a community in which self-realization can be learned. The relationships among its members, being limited, can be clearly defined and given specific meaning. The relationships of students to faculty, freshmen to upperclassmen, one department or major to another are fitted into a definite system. There is a meaningful progression from one year's study to the next, proceeding to the achievement of a degree, which means leaving the community. The standards of achievement and behavior expected of the student are clearly defined. The student can figure out without much difficulty just about where he stands, or ought to stand, in any given relationship.

A college is likely to be a rather stable community, with a strong permanent core of members (the faculty) maintaining a consistent program (the curriculum). Its special atmosphere and traditions are carefully preserved and highly valued. The strong conservative forces in most colleges which preserve their special quality are attributable to the self-perpetuating character of their membership. The faculty controls the selection of new members of the faculty and the admission of students. The effect of such selective measures is to preserve a characteristic, almost a stereotyped, personality pattern among students and faculty.

But faculties, while preserving quality, generally try also to provide for some variety in interests, specialization, and point of view to counteract the tendency toward conformity. Departments try to get as much variety as possible in the interests of faculty members. Admissions committees try to avoid stereotyped standards for students. There is a story about the college admissions officer who received a letter of recommendation about an applicant saying, "I do not think she is a leader, but I believe she is a good follower." The admissions officer wrote back, saying: "We will be glad to have this girl. This college is full of leaders, and we need some good followers." An effort is made to provide for variety in social class, family background, occupational interests and economic levels and for wide geographic distribution, in the student body.

Another conservative factor is the guarantee of membership in the college to faculty and students who meet its standards. Tenure is a very precious privilege for both faculty and students. It can be terminated only for the most serious offenses, principally for failures to meet clearly defined standards of scholarly work. Faculty members may criticise mother, home, and country, publish controversial works, hold radical views, and still continue in membership, provided they act within the canons of scholarship, use valid methods of inquiry, and accept scholarly criticism. The faculty tries to tolerate a broad range of opinions and to protect its members from unwarranted attack, reprisals, or repression. It thus exercises both a liberating and a conserving function.

It may come as a shock to some students to suggest that the quality and the freedom of the student body are protected by the faculty. But the faculty tries to select students who will perpetuate a fairly consistent pattern of interests, abilities, and achievement in the college. The tenure of students is protected, just as the tenure of faculty is preserved. So long as students meet the requirements of scholarly work and honor the regulations and standards of college life, they are protected from reprisal so far as possible.

This is a great advantage to the student, on the whole. For, as an old collegiate aphorism puts it, "The value of the degree depends on the quality of the students who are awarded it after you graduate." Its value can endure only in and through persons who consistently try to represent high standards of scholarly value in their work.

In choosing to attend one college rather than another, the student takes on some responsibility for perpetuating the distinctive character of the college. He will not—Heaven forbid!—take on all of the qualities exemplified in members of the college. He cannot if he would and he should not if he could. "Thank God!" cried one professor, "there are no typical students at this college!" The student rather must find in the college the personal relationships and activities which will help him realize both the personal qualities he desires and the standards of excellence desired in the college. He finds his models among the faculty and students with whom he associates daily. He can improve the quality of his life and work through the responsiveness, help, and counsel of other members of the college. But he must also contribute to the life of the college or a community, meet the standards of academic performance that it sets, and carry on some of the distinctive activities of student life.

The faculty protects the tenure of the student but gives him responsibility for maintaining the standards required in the college. The student's work is graded by his instructors to insure that he meets the standards required. He is protected to some extent from the effects of capriciousness or ill will, on the part of a faculty member, by two safeguards: Acceptable standards of grades and behavior are fairly well defined by agreement among faculty members; and a student cannot as a rule be disqualified for failure under one instructor alone; only a series of failures can be grounds for disqualification. Most college standards and regulations are based on the assumption that a student is responsible for his own behavior, for his program, study habits, interests, and achievement. Grades are given by his instructors, but he earns them. Regulations may be passed by faculty or students, but each student observes them in his own behavior. Like the faculty member, the student is secure against unwarranted attack or interference and free to pursue his own interests. But he is expected to use his security and freedom in the interest of sound scholarship and the achievement of high levels of excellence.

SELF-REALIZATION AS REVEALING AND SHARING ONESELF

There are three elements of self-realization in college life. Each of these elements is two-sided, involving both the inward and the outward, the private and the public aspects of the self. Each requires both self-awareness and self-revelation.

The development of common interests

Community life in the college is based on the activity of small groups of people sharing some common interest. Like-minded students cannot find each other except by making their interests known. In so doing, they have to reveal themselves to each other. Most colleges have developed some procedures for identifying common interests. The college catalogue itself, with its announcement of courses, publishes the interests of instructors by describing the courses they offer to teach. The student chooses the courses which fit his interests. Catalogues or student handbooks offer information about the interests of clubs, societies, performing groups, and governing bodies in which the student may share. There are announcements and invitations for opening meetings, teas, picnics, lectures, special events; it is hard to escape being informed about opportunities to identify with groups sharing a common interest. It is equally hard to select, from all of the opportunities offered, those which will be most rewarding for self-development.

For this reason, the student must have his own inner resources of self-awareness and self-direction. He cannot do everything. He cannot take all of the courses he would like or join every student activity. He has to know his own interests and have an idea of their relative importance to him; he must express his interests and inquire into the interests of others; he must also select the students and faculty members with whom he wishes to share common interests.

Two considerations are important in selecting common interests as a basis for shared activity. One is the nature of the interests; the other is the character of the people with whom they are shared.

Common interests must provide room for growth and development. Mere repetition of familiar experience and activity is boring and stultifying. To be rewarding, shared activity must offer something new, enlarging experience and feeding the self with new ideas and experiences. But common interests must represent more than mere novelty. They must include something continuous with past experience and something familiar on which further development can be based. College courses, for instance, are based on work done in high school, but they open out into broader reaches of ideas and skills. In choosing either courses or student activities, the student has to match his previous experience and interest with the new interests he wishes to develop. This interest must be a public rather than a private interest, related to the subject matter, rather than to the study of himself.

For example, faculty advisers are sometimes apprehensive over the desire of freshmen to enrol in courses such as psychology and philosophy, which attract students because of their novelty since they are not standard high school subjects. Some students hope to use such courses to learn how to understand themselves. Such interests may be commendable, but they cannot be satisfied. Neither subject takes up problems of an individual character. Psychology deals with theories of human behavior in general, philosophy with the general theory of value. These principles apply to the individual in a general way. But the inexperienced student frequently tries to apply everything to himself in the most particular way. As a result, he learns little of the subject and less about himself.

The student wishing to study any subject or participate in group activity has to bring to it more than self-interest. He must understand his own interests well enough to distinguish them from general facts, theories, and activities applying to subjects of common interest. Common interests cannot develop around self-interest. The student has to find interests that are consistent with his inward self, continuous with his past experience, and shared by other students. These interests must open the self to a broader range of ideas, to new experience, to new people. Common interests must move private interests outward into a public world.

Self-realization may be defined as just such a process of growing outward into public life. For in relating himself to others in the pursuit of a common interest, the student reveals himself and develops a public image. He becomes known as a person with special interests in literature, chemistry, art, mathematics, or other fields. He becomes known as a person who can contribute to the life of the college in various ways, from solving calculus problems on up to winning football games and raising campus chest funds.

The public image of the self can develop only in a community. It pictures the person as the community sees him. It is up to his fellow students and faculty members to say whether a student's public image is desirable or acceptable in the college. It is up to the student himself to determine whether his public image is consistent with his inward knowledge of himself and acceptable to him.

Which brings us to the second point—the nature of his associates in shared activity. Interests come attached to people, and the identification of common interests amounts to forming an attachment to others. "Birds of a feather flock together." A common interest is the feather that identifies the flock. People with a common interest *are like* each other, at least in having one like interest. Whether they also *like* each other is another matter, and whether they flock together is determined by considerations over and above the content of their common interests.

For one thing, common interests, shared activities, and groups forming around them must be acceptable to the rest of the college. The college allows so very broad a range of interests that it is hard to conceive of any activity, even the most hazardous or trivial, that cannot be at least tried on some campus. It is better not to tempt fate by trying to give an example since some college students would be sure to try it. Suffice it to say that the college is the kind of community that favors the development of groups around common interests. But acceptable interests must bear some recognizable relation to the purpose of the college and meet its standards of achievement and behavior.

More important, perhaps, is the requirement of some desirable and durable personal relationship over and above the common interest itself. For self-realization, a student needs the encouragement and companionship of friends. They interpose a shield against a hostile world, behind which he can feel secure in revealing himself more fully. The student also needs both approving and critical responses from friends to continue developing his interests. These constitute the essential reward of learning that keeps the process going; and the response that rewards learning has to come from a person who is admired and important, whose response is desired.

This does not mean that the student should try to find common interests and make common cause with just those faculty and students who are perfect. He may, with the intolerance of the young, refuse any personal relationship with anyone whose behavior falls short of his expectations in some respect. In that case, his circle of acquaintances will be extremely small. But he can always find interests that he shares with people whose acquaintance will reward him in some way, and he can find models among faculty and students who exemplify in some respects the kind of person he wants to become. Sometimes a common interest may even be found in a problem or shortcoming that he shares with others. And the relationship he forms with them may be very rewarding if they are willing to recognize the common problem, deal with it realistically, and work toward high standards of attainment.

For example, some years ago, when the average height of students was somewhat less than it is now, taller than average students had rather a hard time on some campuses. The beds were too short, the classroom seats too small, and other students gave them a good deal of teasing and hazing, some of it rather unkind. Tall women had a particularly trying time since the prevailing social standards prescribed that the men they dated should be taller than they. Men who were tall enough were in short supply, and even when available they sometimes failed to provide congenial companionship in other respects.

On one campus, some women over five feet eleven organized a society, the Glamazons, to deal with the common problem. They secured as faculty adviser the dean of women, herself a rather tall woman, generally admired for her personal and professional stature, rather than her height. They called on the departments of physical education, home economics, and psychology for expert help in improving physical coordination, dress, and social relationships. They shared successful ex-

periences with each other and worked with the college administration
to solve problems related to furniture, equipment, and services. The
students did not wish to be like each other, or like the dean. But they
helped each other become attractive and interesting persons. They
protected each other from derision, and the organization gave them
needed prestige and status. Because they cultivated a variety of social
and cultural interests, other students became interested in their activities, and being invited to one of their meetings became rather a mark of
distinction.

Bias and prejudice interfere with the development of common interests and personal relationships in shared activity. These factors tend to
inhibit self-realization. Students are sometimes reluctant to try out a
new idea or suggest a novel activity; they naturally prefer, like other
people, to stick with what is comfortable and familiar. Bias and prejudice are much more serious than simple hesitation over something new.
They are essentially selfish acts. To discuss ideas in terms of personal
prejudices amounts to focusing attention on oneself; since common
interests cannot develop around self-interest, other people are shut out.
To introduce personal prejudices into shared activity is a form of resistance to learning, requiring the outward world to conform to one's inward preferences rather than developing inwardly in response to an
enlarging world of experience and interest. Just as prejudice keeps the
student from enlarging his interests, snobbishness cuts him off from
personal relationships that might advance his development.

Both common interests and the personal relationships developed
around them help to enlarge the scope of learning. For example, the shy
student needs precisely the rough-and-tumble response of more aggressive students, which he "shies away from," in order to develop his social
skills. The prejudiced student needs personal acquaintance with the
very minorities he despises in order to develop needed capacity for
fairness and objectivity. Self-realization means opening the self to
others, not shutting them out, revealing ideas and accepting new interests, not clinging to familiar patterns of life and thought.

The college helps students identify common interests by giving them
security as members of the community and protecting an area of freedom for self-expression and individuality. The student can take advantage of this kind of community only by assuming a relatively detached attitude toward his inward, private self. Some of the limitations
of the self have to be transcended without destroying its essential character. Some of the self's weaknesses have to be revealed with as little
shame as possible; exploring common interests means exploring oneself

more deeply, even at the expense of some embarrassment. Some of the Glamazons, for instance, had to reveal their embarrassing awkwardness in order to help others deal with a common problem. Sharing activity that explores novel or creative fields means deviating from some commonly accepted ideas. The Glamazons, for example, had to deviate from the popular notion that an acceptable date must be taller than the woman in order to find satisfying personal relationships based on some more significant standards. There can be tacit agreement among students that honest errors, mistakes, or deviations from accepted ideas will be understood and forgiven. This does not mean that no criticism is allowed, but often makes it possible to give even more pointed and meaningful criticism than usual. Reprisal and retribution are suspended in the interest of more freedom to try new and unfamiliar tasks or to solve common problems.

We recognize common interests by the matching or fit of their content. The interests seem to go together, and on further examination, it is possible to define particular points at which they are continuous with each other.

Common interests may be recognized by their similarity or identity. "Anyone want to make a fourth at bridge?" "Yes, I do." The interest in bridge is identical; the "fourth" fits in. Of course, there may be some interests, identical in character, which cannot be shared, in the very nature of things—a common interest in dating a beautiful blonde freshman, for example. So identical interests may lead to either shared activity or competition, depending on how many can play.

Common interests must be public, rather than private; it is a nuisance to have someone read over your shoulder, whereas reading aloud to a friend may be a great joy. Common interests give meaning to the relationship between the participants, over and above the meaning in the activity; reading aloud to a friend means sharing a relationship, whereas reading in a reserve room full of other students does not.

Common interests may also be quite different in character, but related to each other. The differences may be necessary to the relationship or the activity. Republicans and Democrats have a common interest in politics, and they need each other for politics to be any fun. Or the differences may be between parts of a whole, which must be brought together before anything meaningful can appear. Sometimes distinctive social roles are required for common interests to develop, as for example, teacher and pupil belong together. Or differences may just be there and be used in the common interest, as in the case of foreign students who contribute to the discussion out of their different cultural background. In some communities, differences in interest, background, or role are used to divide groups of people and keep them apart; race, wealth, political affiliation, sex are sometimes used in such ways. But in the college, the general rule is to use differences as far as possible to relate people to each other in shared activity.

The student will find that he needs to develop skill in identifying common interests in both ways. Expressions of personal interests in conversation and student activity cannot be limited to those which are identical with everybody else's. There must be acceptance of differences of interests and point of view and of the persons who hold them. To enlarge the range of common interests, students must learn to value differences between persons and use them to find meaningful relationships in shared activity.

Two factors make it relatively easy to develop skill in identifying common interests in college. First, compared with other communities, the college has a relatively homogeneous population. Identical or congruent interests are almost built into the college population. And the student body from the beginning is organized into groups that bring out common interests: classes, orientation groups, residence halls, fraternities, clubs on the formal side; and bull sessions, coffee breaks, and various social occasions on the informal side.

Second, students who share similar or identical interests also have other interests that are not similar or identical. As personal acquaintance grows, these differing interests can be more fully expressed. Because the personal relationship is valued, students often begin to see ways in which their differing interests can also be shared. Thus the extent of common interests tends to be enlarged.

Sometimes, too, problems develop in student groups which require for their solution the help of people with divergent points of view. For example, in a commuter college there was a ten o'clock coffee break crowd that settled down to ten or twelve cronies who daily gravitated to the same table in the student union. Soon they became aware that their conversation tended to center on student government. They began to discuss it systematically. They brought in the student body secretary and found that she had some special problems. They got her to bring the student body president in. They attended student council meetings and invited the dean of students to come and talk about the administrative point of view. In the second semester, they got the student council to sponsor some open luncheon sessions where other students could come to talk about student government. As a result, measures were taken to increase participation in self-government by more students of the commuting population. The personal relationship of the original coffee break crowd led to a common interest, which was developed through the expression of differing perspectives on a common problem.

Some very significant developments have come out of the free sharing of divergent interests in student groups with well-established personal relations. The growing interest in interfaith activity and in the study of comparative religion results in large part from the experience of students in discussing their differing religious backgrounds. Personal relationships among the leaders of churches in many nations, begun in their student years, have now flowered into organizations like the World Student Christian Federation and the World Council of Churches. Faculty members, too, have experience in finding common interests out of their differences in point of view. The trend toward interdisciplinary studies has developed out of the faculty's need for a broader concept of method, using differences between various fields of specialization to improve their capacity to solve complex problems.

The college is the kind of community whose purpose is to enlarge the range of common interests. It, therefore, provides both freedom and encouragement for the development of common interests in spite of the profoundest differences of experience and point of view.

The freedom allowed students for exploring interests accounts to some extent for the free, uninhibited character of student discussion, especially in informal groups. The dormitory bull session or union kaffeeklatsch is like nothing else on earth. Its vitality results from its freedom. No parental authority is represented; no reprisals are visited on anybody for his ideas; no grades are given for correct or incorrect answers. There is personal involvement and self-revelation, but interest is directed to something everybody is concerned about. Students concentrate not on themselves, but rather on matters of general importance, such as religion, beauty, sex, the fate of the universe.

Such unsystematic and free-flowing responses help students develop skill in revealing and sharing themselves. On this foundation more systematic disciplines of scholarly work develop. The advanced seminar shares many of the characteristics of the bull session, but it is kept to the main point more consistently. The fine disregard for facts in the bull session is transformed into a disciplined but free imagination, asking new questions and proposing hypotheses but supporting them with facts and observation.

The process of sharing and revealing oneself is the heart of the scholarly enterprise. It holds the college together as a community. Groups form around common interests. Out of a complex of smaller groups, the college is knit together into a community. As an institution, it protects its constituent groups and gives them freedom for self-realization. Colleges provide the content, the ideas, and the atmosphere in which common interests can emerge and be discovered by students.

The growth of generosity

Generosity is required for common interests to grow into shared activity. The student gains much from sharing common interests, but he must also give much. Revealing an interest means giving a good idea away and making it public property. The self must be sturdy enough to survive when interests become common, when ideas that mean a great deal in the private inward world move outward and become public. The public image of the self is built up out of the ideas that are thus revealed, giving away, moved into the public domain. In spite of the fears and anxieties suffered in the process of giving away something of significance to the inward self, the student will find that the self develops in the process. The self develops in its public character through the realization of the self in community life.

Generosity is self-supporting. In sharing his skills and interests, the student develops a whole new public dimension of the self. The more significant the ideas and interests that are shared, the more significant the public image will be to others. The more generous the sharing, the more generous the response of others is likely to be, and the more it will strengthen the self.

But generosity is not an easy virtue, nor are its rewards altogether unmixed blessings. Generosity also demands the gift of time, not only in expressing one's high and noble insights, but also in listening and responding to the low and ignoble thoughts of others. It is easy to feel generous and openhanded when telling the professor all about the marvelous idea for a term paper showing the relative significance of technology in the cultures of Greece, the Holy Roman Empire, the Italian Renaissance, the British Empire, and Soviet Russia. The idea is broad, noble, generous; the student is giving the professor a tremendous insight into a magnificent new historical synthesis. The student finds it more difficult to be generous with his time and response when the professor, in his turn, refers the student to works in which the idea has already been explored and suggests that for a term paper the concept be reduced to one period or technological development. To be generous in listening to criticism and suggestions is difficult; it makes the student suddenly remember a pressing engagement or a nagging cold that has to be treated before the Health Service closes.

Furthermore, generosity begets gratitude, and gratitude is not always a comfortable feeling. The student who patiently listens to his roommate's discourse on the next term paper, and generously offers suggestions that prove to make the paper of B rather than C quality, may be surprised by the roommate's lack of appreciation after the grades come out. Or he may be surprised by his own animosity toward a professor who generously referred him to the source book that modified his concept of a very important paper and forced him to rewrite the whole thing.

Students may take some comfort from the knowledge that generosity, in the long run, is more important to the giver than the receiver. In criticising his roommate's term paper, the student may hit upon an idea that opens up a whole new line for his own work. Nor does generosity always go unrecognized. The Acknowledgments in the front of this book may come as a surprise to some students and faculty members, who could not have known any more than the authors, at the time, that their generous expression of ideas and criticisms over coffee at the student union or dinner at the Chinese restaurant would emerge in this book. "Acknowledge the source" is more than a rule of scholarly good manners; it is an obligation to give credit to the originator of an idea. To fail to do so constitutes plagiarism, the theft of scholarly material, a very grave offense against the scholarly enterprise, for it undermines the generosity in sharing ideas on which scholarship is grounded.

One form of generosity is worth special notice because of its unusual quality. It is the tutorial help given to students by more advanced students. An unfamiliar subject such as psychology sometimes sets the beginning student completely at sea, without a recognizable landmark. He flounders in a welter of facts and concepts, none of which seems to make any sense. The instructor sometimes cannot help very much since the experience of the student generation may be too far removed from his own for him to know the current ideas that might illuminate the subject. But an advanced student is familiar enough with the experience of the freshman to point out some landmarks and give him his bearings. In the process the tutor is rewarded amply. There is no better way to learn a subject than to teach it to someone else, gaining familiarity through making the subject understandable to others.

Students need not be embarrassed about accepting help from others or reluctant to give assistance to them. Generosity is self-rewarding. There is no moral bookkeeping, and no accounts will be rendered at the end of the college year. All that is expected is that students will freely share ideas and interests with one another, and with the faculty, in caring for the really important task of keeping the scholarly enterprise going.

Cooperation

Generosity, which rewards both giver and receiver, is the basis for cooperation. College teaching is cooperative study. Students and faculty alike cooperate in the exploration of the subject. Each may learn something new as he adapts a subject to his own interests, and teach something new as he expresses his own ideas.

Cooperation does have some dull, routine aspects. For the student, it signifies preparing assigned term papers, adapting his interests to stated purposes and content in his courses, and turning his work in on time. For the teacher, it signifies reading heavily padded term papers, trying to find a germ of an idea hidden in each like a needle in a haystack, giving the kind of criticism that the student can understand and use to refine his ideas, and returning the things on time. Meeting deadlines and sticking to the job are onerous but important aspects of cooperation.

Cooperative study is provided, both formally and informally, in college work. Bull sessions on term papers give students a chance to enlarge their interests and increase the range of their ideas. Students sometimes set up regularly scheduled discussion sessions on a course, working together on the development of general concepts and checking factual data. Sometimes group projects are assigned by instructors as part of course work—a survey of student attitudes, an engineering survey of campus facilities, a stage set, the auditing of organization books. Independent study, provided in some colleges, may be conducted in groups as well as by individual students. Collaboration is an important technique of scholarly cooperation.

Cooperation also has both its inward and its outward aspects. The student must find within himself the interests and ideas that he can contribute to the cooperative enterprise in which he is engaged. Outwardly he develops a public image through the skills and ideas that he contributes. And, in return, he is inwardly enriched through the responsiveness and friendship of others and the ideas and interests that they contribute to the common enterprise.

SELF-REALIZATION IN STUDENT ACTIVITIES

In student activities as well as in instruction, the requirements of common interests, generosity, and cooperation are essential to good human relations in the college as a community. The identification of common interests is required for all shared activities from spontaneous pajama parties to the varsity show. Common interests are defined when a student invites another to go along and has his invitation accepted; this is the way that organization membership grows. The generosity of workers with time and donors with money is required for a successful Campus Chest drive. Rather sophisticated levels of cooperation are required to produce an opera, publish a paper, organize a residence hall. Through breaking big projects down into little jobs within the range of a student's competence, groups of students are able cooperatively to produce far beyond their individual capacities and limited time.

Critics of student life have declared open season on queen contests, mock celebrations, and nonsense societies, lumping them together with panty raids, cafeteria riots and jamming into telephone booths, as undesirable if not dangerous activities. Perhaps they are right. Certainly not all student life is maintained on a level of high seriousness. But there may be a useful distinction between frivolous activities requiring a degree of cooperation, and trivialities representing only a sudden yielding to mass impulse. Frivolous activities may enlist the energies and develop the capacities of students who are not yet ready to risk themselves in more serious enterprises. They may be the beginning of self-realization through shared activity.

Apathy is more to be feared than frivolity in college life. Apathy does not mean failure to vote in elections, or absence from hall meetings, or lack of commuter participation in campus events. The kind of apathy that strikes at the community life of the college is failure to respond to others, the withholding of contributions to common interests, and withdrawal from cooperative enterprises. Apathy of this type means preoccupation with the inner self, ignoring others, keeping out of things, and refusing responsibility. There is fortunately little apathy of this sort on the campus. The blasé pose of some upperclassmen, who regard it as infantile to get excited about anything and sophisticated to be cynical about college government and activities, comes close to it.

Apathetic behavior also appears sporadically in some students who encounter really difficult problems in self-realization. Some of them have to withdraw for a while from the give-and-take of college life; they turn inward for a spell in order to find some footing for continuing self-development. Some become almost "professional outsiders," unkempt, uncouth, and unintelligible.

Neither manifestation presents a really serious general problem of apathy. The cynical student is fairly easy to see through and may actually be a useful corrective for the undisciplined enthusiasm of freshmen. And the "outsider" really yearns to be on the "inside," but has to come to terms with himself before he can find a way to cooperate with others. He is barred from student activities not so much by his failure to meet student standards as by his inability to set effective standards of his own. He is not so much afraid of others as afraid of himself—afraid of losing himself or of lacking integrity. He does not reject others' interests or friendship, but he cannot clearly define his personal interests and is afraid he will not be a good friend. When he comes to terms with himself, knows his interests, and finds a way to express them that is inwardly acceptable, he can find his way into participation in college life.

One of the great values of the college as a community is its generous accommodation of people in all stages of self-realization. The hearty, self-confident students find more to do than they can manage; they have to learn to make choices and select activities of value for themselves out of a rich variety. The serious-minded can find serious activity; the frivolous can play with trivialities; the enthusiasts can pursue causes. The cynics may criticise, and the gripers may complain. Those who have lost their way are given a space in which to find themselves; and if they choose, they may find a counselor to help them over the hard task of self-acceptance toward self-realization.*

It is not the business of the college to isolate the scholar and give him an ivory tower where he can keep himself unspotted from the world. Like other communities, the college is a noisy, dirty, hilarious, exciting, infuriating place. Its business is to provide the scholar with a way to make a place for himself as a whole person, just as noisy, careless, and exasperating as the rest, in a very busy and vital enterprise. In the process the student has responsibility for making a place for others, as friends, critics, and collaborators, in a community of work and study.

---

* Erik Erikson describes the "moratorium" provided by societies in which young adults can be relieved of pressures and try to find themselves. The college may be said to provide a "moratorium" for students, and certainly it is tolerant and understanding of those who have trouble establishing their identity and proceeding to self-realization.[2]

SOCIAL COMPETENCE AS AN OUTCOME
OF SELF-REALIZATION

Of course, no one can do everything, respond to everybody, give everything away, or cooperate with everyone. Self-realization is a selective process. It requires expressing some intentions and interests and neglecting or repressing others. Social competence, in effect, amounts to skill in selecting the interests and the contributions that best represent the self. Social competence can develop most fully in a community which allows wide variety of interest and tolerates mistakes without imposing severe punishments upon those who cannot quite do what they intend or express what they mean. The college can be just such a community; although the limits of tolerance vary with each institution, they still provide room for those who are fumbling, awkward, and uncertain in social relationships.

In gaining social competence, the student finds three major resources in college. First, college serves as a mirror, reflecting the effect of his behavior upon others. Second, it serves as an extension of himself, giving greater range and scope to his powers and interests. Third, it enriches the self and provides the constant flow of strengthening response that is needed in self-realization.

The college as a reflection of the self

Self-awareness is certainly not complete when a student enters college—if it is ever complete at any point in life at all. Students need to express private interests publicly so that they can check their realism and consistency and test the integrity that they are developing by comparing their public image with their inward self. Reflection on the effects of one's behavior on other people helps to refine and clarify interests and to develop a public image consistent with inward desires. The student's reaction to others and their responses to him provide a kind of mirror, reflecting the emerging image of himself.

For example, the student's response to the ideas and activities of others reflects his personal interests. "I wish I had thought of that idea," he thinks, hearing another student discuss one of the essay questions on the sociology exam.

"I wish I had a date as gorgeous as she is," he muses, watching a fraternity brother escort a beauty out of the freshman dorm.

"Do you think it would be all right for me to do a paper comparing Hemingway with *Wuthering Heights,* instead of just writing a paper on *Wuthering Heights?*" he asks the English instructor.

"I'm no good at selling things," he tells the ticket manager for the class hop.

Tossed off casually and thoughtlessly, these reactions mean very little. Upon reflection, the student may find that they tell him a good deal about himself. They reflect the content of his interests and his emotional reactions, the kind of ideas that he finds interesting, the qualities he finds desirable in a date, the relations he sees between ideas and his personal limitations. It is important for him to see clearly *what* it is that he is responding to and *what* ideas, people, and experience he can accept or reject in terms of his inner knowledge of himself.

As to performance, there is every reason to recognize envy of the superior performance of another student as a desire to improve his own achievement. As to ideas, they float freely in the college atmosphere, and provided he acknowledges the source, any student may take up what strikes his interest and develop it for himself. As to dates, there is no way of finding out whether one is desirable until the invitation has been offered and accepted. As to assignments, extension of scope may be acceptable within reasonable limits, and the professor can define the reasonable limits.

So the student can take his reactions as giving some leads to possibilities for self-realization. But reflection on oneself can be pretty deceptive, and the student has to correct for errors and distortions. Envy of an idea or a date may be honest covetousness, that is, desire for exactly the same thing for himself. Envy may lead to competition in order to get the desired object in fair, legitimate ways. Or envy may be vicious covetousness, hatred for another, a wish that good things would not happen to the other, without any accompanying desire for good things for himself. Or it may be a mixture of both.

Upon reflection, the student can usually figure out whether he is saying, "I, too, could enjoy being like that, and I will try"; or whether he means, "I want to take away what other people have and will resist doing what they expect of me." What is tricky is that people usually mean a little bit of both. But the student can choose to act on the meaning that is more acceptable to him and to others in the community, rather than on one that is more abhorrent and less desirable.

Motives are almost always mixed, but it is possible to achieve good things in spite of mixed motives by trying to give the better motive as much of an edge as possible. For instance, wanting to write on a topic different from the one assigned—a comparison with Hemingway instead of a straight criticism of *Wuthering Heights*—may represent both a genuine thrust of interest into a broader dimension, rebellion or resentment against the professor, and a desire to test the teacher to see if he is as good a guy as he makes out to be. Legitimate scholarly interests grow out of just such mixed motives more often than we like to admit. If there is any legitimate element in the student's response, it deserves a chance to develop. Asking permission to modify the assignment is an appropriate way to open up a legitimate intellectual interest. And there is every reason why a student should find out precisely the limits of variation in assignments that a professor will accept, without necessarily sitting in judgment on the professor's character.

The reflected image may both please and annoy, perhaps even frighten, the student. At this point, the college offers the other side of the mirror. The reactions of other students and faculty members can be used to check the student's interpretation. If he enjoyed the date, his judgment is confirmed by the reaction of his friends. "Who was the cool blonde you took to the formal? Any chance of meeting her roommate?" He gets an idea of his status from reactions to his choice of major. "Paleontology? That's something really different!" He confirms his feeling that he is a pretty good student after all. "A B from old Chippingdale? That's equivalent to an A from anybody else."

In conference, the student may check his relation to the teacher. He may be a patient counselor who can help the student work out his own ideas or a rigid taskmaster from whom the student can learn carefully disciplined ways of work. The student can get something of value from either type of instructor, but he needs to know what to expect.

The responses of others reflect the public self which the student can compare with his inward intentions and desires. He is not walled off in his own inward view but can see himself in their reactions to him. What is inwardly confused may be outwardly clarified. What is inconsistent may be "trued up" by making another effort to express himself more clearly, or to secure something more like the desired reaction. Social competence is gained as the student learns how to make his ideas clear, how to make his inward self congruent with the reflected image.

But if the student cannot manage to gain such competence by his own effort, he is not left isolated. He can call on the help of a counselor, who can help him spot mistakes, misconceptions, unacceptable elements that keep him from developing the public image he desires. He need not be meshed in confusion. Wise counsel can help him clarify his interests and develop his capacity for self-realization.

The reflection of himself also helps the student sharpen his faculty of self-criticism. Students are usually highly sensitive to the disparity between their ideals and expectations, on the one hand, and the weaknesses and shortcomings in their behavior, on the other. Such sensitivity makes them quick to criticise each other and frequently overzealous in self-criticism. Eventually, they usually find a delicate balance between faultfinding and complacency in more calm, dispassionate, and objective evaluation of themselves and others. But a good deal of experience in shared criticism is needed for the balance to be found. In four years of close association, a great deal can be learned about other students and about themselves.

In the first place, a student is likely to be quick to envy achievements which he would like to emulate; this envy may be a clue to his own interests and goals. He is quick to deplore errors and faults in others; and these may give him a clue to the faults and shortcomings that he most deplores in himself. Acting on the principle that human beings react most strongly to the behavior of others, with either praise or blame, on matters that are of deepest personal interest to them, the student can get some clues to his own expectations of himself. He can even get a rough idea of their relative importance by weighing the relative strength of his reactions to the behavior of others.

Self-correction develops in somewhat the same way. The student observes successful performance in others and gets a model to follow in improving his own work. From observation of others, he can be warned about unsuccessful forms of behavior and action. One important consideration is the selection of an adequate model; it is easy to set sights too low by selecting a person who is popular and emulating his every trait, even an undesirable one. A whole battery of models, each selected for excellence in a particular quality, may be a safeguard against mediocrity and conformity. Furthermore, the student must be careful not to subordinate his personal identity to the slavish imitation of another person.

The example of the group that criticised student government is a case in point. The students recognized that in criticising the student council for its failure to enlist the interest of a commuting student body, they were criticising themselves for failure to participate in student government. They followed a plan designed to correct both aspects of the problem.

The value of a college as a mirror of strengths and weaknesses depends on the student's capacity to reflect on himself and follow the best leads he can get, rather than to fear and try to conceal his weaknesses and mistakes. He can also see things of value to himself and others, new goals, new interests, ways to avoid mistakes and to succeed.

The college as an extension of the self

The relationships that reflect the public image of a student also extend and enlarge the self. Since the student is associating with people who have varied interests and backgrounds, he can find new dimensions for self-realization in the new interests presented by students who differ from him in background and experience.

For example, in most American colleges, the student is likely to encounter people from a wide variety of unfamiliar cultural backgrounds. Trade unionists, the foreign-born, Southerners, Easterners, Negroes, foreign students, Democrats and Republicans, Protestants, Catholics, Jews, Buddhists, agnostics, Mohammedans and goodness knows what other groups may be represented in the college. It may be possible for a student to leave college without encountering personally anyone with a cultural background different from his own; but any student who wishes has the opportunity to cultivate acquaintance with people of many different races, religions, classes, and nationalities. One student told her staunch Republican father, upon graduation, that the most wonderful thing that happened to her in all her college years was rooming with the first Democrat she had ever met. It was rooming with her, she said, that gave her real insight into the Democratic Party. Just before her father exploded, she added, "And it has made me a better Republican!"

Some students avoid the encounter because they wish to avoid the change which extending the self inevitably means. But as the anecdote illustrates, it is not necessarily an unwelcome change. Many values involved in extending the self enhance social competence.

First, there can be a sharpening of sensitivity to the needs and interests of others. At the point where cultural background differs enough to make for differences in manners, sensitivity is required in order to understand other people and establish adequate social relationships with them. For where manners differ, meanings and interests differ. Finding shared activities out of differing interests and in spite of misunderstanding requires a fairly sophisticated level of social competence. Foreign students often criticize American students for failing to create opportunities for them to interpret the culture of their nations. There is too much emphasis, they say, on adjusting the foreigner to American college life and too little on enabling the foreign student to help American students to adjust to intercultural and international relationships. What they suggest is not so much a failure of American colleges as a new field of opportunity for the development of social competence. The

rich resources of cultural difference afford students unparalleled opportunity to understand cultures which they can know better through their
fellow students of other races and nations.

Second, the range of skills and interests in the student body makes it
possible for students to develop social competence in giving and receiving service. Differences in skill become assets needed in organizations and activities; and when a special skill is needed, a student is
needed. Social competence is strengthened in those organizations
where there is both a sense of obligation to a group and experience in
contributing directly to other persons. Both pleasure and generosity
are enhanced by the direct, personal response to the act of giving as
well as by the inner satisfaction of meeting one's obligations to a group.
Fund-raising drives are a case in point; the more successful campaigns
are based on personal solicitation by students who learn to appeal to
the personal interests of contributors and to thank them personally for
their gifts.

Third, students can develop skill in being spectators as well as direct
participants in activity. Students who cannot produce a note of music,
even in the shower, have a world of music opened to them by student
performers in concerts, plays, and recitals. The student audience has
a great deal to gain from going and seeing and extending the range
of personal enjoyment. The worlds of art and science that some students cannot claim as their own can be opened for them by others. The
extension of the self in the spectator role can be developed more easily
in college than at any other time.

The student may develop a very sophisticated level of social competence, in learning how to venture into new areas of enjoyment and interest. Through group activity and personal encounter, he develops his
taste, understanding, and sensitivity. He extends his interests into activities where he has little or no skill through participation in cooperative activity. He can contribute his minimal skills and enjoy the performance of the highly skilled persons with whom he associates. Every
student can find a way to contribute something to the life of the college,
and he can extend himself in relating his gifts to those of others.

The college as a resource for self-realization

Community life in the college enriches as well as enlarges the self.
Self-enrichment is not purely a selfish matter. It is a reciprocal relationship, in which the student gives much and also receives riches from the
gifts of others.

The greatest contribution of the college, of course, is made out of its curriculum, its library, its faculty. But the riches of the college also come to the student through personal relationships, particularly those which free him for self-realization in friendship and intimacy.

The college affords unusual opportunity for friendship, through the enduring personal relationships formed in cooperative activity in and out of class. Superficially, this opportunity is recognized in reference to the value of college "contacts," social and professional, for the advancement of one's career. It is true that one's fellow students are his future professional associates, and the friendships cultivated in college add to the pleasure and opportunities to be found in an occupation. Valuable as such considerations are, the enrichment of life in the college years through friendship goes much deeper.

In friendship, the student adds to his interests and ability those of his friends, not merely by addition, but by a more complex relationship of change and growth. The student does not just adopt a friend's interests, but in a way he makes them his own. He does not merely "own" a new interest; he shares it with the friend. It is easier to follow common interests into new fields when someone else is there to encourage and lend warm support. What is shared goes into a personal relationship as well as an activity; each is a different kind of person when he is with his friend, and there is a different quality in what they do together.

It is hard to tell what constitutes friendship. All that can be said presently is that friendship seems to begin with common interest and goes on from there to bring people closer together. Friends share their differences, their enjoyments, everything they are or wish to be. Joy and sorrow, approval and disapproval, positive and negative responses seem to have equal effect in binding friends to each other. It is hard to measure friendship or to discriminate between factors that make it more or less likely to develop.

For example, roommates sometimes become close friends, sometimes get along all right without particular friendship, and sometimes cannot abide each other. Several years ago at an Eastern university an effort was made to study factors making for successful roommate selection. Students in a large residence hall rated their roommates on the degree to which they agreed with them on each of twenty selected factors. Comparison of these ratings showed significant similarity between roommates on only two points: Roommates tended to agree with each other in the degree of satisfaction they found in their relationship, and on the importance of agreeing to sleep with the windows open or shut.

"Good roommates just happen, I guess," said the graduate student making the study, "I guess there is nothing we can do about it."

There is much truth in the observation. Very little can be done to help friendship ripen among students, except to keep the college going as a community in which students can meet and make friends. Faculty members know that ideas, which are the major business of the college, can develop only in and through personal relationships. Where friendships do not form, ideas cannot live very long. So it is a matter of the gravest concern to faculty members for students to let themselves be grasped by ideas and find strong common interests which ripen into friendship. Recently, a distinguished political scientist voiced his anxiety over what he viewed as a decline in the depth and quality of friendship among students. "Students do not care any more," he said. "They do not care about ideas. They do not know how to let themselves be grasped by problems of truth and value. They cannot fall in love with each other, let alone with ideas. Their hearts are invested at three-and-a-half percent, and their response to love is, 'What's in it for me?' "

The comment may be unfair, for the inward feelings of one generation may not be readily understood by members of another. But it is an astute observation of the essential unity of affection, in spite of the diversity of its objects. Caring for ideas and caring for people essentially require the same thing: giving oneself freely to an absorbing interest. A student cannot be grasped by ideas and remain aloof to people or develop friendship while remaining indifferent to ideas.

The student needs friendships as a source of energy, drive, and support; and others need his friendship to sustain them. In friendship rewarding responses and critical observations are exchanged to support self-realization and insure continuity in learning. For instance, those roommates who develop a good relationship are often most candid with each other about shortcomings and mistakes. A student who had struggled to develop good study habits, working with a counselor to set up a schedule and solve some problems of concentration, was discouraged because he wasn't making any progress. In exasperation after hearing his tale of woe for the thirteenth time, his roommate turned on him and asked, "What are you scheduled to study right now?" "Why, F-F-F-French," the student replied. "Then for Heaven's sake study French, and don't talk to me about your problems!" replied the roommate. Scorned, the student opened his book and put in his first solid hour of study in weeks.

Friendships with persons much like oneself may be easier to form, but the student finds enrichment in friendships with persons different from himself. A memorable example was the friendship formed by three music majors—a singer, a pianist, and a bassoonist—who shared an apartment for the summer, to the horror of people aware of their incompatible temperaments and their inability to cook. The singer was moody and mercurial; the pianist was disgustingly bright and cheerful; the bassoonist was consistently self-deprecatory and shy. One was Catholic, one a Protestant, and one a Jew. Their house rules, however, gave a clue to the success of the friendship. First, they never practiced at home. Second, they never discussed music unless it was related to religion, which was the most acceptable topic of conversation. Third, they thanked the cook, whether they liked the food or not. The bassoonist, not nearly so tongue-tied as he had been at the beginning of the summer, reported that their table talk about religion had got them all much more interested in their own faiths. "I read more about Judaism this summer than I ever read in school," he said. "I got into the habit of going to temple again. I had to, they expected me to tell them something about it. I guess the best way to find out something about yourself is to have to live it out with people who are different."

Encountering people differing from oneself can be a source of stress. Recognizing differences between oneself and others leads to self-doubt and anxiety as well as to pleasure and enrichment. One value of friendship is the comfort and relaxation provided in the midst of stress. Students who care for each other, like the three musicians, can deal with personal differences that otherwise could be very painful sources of stress. Students can be secure and confident of acceptance in sharing ideas and interests of all kinds with friends. And the student is no less himself for accepting the differences of other people.

Out of some friendships, students develop relationships of great strength. They give each other a great deal yet do not demand much. They feel serenely certain of each other's affection and assured of appreciation and support. Where they have common interests, they work together; where they have special interests, each works independently; where one needs privacy, the other respects it. The development of sensitivity, responsiveness, and appreciation in such a relationship is an extremely mature achievement.

Intimate personal relationships grow out of friendships with persons of the opposite sex. A person of the same sex cannot be used as an object of sexual relationships. It is asking too much of friendship to substitute for the complete intimacy of marriage, the rich and fulfilling giving of the self in sexual union. Mature love is not complete without the intimacy of the sexual union of marriage, as a completion of the self.

But it is said, with some truth, that friendship with persons of either sex helps to prepare for intimacy, for fulfillment in marriage. Certainly love is rightly regarded as a single emotion; ways of loving differ as the objects of love differ. One cannot love an idea as he can love a person; but the capacity for giving the self to the idea and following it where it leads is very close to the capacity for loving someone and sharing in a common life regardless of the consequences. It is the expression of devotion that differs: toward ideas, creative work; toward a person of the same sex, common interests, shared activities, shared ideas; toward a lover, all of these things and all of oneself, with sexual union at once the culmination and the beginning of love.

Students seem to tend to overemphasize courtship at the expense of friendship. The student mores lend approval to steady dating, pinning, and early marriage, but they either undervalue or disapprove friendship.

One aspect of this overemphasis on courtship is the overvaluing of coeducation. In New England, and to some extent among upper-class families generally, separate men's and women's colleges are considered acceptable, or preferable. But for much of the country, coeducation is the norm, and men's and women's colleges are considered peculiar deviations. Referring to women's colleges as "convents" rather thinly conceals public contempt of presumed sexual fear or inadequacy among their students. Derisive comments about weekend excursions ("invasions") from men's colleges to nearby women's campuses reveal similar contempt. The men's and women's colleges fight back with contemptuous comments about coeducational "country clubs" or "marriage marts." Sweeping assertions are made that men (or women) have higher intellectual attainments when free from the distraction (or competition) of students of the opposite sex. This slurring match obscures some significant problems in a fog of nonsense generated by both sides.

One factor thus obscured is interference with mature self-development by overemphasis on falling in love. Pressure to conform to standardized patterns of falling in love complicates a highly individualized relationship. Most students do not conform to pattern and are subject to anxiety because their behavior is different from the set standard. Some react to this anxiety by being homesick. Susan and Joe, for example, were in colleges two thousand miles apart. They grieved at ending a close high school friendship. Both were expected, according to prevailing campus patterns, to find a date for the freshman formal during the first two weeks of classes, and preferably to make it a steady date as soon as possible. They were expected to fall out of love with each other and fall in love with somebody else. The prospect made them miserable and homesick. (Homesickness, by the way, is often grief at parting from a boyfriend or girlfriend as well as longing for the family.)

Others react to anxiety with avoidance. Some cannot continue court-ship long enough for it to ripen into love. Alice, for example, collected and returned three fraternity pins in her freshman year, but she could not let herself go and fall in love with any of the three equally desirable men. She got pinned because her sorority sisters expected it but was so anxious to have their approval that she could not wait to see if she really was in love.

Some students withdraw from courtship because they are confused or annoyed by some of the pressures involved and the standards to which they must conform. Sharon, for example, accepted Gil's pin in order to stop her sorority sisters' nagging about getting it in order to keep up the house record. She returned it because she and Gil got bored with each other. Their respective houses frowned on dating anyone else after pinning, and lack of other contacts kept them from having any-body else to talk to about each other or from getting new ideas to intro-duce into their own conversation. Sharon stopped dating altogether, concentrated on study but did poorly at it, and was a wet blanket on the house. Alice was afraid she couldn't fall in love, and didn't; Sharon wanted to fall in love, but her courtship came to a dead end for lack of friendships to help keep it going after she "went out of circulation." Neither had adequate help from their fellow students to meet their per-sonal needs and still satisfy the expectations set in student mores.

A good deal of anxiety normally develops in intimate relationships anyway. We are always a little bit uneasy about caring too much for anyone for fear of being hurt. We fall in and out of love, with several different people, before developing a durable relationship; being brokenhearted is very painful and almost unavoidable. We are also aware that our friends and lovers will eventually be lost through death, if not through separation in other ways. So, foolishly, we try not to care too much, hoping to avoid being hurt too much. Even the deepest and strongest friendships and marriages are subject to some underlying anxiety, due to the fear of loss or the certainty of death. Only the strength of love overcomes anxiety. Love makes it possible to give one-self freely and happily in spite of fear.

Friends are important enough for us to care for them in spite of anxiety; and they help to overcome our uneasiness. We can talk to them about our deepest feelings without so much fear of being hurt. They help us face the inevitable question, "Am I really in love?" and give a reality check that helps us make sure of our feelings and plans. Friends' approval and encouragement help us keep on with courtship, and make it worthwhile to settle quarrels, work out problems, and overcome blocks to a durable relationship. When courtship increases the range of friendships—he likes her friends, she likes his—the relationship is strengthened. When a student wants to fall in love and needs to find a suitable partner, friends often offer an introduction—look at all the women who marry their brothers' fraternity brothers or the men who marry their sisters' college roommates.

But prevailing student attitudes do not seem to take account of the resources of friendship for dealing with anxiety. The mores almost seem to leave anxiety out of account altogether. To judge by typical student behavior, there is nothing to fear except being without a "steady"; the normal anxiety underlying intimacy is not recognized at all. There is a high premium on falling in love, but no provision is made for heartbreak except starting another courtship as soon as possible. No allowances are made for the anxiety generated by "being on the rebound"—through grief, disappointment, wounded pride, and fear of sexual inadequacy. Friendship is not generally approved as a source of comfort and encouragement or as a bulwark against anxiety. It is mistakenly regarded as an escape from courtship rather than a support for it.

The overemphasis on courtship is often carried to such an extent that any other personal relationship, especially intimate friendship, is regarded as undesirable interference with the most important task, falling in love and getting married. Couples who are pinned or engaged "go out of circulation." Fear of competition is partly responsible for this isolationist pattern. The woman might find another man more attractive, should her steady introduce him; her roommate might cut her out with her fiancé, should she let them get too well acquainted. To fear of competition is added fear of sexual inadequacy. Students seem to act on the principle that friends may compete with lovers for affection, as if affection must be exclusive to be acceptable and sexual to be real. Friends seem to be regarded as competition whether they are of the same or the opposite sex. And friendships between persons of the same sex have come to be suspected as being nothing more than a substitute for mature sexual love, developing only between persons who are sexually inadequate, if not actually homosexual. At best, such friendship is disregarded and undervalued; at worst, it may be the occasion for disapproval or slanderous gossip, sanctioned by prevailing student mores.

The irony of it all is that the high premium on courtship actually restricts the capacity for expression of affection and reduces the range of self-realization. Conformity to the mores means rushing into court-ship at the earliest opportunity, rather than selecting the likeliest part-ner out of a number of friends of the opposite sex. Random selection from a small group is less apt to produce good choices than careful selection from a large group. The chances for finding a more suitable partner after an unhappy courtship are reduced by "going out of circula-tion" for the duration. A well-matched couple is deprived of the help and encouragement of friends that would increase their chances of working out a durable relationship. And, if they fall out of love, the re-sources of friendship for dealing with heartbreak are forbidden to them because of the fear of sexual inadequacy. The anxiety that inevitably accompanies affection can thus be increased to the point where it can become a serious block to self-realization. It may interfere with the development of the capacity for feeling or expressing affection. To avoid such anxiety, a student may completely give up trying to make friends or fall in love; or he may deny his feelings and appear cold and unresponsive, shy, cynical, or hostile in his behavior.

Overemphasis on courtship and undervaluing of friendship are par-ticularly damaging to the students who need friendship most: to those like Alice, who need friendship to learn to share themselves deeply; to those like Sharon, who need a friend to help resist the pressure to accept the symbol instead of the substance of love; to those like Gil, who need friends that they can share to enrich their courtship.

Particularly damaging is the fear of homosexuality and the misin-terpretation of friendships with persons of one's own sex as evidence of sexual inadequacy. Same-sex friendships are the norm in college and the most numerous among mature adults. Residence hall living sepa-rates men from women, just at the times when intimate conversation can develop in long interrupted stretches of relative relaxation. So friendships form more easily and frequently in one's own hall and, therefore, with students of one's own sex. But same-sex friendships also predominate in adult life outside of college. Men make friends on the job, in the club, in professional organizations, under conditions where men are both more numerous and more frequently encountered as equals. Women make friends with neighbors who have small children, with fellow PTA members, and with women on the job, who are more readily encountered as equals.

Whether they like it or not, men and women tend to make most of their friendships with persons of their own sex. And this offers some advantage for women. As Dr. Margaret Mead said in a recent talk to students, "When the men have done glorious deeds and died, their wives will very likely survive them, and unless they can make friends with other women, there are going to be lots of lonely widows in the world!" Friendship means just as much for self-development as courtship. To regard friendship as evidence of sexual inadequacy is not just an unfortunate misunderstanding of human needs, it is a factor in building up anxiety that damages self-development.

The bickering over coeducation actually obscures the fact that colleges have not successfully come to terms with the needs of students for expressing affection and love, for making friends and falling in love. Some coeducational colleges might as well be separate men's and women's colleges since the organization of the student body separates students by sex—in residence, in student government, in major fields of study, in dining halls and student unions. Some men's and women's colleges provide more opportunity to meet an acceptable person and fall in love because they have to provide a program of varied social activities that will bring men and women together on campus. Where the management of social programs is left wholly to students, regardless of the type of college, there is likely to be more than adequate provision for dating but neglect of provisions for the growth of friendship.

On most campuses, standards governing dating, the expression of affection between friends, and the display of affection in courtship are in a state of confusion, or worse. The administrative regulations of the college may be so antiquated and so narrowly conceived as to limit rather than encourage friendships of any kind; or else they may be nonexistent. In either case, the standards in effective operation are likely to be student-administered. If they are publicly stated, they are likely to be ambiguous or narrow—in order to be acceptable to the faculty and administration. But they are much more likely to be unformulated, set by the mores and enforced by group pressure, and characterized by conformity to the overvaluation of courtship and the undervaluation of friendship. On the whole, neither official nor unofficial standards in American colleges can be said to encourage the development of friendship and love. Nor do they offer students any help in mastering the task of self-realization through expressing affection.

The complacency with which coeducation is accepted obscures the fact that simple association does not lead to friendship, love, and marriage, unless affection is also approved, and its acceptable development and expression encouraged in students. Jacques Barzun[3] suggests that colleges may be over-intellectualizing, at the expense of students' emotional development, in their customary attitude toward affection and intimacy. The defense mechanism may be a way of avoiding an admission of failure to work out the relation between mind and body, intellect and emotion. The suggestion is worth thinking about. Certainly colleges could do more than they do to help students develop mature patterns of emotional expression as well as effective emotional control. Students need to help each other, and faculty members and counselors need to help students find more generous and suitable ways of expressing affection and forming close personal relationships. But all the mature relationships involving shared affection must be equally provided for. One cannot be allowed to predominate at the expense of another—neither courtship at the expense of friendship, nor friendship at the expense of marriage. As a beginning, some work has to be done on the problem of finding acceptable ways to show affection.

The expression of affection has many appropriate forms in college. There is genuine affection of students for members of the faculty, differing from the affection students feel for each other. One need only listen to alumni recalling the meaningful experiences of the college years to recognize that encountering a gifted teacher profoundly affects the development of a student. Yet the expression of such affection has rather narrow limits; it is shown in patience, fair criticism, receptive counseling by the teacher, in consistent, conscientious, excellent work by the student. The achievement of excellence is, perhaps more than students are willing to admit, an expression of affection for their teachers as much as a passionate interest in scholarly work for its own sake. Forms of faculty-student relationship vary with the conditions of community life in the college. The office coffeepot in the commuter college may be the center of shared friendships just as deep and meaningful as the friendships that grow out of colloquia in the study of the professor's home on a residential campus. Food, talk, and time are the ingredients of affectionate relationships on any campus.

And intimacy takes time to grow out of friendship. Time for understanding one another, time for the growth of confidence and assurance, time for reflection and absorption of shared experience into the fabric of the self, time for the exploration of common and differing interests, time for developing appropriate expressions of affection—everything has to be learned, and learning above all requires time. The deliberate pace of college life, the regular patterns of scholarly discipline, provide an orderly sequence of development which gives time for students to learn. There is time for students to commit themselves to a passionate interest in ideas. There is time for friendships to develop out of common interests, and for one of them to flower into intimacy, devotion, and love. There is a foreseeable end to college life, a foreseeable time for its culmination in entry into an occupation, a marriage, a family of one's own.

Yet there is much in college life that works against the pattern of orderly development in self-realization. There are heavy social pressures for the rapid development of social competence. Pressure to achieve status may force a student into stereotyped personal relationships, into knowing only the "right" people, avoiding those who are different, staying with the prestige-makers instead of establishing the personal relationships based on genuine common interest that lead to enduring friendships. Pressures of social approval and disapproval may force students prematurely into steady dating or early marriage. Fears and anxieties, bred of the uneasy times in which we live, press upon students, who then cling to friends and lovers for comfort. Uncertainty about the future forces a desperate grasping for the forms of affection and intimacy that may prevent the growth of their substance. There is competition for the symbols of maturity, the engagement ring being regarded as a trophy rather than an evidence of love. Heavy petting, "making out," and going steady force the growth of intimacy and limit the time required for casual, tentative, and reflective exploration that leads to more durable relationships.

Students are the principal sufferers from the stresses that interfere with orderly self-development. They are not to be altogether condemned for their efforts to come to terms with these stresses. Despite the desperation, conformity, and anxiety evident in many colleges, many students still find effective ways of pacing themselves and protecting themselves from pressure. They find the time for the casual encounters and shared activity that lead to friendship and the consistent, continuous associations that ripen into enduring love. The college provides a variety of group activity in which students can enlarge acquaintance and friendship. Residence halls, unions, dining rooms, and classrooms provide the continuous personal contact essential to the growth of friendship. There may be no privacy for the practice of sexual relations, but the liberal provision for dating, joint study, and companionship in social settings move just as surely toward intimacy and the maturing of love.

Above all, the members of the college have a gift for overlooking much and accepting much that would be forbidden or condemned in another community. Privacy for courtship is made possible by small courtesies, by a kind of collective blindness, by decent restraint and reticence, by small indulgences and understandings that are generous far beyond anything that could be expected. Students are unfortunately inclined to abuse these provisions. But colleges generally let students set their own pace and find their own way into the meaningful relationships of adult life. Given reasonably decent standards of taste and manners and reasonable respect for others, the student can have a great deal of freedom in exploring ways of love, as well as other ways of knowing himself. The college is not a marriage bureau or a lonely hearts club. But it is a community in which the close personal relationships required in academic work can be expected to ripen into love.

The warmth, acceptance, and cooperation generated in college life are effective in relieving stress. The solidarity and enthusiasm that students generate for special events and high occasions provide an effective use of stress to sustain higher levels of achievement and enjoyment. In friendship, students exchange the affectionate or astringent response that provides a steady flow of assurance and correction, strengthening self-acceptance in the varying fortunes of success and failure in college life. In love, even more than in friendship, students can acknowledge and relieve the stress of anxiety by exchanging reassurance and affection. Friendship and intimacy provide the stability and reward that help students accept the stress resulting from the uncertainty and difficulty of academic life.

The response of others gives the student the reward essential to learning. The response of friends is a very great reward because it comes from the people who mean most to him and who most freely share his interests and aspirations. In its community life, the college must seek to cultivate the personal relationships that will lead students toward enduring friendship as a principal means of support for scholarly work. Personal encounter leads to the identification of common interests. Around common interests, shared activities form. Through giving himself generously to shared activities, the student develops the gift of cooperation in an enterprise of great value. Out of cooperative relationships, friendships emerge. Out of friendships, the student develops the capacity for sharing intimately the life of another person. Intimacy ripens into mature love and culminates in marriage and the founding of a home. Such personal development is necessary for full self-realization. The college contributes to self-realization in the interest of giving the scholar the personal support and satisfaction that will enable him to undertake a long life of productive work.

10

Have briefcase; will travel

Student organizations,
government, and
leadership

STUDENT MORALE AND COMMUNITY LIFE

The patterns of human relationships set the distinctive atmosphere and tone of the college. To the extent that student organizations provide an enduring personal relationship in which the individual feels significant, students have a sense of identification with the college. To the extent that student organizations show vitality, imagination, and variety in common interests, students have a sense of contributing to the college. To the extent that student activities serve the purposes of the college, the student has a way of contributing to the achievement of its goals.

This may be the point at which to say something about the argument over the relative advantages and disadvantages of residential and commuter colleges. The residential college claims advantage through the continuous, twenty-four-hour involvement in college life that leads to more wholehearted commitment and consistency in morale. It is sug-gested that the commuter college cannot achieve equal consistency or depth of involvement; it must compete with family and community in-terests for the student's time and energy, and it has difficulty in bringing students together because of conflicting commitments, travel problems, and lack of loyalty.

The distinction is probably an over-simplification. The residential college may fairly claim that its effect upon the student is more con-centrated, less diluted by other interests and influences. The commuter college may fairly claim that what it saves in "hotel" costs is plowed back into the important business of academic work; student activities, therefore, concentrate specifically upon the most important common interests, related closely to the scholarly purpose of the college. The residential college can fairly claim that continuous separation from the family develops independence and self-direction. The commuter col-lege can fairly claim that during the college years the student is usually dependent on the family for financial support anyway; that full inde-pendence comes only with marriage and establishing a household after college; and that the higher residential fees purchase only relative free-dom from the family, which is a matter of emotional development rather than geographic location.[1]

The claims are fair and have supporting evidence on both sides. There is a distinction between residential and commuter colleges in the length, continuity, and scope of involvement in college life. But it is probably unwise to conclude that they, therefore, make a different impact on student morale and personal development. More time and closer contact with others may be extremely valuable at some colleges for some students, matter very little in other instances, and be com-pletely undesirable elsewhere. Differences in degree of separation from the family may perhaps be better described as cyclical differences in periods of withdrawal and return; and neither the residential nor the commuter student can escape the task of helping his family understand his development as the result of college experience. The quality of college life and the strength of student morale are effects of the interests and energy infused into college life by the student body itself.

Sources of student morale

Regardless of size, location, type of membership, and residential services, colleges depend on two important contributions to student morale from two different sources in the college.

First, the basic social relationship in the college is the classroom. The effect of classroom activities on student morale is the responsibility of the faculty. The responsiveness and interest shown by the faculty toward their students is the most important factor in supporting high levels of aspiration and achievement. Faculty attitudes may be either warmly personal or coldly objective, either flexible or rigorous. The coldly objective and uncompromising teacher may challenge students to higher levels of achievement, just as much as the warmly responsive and patient teacher may encourage improvement. There is no single pattern to which faculty attitudes must conform.

Freidson[2] also finds that distance or closeness of faculty to students in social relationships do not seem to have differing effects on student morale. He concludes that clarity in the definition of the respective roles of faculty and student seems to be much more important in sustaining student morale and achievement.

But faculty members must stimulate interests in students that go beyond the limits of course work. Student activities are strengthened by an infusion of interests from the classroom. These may be interests which cannot be satisfied within the limits of the course; or they may lie in special fields in which the college is not providing instruction. In that case, students can take the initiative in carrying on effective study. For example, a group of physical education majors discovered that they had a common interest in physical therapy, in which the college did not offer instruction. They formed an interest group and worked with the head of the department in securing speakers, making field trips, and finding summer work experience that contributed to the development of their specialized interest.

The faculty can feed ideas into student activities through recognizing special personal interests expressed in course work and encouraging their development in student activities.

Second, the organization of student life in residential living, student government, and extra-curricular activity, is primarily the responsibility of students. Student activities extend the interests of students beyond formal course work. The identification of students with organizations and activities contributes to their loyalty to the college. Particularly in large student bodies, the sense of the college as a whole community is rather vague and diffuse. And on any campus, the student must have some personal relationships which confirm his sense of belonging to the entire college. The student also develops personal identity through group relationships. His major field identifies him as a person with particular interests. His memberships in organizations identify him as a person who has made particular contributions to the college as a whole.

The degree of responsibility delegated to students and the purposes activities are supposed to serve vary from one college to another. Perhaps the best distinction that can be made, and it is rather vague, is between the maintenance of the structure and organization of the college by the faculty, through the administration of college organization, budget, and curriculum, on the one hand, and the introduction by students of variety in content into the program of the college in such areas as social life, residence living, interest groups, and self-government, on the other hand. Freidson[3] gives two lists* of typical areas of student responsibility in the college. Deans of students were asked to check areas in which students were capable of handling organization and activity. The ten items most frequently checked were:

1. Promoting student participation in extra-curricular activities.
2. Planning charity campaigns.
3. Problems of student apathy.
4. Conducting freshmen orientation.
5. Selecting speakers for campus programs.
6. Participating in course and teacher evaluation.
7. Governing rushing and hazing policies.
8. Leadership training.
9. Supervising coordination of religious activities.
10. Handling safety programs.

The ten areas checked least frequently were:

1. College tuition.
2. Admission policy of college.
3. Regulating phases of academic policy (e.g. cuts, examinations).
4. Intercollegiate athletic policies.
5. Setting college calendar (vacations, exams, special events).
6. Dealing with issues in academic freedom.
7. Selecting sites for new buildings or recommending better use for existing facilities.
8. Participating in supervising vocational guidance and placement program.
9. Participation in setting scholarship policy of the college.
10. Participating in setting student loan (or student aid) policy.

These lists bear out the generalization that student responsibility is most appropriate in areas where variety and initiative rather than continuity and structure are important. The faculty have to control the permanent structure of the college, along with standards of academic achievement and the requirements for degrees. But without the initia-

* Freidson's lists omit two important areas, commonly regarded as responsibilities of students: the organization of residence halls, and the coordination of fraternities and sororities. Doubtless, in a more definitive study, others should be added.

tive of students, substantial areas of student need, organization, and interest may go unfulfilled, and much of the flavor of college life may be lost.

Student morale usually tends to be high when there is a good working relationship between faculty and students with clearly defined roles and relationships. Student morale also tends to be high where there are clearly defined patterns of student organization and specified areas of student responsibility. Both students and faculty, therefore, share responsibility for developing strong organizations and programs that give the students opportunities for self-realization and significant responsibility for strengthening the community life of the college.

The development of civic pride

One highly desirable effect of strong group relationships in classroom and student activities is the pride of membership in the college they generate. Students show civic pride by their support of student activities and their conscientious performance of academic work. They take pride in showing, both on and off campus, appearance and behavior that give evidence of the status and prestige that they have as members of the college. They express civic pride in conversation with prospective students, trying to interpret the value and importance of college life to them to influence them to attend college. They try to raise their personal levels of aspiration to conform to the expectations that are generally valued in the college.

Perhaps one of the most important factors in generating civic pride is the atmosphere of sociability and good comradeship. The tone of a campus, its atmosphere of hospitality and enjoyment are set by students in their relationships to each other. Casual greetings on campus set a tone of warmth and friendliness. Students take pride in the social life of the college, competing in producing dances, teas, parties, and receptions, which excel in enjoyment, good taste, and attractiveness. Congeniality and sociability are the responsibility of students, and the general social atmosphere of the campus is a product of their casual, everyday relationships as well as of the spirit generated in high occasions.

"College spirit" is the term usually used for civic pride. Many freshmen come to college expecting to continue the typical "rah-rah" spirit generated in high school athletics, pep rallies, dances, and big games. Of course, intercollegiate athletics generate this familiar college spirit. But big games are not the only forms, or the predominant forms, in which college spirit is expressed. Sometimes freshmen are confused and disappointed, and they find it hard to recognize the vitality of student organization and the strength of student government as appropriate expressions of college spirit. They are sometimes confused by the bewildering variety of activities and find it hard to express their spirit appropriately in college life.

There is some evidence that this confusion arises from changes in predominant patterns of student activity, for colleges and high schools have followed opposite trends over the past few student generations. In one college, a study of the high school activities of entering freshmen showed a definite change in patterns of participation. Following World War II, the number of entering freshmen previously involved in small groups requiring self-direction and participation in planning and carrying out activities declined, as did the number of activities represented. There was a corresponding rise in participation in mass activities, such as pep rallies, or in performance groups (drama and music societies and the like). These activities involved more active direction by teachers or more active leadership by a small number of students.[4] Over the same period, college students were de-emphasizing mass activity and counting more on student-directed groups to generate college spirit, under student leadership.

Apparently, colleges cannot count on freshmen to bring to college as much experience or skill in self-directed group activity as they once did. Student organizations may have to provide more training for entering students in participation in self-directed activity. They may have to work harder at discovering the interests of freshmen and helping them find satisfying group activities. There may have to be more active recruiting of members, through direct personal invitation, and less reliance on general announcements.

Organizations and their members also take pride in providing valuable services to the entire college. Some of the most important events in the college year are provided as special services by student organizations. For example, Religious Emphasis Week, an all-college event on many campuses, is sponsored by student religious groups, frequently in cooperation with fraternities and sororities, residence halls, and student government. Social events often have community service as an important secondary purpose. For example, there are benefit carnivals, dances, or athletic events that raise funds for World University Service, campus chests, and other service projects. Campus cultural life is greatly enriched by performances and exhibits of student groups in the arts.

Other student groups provide an important service through their recognition of outstanding achievement and their support of higher expectations of academic excellence in the student body. To be entirely truthful, however, it must be admitted that academic achievement is not always given as wide recognition as might be wished. Recently, a student editor exhibited a copy of a newspaper from another campus as an example of the undervaluing of academic achievement. The front page was filled by feature stories and pictures publicizing the election of the May Queen. On the back page, in the short column left over from a large cigarette ad, was a brief notice about a student who had been awarded three major national fellowships for graduate study and whose record of academic honors and independent research was extremely distinguished.

Almost unrecognized are the personal services provided to students through various organizations in the student body. Freshman orientation gets a great deal of attention and publicity during orientation week, but the continuing guidance of freshmen by upper-classmen throughout the college year receives very little attention. Another example is the organized tutorial service, the voluntary assistance in developing study skills and dealing with academic difficulties that upperclassmen give to beginning students. The interest of students in helping their colleagues succeed makes it possible for more students to achieve levels of production in which they can take personal pride. And pride in one's own performance is an essential ingredient of pride in the college as a whole.

Civic pride is also expressed in routine attention to needed services in maintaining the facilities and functions of the college. A great deal of "housekeeping" is done by students, both voluntarily as individuals and systematically through organizations. Students serve as election judges, ushers, and guides; they may take responsibility for safety education, fire drills, and Civil Defense measures. The regular grind of the staff in getting out student publications is an indispensable part of the communication system of the campus.

It is the responsibility of students to help one another find ways of effectively expressing and developing civic pride and college spirit through appropriate activities. Civic pride tends to be high when faculty members respect students and give them genuine responsibility for important functions in college life. Pride and morale tend to be high when students organize strong activities serving a variety of interests and form stable groups with a clearly defined relation to the college. When students feel pride and find satisfaction in their participation in student organizations and activities, and when the entire college takes pride in the self-directed activities of students, the resources of human relationships are generously available for the support of individual development and the growth of the college as a community.

DEMOCRATIC CITIZENSHIP IN THE COLLEGE

Student government and college activities are often commended for their value in preparing students for leadership in business or professions, civic groups, and citizenship. Student activities do afford important opportunities for the rehearsal of leadership and membership roles. But in student activities, the practice of citizenship is not merely rehearsal, it is for keeps. It is essential to the community life of the college.

In most colleges, students and faculty expect the procedures and practices, as well as the policy and administrative organization, of the college to be in keeping with the democratic ideals to which it is committed in the service of American society. There is a general understanding that democratic principles are meaningful only if an attempt is made to carry them out in practice.

The extent to which the practices of student organizations and activities agree with democratic ideals always varies. In the areas of student responsibility, the extent of student autonomy is not clearly defined in all cases. For example, many colleges still are trying to settle the question of the extent of student responsibility for selecting speakers for campus groups and the extent to which the faculty must share in the selection. Student groups are also interested in problems of academic freedom; they attempt to take action, either alone or in concert with the faculty, on important issues affecting the freedom of the members of their college. Within student organizations, a continuing effort is made to develop interest in student government and encourage voting in student elections.

But the concern for democratic citizenship and student responsibility goes beyond a concern for elections and voting. There is concern for the quality of participation. Two commonly accepted standards of democratic participation represent goals that student organizations try to achieve, either quite consciously in their planning and programs, or implicitly in the relationship among members. These standards they seem to share with the rest of American society, as ways of evaluating the quality of democratic citizenship.

The first commonly accepted understanding is that in democratic groups membership shall be open, based on objective standards of merit and skill, interest and responsibility. There is an understanding that such factors as sex, racial, national or religious affiliations, which are beyond the control of individuals, are not appropriate standards for membership.

This naturally does not mean that student groups are not selective in their membership. Honorary societies require excellence in academic achievement. Service clubs require standards of responsibility, time, and service to the college. Athletic teams, debate teams, drama, dance, and music groups have to select participants on the basis of skills.

The question of open membership revolves, not around discriminating selection according to skill and achievement, but rather around the struggle against discriminatory practices. In particular, discrimination in membership against members of minority groups is a real problem in the development of high standards of student organization and participation. The continuing discussion of discriminatory membership practices in fraternities and sororities is a case in point. The issue has been settled in some instances by administrative action. For example, the State University of New York several years ago refused administrative approval and use of college facilities under its jurisdiction to groups using discriminatory factors based on race, nationality, or religion in the selection of membership. On other campuses, similar standards of open membership have been set by action of the faculty, the student personnel officers, the president, or other administrative officers responsible for student organization. Student governments have set such policies on other campuses. And in some instances, the coordinating councils for fraternities and sororities, the national fraternities, or campus chapters have set such standards for themselves.

On the whole, student groups seem to be moving toward open rather than exclusive membership. College administrations and faculties themselves have led the way, through efforts to eliminate discrimination against minority groups in admission of students to college. The emphasis seems to be on enlarging the scope of human relationships in college rather than narrowing or limiting it.

This trend is in keeping with the trends in community life generally in the country. But the problem is not solved. Students have a contribution to make to the college in working out more democratic standards of selection and participation of members in student activity. Colleges could actually lead the rest of American society in giving equal access to their services, regardless of status. In some respects they have led the way. For example, the work of students and faculty members of the University of Oklahoma, in accepting the Supreme Court decision in the *Sipuel* case and accepting Negro students into college life, has been most commendable and effective. It can serve as a model for other colleges and for communities.

The second commonly accepted understanding of democratic principles is that the members have the right and responsibility to participate in decisions that affect the activities in which they are jointly engaged. And it is pretty much agreed that access to positions of leadership should be open to members on the basis of personal merit and achievement.

Some students feel, as citizens of many communities feel, that efficiency is lost by submitting programs and practices to review by members. There could be better distinctions between matters of practice which have relatively little effect on the personal development of members and matters of policy which profoundly affect the quality of the organization and its value to the membership. But sometimes the distinctions are a little difficult to make, and it is usually safer to err on the side of referring more matters to the membership than they really may need to review. This practice may lead to unnecessary delay and complications in carrying out plans. But it tends to protect the right of members to participate in planning. For example, arbitrary determination of meeting dates may make it impossible for a majority of members to participate. The device of setting inconvenient times of meetings has actually been employed in student groups, as well as in community organizations, as a political technique for strengthening minority domination.

Sometimes student organizations seem to lose efficiency through having "more chiefs than Indians." The number of leadership positions may be increased beyond those actually necessary for carrying out plans, to enlarge the number of students who can have experience in leadership. Naturally, the very small group in which every member has an important office is rather ridiculous. But pressures on time and interest do appear to make it wise to reduce the amount of responsibility and the time involved in positions of leadership and to delegate smaller blocks of responsibility to an increasing number of people. Such carefully considered division and delegation of responsibility may in the end tend toward greater efficiency, rather than a reduction in effective programing.

Access to higher levels of leadership is expected to be gained through grades of responsibility and initiative. Beginning as a member of a group, a student progresses to membership on a special committee. He may then move into a committee chairmanship and from there into an elective office. At each step, his job becomes more complex, involving increasing responsibility for assuring effective participation by others, as well as producing effective work on his own.

There are many other standards of democratic citizenship used by students in evaluating the effectiveness of organization and activity. But these two seem to be the predominant concerns of students: Open access to membership and leadership, and participation in decision-making.

Student government as the political apparatus of student life

College administrations delegate many different functions to student government. Judiciary councils, disciplinary boards, or student courts very often assume responsibility for judging misdemeanors and violations of college regulations in the first instance. Some colleges invite representatives chosen by the student body or appointed by its governing body to serve on faculty committees in such areas as instruction, student health and welfare, and other areas of faculty or administrative control.

Student government is primarily a political agency, designed to enable students to organize in order to communicate their interests effectively to the administration and to coordinate their activities and keep them in line with college purposes. The most common student governing body is a representative group chosen from various departments, schools, divisions, or from living units such as residence halls, fraternities, and cooperative houses, with provision for representation of non-resident students. Sometimes both academic and residential bases of representation are used. Some colleges have a dual government, one drawing together residence halls and living units, another functioning as an all-campus governing body. Sometimes men's and women's self-government are separated, with some joint planning and policy groups.

From whatever groups representatives are chosen, it is assumed that they will communicate and coordinate. They are expected to report the interests and desires of their constituency to the governing body and to report back its significant action. The representatives are further expected to take responsibility for coordinating the activities of their constituent groups with the campus-wide program planned and directed by the student governing body. For example, a freshman may expect his class or residence hall to organize within the structure of student government. He may stand for election as an officer or representative; upperclassmen cannot do this job.

✓ Coordinating functions which student government exercises vary widely in scope and degree of responsibility. As a rule, however, student governments are responsible for keeping the purposes and programs of student activities related to the general purposes and programs of the college as a whole. Student government is often expected to set standards for acceptable activities, to enforce appropriate regulations, and to coordinate the activities calendar. In some colleges, the student government grants official approval or recognition of organizations and activities, entitling them to use facilities of the college in carrying out their program. Student governments frequently are responsible for sponsoring and financing certain all-campus activities. Many of them administer a budget based on the student activities fee and support publications, athletics, cultural and social events, as well as the apparatus of student government and intercollegiate relationships, out of college funds.

Coordination, of course, cannot be effectively carried out without effective communication. And many leaders in student government feel that the communications problem is the rock on which many student governments come to grief. The basic channel of communication is through the representatives of various groups on the student governing body. Naturally, the effectiveness of their communication with their related groups varies a good deal, because of the individual qualities and skills in the representative himself and the differences in the responsiveness of groups to reports and inquiries from student government.

Status and prestige patterns within student groups account for some of the communications problems. Sometimes the strongest leaders represent student groups on student councils; but often less experienced leaders with lower status serve as representatives, the strongest leaders as officers. So the representative may have more prestige in the student council than he has in his own group. Accordingly, the student council may pay more attention to the needs and interests that he expresses on behalf of his group in the council than the group pays to his reports of council action. Conversely, a representative may have high prestige in the group he represents, but little status in the student council. So the group may readily respond to his reports, but he may not get a hearing for the group's interests and needs in the student council. Status affects communication by determining who listens to whom. Even with the most conscientious and systematic attention to the contributions of members, student councils find it difficult to get an accurate reflection of the concerns of the constituent groups, and student groups have trouble getting a good picture of council activity.

Publication and publicity are also important channels of communication. College newspapers and other publications are frequently controlled by student government, either through administrative direction or financial support. Still, student governments are often dissatisfied with the information given through publications to the student body. One problem is that very often there is little to report. The coordinating functions of student government are administrative rather than legislative in character, for the most part. Much work is routine and repetitive. Through personal negotiation by officers or committees with student groups, faculty committees, and administrative officers, many matters are settled outside the student council and are simply reported for information and review. Although the word can be carried by representatives or published in the college press, there is very little to do, except to be informed. Such activity does not make news.[5]

Consequently, both student government and publications are tempted to make news by stirring up issues, usually in conflict with the college administration, or by magnifying simple administrative problems. For example, overcrowding in residence halls may become a "hot issue" in the college press, but it can only be solved by long-range building programs. These are running behind enrolment increases, and in the end will add to student fees—which the paper does not mention.

When problems arise, the student government has to be able to mobilize the political machinery of the campus in the process of decision-making. In times of crisis, many students feel involved personally in decisions and action, and it is such involvement that they remember and use in judging the effectiveness of student government. If their college years were relatively peaceful and the student government well coordinated, they remember very little about the student government and tend to rate its effectiveness as very low. If there were serious problems requiring active participation in decisions, they tend to remember the student government as being active and strong.

For example, at one college, during a single academic year, the student council took two actions of major significance. First, it revised its constitution, radically changing the basis of representation of student groups on the council. Second, it settled a policy governing the selection of speakers for student organizations. It won from the administration, in a noisy battle, the delegation of responsibility to the student council for approving off-campus speakers for student groups. Constitutional revision passed with very little student discussion and a very light vote. It was hardly mentioned in the college press. The selection of speakers aroused violent argument and involved a much greater number of students in committee work, letters to the editor, surveys, and determination of the final policy. Students remember the student council of that year as being extremely strong and effective, for "standing up to the administration" through its activity in settling the policy on campus speakers; very few remember the basic revision of the constitution and the change in the patterns of representation and communication, which in fact made possible effective solution of the policy matter.

Some student governments try to take responsibility for leadership training among students. The development of leadership is a vexing problem because of its vagueness. A training program may not help student government very much either, because it is handicapped by the competition with other groups to secure effective leaders. Organizations with smaller membership and more limited program offer more immediate personal contacts to students and tend to assume more immediate significance for them. Student government suffers from abstractness, vagueness, lack of immediacy. The student does not know the whole college, the whole student body, the whole student government. He does know the people in his fraternity, the theatre arts club, and the swimming team. He is, therefore, likely to give more time and attention to such groups and to take more seriously the obligation to give them leadership.

There may be a tendency for students with strong political interests to seek leadership in student government, while others gravitate toward interest groups, fraternities, living groups, and the like. Students who prefer to be chosen as leaders, to have responsibility delegated to them at the request of other members, sometimes are reluctant to put themselves forward as candidates or to seek office. Student organizations— even a student government itself—may develop group standards expressed in approval of the modest, self-effacing leader and disapproval of the aggressive office-seeker.

This is not to say that student government draws aggressive, authoritarian or undemocratic leaders, while other groups draw more democratically inclined, stronger, better-qualified leaders. But what is needed in student government is a politician. And in the very nature of things, politicians cannot just emerge by osmosis out of closely-knit group relationships, in which their sterling qualities become apparent through close acquaintance. They have to show themselves, win support, and acquaint themselves with large numbers of students. The freshman who desires to win elective office should be prepared to develop these political skills.

What is incongruous in the position of the leader of student government is that he must be a politician to achieve a position of leadership, but then he must operate primarily through informal relationships with administrative officers and leaders of other student organizations in carrying out his responsibilities. The development of a political machine bears little relation to the control of the apparatus of student government, or to the functions of coordination and communication which are its primary responsibilities.

Leadership workshops and institutes tend to emphasize attentiveness and responsiveness, participation in planning and organization, recruiting on the basis of interest, and maintaining good interpersonal relationships. Such training is also suited to the routine daily activity of student government; therefore, it is good training for most student leaders. A freshman should take advantage of any leadership training program he can get into, but he should be aware that such programs usually do not prepare leadership for the political activities of student government, for political campaigning in order to secure an office, or for the political organization necessary to support student interests in dealing with crises in student life. Leadership training programs, consequently, are more likely to provide consistency in program in student activities than to develop the political techniques needed for maintaining consistency in the leadership of student government itself. In voting for officers, the student should remember that he has to consider political skill as well as the training of candidates for student government.

This incongruity is a serious problem. It makes it difficult for student government to find ways of maintaining consistently good leadership in its offices through democratic procedures of selection. Student government officers often fall back on other selective processes, most frequently on personal succession. Since, as a rule, there is only one campus-wide government, there is no reservoir of politically trained leaders on which to draw. Officers turn to their fraternity, their residence hall, or representatives with whom they work on the student council for promising prospects whom they can groom as their successors, putting their political machine behind them for election. The practice of personal succession, however, afflicts student government with all of the ills historically related to that method of selection. Nor does it provide for open access to positions of leadership, valued as a mark of democratic practice. No one is happy about this, but as yet there

are few successful plans for leadership training that include the development of political skill.

Some form of student government is probably indispensable to
democratic citizenship in the college. It is difficult for students to evaluate its effectiveness; they may feel that it fails to represent their interests. But something has to be put in the place that the student government occupies, if only to function as a symbol of the autonomy and
independence which students desire. It has been suggested that there
may be a relation between the delegation of independent responsibility
to a strong student government and the delegation of responsibility for
independent study to students in the college. In experience, this relation
does not seem universally true, though there may be a tendency to give
independence for self-government in similar measure to the independence given students in academic work. But strength seems to be a function, not of the independence of student government, but of the importance to the college as a whole of the matters on which the student
government can act. And the most important functions often arouse the
least interest and require the dullest work.

Perhaps the strength and effectiveness of student government may
be better evaluated by administrators and faculty members than by
members of the student body. Complaints from administration and
faculty that student government is pushing too fast, distress over its
crises, requests for its help may be interpreted by students as evidence
of its value. On the other hand, many examples may be given of the
appreciation of deans, residence directors, faculty, and college presidents of the loyal and effective work of student government in supporting the interests of the college. They have praised student governments
for acting in support of academic freedom, and winning the allegiance
of students to the purposes of the entire college, both in its corporate
life and in its relations to the community outside the college walls.

Leadership in college life

The effectiveness of leadership in college life must be judged on two
different grounds. First, there are leaders who emerge by personal force
and responsibility, out of small groups with close personal association.
Leaders of student religious groups, interest groups, fraternities, honorary and service societies are frequently of this type. Second, equally
effective leaders secure key positions through political processes, requiring active office-seeking, aggressive drive for positions, and the
development of status and prestige. Leaders in student government,

intercollegiate organizations such as the United States National Student Association and the United Student Christian Council, and political organizations such as Young Republicans and Young Democrats are often of this type. Both aggressive and permissive leaders can be equally effective, and both are probably necessary in student life.

Status and prestige factors in student life affect the selection of both types of leader. Status ratings are attached to membership in different types of student organizations and activities. Membership in a social fraternity may be valued more highly than membership in an honorary, scientific, or literary fraternity on one campus, with the ratings being reversed on another. Athletes may have high prestige on one campus and be regarded as goons on another. Women occupy a peculiar, confused position in ratings on most campuses. Beauty and charm are always assets, but their prestige ratings vary with the campus or the occasion. Prestige and status in women's activities, such as sororities, residence halls, the Women's Athletic Association, or Associated Women Students may not endow a woman leader with similar status or prestige in campus-wide activities. Sometimes status and prestige patterns assign particular positions, often those involving the dullest work, to women leaders. A woman, for example, may frequently be appointed as copy editor of the college paper, while it may never be conceived possible that a woman could be selected editor-in-chief. Positions such as vice-president, especially where membership development is a responsibility, secretary, or treasurer may by tradition or implicit understanding be reserved for a woman. But the presidency of an organization, unless it is exclusively for women, may not be open to a woman candidate. Women seem particularly scarce in leadership positions requiring political acumen although there is some evidence that much more aggressive political leadership may be developing among women students.

Status and prestige ratings may reflect biases related to other minorities. Nationality, race, or religion may affect status, and hence the level of leadership to which a student may aspire. Happily, there are also indications that these limitations may be beginning to break down. However, status and personal prestige tend to restrict or enhance effectiveness in communication, to reduce or increase the effectiveness of a leader's influence upon the judgment of other students, and to affect the nature and weight of his following in the student body.

Status and prestige are not altogether determined by the judgment of groups and the weight of public opinion. There is a capacity for status that students may develop, in varying degrees. It may be reflected in the capacity of the student to assume higher levels of responsibility, requiring the acceptance of higher status. The capacity for status may be reflected in increasing self-confidence and self-esteem and the ability to accept gracefully the admiration and response of others. There are some useful distinctions that can be made between various status and prestige factors as they affect leadership in student groups.

How to tell the Greeks from the Barbarians. The fraternity or sorority pin is a visible mark of distinction by the social standards of most American campuses. It is the mark of social acceptance, signifying that a student has been selected as a member of an exclusive group, which is discriminating in its tastes and standards of membership.

There are also status ratings among the Greek-letter organizations, varying from campus to campus, but tending to assign rankings that are higher for some groups than for others. Some ratings are based on standards of academic excellence, taste and quality in programs, and service to the college and community. Fraternity and sorority members try to support academic achievement and reward excellence in academic work, for chapters as well as for individuals. They maintain projects of philanthropy and community service, which are of very great value to college and community. They try to train leaders and develop skill in administration. The status and prestige earned in these ways are well deserved and contribute a great deal to the strength of student organization.

Because the Greeks are usually well-organized, cohesive, and accustomed to function in closely-knit groups, they have frequently tended to become politically dominant. They can mobilize the necessary votes to elect members to offices in student government, publications, and other important groups.

By contrast, the Barbarian, the independent student, may seem to be an uncouth person of low taste and bad manners. In the past, students not affiliated with fraternities and sororities sometimes did tend to develop ruder manners and appearance than the more cultivated Greeks, perhaps as a symbol of resistance to the well organized, dominant minority. As they were not well organized, they rarely achieved leadership requiring political activity.

The distinction between Greek and Barbarian is no longer so sharp or significant, and probably never was. Independent students have developed some effective organizations. Commuters form luncheon or dinner clubs and coffee societies, some of which have gained enough strength to support effective political campaigns. The growth of college residence halls has introduced a new factor. Well organized halls develop standards of taste, manners, and conduct, which lend status and prestige to their members. They also may form a basis for effective political support. Fraternities and sororities themselves have sometimes recognized the need for strong student organizations outside of their own membership, and they have contributed leadership to the development of service organizations, interest groups, and residence organizations, composed primarily of independents. On other campuses, their fraternity domination of student government has been broken by the development of factions within the fraternity system itself. Groups having low status within the fraternity system have sometimes organized a drive for positions of campus leadership, in an effort to enhance their prestige and attract more desirable members; such competition has tended to break down Greek dominance, and effective political leaders without fraternity affiliation have stepped into the breach.

This is not to say that domination of campus politics by Greek-letter organizations was a bad thing and needed to be broken up. Rather, it indicates that some factors and trends in college life provide more open access to positions of leadership. Leadership has become more widely diffused among students. Status and prestige can be won through many different kinds of group relationships and participation in a variety of student activities. There is a leveling-off and a leveling-up of standards of behavior and conduct. There are no longer such sharp status distinctions between one student group and another, but rather a more commonly accepted set of standards in which all students more or less tend to share.

On the whole, the breaking down of class distinctions, prejudice, and minority status, and the more general diffusion of prestige lend greater support to the development of self-direction and self-confidence in the student body. And out of this broader range of activity, more effective leaders, specifically trained for particular functions in student life, are beginning to emerge.

How to tell the big wheel from the wheel horse. Student leaders, like other leaders in society, differ in their capacity to do sustained work. Status and prestige introduce factors which may bring into positions of leadership students who can do effective work, or these factors may reward less competent students with positions which they cannot fill effectively.

The big wheel is no longer the "pin-boy" who advertises his affiliation with important groups by displaying keys and pins. He may be a big political operator, who enjoys power for its own sake and aggressively seeks offices to advertise his prestige. He may have a great deal of publicity. He may have a long list of activities and positions following his name in the year book.

The wheel horse, on the other hand, is the unrewarded but effective planner. His tasks are likely to be rather dull, at least from the point of view of others, although he may enjoy them very much. He may be the perennial secretary or the perennial treasurer. It is the wheel horse to whom groups turn when there is a committee to be run, relationships to be ironed out, procedures to be settled, policies to be determined, conflicts to be resolved. He may be an effective mediator, able to compose differences of opinion and interest. But he does not work in the limelight, he rarely receives very much publicity, and outside of the immediate group which is supported by his services, he may be very little known.

Both may be great work horses. The big wheel may not be any less energetic and devoted because of the publicity that attends him. He may perform very important functions of cultivating acquaintance, using personal influence to develop intergroup relationships, and coordinating the work of other leaders. The wheel horse may insure effective participation by drawing members into a closer working relationship with the group, delegating responsibility, and involving them significantly in decision-making and program planning. It is an oversimplification to say that the big wheel is merely a symbol, a figurehead. This may be a very important function, in the first place, and there may be a great deal of work attached to it, in the second place. It is not always true that the wheel horse goes unrewarded. In expressing appreciation and rewarding service to the college, student bodies have been known to come up unexpectedly with awards to those diligent souls whose efforts have gone almost unnoticed.

In making judgments about the effectiveness of leaders, students need to distinguish between the types of leaders in terms of their responsibility, their integrity and judgment, their ability to communicate effectively, their responsiveness to the interests of others, and their capacity for work. Other things being equal, the big wheel may add the flair, the panache, that will lend excitement and stimulate enthusiasm while still supplying the capacity for sustained work. At other times, the quiet, efficient, wheel horse may be a more desirable leader to mediate differences, avoid conflict, and develop an efficient working team. "New occasions speak new duties," and students will want to choose leaders that suit the occasions to which they must rise and the duties they must perform.

How to tell the leader from the ringleader. The administration of complex programs with active participation by the membership requires a high degree of responsibility and close relation of the leader's interest to the interest of others. The leader of well organized groups has to serve the common purposes of the members. He must learn to cultivate close working relationships with other students and to understand and support their interests and purposes. This does not require, necessarily, a great deal of self-sacrifice or self-abnegation. Rather it requires sensitivity and responsiveness to others, qualities essential to good human relationships in any community. Whether he pursues an aggressive political campaign or is chosen through consensus, the leader, nevertheless, accepts responsibility to serve common purposes as his own. He has to strengthen personal relationships among members. He must pursue constructive and conservative policies, designed to maintain high levels of interest and carry forward traditions that the group has learned to value.

By contrast, the ringleader is more likely to serve disruptive than constructive purposes. As a rule, he is aggressive, self-confident, strongly devoted to his personal interests. He may have some characteristics of the authoritarian personality, such as dogmatism, humorlessness, intolerance.*

The ringleader often assumes a position of leadership in movements expressing dissatisfaction with college life. He is particularly likely to react against matters which are settled by tradition or custom, in which relationships are intentionally left vague and ambiguous. Another sore spot is likely to be the exercise of discretionary powers by a student, an organization, or an administrative officer. Or he may dislike leaving matters to be settled by precedent or consent rather than detailed policy. His lack of tolerance for ambiguity drives him to insist that everything be cut-and-dried.

The following of the ringleader can rarely be described as an organization. It is more likely to be an aggregation or assemblage. Sometimes the followers are "outsiders." But the real outsider is not likely to associate with any sort of collective activity, for he is preoccupied with inner personal concerns. It is more likely to be the outsider who wishes to move in, who wants to find a place for himself, that follows a ringleader.

---

* Samuel Messick and Norman Frederiksen found significant correlations between low ability and acquiescence. Both acquiescent and authoritarian responses seemed to be negatively correlated with tolerance for ambiguity, altruism, and liking to think.[6]

To some extent, the ringleader may serve a useful purpose. He may call attention to real problems in student life, which can be corrected. But it is usually easier to handle complaints and dissatisfaction through normal channels of communication in the student body, through student government, student committees, administrative officers, or counselors, than to cope with the ringleader and his following. However, student officers and representatives in student government sometimes find it difficult to secure attention to complaints and grievances. Or they may come to value their personal relationship to faculty members and administrative officers so much that they fear to disrupt it by introducing problems and conflicts. Usually, student body officers turn over rapidly enough for this situation to be avoided. In the first weeks of their tenure of office, they tend to act on matters of immediate concern, to prove to the student body that they really are devoted to its interests and communicating its needs. But sometimes an unresolved difficulty may drag along to the point where it becomes unbearable. Then the students with the most volatile reactions will be the first to complain. And if a ringleader takes up the cry, dissatisfied students may flock to him.

At best, the ringleader may be a spur to the official leaders of the college. At worst, he may disrupt orderly procedures by bypassing the leaders who administer them. Responsible leaders may not even be able to get a hearing, let alone win support and understanding from students, because they are literally squeezed out by the attention given to the ringleader. In such circumstances, it may be difficult to re-establish normal communication and coordination in the student body.

The ringleader sometimes points to significant problems, but usually he lacks the capacity to define them clearly. He rarely can organize effective ways to solve problems since he finds it difficult to relate his own interests to common interests of a group. His inner personal concern is paramount; he brings himself to the center of attention.

However, ringleaders sometimes find themselves in a position where they have to develop, very quickly, much more mature skills, and they may become effective leaders. Occasionally, one will surprise the campus by discovering how to respond to the interests of others and how to develop more effective personal relationships and leadership skills.

"Getting on the Bandwagon." Imitation is the sincerest compliment. Effective student leaders are imitated by other students. Effective programs are adopted by other groups. For example, one campus had a rash of jazz concerts. The first was eminently successful in both attendance and income. Surprisingly, the rest were equally successful,

as well organized procedures for selling tickets, promoting attendance, and selecting a distinctive type of band were followed. Everybody "got on the bandwagon," and it was an enjoyable ride. But the campus had had enough jazz concerts to do it for a student generation, and a different theme had to emerge in the following year.

Sometimes, "getting on the bandwagon" does not lead to nearly so successful results. A good idea can be run into the ground; even the best idea can become dull through too much repetition. Imitation of effective programs may develop into a treasured tradition when the activity imitated is a successful one that makes a real contribution to the college. But less desirable forms of activity are sometimes imitated. For example, one college may feel that it has to have a panty raid just because other colleges have had one. Jamming into telephone booths and loading up Renaults are somewhat more desirable forms of "getting on the bandwagon," although they are just as meaningless. The tendency to "get on the bandwagon" is, consequently, regarded by many observers of colleges and universities as conducive to undesirable conformity.

But when an activity is really enjoyable, it is natural for everybody to want at least one ride. And as long as there are any riders, the bandwagon can go as long as the celebrated One-Hoss Shay. "Getting on the bandwagon," consequently, may be desirable when it provides for the diffusion of worthwhile interests, ideas, and tastes throughout the student body.

Bandwagon tendencies also affect the selection of leaders. An effective leader in one group becomes desirable as a leader in other groups. Everybody piles on his bandwagon. Responsibility is piled on responsibility, office upon office.

A certain amount of bandwagon selection is built into the structure of student body organization. Taking on one responsibility usually requires a student to assume additional jobs. A committee chairmanship, for example, may require serving on an executive committee. An organization president may have to serve *ex officio* on coordinating councils or inter-group committees. The organizational pyramid on one campus insures that a sorority president will serve on Panhellenic Council, the Homecoming Committee, the Spring Carnival Committee, and the House Presidents' Council (which includes both sorority and residence hall heads). She must chair a standing committee of Panhellenic. In addition, the chances are four out of eleven that she may be elected an officer of Panhellenic and two out of eleven that she may be its president or vice-president. If she is elected to one of these offices, she will have to serve on either the Student Assembly or the Student

Judicial Committee, the Women's Senate or the Women's Athletic Council. These *ex officio* responsibilities cannot be delegated. Election as president will automatically give her at least five and perhaps eight other jobs.

Systems for classifying offices and limiting the number that one person can hold are fairly effective in controlling the tendency to ride a good leader's bandwagon. They are not so effective in handling the structural problem of *ex officio* representation, which makes bandwagon selection of leaders inescapable. Although *ex officio* assignments are considered in weighting offices under point systems or classifying them by grades of responsibility, these systems do not really unload the bandwagon that key officers are pulling. They are fairly effective in passing the leadership jobs around among more students. But they do not take account of the total leadership load over four years of college or allow for differences in academic load between departments or among individuals. They do not automatically insure that a good leader may find it possible sometime to give up office and just enjoy being a member for a change. They do not make it easier for leaders to change their interests or get needed variety into their activities. These things the leader will have to work out for himself. And one of the hardest things a student leader can undertake is to say no to requests for leadership that he knows are important and that he would enjoy accepting. It is hard to stop a bandwagon once it gets rolling.

Leadership skills. There are five simple skills of leadership that help develop student organization and college life.

First, there is skill in developing the membership of groups. The effective leader influences other students to join. He cultivates a broad range of acquaintance and issues invitations to his friends to join in activities which he thinks they will enjoy. His congeniality and friendliness make him effective in keeping the membership of organizations open and growing.

Second, leadership calls for skill in developing common interests. The effective leader can recognize interests which he has in common with others and can see possibilities for developing these interests in programs. He has imagination and ideas; he can build up procedures for carrying out ideas in action. He is able to draw out the ideas and interests of others and to develop their imagination.

Third, there is skill in defining special roles that different members may play and delegating responsibility to them. If the group is well organized, and members are well acquainted with each other, the effective leader may leave the definition of roles and the assumption of responsibility to volunteers. Other groups may expect more specificity in the definition of roles and assignment of tasks by the leader. The sensitive leader will know how to distinguish one group and one occasion from another. He will avoid stereotyping but will see to it that members have a variety of experience in different kinds of roles. For example, the student who bakes the best brownies may not always be expected to provide brownies for teas, receptions, and parties but may occasionally be asked to chair the social committee or to be a consultant to a student government committee on recreational interests. The effective leader can develop committees, assign functions, and select good chairmen for the tasks involved. He must be able to delegate responsibility to other leaders and help them learn to delegate responsibility to members as well.

Fourth, leadership requires skill in making decisions. The effective leader is decisive, and he is also careful to have his decisions confirmed by other members. The sensitive leader will have to decide when he can make a decision alone and when a question must be submitted to discussion so that members can begin to develop agreement on it. There is no rule of thumb for choosing processes of decision-making. The effective leader will have to learn from experience how to distinguish one occasion from another. The democratic leader will always make sure, however, that the group agrees to support a decision, however it is made.

Finally, leadership requires skill in representation. The leader is a symbol of the group, and he must represent in his conduct and procedures the standards which the whole group wishes to achieve. He must speak for his group. When he is called upon to enlist the support of his group in matters of broader concern, he becomes an important instrument of communication. The effective leader will develop skill in interpreting to other members the interests, problems, causes, in which their support is to be enlisted. He also will develop skill in reflecting to other organizations and officers the interests, concerns, and problems represented in the organization he serves.

The faculty adviser. The custom of asking faculty members to act as advisers to student organizations seems to be a tradition in American colleges. While the faculty adviser is an instrument of administrative control over student activities, he rarely exercises direct control. Instead he tries to develop self-direction and group control by students in line with college purposes.

First of all, he must work as a member of the group. His role, of course, cannot be exactly the same as that of other members. He is not a student. He does not have as much time or energy as students have. But he is a member playing a special kind of role. He is expected to attend meetings. He must be welcome to participate in discussion and planning.

Second, as his title indicates, he is expected to advise. He is an important source of information about college regulations, standards, procedures, which must be taken into account. He is responsible for helping student groups relate their purposes and programs to those of the college. He assumes that students wish to contribute to the college, to the life and traditions of the campus. Students can draw heavily upon his advice and interpretation in increasing the significance and enduring value of their organizations, activities, and government.

Third, the faculty adviser can contribute to programs out of special resources. He has access to other faculty members, whose help may be enlisted in special programs or projects. He can suggest qualified speakers. He may be able to introduce students to opportunities for seeking help or giving service in the community. Sometimes he can help them find financial support.

Perhaps the most important service of the faculty adviser is to provide continuity from one year to the next. Students are transient members of the college; the time they spend in activities is relatively short. Summer vacations are gaps which are difficult to bridge, creating a kind of built-in discontinuity which is difficult for students alone to overcome. But the faculty member can help make sure that the program of one year is consistent with what has gone before and that it represents values that students wish to continue in college traditions.

If, over and above these functions, the faculty adviser also adds to personal enjoyment, warmth, and friendship, this is all to the good. Many faculty members value their relationship as advisors to student groups. It is fun for them, and they can help make college life fun for students. In return, they often give services over and above the call of duty and enable students to take on activities of great complexity and scope. A really good faculty adviser can help students contribute much more than anyone could expect to the life of the college.

The student with brief case. The scope of student leadership is not restricted to the campus. Energetic student leaders seek for broader fields of activity, and they may be sought by groups outside the college for the special contributions they can make.

Intercollegiate relationships have been based on many different interests. Athletics, for example, have led to rivalry and competition among colleges and universities and to the growth of intercollegiate athletic associations, which set the rules and determine the schedules for competition in various sports. The growth of intercollegiate athletics and of income from them has created problems which administrative officers and faculty members have had to solve. So control of inter-collegiate relationships in this area has been vested primarily in the faculty and administration. But students do migrate to other campuses for athletic events, carry the banner, and produce the spirit, in spite of traffic hazards and other perils.

The brief case rather than the banner is standard equipment for leaders in other intercollegiate relationships. Student religious groups, for example, have a long history of intercollegiate organization. State, regional, and national meetings with continuing organizations have grown up around denominational groups, the Y.M.C.A. and Y.W.C.A., and interdenominational groups such as the United Student Christian Council. In these intercollegiate organizations, a very large area of responsibility and leadership in program content, policy, study, and action is reserved for students. Staff directors assist in program develop-ment and direct intercollegiate organizations.

The newest association on the scene is the United States National Student Association, an intercollegiate organization coordinating stu-dent governments. In its second decade, it is still striving for stability in structure and program, but it is an extremely productive organiza-tion. It provides for the exchange of information, services, and ideas between student governing bodies on many campuses. Its national meetings bring together large numbers of student delegates, both in small group meetings and in debates in a general assembly. Its various commissions have worked out suggestions for participation of students in curriculum planning and other aspects of college administration; they have drafted a student Bill of Rights and Responsibilities setting forth desirable standards for maintaining the status of students in col-lege; and they have studied the changing patterns of values and stand-ards in American students.

Nor is the scope of intercollegiate activity limited to the United States. The World University Service, for example, serves as an inter-national clearing house for the exchange of student aid and student leadership among many countries of the world. Its work of rehabilita-tion of colleges destroyed or damaged in war and its service in the development of colleges and universities in emerging nations of Asia and Africa, are also important causes in which colleges and universities and intercollegiate associations in the United States have enlisted.

The United States National Student Association maintains working relationships on an international level, both through World University Service and with national unions of students, in many countries of the world. It brings leaders from other countries to study at American universities and gain experience in leadership and knowledge of patterns of student life in this country. It represents students in government agencies and planning bodies in this country and in international associations and agencies. It is trying to work out a pattern of common interests and purposes in which students in many countries may share in a genuine international community of scholars.

The student with brief case, who will travel, can find great scope for his interests. And he will be involved in settling significant issues. The organizations drawing students together nationally and internationally have addressed themselves to some of the most serious problems in student life: the basic values and purposes which sustain scholarly work and draw scholars together; the needs of students for food, shelter, medical care, books, and laboratories; the raising of standards of academic achievement in colleges and universities both in the United States and elsewhere in the world; the sharing of resources in support of democratic student movements; the training of student leaders. In these organizations, student leaders undertake the important tasks of study and action on their own initiative and responsibility.

The student with brief case, however, may go no farther than the nearest subway station or bus stop. Increasingly, students are being called on to perform important services in the community in which the college is located. The community increasingly has become a subject for study. Public opinion surveys, market research, studies of family relations, observation of pupils and teachers in schools are increasingly part of the course of study for students in social sciences, business, engineering, science, and education.

Students also offer important volunteer leadership in the community. Churches, scouts, "the Y," settlement houses and neighborhood centers, city recreation departments, and other community service agencies need student leaders. Other civic organizations and societies in the community also value student participation: scientific associations and academies, art galleries and museums, symphony societies, political organizations, and many others. The student can find an effective place for himself in voluntary service in the community, just as readily as on the college campus.

In a study of extracurricular activities of students at the University of Buffalo,[7] for example, an attempt was made to discover why there was a relatively low level of participation in campus activities. The membership of the University at that time was heavily weighted on the side of commuters, and there was real concern about increasing student participation in campus affairs. The survey found that about half of the students participated in community activities. They served as volunteer leaders in the "Y" and Scouts; some of them were on the official boards of churches or neighborhood houses. They had, in many instances, continued group activities that they had begun in high school, but they had progressed to higher levels of responsibility and leadership in museums, the symphony society, and all sorts of educational, scientific, and cultural organizations. While campus activities may have needed more participation, students had formed enduring relationships to significant activities in the community and were using effectively their skills in leadership and community service.

The student with brief case may use the resources of the community, national organizations, and international agencies in following his personal interests and developing his skills. By serving the needs of these community groups, the enterprise of scholarship continues to grow. The student who broadens the scope of his activity and gives leadership in the community is also contributing to the growth of the college and the enlargement of the scholarly enterprise.

Of course, he may have nothing in his brief case but his lunch.

11

Something of value

Developing judgments
of value

JUDGMENT AND VALUES IN COLLEGE LIFE

Implicitly or explicitly, colleges assume "that there are civilizing values which need to be communicated to and through any person who goes to college and expects to live primarily by means of a trained mind . . . few deny that they expect college to exert a 'maturing' influence upon students' standards of behavior, quality of judgment, sense of social responsibility, and perspicacity of understanding of themselves and others, in addition to whatever body of skills and facts they acquire."[1]

Furthermore, colleges assume that in the task of developing standards of value students will undergo change and college experience will have lasting consequences for choices of conduct in adult life.

We agree, therefore, . . . (1) that among its responsibilities the American college should include a conscious concern for the character of its students; (2) that it is not desirable to separate the training of the intellect from values which impinge on the life and thought of the student; (3) that basic convictions and values are formed in the early years and primarily in the home, but the college can modify convictions and values both for good and for ill. It can assist in turning vague concepts into convictions by the encouragement of conscious examination and evaluation and by the opportunity for positive practice.[2]

Although values may be expected to change during the college years, the experience need not be unsettling for students. Usually value judgments in one particular area will become unsettled because of personal or social problems. These then have to be resolved, but other values remain fairly stable and can be used in settling immediate problems. Under ordinary circumstances, the student should expect more or less continuous development in most of his values throughout his life.

Rarely does a student undergo the shattering experience of having his entire system of values, or any significant part of it, shaken to its foundations all at once. Even if he should, there is always hope that he can find at least one fixed principle as a hard core around which he can maintain his identity and re-establish orderly development of his values. And he can usually find skilled help and counsel from members of the faculty, the counseling staff, chaplains, ministers and religious advisers, who are ready to help him find a way to reconstruct his system of values and find himself again.

The mature person is able to act in two very different sets of circumstances. He can conduct himself properly in settled situations in which his values are clear and he can act consistently in relation to them. This takes integrity. And he can accept conflicts in which the values involved are not clear, take the best action he can, and reflect upon it in such a way as to settle new values. This takes courage.

The scholarly enterprise takes the student into essentially unknown areas, in which values are unsettled. In fact, the unknown is the very reason for conducting scholarly inquiry. And there is always the uncomfortable possibility that the unknown may turn out to hurt somebody—and that somebody may be the investigator. In venturing into new fields, therefore, it is important to have the basic values that sustain the self fairly well in hand and readily available for self-defense. Then facts can be more readily and correctly interpreted. Should confusion or conflicts in belief appear, they can be more clearly defined, and new values can be more easily developed to resolve the conflict and confusion.

But the college does not present the student with a ready-made set of values. Progress through college may better be viewed as a series of judgments of value, which continually settle one or another area of knowledge or belief by getting new experience or new facts. College life generates confusion and conflict in values as people with differing character and experience learn to work together. The student has no choice but to bring to college the values that he has established in the course of his development, under the influence of his family. These values form the core of his character and enable him to make value judgments and resolve conflicts of value as he progresses through college.

STUDENT MORES AND CONFORMITY

Upon entering college, the student is presented with his first problem in value judgment. He has to come to terms with the mores of the student body, which determine what is acceptable, "what is done." Catalogues and handbooks do not usually carry any statement of the values that students regard as desirable in each other. These are conveyed more by gestures and manners than by systematic description. Sometimes the student does not even know that they are there until he has behaved in an unfitting way and has suffered the consequences. Simply becoming aware of the mores presents a certain problem for students.[3] One feature of the trend toward improved orientation to college is the care with which upperclassmen try to interpret significant mores to entering students.[4]

Even so, every student must determine his own response to campus mores. He has to reject some and accept others as may seem best suited to his inward image of himself. If he does not exercise his own judgment and live "by his own lights," he loses sight of himself and develops inconsistent behavior instead of clear self-direction. On the other hand, if he lives wholly "by his own lights," he may lose contact with the life of the college and lack effective ways of relating himself to others in shared activities, cooperation, and friendship. He has the difficult task of learning to live "by his own lights," responsible for directing his own personal development while using the mores as they light his way to valuable relationships.*

A consequence of the freedom and toleration that the college tries to maintain is the wide range of variation in the values and conduct of its

---

* David Riesman deals with the problem of self-direction, and describes types of character related to major sources of value: the "inner-directed," concentrating on inward sources of value; the "other-directed," adapting to the shifting patterns of value in the community without any consistent inward pattern; the "tradition-directed," conforming to conventions of the culture; and "the autonomous," selecting values to guide behavior that are consistent with the inward self and shared with others.[5]

members. Student mores may differ from the standards held by the faculty; behavior required or tolerated in freshmen may be unacceptable in upperclassmen. Differences among students in values and behavior derive in part from differences in regional, cultural, and family background and in part from differences in level of maturity as students progress through college. Confusion and conflict may be aggravated by the persistence of some patterns of adolescent behavior, perpetuated past their time by some practices in the college itself.

Self-assertiveness as rebellion

One feature of adolescence is self-assertion, through imitating inappropriate or forbidden adult behavior as evidence that one is really grown up and free to act against the dictates of parental authority. Drinking, bragging, rioting, practical joking, panty raids, malicious mischief, and the like express some of the adolescent rebelliousness that carries over into the college years. The tolerance of the college for such manifestations of lingering adolescence is rather generous, and it often puzzles students. They regard it as a trap, or they feel the need—itself another adolescent manifestation—to test it by seeing how far they can go in inventing and carrying out bizarre activities. They are more likely to express rebelliousness in groups than as individuals. The fear of authority is a feature of lingering adolescence, and students seek safety in numbers, as they once sought the protection of the gang or the high school crowd.

Fads

Another feature of lingering adolescence is faddishness in behavior, manners, and dress. Fashion and sales promotion take advantage of it, advertising the Ivy League style, the "campus-tested" product, as the thing to wear or use. But characteristic patterns of dress and manners appear without commercial encouragement. The sloppy look, the casual look, the saddle shoes, the white bucks, the sneakers, the blue jeans, the sweater-and-skirt combination were campus fads before they were advertised as fashions. Advertisement seems to hasten the diffusion of fads, rather than to generate them. Manners, too, get pretty well settled in acceptable local forms, all the way from the roughest to the most refined.[6] Carelessness and indifference about signs of respect and attention may be cultivated in one college, while in another, expressions of regard, politeness, and appreciation may be *de rigueur*.

Conformity

Faddishness and rebellion are not too serious in themselves. Given time and adequate adult models, students tend to grow out of them. But they can be prolonged far beyond their normal span and become hazards to self-realization when they are reinforced in the student mores by a third feature of lingering adolescence, conformity.

Adolescent conformity, like much adolescent behavior, is an extreme form of normal human behavior. Conforming to consistent patterns of manners, customs, and habit is necessary to self-development, community life, and good human relations. In adolescence, however, the need to conform is a far stronger drive, and group pressure to conform is much more severe than the normal adult can tolerate. Conformity determines identity; the adolescent must go along with the crowd and do what they all do to establish his identity or to be accepted as a real person, a regular fellow. Only with the passage of time and the enlargement of his experience does he gain self-confidence and the capacity to set his own standards and try to live up to them. At this point, too, many of his fellows mature sufficiently to assume self-direction; then their dependence on group standards wanes, and the stereotyped behavior characteristic of conformity yields to a more flexible, varied, and tolerant pattern of manners, taste, and conduct.

But wherever lingering adolescent patterns predominate in the student mores, conformity is the rule, rather than the exception, in student life. The weight of student custom and tradition is thrown against individuality, self-realization, self-direction. The student who tries to achieve mature self-direction may find himself deviating from prevailing patterns of student behavior, rigidly enforced by group pressures. Then he has to assert himself not only against adult authority but against his fellow-students in order to win any degree of independence.

All too frequently, reprisals are visited upon students who do not conform to the mores. Sometimes a student who is "different" may be isolated socially, ignored, or just not invited to share in student activities. His reputation may be ruined by idle gossip and criticism or even outright calumny and slander. He may be expelled from a group or made so uncomfortable by harassment and practical jokes that he has to withdraw.

The student who holds to more significant intellectual and social standards, or who models his behavior on the more mature patterns of the faculty and upperclassmen, may find it difficult to defend himself against reprisal. There is an adequate defense; it depends upon finding desirable associates who share common values of a more mature kind. But he must find them for himself. And in some instances, conformity is so strongly supported in the mores that students with high standards do not dare to express them for fear of reprisal. Since they cannot make themselves known, they cannot make common cause in serving their common interests and protecting themselves from group pressures. But there is usually some possibility of finding associates who will support mature interests and self-direction. Occasionally, faculty members can help.

For example, a student whose academic record should have been outstanding, to judge by his aptitudes and high school performance, was on the verge of being disqualified and sought help from a counselor. In the interview, it emerged that he had found himself associated with students who took their academic work very lightly and expected superficial, pseudo-sophisticated social behavior of their friends. He had tried to conceal his real intellectual gifts and practice them on the sly. But others found out his secret. They made life difficult for him through practical jokes and belittling remarks about his social inadequacy. He then gave up his intellectual interests altogether and ran with the crowd. But he was not happy. Finally he realized that he really wanted to do a good job in college and did not enjoy the "country club crowd." So he withdrew from the group altogether and was a lone wolf. But then his grades declined still further. He said that he needed someone else who really cared about him and shared his intellectual interest. With the help of the counselor, he figured out the type of student he wanted to know, found a couple of organizations to join, and developed some new friends with high intellectual standards. To his great pleasure, he found his interest returning and his performance improving. This story has a happy ending, for within two semesters he had achieved a straight A average.

Anti-intellectualism

This student's problem is unfortunately rather common. Conformity to lingering adolescent patterns of behavior results in the undervaluing of intellectual standards and the reduction of levels of expectation and performance. In the lingering stages of rebellion, students assert themselves by refusing to accept the most significant intellectual values of the college, which they identify as rigid requirements enforced by adult authority. (That in conforming to the pattern of rebellion against conformity they are involved in a worse kind of conformity is just one of those booby traps of growing up that many students are not clever enough to recognize.) Deadlines are set for term papers; students brag to each other about sneaking a paper in under the office door or concocting a plausible excuse for filing it late and fooling the professor. Election as a queen is rated as more important than election to Phi Beta Kappa. Cheating is perfected into a system managed by an organization.

Conformity through the neglect of intellectual values is just as hazardous as the reprisals visited upon students who try for high achievement. Both are disastrous in their effects upon the most promising students of real intellectual gifts and energy, who could achieve high levels of excellence. The neglect of intellectual values sets a ceiling to acceptable limits of achievement well below the excellence of which the students are capable. Reprisals for deviation in the direction of excellence add to the stress under which students work. Conformity denies the freedom for maximum individual achievement to which the college is committed. The student who is capable of excellence in achievement needs the warm response of friends to support him, and isolating him or ruining his reputation does very great damage not only to him as an individual but to the whole scholarly enterprise in which students are engaged.*

For even the most modest scholarly achievement requires great emotional strength. Mastery of the stress of academic work requires considerable emotional control. Rising to occasions for high achievement places even greater demand upon adaptive reserves. Stress is increased by the high stakes involved in college work. A good income, a happy home, a satisfying job, a place for himself in community life are all riding on the student's achievement in college. The deplorable fact is that the student who takes these matters seriously very often has to waste strength in resisting pressures and reprisals from his fellow students or in concealing his serious interests behind a façade of con-

---

* The subtler pressures to conform to non-intellectual standards can destroy the intellectual capacity of students, just as surely as reprisals. Jacques Barzun describes the process of "abdication" of intellect:

"Meeting at every turn the same bland, patronizing treatment, the man who feels within himself the wakefulness of intellect comes to think of it as peculiar to himself, a somewhat shaming oddity.

"If by chance he has more than a taste for intellect, an appetite, perhaps a passion, the habits of public opinion may strike him as so stern a rebuke that he succumbs to the disease of denying in oneself what one finds denied outside. . . . He pretends that he is harmless because powerless, yet he rebels against this self-imposed emasculation, the current name of which is conformity. In no sense positive, conformity expresses lack of power—not duress after struggle and loss, but lack of what one has consented to destroy."[7]

formity. He is subject to anxiety that saps his emotional reserves. This anxiety may be aroused by thoughtless or salacious gossip or by awareness of the disparity between his more mature purposes and the late-adolescent fantasies about "date bait," sexual adventures, and pseudo-sophisticated social life that circulate freely among students.

It is hard enough to accept the difficult tasks of scholarly development, to overcome natural tendencies to conform, to find personal identity, and to master tasks of self-realization, without the added burden of resistance to immature group standards. The best students have to wait far too long for the rest to grow up and give them the support they need.

Unfortunately, colleges sometimes contribute to the persistence of adolescent behavior. Since they are recruiting students from high schools in which adolescent mores predominate, representatives sometimes overrate some of the superficial aspects of student life. School spirit, fraternity life, dances, student unions may be emphasized to the neglect of the intellectual values and resources of the college, in an effort to address high school students in their own language. Unfortunately, high school graduates are thus left unprepared for the transition from school to college, the greater self-direction it will require, and the serious academic work that will be necessary.

Furthermore, colleges tend toward standardization in the selection of students, and standardization may lend support to conformity. Colleges use pretty much the same sort of tests in student selection, setting similar requirements for high school grades, and looking for the same qualities of leadership, or social adjustment.[8] Although a beginning has been made, more attention is needed to the selection of good students who may not conform to standardized qualifications of ability and adjustment. Colleges are examining their presuppositions about social adjustment and personality traits and the effects of status and prestige factors on selection. They are trying to pay more attention to culturally or educationally deprived students of good ability, to under-achieving students who need better motivation, and to nonconforming gifted students. The traditional generosity of the college in allowing a wide range of variation in traits and interests can be a valuable counterweight against its tendency to conformity and standardization.

Jacob[9] found differing patterns of conformity among colleges. In some, campus values emphasized aggressiveness, intellectual independence, and skill in controversy. There a passive, self-effacing, accepting student would be nonconforming and would probably find it hard to develop mature values. In some colleges, there appeared to be different curricular and extracurricular patterns of value in the same college. There both aggressive and accepting students could conform to some value system, even though there seemed to be a conflict between the two systems of values. Apparently, inward personal conflicts are not so likely to arise where there are differences, or even conflicts, in the values held by different groups in the college. But inward conflicts seem to arise when group pressures force students to conform to a single set of values. It is easier to resist pressures to conform when another set of nonconforming values is available to live by.

There is a tendency, too, for colleges to perpetuate adolescent behavior by failing to give students responsibility for meaningful scholarly activity. Students may occupy themselves in trivia just because they have nothing else to do. Student governments run queen contests for lack of significant business. Students may rebel against the faculty because they have no other way to take initiative or share in the management of the college. Students on one campus failed to attend a reception for high school students attending a career conference. When the conference director criticized the student body president for failing to persuade students to attend, the president asked, "Sir, how many students were on the planning committee?" "Why, none," replied the director. Students excluded from planning are likely to infer that they are not invited to participate in other aspects of important programs.

Essentially, the administration and faculty must decide what responsibility students need to assume in order to understand and support the values to which the college is devoted. But if they give students no responsibility at all, they are likely to perpetuate adolescent patterns of rebellion, resistance, deception, and conformity. These pose a counterweight to academic standards and perpetuate student mores that interfere with achievement.

But students need not wait for faculties to give them responsibility in the management of their affairs. They can take the initiative, make plans, present proposals. They do not have to wait to be invited to attend a reception for high school students; they can ask to plan it or provide entertainment. Of course, it goes without saying that students are more likely to take the initiative where faculty members and administrative officers are receptive and encouraging. But students need not confine their interests to superficialities if they wish to assume responsibility for introducing mature values into student life and for counteracting the tendency for adolescent standards to linger past their time.

THE APPEARANCE OF MATURE STANDARDS

Since the college includes people in various stages of development, its members actually have a mixture of values and behavior patterns, including both immature and more mature forms. So on most campuses, the task is not so much to introduce new standards as to identify and support those existing standards that have the greatest value. It would be easy to improve the tone of the campus if the less mature students could just be persuaded to be more attentive and less resistant to the serious interests of those who are more mature. Unfortunately, college life is not that simple. Lack of tolerance and pressure to conform are features of lingering adolescence, and they cannot be crushed but must die a natural death. More mature and advanced students are likely to be exposed to reprisals for being in league with the faculty if they undertake to bring about a change by direct action. The matter has to be approached in another way.

Orientation to college life

Given time and adequate leadership, students can develop mature standards, and advanced students are showing evidence of growing tolerance toward younger students. They no longer practice pranks and practical jokes on them to as great an extent as formerly. The humiliation of hazing and initiation, as expressions of superior status and dominance of upperclassmen, are beginning to die out.[10] Instead, upperclassmen are giving greater leadership to activities designed to help entering students establish themselves in the college rapidly and smoothly. Greater emphasis is put on friendly relations between upperclassmen and freshmen, on interpreting student mores and college standards, and on identification of skills and interests valuable in campus organization and community service.

Initiation is giving away to orientation. Freshmen once slaved at menial tasks for domineering upperclassmen; now upperclass advisors write to entering students before registration, meet them, help them get settled and registered, see that they meet other students, inform them about campus traditions, pass on helpful hints on faculty members and courses, and introduce them to campus organizations. The replacement of Hell Week by Help Week in fraternity initiation introduces students to worthwhile opportunities for community service. Some orientation programs actually include interpretation of the educational philosophy of the college or discussion of important books or intellectual issues.

Respect for minorities and acceptance of individual differences

Students are showing increasing maturity of judgment in handling individual differences and establishing relationships among minority groups. Discriminatory practices among students are being replaced by a readier acceptance of individuals on their merits. For example, the initiative in eliminating discriminatory clauses in fraternity constitutions has come from students, often from fraternities themselves. Student religious organizations have given effective leadership in interfaith and intercultural programs. Coeducational activities are the rule rather than the exception; and even though women students may still be considered oddities in some fields of study or activities, at least they are acceptable oddities less subject to ridicule and belittling. There is less idle comment about individual differences and more candid interest in their meaning and value. Though colleges are not free from discriminatory practices and other signs of prejudice, increasing maturity in student life is shown by attempts to make personal relationships more comfortable for people of unusual characteristics and affiliations—the physically handicapped, the foreign students, women, Negroes, Democrats, Republicans, the gifted, and students with peculiar majors.

Support of academic freedom

Respect for differences of opinion and the responsibility that students take for supporting freedom of expression provide further evidence of increasing maturity in judgment. One continuing concern of student government is the development of effective channels of communication within the student body so that conflicts can be resolved and controversies dealt with in an open and effective manner. All-college conferences, town meetings, workshops enlist students in discussion and action on problems of community living.

There have also been occasions on which students have risen to support the freedom of expression and civil rights of scholars for both faculty members and students: for example, student protests at Swarthmore, Harvard, Yale, and many other colleges against the loyalty affidavit required of students receiving Federal loans,[11] and student support from colleges all over the country for freedom of the college press in the case of the *Daily Texan* in 1956. Activity in support of academic freedom is beginning to be coordinated on an intercollegiate basis through the United States National Student Association as student governments become stronger and develop more sophisticated and effective techniques of action in the interest of the college.

Respect for privacy

The protection of privacy is a more subtle matter. Dormitories provide no privacy to speak of; students live in a fish bowl. Some protective devices do appear: signs and symbols ("Quiet, Genius at Work"), the closed door, tacit understandings between roommates and friends. There is a blessed bastion of quiet protected by fierce, professional dragons, the library. Quiet is not the only important aspect of privacy. Students also can support more mature standards by attention to such things as control of gossip and rumor. Freedom from inquiry into personal affairs is an important protection for the privacy essential to scholarship.

Furthermore, mature persons respect privacy of possession. For scholars, this privacy extends to ideas, materials, and problems as well as toothbrushes, typewriters, and books. Ideas are shared among students as freely as clothes; but it is a mark of maturity to acknowledge the source of an idea, while the ownership of a blouse or necktie is not necessarily of grave import. Ideas are part of the student or faculty member or author producing them, while clothing is not. They are given, not loaned, and the gift includes part of the self. So it is the mark of mature scholarship to acknowledge the source. Conversely, the most serious violation of academic standards is plagiarism, the use of another person's material without acknowledgment.

But the protection of privacy for the development of an idea or a problem to its fully ripened form is a matter in which students need increasingly mature responsibility. Borrowing class notes, lab reports, books, term papers are as serious invasions of privacy as cheating, collusion, and plagiarism, and they are much more widespread practices. Faculty members can do very little about it. But students could help by finding ways for ideas to be exchanged and help to be given while protecting the right of others to develop their own line of thought without being badgered by lazy, incompetent, or thoughtless students for assistance to which they are not entitled.

Referral for counseling

A special problem in the protection of privacy is securing help for students having personal problems, without appearing to tattle or tell tales. The distinction between tattling and referral is hard for even the most mature adults to make. People will tell each other their intimate personal problems. Sometimes friends can help them find solutions; sometimes they cannot help; sometimes it would make matters worse for them to try. Many problems require the special privacy afforded by professional counseling. Students can learn to distinguish this class of problems from those which can be solved by friendly advice, and they can learn how to refer a friend to a counselor, without telling tales. But there is no rule of thumb to follow.

Maturity in such judgments is probably better developed by consulting a wiser person—a trusted faculty member, a counselor, or a dean. Each case has to be worked out in its own terms, and the only safe rule to follow is to ask for counsel for oneself if a friend's confidence is too hard to bear or his problem too difficult to solve. A counselor can help a student decide when a friend needs expert help and how the referral can best be made. Maturity of judgment is evidenced by willingness to ask for help in matters beyond one's own competence. Knowledge of one's own limitations has very great social value.

The ability to suspend judgment

Mature standards of value are shown in the suspension of judgment until all the evidence comes in or necessary stages of development are followed. Students will find that part of their course work involves training in the art of thinking otherwise. Being open-minded, in the academic sense, does not mean having fuzzy ideas that change with every new opinion. It means having a clear idea, deliberately thinking otherwise, gathering evidence, and making up one's mind. This process of judgment is more frequently practiced in the classroom than in student life; but it can be introduced into student activities and self-government.

The judgment that has to be suspended for differences of opinion to be expressed or controversy to become really significant is the judgment upon personal character and personal relationships. In American culture, remarks belittling personal character and feelings are considered bad manners and poor taste. But this canon of taste is usually honored, not by excluding personal references from discussion, but by excluding any subject that might arouse strong feelings or offend someone—in other words, by avoiding the only subjects worth talking about. As Barzun points out, attention primarily to feelings excludes the important factual, rational, intellectual content from the discussion of issues and does nothing to resolve and focus the feelings, either.[12] Students can cultivate orderly processes of judgment by taking up controversial matters in orderly discussion. The interest of student governments in group procedures and discussion techniques is a move in this direction.

The town meeting which invites students with differing points of view to participate in orderly discussion is becoming more common. Above all, attention to the conventions of group procedure that eliminate personalities from discussion of issues helps to develop the capacity to suspend judgment in the interest of participation in the settlement of problems of value.

Such suspension of judgment also can be useful in non-academic relationships in the college. Students can give each other a little more freedom for development in the great choices of work, mating, and a way of life by suspending judgment until the proper time has come for a final decision. This does not mean doing nothing or refraining from consideration of choices. Rather it means getting experience, studying alternatives, weighing personal interests while waiting for the final decision to ripen. What students can practice for themselves, they can also practice with each other by exchanging information, experience, and social contacts that are helpful in these decisions and avoiding the intrusion of cynical comment, superficial evaluation, or disapproval into the decisions of other persons. For example, occupational choices can be made easier for students if they can share job experiences either in discussion or by working together on similar jobs. It would be helpful for students to suspend stereotyped judgments of status related to occupations, such as those overvaluing engineering or undervaluing teaching or those regarding artists as odd, both in their personal choice and in evaluating the choices of others.

Freedom for the development of mature personal values is enhanced by the suspension of judgment on personal character. It permits growth and enrichment and provides an atmosphere in which really important differences of opinion can be worked out, as a basis for settled values, in individuals and groups.

THE GROWTH OF VALUES

The growth of mature values cannot be left wholly to chance. Advancing age does not endow students with high standards unless values are generated by the active effort of faculty and students and practiced in the social relationships that bind every college together as a community. Because of their separation from student experience, both in patterns of community living and in the differences between generations, faculty members have little access to important areas of college life in which values are developed. There is no guarantee that even the best standards of value developed in the classroom will be transferred to student life. Faculty members also tend to be very critical of students' judgment, particularly of their judgment of value.* These criticisms are likely to have more acidity because faculty members lack effective contact with students in relationships where important values are developed.

There are four aspects of value development in the student years to which the college as a community gives effective support. And faculty members can contribute effectively to student development, to some extent, in all of them.

Relating social values to self-development

First, the college can provide a community in which there is an unusually close relationship between personal and social values. Both course work and student activities depend upon the recognition of common interests in the development of cooperative enterprises. Consequently, students are led to express personal values in social relationships and to relate the values expressed in social relationships to their inward personal values. Thus, personal and social values become reciprocally related to each other, each feeding the development of the other. As development proceeds, they tend to become consistent with each other, under normal conditions.

Second, students are expected to exercise their growing social competence by serving the college. Responsibility for organizing student life is placed upon them, whether by neglect or by deliberate delegation of responsibility. To discharge this responsibility satisfactorily, students have to develop more or less explicit values sustaining both personal development and effective organization of student life.

Third, since students are transient members of the college, their patterns of social organization are likewise transient and can be more easily changed than is ordinarily the case in community relationships. If higher standards of social competence and more mature values are actively introduced into student life, it is relatively easy to supplant immature behavior with more mature value judgments. (Unfortunately, standards can decay just as rapidly.)

---

* Although he also cites evidence that many students are concerned with values that sustain community life, Jacob, for example, takes exception to the self-centered values of students, whose concerns for a happy marriage, a good income, a secure job predominate in their value systems.[13] But just these self-sustaining values are needed as a base for effective development of standards of tolerance, generosity, and responsibility in social and political life. If self-sustaining values predominate, it may very well be because students face the choices of a career, a mate, a way of life, in which these values are immediately involved.

The development of personal and social values is a reciprocal process. The stronger the inward self, the more social competence may develop. The more social competence develops in student life, the more mature judgments of value are strengthened. The stronger and more mature the group judgments of value, the more reinforcement can be given to mature values in individual behavior early in the college years. Both personal and social values are strengthened in college to the extent that there is conscious effort on the part of both students and faculty to develop relationships in which the values that sustain mature self-realization can be expressed in college life.

Evaluation based on behavior

Both personal and social values are expressed, as they are learned, in behavior. And the college proceeds on an unwritten assumption that action, not just words, is the evidence of personal character. The suspension of judgment allows room for the broadest range of opinions and beliefs to be shared in study, without fear of reprisals. By keeping discussion going on controversial matters, the college makes it possible for the student to try out value judgments without exposing himself to the practical consequences. In the intellectual rehearsal of social values, the student can test their consistency with his personal values.

Here again, conformity is a real hazard. For if the student is forced to conform his personal values to rigid, stereotyped, prejudiced mores, he may face an impossible choice. He may yield to pressure and conform outwardly to the mores, while inwardly holding to different personal values. Or he may give up the struggle to develop personal values and accept the values given in the student culture as his own. In the first instance, he will suffer from the shame of knowing his own duplicity; he will lose integrity. In the second instance, he will lack courage. But both integrity and courage are required for the vocation of scholarship, and conformity may end in loss of capacity for scholarly work.

In the end, the student must commit himself; he must produce or secure something of value. Then he is subject to evaluation on the basis of his performance. His performance must meet intellectual standards of clarity, logic, fact, accuracy, style, taste in academic work. In human relationships, his behavior must meet standards of sensitivity, responsiveness, integrity, consistency, courage. The suspension of judgment during the study and discussion of values is not intended to relieve the student of responsibility for his behavior. On the contrary, without forcing the pace of development or inducing narrow conformity, the college tries to bring the student gently but inexorably to make choices and take action that commit him to the vocation of scholarship, with the great values it serves. Freedom is given to explore different values and to get needed practice in improving behavior and performance. But in the end, choices must be made, work must be done, and their quality must be evaluated.

The academic performance and conduct that are evaluated in college serve as an index to the capacity of the student for expressing his values in behavior. They test his ability to make his beliefs consistent with his practice. But it is on the practice of academic skills and human relationships that the student is evaluated, not on the basis of his conformity to group standards.

Consistency of values with practices: The religious way of life

Consistency of belief with practice is of crucial significance in the development of a way of life. The Judean-Christian tradition particularly emphasizes this principle of harmony. In this view, being good, doing good, and feeling good are continuous with one another. Naturally, there is never perfect consistency between private and public values, individual and social values, faith and practice, feelings and behavior, intentions and consequences. Conflicts, therefore, appear within the self, through the disparity between values and behavior. These conflicts are complicated further in community life by conflicting beliefs held by different people. Inconsistency and conflict are to be anticipated in the course of self-development. The development of a way of life depends not so much on success in resolving conflicts as on keeping up the struggle to bring them into some consistent relationship, to settle some problems of value, and to apply values in practice as far as possible. This is the way proposed in religious tradition, from which the vocation of scholarship draws most of its principles of value judgment.

During the college years, conflicting religious values are a common feature of student life. In a way, the college aggravates matters by bringing together in a closely knit community students with widely varying religious beliefs and values. Yet it provides a community in which religious differences are not merely tolerated but used as a basis for shared learning. At the point where comparable levels of performance and patterns of behavior are shown by students whose beliefs differ, the search for common values consistent with their differing religious orientations can begin. This becomes a common intellectual task.

The relation of personal religious beliefs to the academic enterprise is wisely regarded by most colleges as a private matter. In working out the problem of developing consistency between his religious beliefs and his practices as a scholar, the student can get a great deal of help. The college chaplain is a very valuable source of counseling, and many churches have followed their students to the campus, establishing religious foundations in which not only counseling but group discussion and shared study can be made available to students. But the college itself generally does not demand allegiance to a particular faith or even to any faith at all. It simply expects that the student will try to make his religious beliefs consistent with his practice, both in the classroom and in student life, and that he will share his best religious insights with other students as a way of helping them.[14]

Furthermore, the college has a settled core of values in its intellectual standards for evaluating scholarly work. Integrity, truthfulness and honesty, critical judgment, generosity and cooperation, are only a few of the intellectual values which form the core of mature social values in the college as a community. In meeting these standards of value in his academic work, the student knows in a practical way about where he stands in the college. And he also takes a step toward bringing his practice into line with his values. Allegiance to this core of settled intellectual values in the college makes it much easier for the student to take up the task of resolving conflicts of value for himself.

For example, a devout Catholic student came to a counselor very deeply troubled because he felt his religious faith was being shaken by the study in a European history course of the Protestant Reformation. He had talked it over with the local parish priest, who had advised him to continue both the course and his religious devotions in the hope that eventually the difficulty would resolve itself. But he felt his religious practices were becoming empty and meaningless for him because of their inconsistency with the things he was learning about the Church in the period of the Reformation. The counselor suggested that the student examine the values to which he was committed as a member of the college—the concern for truth, the willingness to follow ideas wherever they might lead, the capacity for critical judgment on a rational basis—in terms of their roots in Catholic tradition. The student then conceived the idea of studying the effect of the Reformation on the Catholic Church and the counselor suggested that he arrange with the instructor a program of reading and papers which would lead him into this aspect of the subject. He also urged the student to take the advice of the priest and keep up his regular religious disciplines. As the semester wore along, the student began to feel more comfortable. His religious disciplines began to take on more meaning, as he saw them as a response to enduring needs of men and society. He discovered in the Catholic tradition a whole system of intellectual values of which he had not been aware that gave him help in improving his scholarly disciplines. What he discovered, in essence, was the tremendous resource in intellectual disciplines for the resolution of conflicts of value. He did not change his beliefs, but he enlarged them. And he learned how to make effective use of them in guiding his academic work.

In thus freeing the student to explore new ideas and new interests and in making the resources of scholarship readily available to him, the college makes it possible for the student to develop skill in resolving conflicts of belief and practice that will be immeasurably valuable throughout life. Without any shame or sense of inadequacy, the student may change his beliefs, enlarge them, apply them in new ways, develop their depth and range to support him in new tasks that he must face. And the student is rewarded by improvement in behavior and academic performance when he makes more effective use of his personal standards of value. The college does provide a solid core of values upon which the student can depend when confronted with confusion and conflict in other areas of value. But its task is to confront him with the great developmental task of maturity, the achievement of consistency between values and performance in an enduring way of life.

The growth of loyalty

Finally, in the college and in the community, the student is confronted with social needs and historical and religious traditions that claim his allegiance and devotion. He is confronted with great causes in which he is invited to invest himself. With the mature development of values comes the capacity for investing himself in causes. Adolescent group loyalties ripen into mature loyalty to the purposes and causes that groups serve. Adolescent pressures to conformity yield to self-directed acceptance of common values in the scholarly enterprise. Narrow self-interest yields to a more generous sharing of interests as personal values become related to social values. As the student develops behavior consistent with his values, he can commit himself to the service of broader purposes and great causes.

In both course work and student activities, the student is confronted with great causes that he would be proud to serve, based on a core of common values refined in a long tradition of scholarly work. These causes claim his loyalty and commitment, not for a semester or a college generation, but for a long, productive lifetime. Colleges worthy of the name have as one common purpose the enlargement of loyalty, not to themselves as institutions but to the great causes they serve: such great causes as the advancement of science, the enlargement of freedom, the enrichment of culture, the extension of ethical practices in human relations, to mention only a few.

One significant advantage of settled values is their unobtrusiveness. When values are settled and incorporated into the essential structure of the inward self, it is possible to act upon them without noticing them very much. As the psychologists put it, they are unconscious, meaning that they are ordinarily expressed in behavior rather than discourse. We know, and other people know, that we hold to certain values because we act in a way that is consistent with them. We do not have to talk about values every time we act on them. Unless actions are called into question we do not have to work out complicated decisions in order to act in a way that is consistent with our fundamental beliefs.

Sometimes it appears to the student that everything of value is being questioned, that nothing is settled because everything has to be discussed in order to learn how to use intellectual method. But in the discussion, it is assumed that there are values to which the college is very deeply committed, and these assumptions may, therefore, be unvoiced. Often it is only by figuring out what is *not* said in the discussion of values that the student can discover the principles to which the college is committed.

There are occasions on which the most deeply rooted values of the college are challenged. And then there is no mistake about the causes to which the college is committed. Students and faculty members may not be able to define them with any degree of clarity. But they know where their loyalty lies, and what action they have to take.

Take academic freedom, for example. It has never successfully been defined with any great precision. Its legal and procedural formulations are pretty general, abstract, and vague. The members of the college cannot say very clearly exactly what it means or why it is so desirable. But they know inwardly when they are honoring its requirements and when they are loyal to its principles. And when they have lost it, there is no doubt in their minds about the matter. They can define clearly the manner of its loss and devise a program of action for its restoration.

The capacity for investing oneself in causes depends on both caring enough for ideas to invest intellectual effort in them and caring enough for people to invest physical effort in service to them. The enduring personal relationships which are formed in college give the emotional support that enables scholars to undertake difficult tasks in the service of causes that are important to the whole college—or to society generally. The friendships formed in the college years grow into loyalty to common values. Scholars know they can count on each other, not only to adhere to common beliefs but to act on them, investing their lives and fortunes in the service of great causes.

THE SERVICE OF GREAT CAUSES

There are, of course, causes and causes. Some are worthy of the total investment of the self; others are trivial and in the long run insignificant; others are spurious or positively deleterious. In the choice of causes to which he commits himself, the student may in the beginning make some mistakes. He may choose causes that are worthy or serve worthy causes in ways that are not consistent with the values they serve. One great advantage of the college to the student is the protection it affords against the consequences of mistakes and bad judgment in choosing the causes he will serve. There are penalties, but for the most part they are corrective rather than retributive. The general principle is not the eradication of bad causes, but the provision of good ones. If the student is to learn to choose good causes, there must be real alternatives, and he must be able to make mistakes from which he can learn. In the process of finding causes that are worthy of himself, he must work out some principles by which his choices can be guided.

First, the great cause, worthy of wholehearted investment of the self, is of enduring, rather than transient value. It extends, rather than limits, the possibilities for securing something valuable. The great causes which claim a student's commitment during the college years are continuous with significant enterprises in the community. For example, the election of a campus beauty queen serves transient status factors that pass out of the student's life when he leaves college and must confront a totally different status system in another community. In contrast, the United States National Student Association has confronted student governments with causes of real concern: the struggle between totalitarian and democratic interests for control of the intellectual enterprise, through its working relationships with national unions of students all over the world; the enlargement of individual freedom in support of civil rights, through programs on academic freedom, reducing discriminatory practices, and developing intercultural relations; the representation of the interests of college students in the discussion of political issues, such as Federal support for public education.

The college curriculum, at its best, represents a systematic effort to introduce students to enduring causes, which enlist the personal commitment of students. Both the liberal and practical aspects of the curriculum are equally valuable in this regard. This does not mean that courses are more effective if they deal with current events and current issues. On the contrary, the discussion of current issues, without reference to the historic causes, values, and traditions that they exemplify, makes it more difficult for students to understand the values involved. Discussion easily degenerates into an exchange of superficial opinion, rather than the examination of values. Novelty and immediacy in problems of value are not nearly so important as getting some idea of what a particular specialty is good for in the long run, in the course of human life. The civil engineer needs to see what human values are involved in river basin development, over and above the technical considerations of dam sites, typography, water storage, soil types, and the like. The artist needs to have some idea of how to answer the question, "It's pretty, but is it art?" The great teacher is distinguished in part by his capacity to open up for students the relation of his subject to the great causes which support the development of human values. The colleges that seem most effective in developing student values appear to be those that mobilize substantial support from faculty and students for worthy causes and open up possibilities for students to express significant values in the service of enduring causes.[15]

Second, great causes are never limited to expression in any particular institution. They also require the criticism of institutions in terms of the consistency with which they serve the causes to which they claim to be committed. The mature capacity for investing oneself in causes requires skill in making the distinction between loyalty to an institution and loyalty to the cause which it serves. In the beginning students easily mistake the former for the latter and settle for unquestioning loyalty to a college without paying much attention to the causes which that college tries to serve. The student may discover that he has taken up a significant cause when he finds himself critical of the college to which he is loyal. The gentle art of petitioning the administration for the redress of student grievances is sometimes evidence of loyalty to a cause rather than to a college. For example, the recent petition of the students of the University of Wisconsin to the faculty shows an extremely mature level of intellectual values and the readiness of students to invest themselves in the important intellectual causes which the college serves.

We undersigned students at the University of Wisconsin are sincerely concerned with the problems faced by the University. It is our belief that students and faculty should work together to find solutions to the problems which are shared alike by all members of the academic community. It is this interest in the community which prompts us to seek your understanding as we strive to make the University of Wisconsin a great academic leader of the Nation. . . .

The primary responsibility of any university is to create an academic atmosphere and to engender in its students the desire for knowledge. On the basis of our observations, however, we feel that the University does not hold the position of eminence that it could enjoy in the world of education and that it must step beyond itself into new realms of educational creativity.

Although the University is constantly making attempts to improve its standards, we believe that it has failed to challenge its students sufficiently. . . . Students on all levels of attainment feel that they have not worked to the limits of their ability and time.

The University must raise its standards. In some cases this means simply requiring more work; in many more it means emphasizing an improved quality of work and an intelligent and analytical approach to the subject matter.

Students must extend themselves to achieve a deep and meaningful understanding of material. But this is possible only if the faculty seeks to help us by challenging us more fully. . . .

In more courses definite facilities should be established to enable those students with intensive interests in the subject to probe beyond the attainment requirements of the course, which are in most cases aimed at providing only a general survey of the subject matter. . . .

We realize that many of us have failed to accept the academic challenge offered by the University. We must accept a good share of the responsibility for our failure to reach the limits of our potential. But the University must assume its measure of responsibility as well. Many standards throughout the University program seriously need a regeneration in excellence. . . .

We are proud of our University for its outstanding record in the graduate field, for its progress in technological fields, and for its defense of intellectual freedom.

We are enthusiastic about the steps which the University has taken to correct some of Wisconsin's serious faults. We believe that these steps will do much to provide a better atmosphere for intellectual growth. Our own student government has made progress with the University in this field.

We ask that this progress be looked at as only the beginning in the creation of a challenging, creative, and scholarly atmosphere of academic excellence at the University.

We sign the statement in the belief that the most important function of education is to encourage serious and constructive criticism.

We trust that our views will be judged in the same serious spirit in which they are given. We hope that at the very least they may provide an index of student opinion which will serve as an impetus to those who determine university policy.[16]

Students may encounter demands for absolute loyalty to a group or institution, regardless of the cause it serves. For example, in some situations involving questions of academic freedom, students and faculty members have been advised against supporting associates whose freedom has been violated, on the grounds that such action would create dissension in the faculty, ruin student morale, or reduce the likelihood of getting an adequate legislative appropriation. The idea that lack of academic freedom would destroy the college, create dissension in the faculty, ruin student morale, or make the university less worthy of the investment of public funds is sometimes overlooked. During one such controversy, students were told by an official, "Your primary loyalty is to the University," upon which a faculty member commented, "My primary loyalty is to God Almighty, and I want this University to serve him in freedom." Great causes are known by their transcendence of immediate institutional loyalties; they endow institutions with greatness. Great institutions are known by the great causes they serve and to which their members give their loyalty.

The capacity for investing oneself in great causes rests in part upon the development of skill in accepting stress, adapting to it, and using it effectively in the support of high levels of attainment. Adequate adaptation to stress is made easier by the use of sound intellectual methods in dealing with conflicting values. The suspension of judgment on personal character, for example, makes it possible to center attention on the ideas, beliefs, and values—the content—involved in the controversy, rather than on personal relationships. This suspension of judgment puts stress in the right place. Energy can be used in the important tasks of resolving conflicts and taking action without greatly disrupting the fabric of community life.[17] The prospect of a richer common life makes it worth while to accept the stress involved in dealing with problems and conflicts of values.

A useful index to the worthiness of a cause may be the peace of mind that comes with settling value judgments and the sense of integrity that comes from undertaking action consistent with them. One of the ultimate purposes of the cause, for instance, must be to broaden and deepen human relationships and to reduce tensions between groups. For example, the Supreme Court decisions regarding segregation in colleges and universities did not, as many people expected, aggravate tensions, but rather they settled certain questions that had troubled students and faculty for some time.

"Lost causes" are sometimes very attractive to students, particularly those who still feel the need to assert themselves in some of the less desirable features of adult behavior. But the "lost cause" betrays itself by its destructiveness. It arouses anxiety and tension without alleviating them. It may be known by its lack of realism or by its sheer irrelevance. For example, the introduction of Southern chauvinism into college life may be regarded as a "lost cause." The doctrine of interposition may be argued, the Confederate flag may be flown, the Civil War may be fought all over again, but there is no relevance in these things to the purposes of the college today. At best, "the lost cause" is in bad taste. At worst, it wastes energy and destroys the capacity for investment in important causes.

Where the "lost cause" often aims at failure in certain human purposes or sets limits to certain human relationships, the great cause proposes to succeed and to enlarge human values. Where the "lost cause" aims to change human nature, the great cause proposes to use human nature effectively, even with all its shortcomings, in the service of great values. The student will know that he is engaged in a cause worthy of his service when he is accepted as he is, without having to be perfect. He will know that he has found a great cause by the generosity, cooperativeness, and confidence of people who help one another achieve success in the common cause.

What these great causes are, the student must decide for himself. But he may know them by the enlargement of his spirit, the warmth of his friendships, the breadth of his interests, and the freedom that comes with release from anxiety. The touchstone of the great cause is the breadth of possibility it offers for self-realization, not only for himself but for all of the people whose lives it touches.

THE INTELLECTUAL ANALYSIS OF VALUE

The unity of the self and some fallacies of analysis

In serving particular values, we exercise preferences for behaving in ways that require particular kinds of physical reactions, emotional responses, ideas and meanings, and purposes to be achieved. These elements cannot be separated from each other. The self cannot be chopped up into physical, emotional, intellectual, or social segments. In our value judgments and in the service of causes, we express perhaps more than in any other way the essential unity of the self.

The unity of the self is recognized in our common-sense understanding that when anything in life is unsettled, there is a tendency for people to feel unsettled all the way down the line, physically and emotionally as well as intellectually. The study of stress conducted at Harvard University[18] shows evidence of this tendency for the whole self to be involved in behavior. Students in the study were subjected to stress through frustration of efforts to solve problems. They all showed a generally unsettled alarm reaction, involving physiological, emotional, and intellectual elements. Three distinctive types of alarm reaction were identified: "Anger-Out," directed toward the external situation; "Anger-In," directed toward the self; and "Anxiety," diffuse feelings of repressed anger and tension. Each type was found to be related to distinctive differences in physiological reaction. And students in each group tended to give distinctive interpretations of the stress situation, emphasizing different content. Differences in type of reaction were found to be related to differences in social background and personality factors. Apparently, in the alarm reaction to stress, the whole self was involved, and the distinctive effects of stress could be consistently observed in all elements of behavior.

The study also indicated that these differences in type of alarm reaction were not necessarily related to the capacity for mastering stress in the long run. When the stress situation was repeated, some students in all three groups succeeded in mastering stress, after varying lengths of time, while others were unsuccessful. Differences in type of alarm reaction, physiology, emotional reaction, personality, and cultural background did not seem to affect mastery of stress. But mastery of stress did appear to be related to the successful integration of all these elements into the functioning of the whole self. The strength of the self and integration of its resources seemed to affect ability to master stress in the long run. Failure to master stress seemed related to weaknesses in the functioning of the ego.

Thus, the study bears out our common-sense impression that the whole self is involved in standing up to the wear and tear of life. The self functions as a unit, not as separate parts. If the self is strong and well integrated, a person can rapidly find the resources of habit or skill that will carry the load of adaptation to stress. Otherwise, he may exhaust himself in the effort to "pull himself together" before he can cope with the stress situation.

In other common-sense expressions we pay tribute to the unity of the self. We speak of commitment to values as being "wholehearted," involving all of oneself. Or we may speak of a "halfhearted" person, whose commitment to values or service of causes seems not to be genuine because he does not put all of himself into it.

Furthermore, we seem to have a feeling that values have something to do with the structure of the self. We speak of them as foundations, or something that binds the self together. If the experimental evidence is any indication, we may very well think of values as the most deeply rooted elements of the self, as having some relation to all of its aspects, physical as well as intellectual, and as the most persistent patterns of thinking and acting that hold the self together.

Still, it is customary to make distinctions between various elements of the self. Values are often thought to be abstract ideas without any physical elements. Distinctions are made between mind and body, intellect and emotion, feelings and ideas, values and actions. Such distinctions are useful for purposes of intellectual analysis. But fallacies may result from forgetting the essential unity of the self, and beginning to think of each element as independent of the others.

Two fallacies proceed from this habit of differentiating between things which are essentially continuous. First, we sometimes conclude that, because values are grounded in unconscious physical and emotional elements of the self, rational control and intellectual analysis have no ultimate effect upon the values expressed in behavior. Second, we sometimes draw the opposite conclusion, that values are intellectual elements clearly differentiated from our bodily functions and emotions, and therefore, we must reduce or eliminate the physical and emotional elements of the self that interfere with our attainment of values.

Both points of view oversimplify the problem by reducing the number of elements in it below what is required to understand it adequately. From the first point of view, we are supposed to settle value judgments by acting as if we were merely physical organisms. From the second point of view, we should act as if we were purely rational beings. But we are neither *mere* physical organisms, nor *pure* intellectual beings. Both common sense and behavioral science seem to confirm the fact that we are both. Apparently we might as well conclude that in settling our judgments of value, we must settle our feelings and our bodily functions as well. Physical and emotional comfort is evidence of effectiveness in settling value judgments, just as much as are ethical or logical tests of adequacy. And we have to use both tests.

But there are real deterrents to the settlement of judgments of value. We are always happier when we can act by habit or settled values, because we are less likely to feel uncomfortable. We are inclined to avoid doing anything new or unfamiliar, because we know the discomfort it will entail. We prefer to ignore problems or avoid trying to achieve something of value, because we are perfectly aware that we will be placed under real stress. For example, many students will attest to the real physical disturbances occasioned by examinations. They cannot eat breakfast on the morning of an exam or expect to lose their lunch afterwards. Intellectual achievements are the least tangible of values, and yet they occasion genuine physical stress. Some students, consequently, settle for "gentlemanly C's," because excellence in performance is a value that is both vaguely defined and difficult to achieve. They prefer to be comfortable and mediocre, rather than uncomfortable and excellent.

Some people abstain from the intellectual analysis of value because they are convinced that it simply stirs up more problems than it solves. It is certainly true that intellectual analysis complicates things. Defining the problem to be solved is itself a problem, and the choice of a proper method is an additional problem. If any action is to be taken, mobilizing the necessary resources, involving the necessary number of people, finding the necessary resources of money and time further complicate the problem. Moreover, from a common-sense point of view, people have always realized that "things have to get worse, before they can get better." Intellectual analysis often brings to light complicating aspects of the problem which were unsuspected. But if it is adequate, it will settle things, even the complications it introduces.

To be sure, matters are sometimes aggravated by the unfortunate tendency of some intellectuals to raise unnecessary questions, just for the fun of it or out of pride in displaying their powers. Necessary elements should not be left out just because they will complicate matters further. But simplicity rather than complexity, elegance rather than untidiness are marks of good intellectual method. They prevent the scholar from wasting energy in settling questions that do not have to be settled, raising questions that do not have to be raised, and bothering people who do not have to be involved.

The scholar also has to keep in mind that values have a social aspect; they have to be confirmed by acceptance in a community if they are really adequate. And resistance to new principles of conduct or new concepts of value is considerably reduced by limiting the scope of these new principles and concepts. The more settled values are left intact, the greater are the physical, emotional, and intellectual resources of the community for accommodating new values, beliefs, and practices.

The choice of methods of intellectual analysis

In the process of settling some of the values involved in the conflicts and tensions of life, at present writing it seems more desirable to use our intellectual powers than to rely wholly on our capacity to work physical violence upon each other. The chances of survival seem considerably greater in discussion than war. And there seems to be increasing evidence that, in the long run, intellectual methods of coping with conflicts promise much more in the way of practical results than the recourse to violence. There is no longer any assurance that we can settle matters by physical means.*

We must choose a suitable intellectual method for dealing with problems of value. Because the most urgent questions are posed in terms of national survival and the maintenance of stable community life, the fields of study that are primarily concerned with human behavior are presently in great vogue. Psychology, anthropology, sociology, economics, political science seem to be preferred intellectual methods of analysis of immediate problems of value in social life. There is also a great deal of reliance on natural science in its various theoretical and applied forms. Medicine and public health are looked to as preferred approaches, because in them the connection between physical well-being and social values is obvious, or seems to be so. But we are also promised a world of "better living through chemistry"; and physics, astrophysics, astronomy, and agriculture are also looked to for help in unraveling some puzzles. Even such practical disciplines as engineering, home economics, business administration, journalism, advertising, and the lowly art of plumbing sometimes claim to offer approaches to the solution of problems of value.

The truth of the matter probably is that we are going to have to use every single specialty we can develop, and perhaps develop some more, in order to cope with problems of value.

Of course, the student's world is not bounded by the college walls. But the problems of value that are of the most immediate concern to him arise out of his immediate developmental tasks and his membership in the college. Psychology and sociology, in particular, are helpful to him in coming to terms with his immediate problems. These specialties deal with the physiological, emotional, social nature of the self, the developmental stages of growth, and the cultural factors which affect the nature and function of the self and afford available objects of value.

We would suggest these as preferred intellectual methods for the analysis of values, for students, not only because of their content and technique, but for certain practical reasons. The help that colleges gen-

* Karl Deutsch points to the fallacy of national sovereignty as a protection for the individual citizen, or any significant group of them. The national state up to this point has successfully claimed allegiance in return for its protection in time of war. Soldiers and citizens would fight and sacrifice for the State, in the expectation that even though some of them failed to survive, the rest of the nation would continue to exist. Nuclear weapons make these expectations unrealistic. He suggests that nations need to find some other values around which political life can be organized and the loyalty of citizens developed.[19]

erally give students in solving their personal problems is made available by experts in these fields.

The college counseling service, both in vocational guidance and in personal counseling, is essentially psychologically oriented. The professionally trained counselors, who are prepared to go beyond giving advice and interpretating college regulations, are likely to be trained in clinical psychology or counseling psychology. In working with such counselors, the student can expect to get some insight into his own physical and emotional reactions and learn to control their effects. He may get some understanding of the process of learning and improve his control of academic performance. He can get help in assessing his abilities and relating them to occupational choice and placement in a first job. In a sense, what happens in counseling is that the student learns just as much of psychological method as he needs to know in order to control his behavior. And with the help of an expert, he is able to use it to clarify his values and apply them in personal development, occupational choice, and learning.

Sociological methods are similarly useful in the analysis of student life. By studying the college as a community, it is possible to understand the values expressed in student mores and in faculty-student relationships and to use them in improving the organization and social relationships of the college. Student governments, for example, have made effective use of group dynamics both in improving their own ways of conducting governmental affairs and in establishing more effective relationships with other groups of students, such as commuters, fraternities, foreign students.

The sociological study of class affiliations, status, and prestige patterns has revealed various factors that determine the values which students express in their behavior. It has suggested ways to change patterns of social relationships to permit other values, more in keeping with purposes of the college, to develop. For example, such insight has brought some notable changes in the purposes and program of fraternities and sororities; it has brought more emphasis on intellectual values and democratic practices, the elimination of discriminatory membership requirements, and emphasis on individual merit rather than wealth and social class and the values associated with them. National studies[20] have applied the methods of sociology and social psychology to the study of student values; and they are extremely helpful to students and faculty members in defining problems in college life that need to be solved and in reconciling the performance of students and the values which the college needs to serve.

These psychological and sociological methods are in vogue among students, as well as in other communities, because they have immediate applicability to the pressing practical problems with which students are confronted. We are convinced that the skilled use of these methods, with the help of a professionally trained counselor, is one of the most important resources for developing personal and social values in college.

Limitations of intellectual analysis

But a word of caution: any intellectual method has its limitations. Psychology and sociology divide human behavior between them on a personal and social basis, but personal behavior is continuous with social relationships. Both methods divide the self into physical, emotional, intellectual, and social aspects for purposes of analysis, but the self involves all of these elements. The methods are good for analysis, but not for motivation. And analysis is an aid, but not a substitute for action. Analysis is helpful in understanding the elements of behavior and planning ahead to improve it. But integrating the self around a strong system of values demands more than just intellectual analysis. The student has to act on the values he holds.

It is tempting to undertake intellectual analysis after the event, rationalizing or justifying behavior after one has already gone ahead and done what he was going to do in the first place. Intellectual analysis may simply make the student more adept in the gentle art of making excuses for himself. He cannot make better grades because his test scores were too low. The fact that a great many students with low test scores nevertheless make excellent grades is not taken into account. He is not making value judgments; he is making excuses.

Many students discontinue counseling just at the point where they have learned enough to make effective excuses. From that point on, the going gets rough. The skilled counselor is not going to let a student rationalize his way out of his difficulties. He agrees to stick with the student until he solves his problems and to protect him so far as possible from any injurious effects of the stress that is going to be involved. But just at the point where the problem is clearly defined and is about to be solved, stress really sets in, and the student ducks out. If the resources of intellectual analysis are going to be used in solving problems and settling values, the student must be prepared to see them through. In asking help from a counselor, he must be prepared to continue until he actually has settled the question of the values that are most important to him and brought his behavior into some consistent relationship to those values. The same principle holds in organized activity. For instance, when student government undertakes to organize campus life to support the significant values of the college, it cannot stop with revising its constitution, but it must go on until programs are actually undertaken and carried out to produce the things which the constitution says are valuable.

The trouble with stopping at the point where things really begin to get difficult is that matters are not settled and equilibrium is not restored. Persuading oneself into suitable feelings or producing a good constitution does not settle anything. This may actually make matters worse by concealing or camouflaging the real conflicts of value that are at the bottom of the matter.

So we would like to state a few simple rules for the use of intellectual analysis in settling personal and social problems of value.

First, try to finish what you start. One student came in to talk with the counselor about a problem in forming effective study habits. With the counselor's help, she worked out a study schedule and revised it, making refinements and improvements that would make study more effective. The next week, she came in to report that she had followed the schedule, found it very comfortable, and felt that everything was all right. Nothing was heard from her until the end of the academic year when her name appeared on the list of students disqualified for failure to achieve the required grade point average. Then she came in to say goodbye to the counselor. She reported that she had followed the schedule faithfully but had had trouble concentrating and could not understand a great many of the subjects that were new to her. She had not come back to talk to the counselor because she felt her test scores were so low that she simply did not have the intellectual capacity to solve the problem of concentration. *

Second, master the method you need to use. Call on an expert counselor to help you in the process of intellectual analysis if you need to use a method that you are not thoroughly familiar with. Common-sense methods and good advice carry students pretty far in settling questions of value and improving performance. There is no point to using psychological and sociological methods, in particular, just because they are there. It is dangerous to try to use them yourself without considerable

---

* Students who voluntarily enrolled in a course for reading improvement indicated that actual improvement in reading and improvement in related academic work did not necessarily follow from mastery of improved techniques for reading. Rather, the students who improved both in reading and in grades seemed to be those who thought of themselves as the kind of persons who could improve performance; those who improved in reading, but not in grades, or who failed to improve in reading, thought of themselves as ineffective people likely to fail.[21]

familiarity with them. One of the great horrors of the college campus is the beginning "psych" major who analyzes himself and all his friends. He is ridiculous, but worse than that, he is a menace. For he stirs up problems that do not need to be stirred up and which he cannot solve. Avoid him like the plague. Use psychological methods to understand yourself, not to analyze others.

Third, respect the privacy of others. If you are a beginning "psych" major, avoid analyzing other people as if it were the plague. Value judgments are strictly do-it-yourself. Horning in on the process is an invasion of privacy. It is not wise to help others with their problems, even if they ask, if you are not an expert counselor in the appropriate intellectual method. If asked for help which you cannot or should not give, refer the student to an expert. If none is available, it is better for no help to be given than for matters to be further complicated by the application of more ignorance.

Fourth, form stable friendships. It is in friendships that values can be settled, not so much by intellectual analysis, as by the enjoyment of working out good human relationships. Where values can be worked out, they may not have to be talked out. And the warmth of friendship sustains the self in periods of stress, when values are unsettled. Friendship gives the assurance of warm acceptance. It insures that problems, failures, and conflicts do not destroy the self but can be accepted by another person as a part of oneself. Friendship gives assurance that the self is really there, in spite of unbalance, uncertainty, and confusion. This assurance we all very much need, and it is the greatest gift we can give to each other.

Fifth, analyze alternatives for behavior before you take action, instead of excusing yourself afterwards. Planning ahead is what the intellect is good for. Methods of intellectual analysis are learned by hindsight, but they are supposed to be used in foresight. Many difficulties can be avoided or controlled by planning ahead. It is unnecessary to excuse oneself for accidents which could not be foreseen. These can happen to anybody. But it is impossible to excuse stupidity. Use the intellectual skills you have to figure things out in advance, and save the energy you would use in making excuses for the arduous work of acting upon the best plan you can make.

THE USES OF THE HUMANITIES

Some other fields of study may have a great deal to offer in the development of a way of life based on high values, although they do not enjoy the current popularity of the behavioral sciences.

First of all, philosophy has something to contribute to the study of values. Logical tests of consistency and form in value can be extremely helpful. For example, in working out problems of civil rights and minority relationships, logic has been an extremely helpful instrument in making sure that the basic principles have actually been applied to community life. It is just not logical to have a public school system for all children supported by tax contributions from everybody in the community and then to set up two public school systems in which one group of children is separated from another. The sheer mathematics of it is illogical; one is not two. Two systems cost more than one.

There is more to philosophy than logic. It also embodies a long tradition in fields such as esthetics, ethics, and epistemology. Is it good? Is it true? Is it beautiful? These are the questions which philosophy tries to ask. And the body of knowledge with which philosophy deals has been refined out of the experience of the human race as it has found, or failed to find, answers to these questions. There is no use repeating the mistakes, and it is helpful to repeat the successes, using the values that have been settled.

We would be tempted to suggest that all students ought to study a little philosophy. But like a little psychology or a little sociology, a little philosophy is an extremely dangerous and explosive thing. We would rather suggest that the student might avail himself of the expert help of philosophers in dealing with conflicting judgments about what is good, true, and beautiful.

It is also possible to settle questions of value by doing something about them rather than by starting out to analyze them. We would humbly suggest that producing and enjoying things that are good, true, and beautiful settles the question right there, by producing valuables, rather than discussing questions of value. Human values are expressed, directly and immediately, in works of literature, art, drama, poetry, music, and dance. Moreover, the enlargement of experience through the study of history and the ability to read literary works of other cultures in their own language certainly extends the range of personal and social values that people can understand and express.

Perhaps the humanities are neglected in times of trouble like these because they do not seem to contribute to the analysis of value. The values they offer are just there to be had. From the study of history or literature or the enjoyment of art, the student can get a feeling of what it is like when things are settled. Sometimes this is very helpful, especially when many unsettled matters occupy the rest of his attention.

He may in fact renew his energy by thus securing a period of relief from the stress of more strenuous intellectual activity.

Not everything is settled in the humanities, any more than in any other field. A literary or dramatic plot, for example, is built around some unsettled situation and proceeds to final resolution. Sometimes the process by which the plot is worked out may give a clue to the working out of a problem in one's experience. At least, a great deal is gained and no harm is done by seeing how unsettled situations are resolved. At least, for a little time, the student is a participant in a successful process of resolving problems or an unscathed observer of tragic failure. He stands to gain some insight which he may find valuable in his own experience; and his experience is enlarged by the dimensions added to it in art, literature, and history.

THE RESOURCES OF RELIGION

In developing and sustaining a way of life, the resources of religion take on extreme importance. The very term *religion* means a rule or a way of life. Many of the high religions of the world refer in their teaching and doctrine to "the way." Even some people who do not like to think of themselves as religious, who are not comfortable as members of a church, or who cannot stomach the deviations of institutional religious practice from the values expressed in religious doctrines, nevertheless may have a religion, in the broader sense of a way of life which is consistent with their system of values and with the image of the self which they would like to become.

We think of this way of life as enduring. While we realize that human life is subject to crises, conflicts, changes, disasters, we nevertheless feel that we ought to face all the ups and downs of life in such a way as to preserve our way of life. If we value ourselves, we want our way of life to endure. If we value our relationships with other people and share a common way of life, we feel that we are committed to each other to preserve it and strengthen it.

There is a difference between being religious in this "natural" sense and having a religion. For having a religion means not only developing values that are organized into a definable way of life but also belonging to a body of believers. The great religions have an institutional embodiment, a church of some sort, in which believers are joined in mutual service and support. As evidence of their common belief and as a way of practicing the common way of life, the body of believers develops a ritual, which provides for the expression of the values that they share.

They worship together. And in worship they express the significant values that sustain the way of life in creeds and symbols of value, in the philosophy, history, and literature preserved in written works or oral tradition. The values underlying the stages of human development are marked by ceremonials and celebrations: birth, coming of age, marriage, death.

The church is also interested in people who have not had a church relationship or who have lost it somewhere in the course of their lives. More members do mean more power, more financial strength, and more influence in the community. But there are other reasons for wishing to enlarge the membership of the church and other values that prompt its members to bring in their friends and win new believers to the faith. For there is a difference between having a religion and being religious. The adherents to a particular faith sincerely and earnestly believe that the body of believers has something to offer that is of great value to others, something that they want to share.

What adherents to a faith have to offer each other is a tremendously enriched form of personal relationship. They are bound to each other by ties of common faith and belief, ritual and tradition, and also in practical ways. They are bound to help each other deal with the uncertainties of life and to help each other meet difficulties and disasters, which beset us all. Despite all of its shortcomings, bickerings, shameful failures, and power politics, the church tries to help its members follow a way of compassion and love. Particularly in the Judean-Christian tradition, there is the simple conviction that the church ought to exemplify in its common life the values to which it is committed in its faith—above all, the values of compassion and love.

Compassion may be regarded as another term for the responsiveness, generosity, and cooperation which are marks of social competence in any context; but it goes beyond these things. The religious way of life requires the compassion that is responsive to the shy or the hostile person, generous toward the ungrateful, cooperative even with enemies. It goes beyond sensitivity and requires the capacity to understand and accept the feelings and interests of others as if they were one's own. It is not abnegation or denial of one's own interest, but an enlargement of it through a relationship to the interest of others.

Along with compassion, the religious way of life requires love. It means caring deeply for other persons and finding effective ways to show it. Sloppy sentimentality is not the kind of love that is meant. Real love is enduring affection, genuine concern for other people. It requires the capacity to see, behind even distasteful, despicable, loathsome forms of human behavior, the need for self-realization and the desire for something of greater value and greater satisfaction to the self and to others.

Compassion and love of this sort are truly unattainable ideals. If these things were attainable, there would be no point to all our striving. One of the values of the religious way of life is that it pitches the expectations, the desires, the ambitions of men at a very high level, high enough to keep men growing and developing throughout a long and productive life.

Because of the absolute demands that the religious way of life places upon people in relation to values, they always feel that they have failed and come short of their purposes. But implicit in the religious way of life is the conviction that it is better to fail in the attainment of high purposes than to attain ignoble ones. The high religions seem to take a very dim view of human nature since they hold that men are doomed to failure anyway and that they had better fail in the greatest causes. But they do not leave the matter there.

The great religions also offer a way of dealing with shame and failure. And these common consequences of human life are, because of their very frequency, the things that are most important for us to deal with effectively. We need to know how to keep on going, in spite of shame and failure. Religion offers two ways of dealing with these common and disastrous human experiences—through confession and forgiveness.

There is no sloppy sentimentality about these ways of dealing with shortcomings and failures, either. Confession requires an open admission of faults and a readiness to change behavior in order to avoid their repetition. Forgiveness requires readiness on the part of everybody concerned to accept the possibility of change and improvement, rather than regarding past shortcomings and failures as ingrained in individual character. A certain amount of hardheadedness and toughness is involved. Not just intentions but behavior must change. Failures must be both admitted and overcome, mistakes both acknowledged and corrected.

High religion also offers ways to deal with meaninglessness and despair. Doubt, despair, and futility are not denied but are to be overcome by positive action. The sense of meaninglessness and despair is not a sign that it is time to give up and quit trying, but rather a sign that a way will be opened, that it is worth going on. In worship, believers individually and collectively express the meanings which they feel are firmly fixed in human life, even at its worst. The ceremonials and rituals of worship are not only ways of celebrating meaningful events and high occasions of achievement, but also ways of holding on to the essential meaning of life in the midst of confusion, conflict, and failure. In time of doubt and despair, the religious way of life offers the discipline of study: study of tradition, to see what practical experience others had in dealing with despair; study of the present situation, to see what resources it may afford; study of the doctrines and ideals of the faith, to see what values can be applied to overcome frustration and futility. The disciplines of worship and study are not merely proposed as exercises for their intrinsic value. They are directed toward action and toward changes in patterns of behavior, in the environment, and in community life. Such action will express necessary meanings and break the bonds of despair.

The vocation of scholarship is peculiarly beset by conditions of shame and failure, meaninglessness and despair. Learning proceeds by way of mistakes, and scholars are ashamed of the mistakes they make. They fail to master intellectual tasks, their experiments do not come off, the hypotheses they present turn out to be empty of meaning. They all, at some time or other, despair of ever learning or teaching anything, of doing productive work. In the scholarly enterprise, there are periods of sterility and staleness when the scholar feels he is not accomplishing anything and might as well give up.

The way of life for the scholar must afford ways of dealing with these very common experiences. The religious way of life provides precisely the disciplines that are most needed to keep on trying to learn something and to teach something of value. And when these disciplines are reinforced by the compassion and love of the community of believers, the scholarly way of life is vastly strengthened.

This is not to say that to be a scholar one must belong to a church. Neither is it meant to imply that the church has a monopoly on the disciplines which make the vocation of scholarship possible. One of the strengths of the great religions is the diffusion of their disciplines, traditions, and values in the community, so that people who are not of the faith share its fruits. Historically, the disciplines of scholarship have in fact been derived from the disciplines of the church, for the universities in the beginning were arms of the church. Even though the institutional ties to the church have loosened, the disciplines have been maintained in the scholarly tradition of the college.

It is to the advantage of the scholar and the college to maintain as close a relationship as possible to the church. The refinement and enrichment of the religious way of life is proceeding both in the church and in the college. It is to the advantage of both to advance along together, sharing the new insights and methods which they find valuable in sustaining the values which they hold in common.

Moreover, scholarship is, after all, one occupation among many, and as an occupation it can fulfill only a limited part of human need. Scholars share with other people in the community a great many needs for personal and social development which continue after college. In the support of these common human interests and values, the resources of religion are made most readily available to the scholar through the church. And he has a certain obligation to share his insights, disciplines, and practices with people in other walks of life who share a common human lot.

The vocation of scholarship is exercised in many occupations, in business, industry, politics, community service, as well as in teaching and research. The college graduate will not necessarily be living in a community designed to give the special guidance, the program, and the rewards that the college offers. He must seek strength and guidance in other ways. It is important for the scholarly way of life to become part of the self and to become one of the inner resources on which a person can draw for guidance and strength in continuing his work.

Personal development does not cease with college. College, rather, opens up a way of life in which the disciplines of scholarship can be applied in a long and productive career. The student will find many tasks to which his scholarly skill can be applied. As he finds groups of people, not only in the church but in other institutions, who share intellectual values and high purposes, he can also draw on them for increasing inner strength to support his way of life. The student who finds the true value of the college experience will go on growing after college.

SUGGESTED READINGS

Armstrong, William H., *Study is Hard Work*. New York, Harper & Brothers, 1956.

Beer, M. F. and Roeber, E. C., *Occupational Information*, 2nd Edition. Chicago: Science Research Associates, Professional Guidance Series, 1958.

Borow, H. and Lindsey, R. V., *Vocational Planning for College Students*. Englewood Cliffs, N.J.: Prentice-Hall, Inc., 1959.

Craig, William B., *How to Finance a College Education*. New York: Henry Holt & Co., Inc., 1959.

Garrison, Roger H., *The Adventure of Learning in College*. New York: Harper & Brothers, 1959.

Ginzberg, Eli (ed.) *The Nation's Children* (Vol. I, II and III). Published in 1960 for the Golden Anniversary White House Conference on Children and Youth by Columbia University Press, New York.

Haiman, Franklyn S., *Group Leadership and Democratic Action*. Boston: Houghton Mifflin Company, 1951.

Jones, Edward S., *Improvement of Study Habits*, 2nd Edition. Buffalo, N.Y.: Henry Stuart, Inc., 1960.

Jung, Carl G., *The Undiscovered Self*. New York: Harper & Brothers, 1960.

Klopf, Gordon, *College Student Government*. New York: Harper & Brothers, 1960.

Lipton, Lawrence, *The Holy Barbarians*. New York: Julian Messner, Inc., 1959.

Livingstone, Sir Richard, *Some Thoughts on University Education*. New York: Cambridge University Press, 1948.

McCary, James L. (ed.), *Understanding Testing*. Washington, D.C.: Office of Education, U.S. Department of Health, Education, and Welfare, 1960.

May, Rollo, *Man's Search for Himself*. New York: W. W. Norton & Co., Inc., 1953.

Miller, Alexander, *Christian Faith and My Job*. New York: Association Press, Reflection Books, 1959.

Riesman, David, *Constraint and Variety in American Education*. New York: Doubleday Anchor Books, 1958.

Shuster, George N., *Education and Moral Wisdom*. New York: Harper & Brothers, 1960.

Smith, Leonard J., *Career Planning*. New York: Harper & Brothers, 1959.

Snow, Sir Charles Percy, *Two Cultures and the Scientific Revolution*, The Rede Lectures. New York: Cambridge University Press, 1959.

Symonds, Percival M., *What Education Has to Learn from Psychology*. New York: Bureau of Publications, Teachers College, Columbia University, 1958.

Thruelsen, Richard, and Kobler, John, (ed.) *Adventures of the Mind*. New York: Alfred Knopf, 1959.

Townsend, Agatha, (ed.), *College Freshmen Speak Out*. New York: Harper & Brothers, 1959.

Van Doren, Mark, *Liberal Education*. Boston: Beacon Press, 1959.

Vaughan, Wayland F., *Personal and Social Adjustment*. New York: The Odyssey Press, 1952.

Whitehead, Alfred North, *Aims of Education and Other Essays*. New York: The Macmillan Co., 1959. Also New York: New American Library, 1949.

NOTES

Introduction

1. Eli Ginzberg, Sol W. Ginsburg, Sidney Axelrad, and John L. Herma, *Occupational Choice* (New York: Columbia University Press, 1951), pp. 108–10, 129–30, give other examples of avoiding decisions.

Chapter 1

1. Otto Butz, *The Unsilent Generation* (New York: Rinehart & Co., Inc., 1958), p. 134.
2. William C. Menninger, *Understanding Yourself* (Chicago: Science Research Associates, Inc., 1948), p. 4.
3. O. Spurgeon English and G. H. J. Pearson, *Emotional Problems of Living* (New York: W. W. Norton & Co., 1955), p. 366.
4. L. P. Thorpe, *Mental Health Practices at the College Level, Fifty-fourth Yearbook* (Chicago: National Society for the Study of Education, 1955), pp. 269–70.
5. Herbert Carroll, *Mental Hygiene* (New York: Prentice-Hall, Inc., 1956), pp. 11–12.
6. William James, *The Principles of Psychology,* Vol. I (New York: Dover Publications, Inc., 1950), chap. x, gives an excellent analysis of self-consciousness. See especially pp. 291–305.
7. Arthur T. Jersild, *Child Psychology* (Englewood Cliffs, N.J.: Prentice-Hall, Inc., 1954), p. 179.
8. Karen Horney, *Neurosis and Growth* (New York: W. W. Norton & Company, Inc., 1950), p. 158.
9. *Ibid.,* p. 159.
10. *Ibid.,* p. 158.
11. *Ibid.,* p. 17.
12. *Ibid.,* p. 15.
13. Robert J. Havighurst and D. V. MacDonald, "Development of the Ideal Self in New Zealand and American Children," *Journal of Educational Research,* Vol. XLIX (December 1955), pp. 263–73.
14. *The Pursuit of Excellence,* Special Studies Project Report V, Rockefeller Brothers Fund (New York: Doubleday & Company, Inc., 1958), p. 47.
15. For a more detailed account of heredity and environment see Millie A. Almy, *Child Development* (New York: Henry Holt & Co., 1955), chap. 1.
16. Roger J. Williams, *Free and Unequal* (Austin: University of Texas Press, 1953), p. 52.
17. Booker T. Washington, *Up from Slavery* (New York: Doubleday Page & Co., 1909).
18. Meyer Levin, *Compulsion* (New York: Simon and Shuster, 1956).

19. *Life,* Vol. XLV, No. 23 (Dec. 8, 1958), pp. 101–2, 104.

20. Horney, p. 18.

21. Almy, p. 74.

22. Erik Erikson, "Growth and Crises of the Healthy Personality," *Personality in Nature, Society, and Culture,* 2nd ed., Clyde Kluckhohn and Henry Murray, eds. (New York: Alfred A. Knopf, 1953), p. 187.

23. Stone and Church, pp. 328–29.

24. Kate Hevner Mueller, *Educating Women for a Changing World* (Minneapolis: University of Minnesota Press, 1954), p. 19.

25. Robert R. Sears *et al., Patterns of Child Rearing* (Evanston, Ill.: Row, Peterson & Co., 1957), Chapter XIII. See especially pp. 480–82.

26. Robert J. Havighurst, "Who Should Go Where to College?", *Student Personnel Work as Deeper Teaching,* Esther Lloyd-Jones and Margaret Ruth Smith, eds. (New York: Harper & Bros., 1954), pp. 15–31.

27. Allison Davis, *Social-Class Influences Upon Learning* (Cambridge: Harvard University Press, 1955), pp. 2–3.

28. John Carson McGuire, *Adolescent Society and Social Mobility* (unpublished doctoral thesis, University of Chicago, 1949).

29. Davis, pp. 2–3.

Chapter 2

1. Robert Havighurst, "Research on the Developmental Task Concept," *The School Review,* Vol. LXIV (May 1956), pp. 216–17.

2. *Ibid.,* p. 216.

3. *Ibid.,* pp. 216–18.

4. See John H. Rohrer and Muzafer Sherif, *Social Psychology at the Crossroads* (New York: Harper & Brothers, 1951), pp. 420–21.

5. George Gardner, "Present-Day Society and the Adolescent," *American Journal of Orthopsychiatry,* Vol. XXVII (July 1957), p. 510.

6. *Ibid.,* p. 511.

7. Rose Butler, "Mother Attitudes toward the Social Development of Their Adolescents," Part II, *Journal of Social Casework* (May–June 1956), pp. 280–88.

8. Myron S. Kaufman, *Remember Me to God* (New York: Lippincott, 1957), pp. 167–68.

9. Butler, p. 280.

10. Gardner, p. 510.

11. Willis H. McCann, "Nostalgia: A Review of the Literature," *Psychological Bulletin,* Vol. XXXVIII (Mar. 1941), 165–82.

12. *Ibid.,* p. 175.

13. Annelies A. Rose, "A Study in College Freshmen," *Journal of Social Psychology,* Vol. XXVI (Nov. 1947), pp. 195–97.

14. Arthur T. Jersild, *The Psychology of Adolescence* (New York: The Macmillan Company, 1957), p. 29.

15. S. M. Jourard, "Body-Cathexis and the Ideal Female Image," *Journal of Consulting Psychology,* Vol. XVIII (June 1954), p. 184.

16. Jersild, *The Psychology of Adolescence,* p. 30.

17. Paul Secord and Sidney Jourard, "The Appraisal of Body-Cathexis: Body-Cathexis and the Self," *Journal of Consulting Psychology,* Vol. XVII (Oct. 1953), pp. 343–47.

18. Jersild, *The Psychology of Adolescence,* p. 55.

19. *Ibid.*

20. *Ibid.,* p. 32.

21. Ruth Tasch, "Preliminary Report on Interpersonal Perceptions of Marriage Roles" (Paper presented at the annual meeting of the Kansas Psychological Association, Wichita, Kansas, April, 1958).

22. Russell R. Dynes and Alfred Clarke, "Correlates of Marital and Sex Roles," *The Graduate School Record* (Ohio State University), (1957), pp. 9–10.

23. A. R. Mangus, "Role Theory and Marriage Counseling," *Social Forces*, Vol. XXXV (Mar. 1957), p. 202.

24. Margaret Mead, *Sex and Temperament in Three Primitive Societies* (New York: New American Library, 1950), pp. 209–218, describes various ways in which biological sex might be used to differentiate social roles, discusses its limitations, and suggests individual merit as a possible alternative in certain areas.

25. Jeanne L. Noble and Opal D. David, "Current Research on Women's Roles," *Journal of National Association of Women Deans and Counselors*, Vol. XXII (Jan. 1959), pp. 93–96.

26. Franklin Shaw and Robert Ort, *Personal Adjustment in the American Culture*, (New York, Harper, 1957), p. 252.

27. Robert Coughlan, "Changing Roles in Modern Marriage," *Life*, Vol. LVI (December 24, 1956), p. 109.

28. Karen Horney, *New Ways in Psychoanalysis* (New York: W. W. Norton and Company, Inc., 1939), pp. 113–15.

29. Mead, pp. 103–4, 190–96.

30. Lois Stolz, "Patterns of Living for Women Today," Address to the California Association of Women Deans and Vice-Principals (Palo Alto, March 15–16, 1958).

31. Eleanor Metheny and James A. Peterson, *The Trouble with Women* (New York: Vantage Press, 1957), pp. 22–62.

32. Coughlan, p. 109.

33. Horney, pp. 116–17.

34. Daniel H. Funkenstein, Stanley H. King, and Margaret E. Drolette, *Mastery of Stress* (Cambridge: Harvard University Press, 1957), pp. 283–84.

35. W. A. Davis and R. J. Havighurst, *Father of the Man* (Cambridge: The Houghton-Mifflin Company, 1947), pp. 146–68.

36. Daniel C. Brown, "Masculinity-Femininity Development in Children," *Journal of Consulting Psychology*, Vol. XXI (June 1957), pp. 197–202.

37. Alice K. Leopold, "Today's Women College Graduates," *Personnel and Guidance Journal*, Vol. XXXVIII (Dec. 1959), pp. 281–82.

38. Donald Brown, "Some Educational Patterns in Personality Development during College Years," *Journal of Social Issues*, Vol. XII, No. 4 (1956), pp. 44–60.

39. Nevitt Sanford, "Motivation of High Achievers," *The Education of Women: Signs for the Future* (Report of a Conference on the Present Status and Prospective Trends of Research on the Education of Women, sponsored by the American Council on Education, Rye, New York, October 27–30, 1957), Opal D. David, ed. (Washington, D.C.: American Council on Education, 1959), p. 35.

40. Kate Hevner Mueller, "The Cultural Pressures on Women," *The Education of Women*, p. 49.

41. Sanford, "Motivation of High Achievers," *The Education of Women*, p. 37.

42. Paul C. Glick, "The Life Cycle of the Family," *Marriage and Family Living*, Vol. XVII (Feb. 1955), pp. 3–9.

43. National Manpower Council, *Womanpower* (New York: Columbia University Press, 1957), pp. 7–39.

44. L. D. Rockwood and M. E. Ford, *Youth, Marriage and Parenthood* (New York: John Wiley & Sons, 1945), p. 37.

45. Alfred C. Kinsey, B. P. Wardell, and C. E. Martin, *Sexual Behavior in the Human Male* (Philadelphia: W. B. Saunders Co., 1948), p. 650 (this study is hereafter

referred to as *Male* in footnotes), and Alfred C. Kinsey, B. P. Wardell, C. E. Martin, and P. H. Gebhard, *Sexual Behavior in the Human Female*, (Philadelphia: W. B. Saunders, 1953), (hereafter referred to as *Female*).

46. Kinsey, *Male*, pp. 650–51.
47. Kinsey, *Female*, pp. 453–59.
48. Kinsey, *Male*, p. 171.
49. Willard Waller, "The Rating and Dating Complex," *American Sociological Review*, Vol. II (Oct. 1937), pp. 727–34.
50. Robert O. Blood, "A Retest of Waller's Rating Complex," *Marriage and Family Living*, Vol. XVII (Feb. 1955), p. 47.
51. Robert O. Blood, "Uniformities and Diversities in Campus Dating Preferences," *Marriage and Family Living*, Vol. XVII (Feb. 1956), p. 37.
52. Kinsey, *Male*, p. 541.
53. *Ibid.*, p. 531.
54. *Ibid.*, p. 537.
55. *Ibid.*, p. 542.
56. Kinsey, *Female*, pp. 233–34.
57. Blood, "Uniformities and Diversities in Campus Dating Practices," pp. 37–43.
58. *Ibid.*, p. 44.
59. Charles W. Cole, "American Youth Goes Monogamous," *Harpers*, Vol. CCXIV (Mar. 1957), pp. 29–30.
60. Robert Herman, "The 'Going Steady' Complex: A Re-examination," *Marriage and Family Living*, Vol. XVII (Feb. 1955), pp. 36–37.
61. Erik H. Erikson, "The Problem of Ego Identity," *Journal of the American Psychoanalytic Association*, Vol. IV (Jan. 1956), pp. 56–121.
62. Sanford, "Motivation of High Achievers," p. 21.
63. Mueller, "The Cultural Pressures on Women," p. 50.
64. David V. Tiedeman, "Career Development of Women: Some Propositions," *The Education of Women*, p. 68.
65. Samuel H. Lowrie, "Dating Theories and Student Responses," *American Sociological Review*, Vol. XVI (June 1951), pp. 334–40.
66. Mueller, "The Cultural Pressures on Women," p. 77.
67. Everett Rogers, "The Effect of Campus Marriages on Participation in College Life," *College and University*, Vol. XXXIII, No. 2 (Winter 1958), p. 194.
68. Mueller, "The Cultural Pressures on Women," p. 78.
69. Rogers, pp. 194, 198.
70. Mueller, "The Cultural Pressures on Women," p. 77.
71. Mueller, "The Cultural Pressures on Women," p. 78.
72. W. L. Slocum, "Social Factors Involved in Academic Mortality," *College and University*, Vol. XXXII, No. 1 (Spring 1956), pp. 53–64.
73. Rogers, p. 198.
74. Esther Lloyd-Jones, "Women Today and Their Education," *Teachers College Record*, Vol. LVII (Apr. 1956), pp. 431–37.

Chapter 3

1. Jersild, *Child Psychology*, p. 299.
2. William James, *The Principles of Psychology*, Vol. II (New York: Dover Publications, Inc., 1950), pp. 449–50.
3. R. Lunger and J. D. Page, "The Worries of College Freshmen," *Journal of Genetic Psychology*, (June 1939), pp. 54, 457–60.

4. Karen Horney, *The Neurotic Personality of Our Time* (New York: W. W. Norton & Company, Inc.), p. 41.

5. *Ibid.,* p. 44.

6. *Ibid.,* p. 45.

7. These three points are paraphrased from Horney, *The Neurotic Personality,* pp. 46–47.

8. Joanna Field, *A Life of One's Own* (Harmondsworth, Middlesex: Penguin Books, Ltd., 1955), pp. 122–31, gives an excellent description of the "blind thinking" which springs from anxiety.

9. Jersild, *The Psychology of Adolescence* (New York: The Macmillan Company, 1957), pp. 171–72.

10. N. and Margaret A. Cameron, *Behavior Pathology* (Cambridge: Houghton Mifflin, 1951), pp. 280–91.

11. Roger W. Heynes, *The Psychology of Personal Adjustment* (New York: The Dryden Press, 1958), p. 26.

12. *Ibid.,* p. 33.

13. S. Rozenzweig, "An Outline of Frustration Theory," *Personality and the Behavior Disorders,* J. McV. Hunt, ed. (New York: Ronald Press, 1944), pp. 379–88.

14. O. H. Mowrer and Clyde Kluckhohn, "Dynamic Theory of Personality," *Personality and the Behavior Disorders,* p. 72.

15. L. F. Shaffer, *Psychology of Adjustment* (Boston, Houghton Mifflin Company, 1956), p. 206.

16. Jersild, *The Psychology of Adolescence,* pp. 371–84.

Chapter 4

1. Robert L. Thorndike and Elizabeth Hagen, *Measurement and Evaluation in Psychology and Education* (New York: John Wiley & Sons, Inc., 1955), p. 7.

2. David Wechsler, *The Measurement of Adult Intelligence* (Baltimore: The Williams and Wilkins Co., 1944), p. 3.

3. *Ibid.,* p. 3.

4. *Ibid.,* p. 24.

5. Arthur Traxler, "What Is a Satisfactory I.Q. for Admission to College?," *School and Society,* Vol. LI (1946), pp. 462–64.

6. Nancy Bayley, "Data on the Growth of Intelligence between 16 and 21 years of Age as Measured by the Wechsler-Bellevue Scale," *Journal of Genetic Psychology,* Vol. XC (Jan. 1957), pp. 3–15; and Nancy Bayley, "Consistency and in the Growth of Intelligence from Birth to Eighteen Years," *Journal of Genetic Psychology,* Vol. LXXV (Dec. 1949), pp. 165–96.

7. Cyril Burt, "The Inheritance of Mental Ability," *The American Psychologist,* Vol. XIII, (Jan. 1958), p. 19.

8. Allison Davis, "The Relevance of Intelligence Test Scores and Achievement Test Scores for Desegregation of Students Enrolled in the Public Schools." (A paper delivered at the Indianapolis Conference for Counselors sponsored by Delta Sigma Theta Sorority, May 10, 1958).

9. Burt, p. 10.

10. For a detailed analysis of which the following is in part a summary, see Donald Super, *The Psychology of Careers, An Introduction to Vocational Development* (New York: Harper & Bros., 1957), pp. 199–218, by permission.

11. H. D. Kitson and L. Culbertson, "The Vocational Changes of One Thousand Eminent Americans," *National Vocational Guidance Bulletin,* Vol. I (1923), pp. 128–30.

12. Eli Ginzberg *et al., Occupational Choice* (New York: Columbia University Press, 1951), pp. 185–86.

13. Edward T. Strong, *Manual for Vocational Interest Blank for Women,* (*Revised Blank—Form W*) (Stanford University, California: Stanford University Press, 1951).

14. Irwin Berg, "Test Score Interpretation and Client Confusion," *Personnel and Guidance Journal,* Vol. XXXIV, Number 9 (May, 1956), pp. 574–75.

15. Alice L. Dement, "Good Students Want Counseling Too," *Journal of Counseling Psychology,* Vol. 4, No. 2 (Fall, 1957), pp. 113–18.

16. Miriam Faries, "Short Term Counseling," *Journal of Counseling Psychology,* Vol. II, No. 3 (Fall, 1955), pp. 182–84.

Chapter 5

1. United States Department of Health, Education and Welfare, *Biennial Survey of Education in the United States* (Washington, D.C.: Government Printing Office, 1955), pp. 10–11.

2. Josephine Rathbone, *Relaxation* (New York: Bureau of Publications, Teachers College, Columbia University, 1943), p. 33. This short study is recommended to students as a useful analysis of the hazards of mental fatigue, and suggests appropriate techniques for using recreation and relaxation to overcome them.

3. *Ibid.,* p. 66.

4. Hans Selye, *The Stress of Life* (New York: The McGraw-Hill Book Company, 1956), pp. 264–65, by permission. Dr. Selye's theory of stress is summarized in this work, and some of its practical applications to everyday life are suggested. Detailed experimental reports are available in his volume, *Stress* (Montreal: ACTA, 1950); and he issues an *Annual Report on Stress* (Montreal: ACTA, 1951 ff.).

5. *Ibid.,* pp. 47–54, by permission.

6. *Ibid.,* p. 31, by permission.

7. *Ibid.,* p. 120, by permission.

8. Flanders Dunbar, *Emotions and Bodily Changes,* 4th ed. (New York: Columbia University Press, 1954), pp. 3–80.

9. Selye, p. 66, by permission.

10. *Ibid.,* p. 91, by permission.

11. *Ibid.,* pp. 263–67, by permission.

12. L. F. Cain and R. Willey, "The Effect of Spaced Learning on the Curve of Retention," *Journal of Experimental Psychology,* Vol. XXV (Aug. 1939), pp. 209–14.

13. H. E. Garrett, "Variability in Learning under Massed and Spaced Practice," *Journal of Experimental Psychology,* Vol. XXVI (June 1940), pp. 547–67.

14. Rathbone, p. 70 and Selye, pp. 267–68.

15. E. L. Thorndike, *Educational Psychology, Briefer Course* (New York: Bureau of Publications, Teachers College, Columbia University, 1914), pp. 55–72.

16. Percival Symonds, "What Education Can Learn From Psychology," *Teachers College Record,* Vol. LVII (Feb. 1955), pp. 15–25.

17. C. J. Leuba and D. Bateman, "Learning During Sleep," *American Journal of Psychology,* Vol. LXV (Apr. 1952), pp. 301–2 and J. G. Jenkins and K. M. Dallenbach, "Forgetting as a Function of Retroactive Inhibition," *American Journal of Psychology,* Vol. XXXV (Oct. 1924), pp. 609–10.

18. Symonds, p. 25.

19. Rathbone, p. 77. The relaxation techniques described on pp. 110–26 can be easily used without particular training.

20. E. M. F. Weaver *et al.,* "Medical Problems of Long Range Fighter Missions," *Journal of Aviation Medicine,* Vol. XVIII (Aug. 1947), pp. 341–51 and Kenneth G. Bergin, *Aviation Medicine, Its Theory and Application* (Baltimore: The Williams and Wilkins Company for John Wright & Son, Ltd., Bristol, England, 1949), pp. 260–70, by permission.

21. Rathbone, pp. 94–98.

22. Bergin, pp. 260–62, by permission.

23. Selye, pp. 66, 269, 275.

24. David S. Palermo, Alfred Castaneda, and Boyd R. McCandless, "The Relationship of Anxiety in Children to Performance in a Complex Learning Task," *Child Development*, Vol. XXVII (Sept. 1956), pp. 333–37, by permission. See also Alfred Castaneda, David S. Palermo, and Boyd R. McCandless, "Complex Learning and Performance as a Function of Anxiety in Children and Task Difficulty," *Child Development*, Vol. XXVII (Sept. 1956), pp. 327–32. David P. Ausubel *et al.*, "Qualitative Characteristics in the Learning Process Connected with Anxiety," *Journal of Abnormal and Social Psychology*, Vol. XLVIII (Oct. 1953), pp. 537–47, deals with similar patterns in adult learning.

25. Dunbar, p. 124.

26. Nevitt Sanford, "Uncertain Seniors," *Journal of the National Association of Women Deans and Counselors*, Vol. XXI (Oct. 1957), pp. 9–15. See also M. B. Freedman, "The Passage through College," *Journal of Social Issues*, Vol. XII, No. 4 (1956), p. 25.

27. Yale University, *Bulletin, Undergraduate Courses of Study, 1958–1959*, Series 4, no. 6 (March 1958), pp. 201–2, describes the "Scholars of the House" program. The "Directed Studies" program for general education in the freshman and sophomore years is described on pp. 9–10.

28. E. S. Jones and G. K. Ortner, "Advanced Study for Superior Students," *Journal of the National Education Association*, Vol. XLIII (Feb. 1954), pp. 107–8 and *College Credit by Examination: Evaluation of the University of Buffalo Program*, Vol. XXI, No. 3 (Buffalo: University of Buffalo College of Arts and Sciences Studies, 1954).

29. Mills College, *Bulletin of Mills College, Catalog Issue* (March, 1957), p. 50.

30. Thomas F. Staton, *How to Study* (2208 Woodley Road, Montgomery, Alabama, 1954). A manual, written for Air Force officers returning to academic work, gives a good rule of thumb for study patterns, reading, and review.

31. "Personality Development During the College Years," *Journal of Social Issues*, Nevitt Sanford, Vol. XII, No. 4 (1956), p. 4.

32. Philip Jacob, *Changing Values in College* (New York: Harper & Brothers, 1957), pp. 1–11, 135–37.

Chapter 6

1. Donald L. Thistlewaite, "College Environments and the Development of Talent," *Science*, Vol. CXXX (July 10, 1959), pp. 71–76, by permission.

2. *Ibid.*, p. 74, by permission.

3. *Ibid.*, p. 75, by permission.

4. M. B. Freedman, "The Passage through College," *Journal of Social Issues*, Vol. XII, No. 4 (1956), p. 20.

5. Selye, *The Stress of Life*, pp. 14–43, gives an excellent illustration of the value of idle curiosity—the development of his stress theory grew out of his wondering what made people feel sick when their ailment couldn't be diagnosed.

Chapter 7

1. Homer L. J. Carter and Dorothy J. McGinnis, *Effective Reading for College Students* (New York: The Dryden Press, Inc., 1957), pp. 189–201.

2. R. Bruce Raup, *et al, The Improvement of Practical Judgment* (New York: Harper and Bros., 1950), pp. 85–91.

3. Charles S. Peirce, "The Fixation of Belief," *Values in a Universe of Chance; Selected Writings of Charles S. Peirce*, Philip Weiner, ed. (Garden City: Doubleday Anchor Books, 1958), p. 103.

4. John B. Kemeny, J. Laurie Snell and Gerald L. Thompson, *Introduction to Finite Mathematics* (Englewood Cliffs: Prentice-Hall, Inc., 1957), pp. 1–53, gives examples of systems of logical notation for complex ideas.

5. Hans Reichenbach, *The Rise of Scientific Philosophy* (Berkeley: The University of California Press, 1957), pp. 125–43, describes different types of geometry having various relations to the world we experience.

6. Norbert Weiner, *The Human Use of Human Beings: Cybernetics and Society* (Garden City: Doubleday Anchor Books, 1954), pp. 160–61, 177–86, describes the range of matters which can be settled by calculation and suggests the limits of this range.

7. Lewis Carroll (Charles Lutwidge Dodgson), *Symbolic Logic, Part I, Elementary* (London: Macmillan, 1896). The examples of syllogisms and relational propositions are good nonsense, good logic, and good fun—as good as anything in *Alice in Wonderland*.

8. Harold F. Clark and Harold S. Sloan, *Classrooms in the Factories: An Account of Educational Activities Conducted by American Industry* (Rutherford, N.J.: Institute of Research, Fairleigh Dickinson University, 1958).

9. Margaret B. Fisher, *Leadership and Intelligence* (New York: Bureau of Publications, Teachers College, Columbia University, 1954), pp. 98–118, defines the phases or modes of practical judgment which the student may wish to master.

Chapter 8

1. Eli Ginzberg, Sol W. Ginsburg, Sidney Axelrad, and John L. Herma, *Occupational Choice; an Approach to a General Theory* (New York: Columbia University Press, 1951). The "period of realistic choices," the college years, with its three developmental stages of exploration, crystallization and specificity, is described in chap. ix, pp. 95–117, by permission.

2. Donald E. Super, *The Psychology of Careers: An Introduction to Vocational Development* (New York: Harper & Bros., 1957), p. 207, by permission. Robert L. Thorndike and Elizabeth Hagen, *Ten Thousand Careers* (New York: John Wiley & Sons, Inc., 1959), pp. 45, 48, 50, show similar findings. There seems to be no relation between measured aptitudes and success in a particular occupation.

3. *Ibid.*, pp. 218–9, by permission.

4. Rose K. Goldsen, *Report on the Cornell Student Body* (Ithaca, N.Y.: Cornell University Social Science Research Center, 1951), Paul L. Dressel and Lewis B. Mayhew, *General Education: Explorations in Evaluation* (Washington, D.C.: American Council on Education, 1954), and Gordon W. Allport, Philip E. Vernon, and Gardner Lindzey, *Study of Values: Manual of Directions* (Boston: Houghton Mifflin Co., 1951).

5. Super, pp. 240–41.

6. *Ibid.*, pp. 241–53, analyzes a variety of family factors, including independence training, which shape the occupational expectations of students.

7. Donald Super, *et al.*, *Vocational Development* (New York: Teachers College, Columbia University Bureau of Publications, 1957), p. 76.

8. Ernest Havemann and Patricia West, *They Went to College* (New York: Harcourt, Brace and Co., 1952), pp. 27, 72–74.

9. Women's Bureau, U.S. Department of Labor, *College Women Go to Work: Report on Women Graduates, Class of 1956*, Women's Bureau Bulletin No. 264 (Washington, D.C.: U.S. Government Printing Office, 1958), p. 4.

10. Theodore Caplow, *The Sociology of Work* (Minneapolis: The University of Minnesota Press, 1954), pp. 42–43, by permission.

11. Richard Centers, *The Psychology of Social Classes* (Princeton: Princeton University Press, 1949), p. 91.

12. *Class, Status, and Power,* R. Bendix and S. M. Lipset, eds. (Glencoe: Free Press, 1955), pp. 224–55. See also Anne Roe, *The Psychology of Occupations* (New York: Wiley, 1946).

13. Eleanor Metheny and James E. Peterson, *The Trouble with Women* (New York: Vantage Press, 1957), pp. 133–64, by permission.

14. Robert Hoppock, *Occupational Information* (New York: McGraw-Hill, 1957), is a useful reference book.

15. The National Manpower Council has published a series of studies of national manpower needs. Of greatest interest to students are those on *A Policy for Scientific and Professional Manpower* (1953), *Womanpower* (1957) and the (1959) study on governmental manpower problems and policies. All are published by the Columbia University Press, New York.

16. William H. Whyte, Jr., *The Organization Man* (Garden City: Doubleday Anchor Books, 1957), deals with these problems in great detail.

17. Women's Bureau, U.S. Department of Labor, *College Women Go To Work: Report on Women Graduates, Class of 1956,* p. 5.

18. Helen Waddell, *The Wandering Scholars* (New York: Doubleday & Company, Inc., 1955), pp. 154–55 (Anchor Books edition).

19. Kate Hevner Mueller, *Educating Women for a Changing World* (Minneapolis: University of Minnesota Press, 1954), pp. 134–37.

20. National Manpower Council, *Work in the Lives of Married Women* (New York: Columbia University Press, 1958), pp. 16–19, by permission.

21. Super, *The Psychology of Careers: An Introduction to Vocational Development,* pp. 76–8, and Super, *et al., Vocational Development,* p. 46.

22. Ginzberg, *et al., Occupational Choice,* pp. 163–67.

23. For an example of a couple that has successfully come to terms with these factors, see Metheny and Peterson, *The Trouble with Women,* pp. 219–22.

24. Gardiner Murphy, *Human Potentialities* (New York: Basic Books, Inc.), pp. 65–67.

Chapter 9

1. Arthur T. Jersild, *The Psychology of Adolescence* (New York: The Macmillan Company, 1957), pp. 7, 17–27.

2. Erik Erikson, "The Problem of Ego Identity," *Psychological Issues,* Monograph 1, Vol. I, no. 1 (1959), pp. 110–12.

3. Jacques Barzun, *The House of Intellect* (New York: Harper & Brothers, 1959), pp. 255–57.

Chapter 10

1. Grace and Fred Hechinger, "The Case for Campus Life," *New York Times Magazine,* Vol. CVIII, No. 36, 946, March 29, 1959, VI pp. 31–34.

2. *Student Government, Student Leaders and the American College,* Eliot Freidson, ed. (Philadelphia: United States National Students Association, 1955), pp. 48–51, by permission.

3. *Ibid.,* pp. 20–21, by permission.

4. Edward S. Jones, *Shifts in Types of Students, 1935–1953,* unpublished study (University of Buffalo, 1954), by permission.

5. Friedson, pp. 40, 75.

6. Samuel Messick and Norman Frederiksen, "Ability, Acquiescence, and Authoritarianism," *Psychological Reports,* Vol. IV (1958), pp. 687–97, by permission.

7. Margaret B. Fisher, *Survey of Student Interests,* unpublished survey (University of Buffalo, 1954).

Chapter 11

1. Philip E. Jacob, *Changing Values in College* (New York: Harper & Bros., 1957), pp. xi–xii, by permission.
2. Edward D. Eddy, Jr., *The College Influence on Student Character* (Washington, D.C.: American Council on Education, 1959), pp. 3–4, by permission.
3. Janet Kelley, *College Life and the Mores* (New York: Bureau of Publications, Teachers College, Columbia University, 1949), pp. 6–7, 56–57.
4. Fred Werner, *Freshmen Orientation* (Philadelphia: United States National Student Association, 1959), pp. 1–7.
5. David Riesman, *The Lonely Crowd* (New Haven: Yale University Press, 1950), pp. 6–31, by permission.
6. Louise Price, *Creative Group Work on the Campus* (New York: Bureau of Publications, Teachers College, Columbia University, 1941), pp. 212–17, describes the evolution and control of the "Stanford rough," an interesting pattern of conformity.
7. Jacques Barzun, *The House of Intellect,* pp. 50–51, by permission.
8. Eunice C. Roberts, "Crises to Try Our Edge" *Journal of National Association of Women Deans and Counselors,* Vol. XXII (June 1959), pp. 150–52.
9. Jacob, pp. 120–21, by permission.
10. Werner, p. 2, gives horrible examples of a passing way of life.
11. *Worse than Futile,* Craig K. Comstock, ed. (Cambridge: The Harvard *Crimson,* undated pamphlet), summarizes the reaction to the "loyalty" provision of the National Defense Education Act.
12. Barzun, pp. 62–77.
13. Jacob, pp. 24–28; and compare with pp. 38–57.
14. Waldo Beach, *Conscience on Campus* (New York: Association Press, 1958), gives a good analysis of the relation of Christian ethics to student behavior and campus life.
15. Jacob, especially chap. vi, pp. 99–116. There is an excellent analysis in this chapter of the variation among American colleges in terms of the predominant values which they serve and the success which they have in overcoming the tendency to self-limiting conformity.
16. Edward D. Eddy, Jr., *The College Influence on Student Character,* pp. 14–16, by permission. The petition was signed by over 200 students active in campus affairs.
17. Walter Bagehot, *Physics and Politics* (Boston: Beacon Press, 1956), pp. 114–48.
18. Daniel Funkenstein, Stanley H. King, and Margaret E. Drolette, *Mastery of Stress* (Cambridge: Harvard University Press, 1957), pp. 273–313. See especially pp. 289–92. By permission.
19. Karl Deutsch, "The Impact of Scientific and Technological Developments on Politics and International Affairs," Address to the American Political Science Association at the meeting of the American Association for the Advancement of Science, Washington, D.C., December 27, 1958; published in part as "The Impact of Science and Technology on International Politics," *Daedalus,* Volume LXXXVIII (1959), pp. 669–85.
20. Jacob, *Changing Values in College,* summarizes the findings of many studies of student values made in recent years.
21. Robert M. Roth, "The Role of Self Concept in Achievement," *Journal of Experimental Education,* Vol. XXVII, no. 4 (Summer, 1959), pp. 255–81, by permission.

Index